Ashley J. Bohrer
Marxism and Intersectionality

Philosophy

Ashley J. Bohrer (PhD) is an academic, activist, and public intellectual. She is an Assistant Professor at the University of Notre Dame and previously held a postdoctoral position at Hamilton College. Her research in the fields of philosophy, critical race studies, decolonial theory, intersectional feminism, and Marxism explores the intersections of capitalism, colonialism, racism and hetero/sexism. As an activist, she is affiliated with various feminist, anti-racist and anti-capitalist grassroots collectives.

ASHLEY J. BOHRER
Marxism and Intersectionality
Race, Gender, Class and Sexuality under Contemporary Capitalism

[transcript]

Bibliographic information published by the Deutsche Nationalbibliothek
The Deutsche Nationalbibliothek lists this publication in the Deutsche Nationalbibliografie; detailed bibliographic data are available in the Internet at http://dnb.d-nb.de

© 2019 transcript Verlag, Bielefeld
transcript Verlag | Hermannstraße 26 | D-33602 Bielefeld | live@transcript-verlag.de

Cover layout: Kordula Röckenhaus, Bielefeld
Typeset by Francisco Bragança, Bielefeld
Printed by Druckhaus Bechstein GmbH, Wetzlar
Print-ISBN 978-3-8376-4160-8
PDF-ISBN 978-3-8394-4160-2
https://doi.org/10.14361/9783839441602

Table of Contents

Acknowledgements | 7

Dedication | 11

Introduction | 13

PART ONE: HISTORIES

Chapter Zero: The Shared History of the Intersectional and Marxist Traditions | 31

PART TWO: DEBATES

Chapter One: The Intersectional Tradition | 81

Chapter Two: Marxist Critiques of Intersectionality | 101

Chapter Three: Queer, Feminist, Anti-Racist, and Anti-Imperialist Marxisms | 123

Chapter Four: Intersectional Critiques of Marxism | 159

Part Three: Possibilities

Chapter Five: Oppression and Exploitation Beyond Reductions | 185

Chapter Six: Dialectics of Difference | 207

Chapter Seven: Solidarity in the House of Difference | 231

Bibliography | 261

Acknowledgements

I owe a great debt to many people who contributed, in ways big and small, explicitly and implicitly, to the production of this manuscript.

This manuscript in many ways began as a series of conversations between myself, Nikeeta Slade, Trish Kahle, and Crystal Stella Becceril in 2013 and 2014. All of us were comitted Marxists with anti-racist, anti-imperialist, feminist, queer, trans-inclusive, prison abolitionist politics, and we were searching for a way to bring contemporary intersectional frameworks to rework Marxism beyond the many reductionisms we had all found in writings of prominent Marxists and in the course of organizing on the left. I am forever grateful for the time, conversations, reading suggestions, call ins, and corrections from that time, and more than anything, for the ways in which they showed me and continue still to show me how to live, breathe, imagine, and think the possibilities of another world.

It was a pleasure and an endless fount of energy when I realized that it was not just myself and these three collaborators who were interested in deep, sympathetic, and integrative thinking along these lines. Over the years, this manuscript and my own thinking has been deeply enriched by conversations with Sara Salem, Michelle O'Brien, Kate Doyle Griffiths, Jules Gleeson, Paul Reynolds, Cinzia Arruzza, Tithi Bhattacharya, Holly Lewis, Rosie Warren, Kojo Koram, Frankie Mace, Matt Cole, and many other folks orbiting around the Historical Materialism Sexuality and Political Economy Network.

Pieces of this research were also developed while I was still a graduate student at DePaul University in Chicago and I owe a great debt to many teachers and colleagues there. My first attempt at tracing the relationship between intersectionality and Marxism came in a graduate seminar in the Women, Gender, and Sexuality Studies Department taught by Ann Russo. I am thankful for her comments on that paper, as well as the comments of my fellow classmates, especially Gil Morejón and Pidgeon Pagonis. Richard A. Lee Jr. has been one of my closest interlocutors over the years, and for the many hours of conversation, questions, and disagreements, I will always be grateful.

It would be impossible to overstate the influence that William Meyerowitz had on my thinking about Marxism, race, gender, and sexuality; indeed, Will was my first exposure to Marxist-feminism at all, when, at the corner of Jackson and LaSalle during Occupy Chicago, he placed in my hands a copy of Mariarosa Dalla Costa and Selma James' *The Power of Women and the Subversion of the Community*. I did not know at that moment that this profound act of intellectual generosity would radically change my academic and activist life, but I could not be more grateful that it did.

Miguel Gualdrón, Nathalia Hernandez, and the entire Grupo de Pensamiento Latinoamericano influenced so much of my thinking that I feel them present, even when I am not directly writing about Latin American philosophy. Muchas gracias, queridxs.

Katie Feyh pushed me through many crises, in addition to listening to my half-formulated arguments, dead ends, and vexed rants at all hours of the day and night. Jess Elkayam Backus offered friendship and empathy through the many low points, personal and professional, that accompanied me through completing this manuscript. Mathias Kiltgaard, Jules Gleeson, and Cinzia Arruzza all read pieces of the manuscript and offered incredibly helpful comments. Frankie Mace edited the entire manuscript from beginning to end, greatly enriching each line of the manuscript.

Large parts of chapters two and five of this text were completed at the Atelier du Théorie Critique in Paris. I am grateful to Gabriel Rockhill for the space, and to all of my colleagues there, but especially to: Jasmine Wallace, Jonathan Liebembuk, Gil Morejón, Vilde Aavitsland, Jeta Mulaj, Owen Glyn-Williams, Amanda Kaplan, Agatha Slupek, and Theodora Bane.

Parts of this book project were presented at various conferences of Historical Materialism, both in London and in Toronto. I thank the conference organizers, my co-panelists, and all of the audience members of each of those presentations, whose thoughtful remarks reminded me this was a project worth pursuing even when I myself was doubtful and whose sharp questions pushed this project further than it ever would have gone otherwise.

Nearly all of this manuscript was written during my time as a Postdoctoral Fellow at Hamilton College. I sincerely thank the College, the Philosophy Department, and the Arthur Levitt Center for the material and collegial support that allowed me to finish this manuscript. I never felt anything but support from my Philosophy Department colleagues—Marianne Janack, Katheryn Doran, A. Todd Franklin, Russell Marcus, Alex Plakias, and Doug Edwards. Margo Okazawa-Rey was a light and an inspiration, as well as a crucial thought-partner in much of this project. I am so grateful to learn from, to teach with, to present with, and to question with you.

Acknowledgements

In the fall of 2016, I taught a small seminar called "Marxism, Feminism, Anti-Racism: An Encounter" in which we read many of the texts under discussion here and during which I worked out many of the arguments presented here. I am so deeply grateful to my students in that course—Victor Bene, Ana Reynoso-Castro, and Sebastian Lissarrague—who always showed up with thoughtful questions, were never afraid to push me or the texts, and who told me when my arguments made no sense (which was more often than I would care to admit!). They were the first to hear, to question, and to comment on much of the material in this text and it is entirely fair to say that I learned as much from them as they from me.

As much as this book is an academic work, my interest in both Marxism and intersectionality was really born out of my work in activist communities and collectives. My (often flawed) work over the years with Occupy Chicago, Slutwalk Chicago, FURIE, Jewish Voice for Peace, Jews for Justice in Palestine, the Center for Jewish Nonviolence, the International Women's Strike, HYSTERIA, the Global Feminist Anti-Fascist Front, the Coalition Against Corporate Higher Education (CACHE), the Campus Anti-Fascist Network (CAN), and others taught me nearly everything of value in this book. I learned as much from our successes as from our failures. My co-organizers at CJNV in particular held me through the process of writing this book, even when it meant each of them doing more work so I could take space and time to write. Oriel Eisner, Isaac Kates Rose, Erez Bleicher, Elisheva Goldberg, Alice Mishkin, Daniel Roth and Shlomo Roth in particular made space in their lives to pick up my slack and I could not be more grateful. Sarah Brammer-Shlay, Scout Bratt, Ella Mason, and Sue Beardon provided deep wells of support when I needed it most.

Of all of my activist experiences, I have learned the most about the painful, complicated, conflictual and often messy process of solidarity and coalition building through my work in Palestine. Deep thanks and profound gratitude is due to the innumerable activists in that struggle, especially the members of following organizations: Youth Against Settlements, the Rural Women's Collective, All That's Left, Grassroots Jerusalem, Holy Land Trust, the Tent of Nations, the communities of Umm al-Kheir and Susiya, Breaking the Silence, and the members of various Jewish international anti-occupation groups that joined us in these journeys and projects of speaking truth to power, channeling righteous rage, and finding pockets of love and joy in the project of changing the world.

This book certainly would never have come in to being without the endless encouragement and boundless work of its editor, Jakob Hortsmann. He saw a book in a 20-minute conference presentation and for that, I will always be grateful.

Daniel Kroop and Brian Grady continually reminded me to work on the book (and to just finish it already!) when I otherwise would have been distracted by other projects. It is so special to share a queer, communist, chosen family with these two. My dear sister, Caressa Starshine, is also part of this family, and it is truly wonderful to have a sister whose deep wells of positivity, optimism, and empathy have, for decades, shone a light in a world otherwise full of darkness and cynicism.

Andrés Fabián Henao Castro, my partner in life and in all things, was also my partner in this project in ways that words will always fail to capture. The entire Henao Castro family—Marlene, Juan Carlos, Astrid, Felipe, and little Antonio—sustained me with generous love and endless support throughout the drafting of this manuscript.

Despite the brilliant minds and sensitive souls that influenced this work, it is bound to have errors, omissions, confusions, and elisions. Those are, of course, my fault and mine alone.

Dedication

If I were to give a materialist analysis of this book, it, like any other object in this world, would reveal an entire, hidden chain of producers of which I am only one small part. This book would have been impossible without many generations of thinkers, activists, organizers, scholars, shit-talkers, and no-shit takers. It would have been impossible without the millions of forgotten choices of people to survive the horrors of this world. It would have been impossible without the farmworkers who grew and harvested my food and without the environmental and labor activists who militate to ensure that achieving sustenance does not entail world destruction. It would have been impossible without the workers who assembled the computer on which it was written or the books it references. It would have been impossible without the letter carriers who delivered both to me. It would have been impossible without the construction workers who built my residence and my office, the factory workers who produced my furniture, the baristas who poured my coffee, the musicians who crafted my writing soundtrack, the educators who taught me things I don't even remember, the activists and social movements around the world who inspire me to do better and work harder. It would have been impossible without the internet radicals who posted memes, pictures, reminders, tweets, and articles that challenged and changed me. It would have been impossible without the innumerable failures, mine and others', that push me to be more accountable. The resistors, partisans, revolutionaries, militants, strikers, and fighters, the mothers, nannies, nurses, sex workers, students, street artists, organizers, sympathizers, radicals of every stripe and kind, those who build coalitions and those who tear down walls, communists, socialists, anarchists, freedom dreamers, freedom fighters, the youth who always know that things could be different, and the elders who always know that history is our strongest ally—I would say this book is *for* them, but this would overlook the fact that it is already *of* them. May we all learn from the lessons they are already teaching.

Introduction

I want to begin by speaking about two moments, themselves rather far apart chronologically, that motivated me to write this book. I was at a conference a few years ago in which three leading Marxist scholars spoke on a panel about intersectionality. The room was packed. I watched one of the scholars begin their talk by confessing that they had never heard of intersectionality until one month before the event. Unsurprisingly, the talk proceeded to be riddled with errors, caricatures, and hubristic pronouncements about a large and varied body of literature that the speaker admitted to knowing nearly nothing about. The second scholar continued the trend of bombastic but ungrounded critique, declaring toward the end of their talk that the problem with intersectionality was that it had no account of how oppressions "interacted"; they seem to "bounce off one another like billiard balls" but without any conceptual explanation. This remark was met by a room full of self-satisfied chuckles of derision. The third speaker rattled off a series of criticisms that, while articulated with less derision, were no more accurate; I deal with many of this person's critiques throughout the manuscript that follows. All three speakers were white, well-respected, and were speaking far outside of their areas of expertise. It showed. The Q&A that followed this panel was itself almost comically bad; the moderator proceeded to call on nearly every white man over 40 in the crowd, while ignoring the hands of the many young people, people of color, and women in the room, some of whom were visibly fuming at the spectacle they had witnessed.

A few years before this conference, I was sitting in a seminar classroom in graduate school, discussing the work of a prominent non-white scholar who was very highly regarded in the post-colonial cannon. In many of the discussions I had witnessed about this person's work, their Marxist politics, and their deep commitment to a critique of capitalism had been overlooked, which I raised in the discussion. A colleague responded, "But why does it *have to be* Marxist?" Their exasperation was clear; to them it seemed as though a white anti-capitalist was imposing Marxism (assumed itself to be Eurocentric, teleological, and ultimately fascist) on the thought and activism of a person of color, who, as an anti-colonial revolutionary, seemingly couldn't also employ the work of a dead white man to these ends. The fact that numerous militant decolonial and feminist struggles had made use of Marxism was either unknown or discounted in the subtext of this pointed and rhetorical question.

I point to these two moments, years apart, because they, more or less, characterize much of the 'conversation' that has surrounded intersectionality and Marxism in recent years. Rife with derision, I have found most engagements between these two perspectives to be grounded more in caricature than in close reading, often discounting in advance that anything useful could come from one or the other framework. And so, after years of defending intersectionality in Marxist circles, and of defending historical materialism in intersectional ones, I became convinced that these conversations would continue to stall without a piece of scholarship that placed the two into actual conversation, leaving behind the various straw persons and scarecrows that too often form a barricade between these two perspectives. This book is thus, in one way, a rather long response to both of these moments and an articulation of how and why each of these modes of engagement are ultimately insufficient, not only for capturing the breadth and profundity of their concepts, but also for the project of uprooting the systems of domination that structure our world. If we are really to intervene against racism, cis/sexism, heteropatriarchy, and capitalism—and it is one of the arguments of this book that if we are to destroy one, we must destroy them all—then we must move beyond this intra-left stalemate. Rather than fighting each other, we must find modes of engagement that do justice to the insights of multiple traditions, multiple experiences, and multiple positions.

Setting the Terms

In order to engage in a project such as this, I must begin by clarifying three of the central terms in the title of this book: capitalism, intersectionality, and Marxism. It is only through doing so that, in the rest of this book, we might some to some kind of understanding about what the other terms—race, gender, sexuality, and class—mean.

Capitalism

Capitalism is the grammar of our world. But for all of its ubiquity, it is a concept and system that is rarely understood. While often capitalism is taken to refer to a purely economic system, marked by markets and exchange, this characterization only begins to scratch the surface. Capitalism is an economic system, one that continually uses violence, brutality, and exclusion to ensure that the relatively few live off the endless labors of the many. But it is much more than this: capitalism is also a series of connected narratives and social practices, it is a system that produces and reproduces inequalities at every turn, not only in the economic realm, but in the political, social, academic, intimate, educational, and imaginative dimensions of contemporary life. And this system, which is overall based in the justification of domination and dominion, came into being and continues to exist, in and through a whole series of oppressive practices and discourses. Far from being a single, univocal operation of power, capitalism is a web of institutions, inherited histories, modes of access, strategies of confinement, and tactics of accumulation, with different and varying configurations across history and across the world. In this sense, I follow the analysis of Silvia Federici, who argues that capitalism "has been above all an accumulation of differences, inequalities, hierarchies, divisions, which have alienated workers from each other and even from themselves."[1]

This "accumulation of differences" in conjunction with the accumulation of power and wealth together is the system of capitalism. In this sense, capitalism, far from being a purely economic system, cannot operate outside of the complicated dynamics of race, gender, sexuality, and nationality. Anievas and Nisancioglu reinforce this point, asserting that

capitalism utilises exploitation and oppression—beyond the formally free exchange of labour-power for wages—as (re)sources for its reproduction. The violence that inheres in forms of exploitation such as slavery, debt peonage and domestic labour, practices such as state coercion, 'just wars' and territorial divisions, and structures of racism and patriarchy is not external to capitalism as a mode of production, but constitutive of its very ontology. When tied to the critique of Eurocentrism, we should thus be wary of any account of the origins of capitalism that posits Europeans or Westerners as harbingers of a normatively and developmentally privileged 'civilization'—an exceptionally 'enlightened' group that dragged the world out of 'savagery'. The history of violence upon which the social relations of capitalism were built should lead us to question the idealised self-image of capitalism as a world of expanding fulfilment and freedom, achieved through the abstract mechanisms of exchange. The invisible hand of the market has always been undergirded by the iron fist of the state, and an array of systemic separations between the subjugated and exploited—patriarchy, 'race', class and so on.[2]

In capitalism, we find a whole host of exploitative and oppressive practices, ones wholly structured through the inter-relations not only of class, but of race, gender, sexuality, and nationality. Let me be clear: I do not argue in this book that capitalism is itself sufficient in explaining the entire phenomena

---

1 | Silvia Federici, *Caliban and the Witch: Women, the Body and Primitive Accumulation*, 1st edition (New York; London: Autonomedia, 2004), 116.
2 | Alexander Anievas and Kerem Nisancioglu, *How the West Came to Rule: The Geopolitical Origins of Capitalism* (London: Pluto Press, 2015), 278-79.

of racism, colonization, heteropatriarchy, and/or sexism. These systems are complex, complicated, and changing; they mobilize pre-existing discourses, emergent practices, and even resistances to them in the continual innovation that has made them so difficult to uproot. Rather this book argues that capitalism was and still is deeply complicit in and structured by the particular shape of multiple, interlocked oppressions at the political, economic, social, and ideological levels. As I am sure will be clear to readers, I maintain the conviction that a systematic analysis of capitalism as a structure is urgently relevant to combatting these systems as they persist today. But unlike many class-reductionist Marxists, I argue that race, class, sexuality, and gender are completely inseparable systems. In this sense, I do not endorse the idea that racism, colonialism, or heterosexism are themselves *reducible* to capitalism's specific class relations; rather I argue that capitalism is a necessary element to an analysis of race, gender, sexuality, and class, just as an analysis of these latter is crucial to understanding the ideology, historical practice, and logical structure of capitalism.

Intersectionality
Intersectionality is a term that used in a whole variety of mobile ways and deployed to many different ends. While I undertake a systematic analysis of many of the key touchstone texts of intersectionality in Chapter One, throughout most of the book I use the term *the intersectional tradition* in order to highlight that intersectionality operates in two ways at once: intersectionality is both a definite, specific concept, named and elaborated by particular people and at a particular moment *and* it is something that is much broader than this. Especially from the present vantage point, in which the specific boundaries of intersectionality have become slippery, plastic, and quickly expanding, it may be more helpful to speak about an intersectional tradition: a group of texts and activist practices that gave rise to the discrete concept of intersectionality, are and were in dialogue with it, and who have been influenced by it. Thinking about intersectionality as both a concept and a tradition is my way of staking out a space to write this text amidst significant debate within scholars who call their work intersectional, about exactly who 'founded' intersectionality, exactly what 'work is does', and exactly to whom it is (and should be) available and accessible.

Thinking about the intersectional tradition allows us to really think about the constellation of concepts and theories and questions and concerns that are deeply *related* to the particular conceptual arrangement of intersectionality, while still marking a difference between them. Hence, in order to understand the moment, the theory, and the history of intersectionality as a concept, one must also understand the variety of names and concepts that feminist women of color had been using to try to address some of the very same issues that today are more likely to be investigated through/under/with/by intersectionality. Thus, it is quite clear that Patricia Hill Collins' "matrix of oppression," Deborah King's "multiple jeopardy," and even bell hooks' "white supremacist capitalist patriarchy" are certainly part of the intersectional tradition even if they are not the same as Kimberlé Crenshaw's particular conceptual formation of "intersectionality." Any account of what intersectionality means to Crenshaw, the explosion in the use of it, the resistance it initially faced (and still sometimes faces, despite its widespread currency on the contemporary left) would be woefully incomplete without the context of struggle, organizing, and theorizing given by these figures and many others besides. It is in this sense that I refer to "the intersectional tradition" as a group of histories, texts, theories, organizing strategies, and struggles that form an internally heterogenous and non-uniform set. It is crucial to think both about the differences and the similarities between articulations of the structures, experiences, identities, and oppressions that all of these figures were trying to name and analyze.

In addition to debates about what intersectionality *is,* whether the intersectional tradition is itself the exclusive domain of black women is an equally contentious aspect of the histories of intersectionality. There are clear dangers in asserting that intersectionality was itself a multi-racial tradition from its origin; the threat of "whitening intersectionality"[3] could contribute to the continual underestimation of black women's theoretical ingenuity, therefore alienating black women from the products of their own intellectual production. However, centering black women in this history does not need to entail erasing the historical fact that many of the theorists of the intersectional tradition were themselves engaged in organizing and theorizing with a multi-racial group of women, who were themselves involved in the production of this tradition. Latinas Gloria Anzaldúa and Cherrie Moraga, the editors of the volume *This Bridge Called My Back,* were centrally important in the development and facilitation of the spread and connection between the thinkers and ideas that would come to be called intersectionality. Elizabeth "Betita" Martínez was a central organizer in the black liberation struggle and influenced many of the black feminist scholars in the intersectional tradition. Argentine-born philosopher María Lugones is also often cited in histories of intersectionality, as is Chela Sandoval, Chandra Mohanty, Urvashi Vaid, and others. The Third World Women's Alliance, whose importance to the development of the intersectional tradition will be discussed below, was composed of black, indigenous, latinx, and Asian-American feminists. The intersectional tradition, especially as it took hold within the field of legal studies, was impacted through not only Crenshaw's powerful articu-

---

3 | Sirma Bilge, "Whitening Intersectionality: Evanescence of Race in Intersectionality Scholarship," in *Racism and Sociology: Racism Analysis Yearbook 5-2014,* ed. Wulf D. Hund and Alana Lentin (Berlin: Lit Verlag/Routledge, 2014), 175-205.

lation, but through her conversations and collaborations with Mari Matsuda, Trina Grillo and others.[4] Equally important to not overlook, many of the women involved in all of these projects were themselves biracial and multiracial. The best way to honor the women of color who are the foundational thinkers of intersectionality is to recognize them in their complexities: Crenshaw, Collins, Thornton Dill, and the many others who have been variously crowned as the originators of intersectionality were themselves engaged in activism, conversation, coalition, and collaboration with many activists, academics, and thinkers, some of whom were non-black women of color. The narrative that intersectionality was or is only about black women reduces the plurality, expansiveness, and coalitional work that these black women were engaged in. Indeed, Ange-Marie Hancock explains that it is essential both to pluralize the foundational narrative of intersectionality and to think about the ways in which non-black women of color were specifically integral parts of these conversations.[5]

Marxism

I treat intersectionality as the name for a tradition in much the same way that I treat Marxism in a rather heterodox fashion, as a group of texts, thinkers, and organizing histories that are widely heterogeneous and often internally conflictual. While it would be wrong to collapse all thinkers or organizers who call themselves "Marxist" into the same set of positions—indeed, I argue against doing precisely this in much of this book—there is some manner of internal related-ness to the group of texts, positions, ideas, thinkers, and organizations grouped under this heading; while I have included mostly only those self-identified as Marxists, I have also included those who have called themselves "socialist" or "communist". In the same sense in which I speak of an intersectional tradition, I am also interested not only in Marxist thinkers, but in Marx*ish* thinkers—academics and activists who use, deploy, work, and rework concepts from Marx or the Marxist tradition in order to explore new problems, expose different arrangements of exploitation, and excavate the vast and varied topography of capitalism. While in the literature on left feminism one often

---

4 | Jennifer Nash has repeatedly highlighted this point in her analysis of intersectionality: "intersectionality is not the exclusive terrain of black feminism, though black feminists have long been invested in examining how structures of domination collide to produce experiences of oppression and identity. Scholar-activists like Gloria Anzaldúa and Cherrie Moraga, among others, have organized their theory and politics around the intimate connections between race, ethnicity, and gender. Moreover, many of the organizations ... including the Third World Women's Alliance, were explicitly interested in "third world women" coalition building" (Nash, "Home Truths," 451).

5 | Ange-Marie Hancock, *Intersectionality: An Intellectual History*, 1 edition (New York, NY: Oxford University Press, 2016).

finds a distinction between 'Marxist feminism' and 'socialist feminism', I have not found the uses of these terms to be so consistent as to mark a useful division. They thus appear interchangeably in this text, as they appear interchangeably in the texts I analyze.

Those who are looking for a deep or systematic account of the writings of Marx or his collaborator Engels are bound to be disappointed by the approach I take here. While I do believe that Marx's own writings still contain many helpful tools, this book is quite a far cry from an exhaustive inventory of Marx's writings on many of the issues that I raise here. There are quite excellent books that already exist about Marx's own perspectives on gender, the family, slavery, colonization, and the like, and while many of these questions appear at points in the text, the focus of this book is elsewhere.[6]

Intersectionality and Marxism
As two traditions on the left, each deeply committed to thinking about the structure of injustice in the world, it is not surprising that these traditions should themselves share figures, texts, conceptualizations, or that the traditions themselves intersect and interact, that they read and respond to each other, and that at many points, they diverge from one another. In places where I speak of shared figures of these traditions, this is not to suggest that these figures have been taken up in the same ways by both traditions; indeed, in many cases, these traditions themselves, at least in their internal self-narratives, have often overlooked the existence of any shared conceptualizations or figures in such traditions.

As such, the terms and divisions at issue in this book—Marxism and intersectionality—sometimes become blurry and difficult to parse. Part of this is because, I argue, there has been a significant strand of intellectual and activist work that influences each of these perspectives and another significant strand that attempts to blend them. If an intersectional author is deeply influenced by Marxist texts or if a self-identified Marxist defines her ideas in and through dialogue with intersectionality, it is very difficult sometimes to say in which chapter or camp that author belongs, as the truth is in this case, as it is for most of us, that we are influenced and hence 'belong' to multiple traditions, multiple perspectives, and multiple camps. When we feel the need to separate clearly, to draw lines, to have arguments about whether or not an author *really* is Marxist enough or intersectional enough to be considered part of that tradition, often those conversations say more about the politics and objectives of those

---

6 | For those who are interested in such questions, I suggest beginning with the following texts: Heather Brown, *Marx on Gender and the Family: A Critical Study* (Chicago: Haymarket Books, 2013); Kevin B. Anderson, *Marx at the Margins: On Nationalism, Ethnicity, and Non-Western Societies* (Chicago: University of Chicago Press, 2010).

engaged in the conversation than they do about the work of the authors under discussion. Those conversations may sometimes be important and necessary, but they are not the subject of this book.

Delimiting terms in order to complete this project was particularly challenging. Both Marxism and intersectionality are internally heterogenous and dynamic bodies of literature. There are significant internal debates and disputes about the boundaries, core principles, and political commitments of each perspective. I decided not to intervene in these debates or to contribute to policing the boundaries of Marxism or intersectionality. I am not sure how useful my voice would or could be in such debates, and in any case, intervening felt like it would have taken this project in a different direction.

Initially, I was very invested in proving to Marxists that the reductive notion that many of them have of post-structural identity politics is not intersectionality. I was also rather invested in proving to intersectionality theorists that Marxism is not the kind of economically-reductive, oppression-blind theory of so many left caricatures. But in order to make those arguments, to show that something is or is not intersectionality and is or is not Marxism, I would have had to narrow and circumscribe both fields significantly, cutting off many strands, traditions, and uses of each theory.

I think the real truth of the matter is that there is a certain affinity between the best versions of both schools of thought reflected in their theories and the worst, reflected in their caricatures. There are structural conditions that lead Marxism into being taken as a self-righteous, Eurocentric bludgeon for white men to use in organizing spaces, and there are structural conditions that lead intersectionality into being used as a merely descriptive, hyper-fragmentary, essentialized notion of multiply-oppressed identity. To be clear, I don't think that these caricatures are the best version of either of those theories. But rather than treating the caricatures as just a simply errancy, I wanted to treat the caricatures as themselves symptomatic of something broader and pressing: the dangers of the theories themselves, the structural and historical conditions of their elaboration, the lack of translation of increasingly insular and self-referential terminology, the institutionalized uses of them that were specifically intended to make them less dangerous. In other words, I found there was something theoretically interesting in the misunderstandings of these theories and moreover, something urgent to think through.

So rather than trying to circumscribe some parts of Marxism as the "real Marxism" and some parts of intersectionality as "the real intersectionality", I decided rather to distinguish between multiple forms of intersectionality and multiple forms of Marxism. In what follows, I show how much of the contemporary antipathy between Marxism and intersectionality is derived from what we might call a "synecdochal straw person fallacy": substituting the weakest part for the whole and dismissing the rest.

Theories and practices of social justice and liberation need to be aware of their own caricatures, of their own worst versions, of the dangers of what they propose and of the vision of the just world they strive for. It does no one any good to pretend that we, all of us, built and shaped as we were in a world of white supremacist, patriarchal, settler colonial capitalism, somehow escaped it with a pure and perfect vision for a world made otherwise, as if by sheer force of will we could wipe clean the deep processes that made us in its image. It is important to proceed with caution and self-reflection, with deep self-criticism and self-skepticism with visions, plans, actions, and campaigns that are expansive, transformative, and world re-making.

Sources and Other Citational Politics

Marxism and intersectionality are intellectual currents or conceptual frameworks that are ultimately oriented toward activism, agitation, and transformational practice. This means that questions of strategy are always central. As Nancy Hartsock reminds us, "Marxism is fundamentally about building movements for social change, movements that recognize that injustice and domination are systematic. These movements need both political organizing and theoretical analysis to do the work of supporting the insights as well as the struggles of the many who are oppressed, exploited, and marginalized."[7] The same is true for intersectionality, and as the book unfolds it will be clearer and clearer that speaking about the intersectional tradition in the absence of deep understanding of its relationship to social movement work and activism will lead only to confusions and mischaracterizations. Both of these theories are, first and foremost, ways of reading, understanding, thinking, and dreaming beyond the deep structures of exploitation and oppression that frame our world. Thus, for a book about theory, actual struggles, organizations, and movements appear, not only as phenomena to be interpreted, but as the sources and sites of theoretical production; words, ideas, concepts, and arguments produced in the street are no less theoretical than those produced in the academy, and the former often speak with more clarity and precision. I thus take the positions, pamphlets, movement newspapers, flyers, and other movement sources as equally important for understanding what both traditions are about, and what they mean in practice, in the world. I take it as a matter of principle, moreover, to refuse the artificial distinctions between activism and academia that posit the former as the agents of political change and the latter as the guardians of theoretical discourse; both the Marxist and the intersectional traditions have their own critiques of this separation.

---

7 | Nancy Hartsock, "Marxist Feminist Dialectics for the 21st Century," *Science and Society* 62, no. 3 (1998): 401.

In addition to including 'movement sources' in this largely theoretical work, I approached this project with a deep commitment to an emancipatory politics of citation. As Vivian May argues, "Citational practices in intersectional work are thus especially important: they offer a way to make collectivity, delineate historical precedence, and claim legacies of struggle."[8] Especially in current conditions, when more and more work claiming to be intersectional engages little or not at all with the texts, groups, and practices that ground it, I remain committed to close readings and deep investigations, tracing the development of concepts and their lines of inheritance. Perhaps that has led to more citations than strictly necessary, but in a world in which oppressed people have less access to academic spaces, in which their ideas continue to be taken less seriously, and in which political work is constantly derided as 'not theoretical enough', fidelity to citations is itself a political choice. This remains true in the Marxist tradition as well, where despite decades of deep and exciting analysis by queer, feminist, anti-racist, anti-colonial, and Global South Marxisms, these voices and their ideas are nearly everywhere buried by more visible and notable Marxists. We must remember that academic and theoretical production happens inside systems of marginalization, silencing, and structural ignorance to the concerns and ideas of oppressed people; the absolute least we can do is engage, deeply, generously, and thoughtfully with these bodies of literature.

It is in this vein that I engage with the theories, ideas, authors, and voices cited here. Jennifer Nash, Tricia Rose, and Anna Carastathis have all used the term "loving critique" to explain a mode of engaging with debates and disagreements in generous and open ways. Carasthathis figures her own critical engagement with intersectionality in the following terms:

> In adducing these critiques, I do not assume[...]that their intent is always to undermine the project of critiquing insubordination or even intersectionality as such. Indeed, I grant the possibility[...]of immanent critiques, and indeed—to use Jennifer Nash's and Tricia Roses' formulation—of 'loving critiques.' Conversely, the apparent absence of critical engagement in celebratory invocations or operationalizations of intersectionality does not demonstrate any greater 'fidelity' or attention to the concept and may be just as (if not more) 'careless.'[9]

While my engagement with many thinkers in both traditions is at times critical, it is always loving, grounding in the fundamental commitment that questioning, stretching, and pushing each of these theories is the highest incarna-

---

8 | Vivian May, *Pursuing Intersectionality, Unsettling Dominant Imaginaries* (New York: Routledge, 2015), 55.

9 | Anna Carastathis, *Intersectionality: Origins, Contestations, Horizons* (Lincoln: University of Nebraska Press, 2016), 127.

tion of respect an academic can offer. This book is just such an offering, a hope that by bringing together and deeply engaging with these modes of thinking, that we may find new, exciting, and world opening possibilities for building the world in a more just and liberated image.

Over these past months and years, as I have spoken to many people about this project, they have, in more and less subtle ways, posed the question "but in the end, which perspective wins?" as a way, I think, of interrogating my position. I find this question now somewhat comical, as if the only way to bring two lines of thought into conversation is to vanquish one and declare the other the victor. As I hope becomes clear throughout this text, approaching these traditions through the framework of either Marxism or intersectionality,would vanquish the revolutionary and revelatory potential of their conjunction.

But refusing to choose between these frameworks does not necessarily entail their integration into one, unified whole perspective. It is not my position that intersectionality can or should absorb anything 'useful' from Marxism, nor that Marxism should cannibalize the 'best' from intersectionality, ultimately jettisoning one framework or the other to the dustbin of theories-that-once-were-helpful. What I have thus attempted to stage in this project is not the unproblematic unification of intersectionality and Marxism into one uber-theory; the erasure of differences in these approaches would forestall the creative and dynamic tensions between them. Fredric Jameson, speaking of an altogether different set of concerns, nonetheless illuminates what different theoretical perspectives can bring to the fore if a truly dialectical analysis is embraced[10]: "the two codes must criticize each other, must systematically be translated back and forth into one another in a ceaseless alternation, which foregrounds what each code cannot fully say as much as what it can."[11] This is, I think, the position I take in regards to the relationship between Marxism and intersectionality: it is not about unifying these perspectives as an unproblematic whole, of excising that which is foreign to the other tradition in order to ground a lowest common denominator of their similarity. What I am seeking rather to do is to ground the basis for what we might call a *theoretical coalition* between perspectives, in which the strengths of each perspective are preserved.[12] We can, thus, embrace a "both/and" perspective without eliminating the need for this conjunction.

A concluding remark: In some of the historical references at issue in this book, some of the terminology might strike the reader as anachronistic or imprecise. In speaking of late nineteenth and early twentieth century commu-

---

10 | For those who view the term 'dialectics' as a specifically Marxist figure, I argue against this position in Chapter 6.
11 | Fredric Jameson, *Valences of the Dialectic* (London: Verso, 2009), 47.
12 | For more about what I mean by coalition, see Chapter 7.

nist women of color I often take their analyses and critiques of capitalism under the banner of Marxism, even when they more often used the terms "socialist" and "communist"; some of them, like Lucy Parsons, might even have called themselves anarchists. Throughout much of the nineteenth and twentieth centuries, these terms did not hold or have the same kind of sharp analytical distinctions that they do now, and many of the historical sources under discussion used the terms interchangeably and complementarily. I have used contemporary terms in order to interpret the identities of those in the past, even when the people under discussion might not have used terms like 'intersectional' or 'woman of color' to refer to themselves.

Plan of the Book

While in philosophy, my home discipline, there is often a premium put on figuring out what exactly it is an author *said* or *meant to say*, I take a rather different approach in this book. While some of the book, especially the chapters in Parts One and Two are interested in portraying with greater fidelity what authors from both traditions have said and are saying—much of the contemporary debate between these traditions arises out of a mutual dismissal based on *not reading* or *not understanding* what is read—the rest of the book engages with what Hancock has called "guerilla readings" of texts.[13] Guerilla readings, a hallmark of the intersectional tradition, emerge when we read authors' texts beyond or even against their stated goals or intentions, mining them for strategic openings of thought and action. The third part of this book is engaged in precisely such a set of readings, searching for openings not only that can bridge the gap between traditions of liberatory thinking. The term "guerilla reading" is a particularly apt descriptor for this project. The guerilla is the small, insurgent phalanx, a form of popular militancy, often the incarnation of the diversity of tactics, with environmentally-dependent strategies. It was the chosen form of many anti-capitalist and anti-imperialist struggles for liberation. It is in a series of these readings that I hope new possibilities for thought and for action will emerge.

This book is divided into three parts. The first part "Histories" comprises one chapter that looks at the relationship between the Marxist tradition and the intersectional tradition, concentrating on the decades and centuries before intersectionality emerged as a specific name for a specific theory. This chapter looks at the touchstone figures of intersectionality's history in the nineteenth and twentieth century, examining how black women conceived of the relationship between gender, race, class, and capitalism from Anna Julia Cooper to intersectionality's founding. It specifically probes the vast and dynamic organizing and writing of black communist women throughout this time period.

---

13 | Hancock, *Intersectionality*, 2.

I begin here because, if we are to refuse the assumption that intersectionality and Marxism share no common ground, we must first recognize what historical common ground already exists, what figures these traditions share and what experiences and perspectives, both theoretical and political, framed the pre-history of this rather acrimonious divergence. This is "Chapter Zero" because it is the preparatory work and baseline understanding necessary in order to really approach the differences, debates, and critiques between the two traditions with historical accuracy and theoretical generosity. In that spirit, this chapter also differentiates intersectionality from many of the theories with which it is often conflated: double and triple jeopardy, standpoint theory, and others. McDuffie, for his part, offers a historical explanation for the obscurity of black left feminism the political repression of communism throughout the Cold War (and, indeed, in its aftermath) led to the broader repression of leftist political ideas, histories, and legacies. In addition, the general marginalization of black women from the dominant interpretation of the history of anti-racist and black liberationist struggle meant that the long and vibrant history and ideas of black women on the left have not attracted anywhere near the time, care, and attention that their innovation, clarity, and profundity demand.[14]

Part Two of this text dives deeply into Marxism and intersectionality and the debates between them. Explaining the basic contours of Marxist and intersectional traditions each comprises an independent chapter. In each of these chapters, I have sought to thematize both the continuities within these traditions, as well as the ongoing differences, divergences, and debates within each framework. Having spent a large part of Chapter Zero explaining conceptualizations of race and gender that are not *quite* intersectionality, Chapter One fleshes out a fuller understanding of what the term means and what unique theoretical contributions it has made to the long traditions of black feminist and womanist critique. Chapter Three looks at the Marxist tradition, specifically highlighting the work of queer, feminist, and anti-racist Marxisms that seek to thematize the ways in which capitalism, gender, race, and sexuality are tied together. It thus principally engages with many lesser-known and understudied Marxist figures, forgoing discussions of many of the most famous figures in that tradition.

Part Two also comprises two chapters that focus specifically on points of contention and critique between these traditions. Chapter Two explains Marxist critiques of intersectionality and Chapter Four looks at intersectional critiques of Marxism. In both of these 'critique' chapters, I have included a wide array of points, all of which are organized thematically. These critique chapters address both potent and helpful concerns as well as blatant misreadings. I thus see

---

14 | Erik S. McDuffie, *Sojourning for Freedom: Black Women, American Communism, and the Making of Black Left Feminism* (Durham: Duke University Press, 2011).

these 'critique' chapters as helping us to simultaneously clarify the places in which further work in each of these traditions is necessary, and to allow us to move beyond some of the hackneyed stereotypes that prevent real engagement across traditions.

Part Three charts new possible directions, for both theory and for organizing, that might emerge by allowing intersectionality and Marxism to really engage in deep conversation and cross-pollination. Chapter Five asks how we might approach the question of the relationship between exploitation and oppression if we worked between the intersectional and Marxist traditions. In that chapter, I consider the various ways that figures from both traditions have thought through this relationship, and, finding them lacking, attempt to chart the contours for a new conception, one that integrates insights from both Marxism and intersectionality.

Chapter Six considers the question of contradiction, binaries, and dialectics from a similar perspective. While dialectics is often associated with Marxism, a close reading of many intersectional texts shows that contradiction and dialectics are frequent figures in that tradition as well. Mobilizing insights from both frameworks, I approach the question of how to think difference and structure at one and the same time; ultimately, I argue that both Marxism and intersectionality provide the foundation for thinking difference dialectically in ways that can be mobilized particularly powerfully against contemporary structures of capitalist domination.

In light of this, Chapter Seven meditates on the question of solidarity, what it means, and what happens when it goes dangerously awry. I diagnose in contemporary organizing a tendency to think about solidarity as constituted through some sort of shared condition or a recognition of sameness despite different circumstances. Explaining the ways in which this produces a politics of the "lowest common denominator", I articulate an alternative conception of solidarity, one grounded in differences and relations rather than sameness. Rather than organizing from the lowest common denominator, I argue that revisiting the question of coalitions can provide us with a way of organizing towards our highest and most expansive goals, even when, indeed, especially when, we might need differential demands in order to do so.

As Iris Marion Young wrote in the introduction to her own volume on difference, social movements, and theories of social transformation, "I cannot claim to speak for radical movements of Blacks, Latinos, American Indians, poor people, lesbians, old people, or the disabled. But the political commitment to social justice which motivates my philosophical reflection tells me that I also cannot speak without them." [15] I think of my work in this book, not as *speaking*

---

15 | Iris Marion Young, *Justice and the Politics of Difference* (Princeton, N.J: Princeton University Press, 1990), 14.

for either Marxism or intersectionality, but rather as *speaking with*, of trying to find a way of clearing the space for deeper, more productive conversations, for thinking new horizons, for organizing stronger and more resilient movements, for being more open and more accountable for the deep criticism and reflection that changing the world requires. The work of changing this world will have to be done in conversation with both of these theories.

Part One: Histories

Chapter Zero: The Shared History of the Intersectional and Marxist Traditions

While the contemporary debates between Marxism and intersectionality are themselves rich and important, it is equally important to ground these debates in the often-overlooked fact that intersectionality and Marxism partially share a history, a set of theoretical inheritances, and that, for some time, some of the most innovative and interesting work being done in both traditions was done at their overlap.

From the 1920s to the 1980s in the United States of America, there was a significant amount of overlap, discussion, and cross-pollination between the intersectional tradition and the Marxist tradition. Of course, in other national contexts, where Marxism formed a central part of national liberationist and anti-imperialist theorizing, feminist concerns were often even more directly in dialogue with ideas of socialist revolution. In order to better understand the contemporary divergence between the intersectional and Marxist traditions, it is necessary to historicize this divergence by considering their shared history. Moreover, sketching the history of the relationship between these traditions will allow us to see more clearly how both contemporary Marxist writings on oppression and contemporary writings on intersectionality have developed over time, avoiding the all-too-common mistake of hypostatizing and reifying each of these traditions. We will thus find that "critiques of capitalism and imperialism have been at the heart of black feminism since its beginnings and hasty associations of black feminist scholarship with an unrefined U.S. multiculturalism mask this intricate history."[1]

Many of the intellectual precursors of intersectionality were committed Marxists and/or socialists. Carastathis notes that "Black Communist feminists are its [intersectionality's] unacknowledged historical precursors" while also noting that many Marxists' attempts to integrate intersectionality into Marxism

---

1 | Kelly Coogan-Gehr, "The Politics of Race in US Feminist Scholarship: An Archaeology," *Signs: Journal of Women in Culture & Society* 37, no. 1 (2011): 95.

have problematically minimized or rejected the central claim that oppressions cannot be hierarchized."[2]

In particular, both Katheryn Gines and Eric S. McDuffie recuperate the history of black women communists as founding the often-unacknowledged intellectual precursors of intersectionality.[3] McDuffie names Claudia Jones, Louise Thompson Patterson, Beulah Richardson and Esther Cooper as "proto-intersectional" thinkers, all of whom were active in forms of socialist and Marxist activism in the US. Gines makes a similar claim about Maria Stewart, Sojourner Truth, Anna Julia Cooper, Ida B. Wells, and Sadie Tanner. It is noteworthy that both Gines and McDuffie's accounts are disputed,[4] even if there seems to be broader consensus about Stewart, Truth, and Cooper's status as intellectual forebears of intersectionality.[5] Vivian May argues that Claudia Jones, a prominent member of the Communist Party (CPUSA) in particular articulated "an intersectional race-gender-class analytic" that "reject[ed] a class-primary Marxist approach and androcentric notions of Blackness and Black liberation."[6] The Combahee River Collective situated their intervention with reference to Sojourner Truth, Harriet Tubman, Frances Harper, Ida B. Wells-Barnett, and Mary Church Terrell.[7] Hancock notes that attention to capitalism and its intertwining with both slavery and colonialism formed central aspects of intersec-

---

[2] | Carastathis, *Intersectionality*, 56.

[3] | Kathryn T. Gines, "Race Women, Race Men, and Early Expressions of Proto-Intersectionality," in *Why Race and Gender Still Matter: An Intersectional Approach*, ed. Namita Goswami, Maeve O'Donovan, and Lisa Yount (London: Pickering & Chatto, 2014), 13-26; McDuffie, *Sojourning for Freedom: Black Women, American Communism, and the Making of Black Left Feminism*.

[4] | Carastathis, *Intersectionality*, 18.

[5] | May, *Pursuing Intersectionality, Unsettling Dominant Imaginaries*, 96; Hazel Carby, *Reconstructing Womanhood: The Emergence of the Afro-American Woman Novelist* (New York: Oxford University Press, 1987); Valerie Smith, "Black Feminist Theory and the Representation of the 'Other,'" in *The Woman That I Am: The Literature and Culture of Contemporary Women of Color*, ed. D. Soyini Madison (New York: St. Martin's, 1994), xii-4. Hancock argues that "while Crenshaw, Collins, hooks, Guy-Sheftall, and others have alluded to the contributions of Sojourner Truth," there are many other, less often cited theorists that connect intersectionality theorists to earlier articulations of what she calls "intersectionality-like thinking" throughout the nineteenth and twentieth centuries. I read this claim as being harmonious with McDuffie and Gines' emphasis on the Marxist, socialist, and anti-capitalist thinkers they survey.

[6] | May, *Pursuing Intersectionality, Unsettling Dominant Imaginaries*, 55.

[7] | Combahee River Collective, "A Black Feminist Statement," in *Capitalist Patriarchy and the Case for Socialist Feminism*, ed. Zillah Eisenstein (New York and London: Monthly Review Press, 1979), 363.

tionality's analysis of how oppression, inequality, exploitation, and injustice were organized in the contemporary world; she notes that "while more recent intersectionality scholarship has been criticized for neglecting class, the more complicated history of intersectionality suggests that it has instead fallen out of the discussion of intersectionality among the interpretive community, a different dilemma worth wrangling on its own terms."[8] Here, however, I argue that there is a partially shared history between Marxism and intersectionality. There is a way in which my argument here could be misconstrued to mean that the intersectional tradition came from Marxism, or developed out of it, or is essentially Marxist. Marxism was an influence on the intersectional tradition, or at least on large parts of it, one that is rather consistently under-theorized. But it was far from the only influence on the development of this tradition: the traditions of non-Marxist feminist women of color, national liberation movements (whether or not they were anti-sexist), Harlem Renaissance art and literature, and a million other people, movements, histories, and traditions, as well as the perceptiveness, experiences, and determination of the individual theorists of intersectionality were all part of the necessary conditions of this tradition's emergence and course. Nor, we should note, is influence unidirectional. As we will see, sharing a history evidences influence in multiple ways, in multiple temporalities at once. To posit a relationship between two traditions, to highlight the figures shared between the traditions, to examine the mutual and reciprocal lines of influence, is not to collapse these traditions into a single whole or to argue for the primacy of one over the other; if anything, it is to demonstrate the immense benefits of reading outside one's narrow tradition, of openness to influence from multiple sources, of reading generously and openly, and of "loving critique" when necessary and appropriate.

It is important to note that the argument I make here—that there is a certain overlap in the history of Marxism and intersectionality—is not an uncontested one, though also not an unprecedented one. Gines argues that much of the black feminist tradition through the nineteenth and twentieth centuries are best conceived as "proto-intersectional," deploying the key methodological insights of intersectionality long before it was so named.[9] In his intricate portrait of black women's communist organizing in the United States, McDuffie identifies multiple theories of multi-axis oppression that Black women communists used to understand and explain their own situation since at least the turn of the twentieth century; McDuffie argues that intersectionality has long been a part of the black feminist communist tradition because "early black feminists clearly understood the uniquely cruel, interlocking oppressions experienced

---

8 | Hancock, *Intersectionality*, 44.
9 | Gines, "Race Women, Race Men, and Early Expressions of Proto-Intersectionality."

by black women under capitalism."[10] McDuffie uses "black left feminism" as his umbrella term to group together multiple theories of black women's unique situation under capitalism in particular. For him, intersectionality is only the latest name of this long, vibrant, and internally heterogeneous history.

Jennifer Nash critiques the way that the history of intersectionality is often told collapses the distinction between black feminism and intersectionality, asserting that they are one and the same, whereas, on her account, the latter is one strand among many of the former.[11] Carasthatis in particular worries about this trend in historiography, of subsuming intersectionality as merely the latest term for a long-existing concept, as if intersectionality were the mere assignation of a new term with little or no novel theoretical import: to treat intersectionality as synonymous with other, earlier, and contemporaneous formulations of black women's oppression and exploitation, she argues, "is to assume the superfluousness of concepts, that is, to see them as 'terms' that do not fundamentally alter, and reflect the nature of the analysis being advanced."[12] To assert that the various formulations discussed below—double, triple, or multiple jeopardy, standpoint theory, superexploitation, sexist racism—are *exactly the same* as intersectionality as a theory would itself fall prey to precisely this inattentive generalization. Hancock uses "intersectionality-like thought" to describe the history of black feminist theorizing in her book on the history of intersectionality[13] and Carastathis uses "precursor concepts" to refer to this history.[14] Broadly speaking, the idea of precursor concepts marks ideas, discourses, and analyses that came before intersectionality, but that were instrumental to its development.[15] I speak of 'the intersectional tradition' rather than

---

10 | McDuffie, *Sojourning for Freedom: Black Women, American Communism, and the Making of Black Left Feminism*, 48.
11 | Jennifer Nash, "Home Truths on Intersectionality," *Yale Journal of Law and Feminism* 23, no. 2 (2011): 445.
12 | Carastathis, *Intersectionality*, 18.
13 | Hancock, *Intersectionality*.
14 | Carastathis, *Intersectionality*, 26.
15 | In Carasthathis' account, these four precursor concepts are: double jeopardy, triple jeopardy, multiple jeopardy, and interlocking oppressions. The last of these, Carastathis takes to be representative of the Combahee River Collective account, which Carasthatis discounts as being intersectional because of its understanding of women of color as constituting the vanguard of liberation—in other words, Carastathis does not count the CRC as properly 'intersectional' *because of* the Marxist language they use and their commitment of socialist politics. As is clear, I disagree with this characterization, as it seems to rest on the premise that Marxism and intersectionality are mutually incompatible frameworks, though, we should note, this premise in Carastathis' work is assumed and never explicitly argued for.

'precursor concepts' or 'intersectionality-like' thinking because both of these terms seem to suggest a kind of natural, determined teleology, the idea that all of these concepts were partial, incomplete, waiting to be overtaken by intersectionality, which is the correct, contemporary, complete version that has evolved beyond the errors of previous articulations. As will become clear throughout this chapter and this book, in some ways intersectionality has decisive advantages as a theory, especially as compared to some of these other articulations; but I also argue that some of the insights of these earlier positions has been, explicitly or implicitly, forgotten or evacuated of some of its radical potential. We must move away from the fetishization of the contemporary, from the often implicit belief that the newest theory is always the most complete or correct.

This chapter is divided into four sections, organized more or less chronologically. The first section considers the writing and speeches of three black women writers in the nineteenth century—Maria Stewart, Sojourner Truth, and Ida B. Wells-Barnett—to show the way in which these figures, central to the development of the intersectional tradition, were significantly interested in themes that have strong resonance with Marxist concerns of labor, class, capitalism, and political economy. Reading these women's work in this light does not seek to subsume them into the Marxist tradition, only to highlight the centrality of anti-capitalist themes in their work.

Section Two turns to the first half of the twentieth century in order to explore many of the black women communists whose pioneering work dealt with the interaction between race and gender under capitalism, specifically Louise Thompson Patterson and Claudia Jones. Grounding an analysis of their work in the significant activism of black women communists at the time highlights how at one and the same time Marxism was an important source (but never the sole source) of their theorizing and how their work in Marxist organizations was never free of racism and sexism within those parties. W.E.B. Du Bois is also a pivotal figure of this time period, who has been identified by multiple intersectional theorists as an important 'forefather' of intersectionality.

Section Three looks at roughly the period between 1960 and 1980, exploring some of the concepts and theories that were both central to the development of the intersectional tradition, and yet still distinct from a full theory of intersectionality: double and triple jeopardy, standpoint theory, and racist-sexism. Specifically, I underscore the relationship between gender and race in these theories and class or capitalism. The last section constitutes a brief survey of the ways in which prominent intersectional theorists are specifically concerned with class and capitalism, contrary to the popular belief of many on the Marxist left. By highlighting the centrality of class and capitalism to the theory of intersectionality, it lays the foundation for a more sensitive and nuanced discussion around the productive possibilities of re-integrating these conceptual perspectives.

SECTION ONE: NINETEENTH-CENTURY APPROACHES

Both the intersectional tradition and the Marxist tradition have their roots in the nineteenth century. In the case of Marxism, this periodization is rather uncontested: Marx's first published writings appeared in 1841, *The Communist Manifesto* in 1848, and his magnum opus, *Capital*, was first published in 1867. While an exhaustive account of Marx and Engels' writings on slavery, imperialism, colonization, and gender would take us far afield here, it is important to note that both thinkers were committed to thinking of capitalism as a structure with deep roots in the oppression of women, as well as in the racist and militaristic expansion of European capitalism through slavery, colonization, and imperialism.[16] In the case of the intersectional tradition, many black women's work of the nineteenth century, both political and intellectual, have been identified as some of the first anchors of the tradition. Harriet Tubman, Anna Julia Cooper, and Sojourner Truth are often cited among the pioneers of this tradition. Indeed, the Combahee River Collective takes their name from the Combahee River Raid of 1863, led by Harriet Tubman. In the case of Stewart, Cooper and Truth, my analysis will focus on the centrality of labor to their understanding of the particular situation of black women, both during and after slavery, tracing the ways in which this emphasis influenced the development of the intersectional tradition in the twentieth century and beyond. While it would be patently ridiculous to claim that any of these women were themselves Marxists, their thinking is grounded in a perspective that could be described as historical-materialist, albeit in a different articulation than that given by Marx and Engels.

---

16 | For direct readings of Marx and Engels' theories see: Brown, *Marx on Gender and the Family: A Critical Study*; Anderson, *Marx at the Margins*; Lise Vogel, *Marxism and the Oppression of Women: Toward a Unitary Theory*, ed. Susan Ferguson and David McNally, Reprint edition (Historical Materialism, 2014). Chapter Three, as well as subsequent chapters will deal more directly with Marx and Engels' own views, even if this project is not specifically about them. I omit them here because while they were quite interested in thinking the relationship between each of these structures and capitalism, they never thought them *in relation to each other*, omitting, for example an analysis of women's oppression under capitalist slavery or colonization; likewise, while both Marx and Engels quite explicitly descried slavery, imperialism, and colonization, they rather lacked any substantive analysis of *race* in this regard.

Maria Stewart

Maria Stewart was the first black woman to lecture publicly about politics in the United States, as far as the historical record shows. A significant number of intersectional theorists have drawn on her work as an inspiration for their own. As someone who spoke repeatedly about the specific situation of black women, and especially enslaved black women, Stewart contributed significantly to the intersectional tradition that was to follow. As Patricia Hill Collins notes, Stewart understood black women's position to be framed not only by race and gender, but also by class.[17] In an 1833 speech, she explained "We have pursued the shadow, they have obtained the substance; we have performed the labor, they have received the profits; we have planted the vines, they have eaten the fruits of them."[18] Here Stewart elaborates the outline of a theory of surplus value two decades before Marx: the cause of black women's impoverishment is that it is black women who do the work, yet the profits and products of their labor are expropriated by a ruling class of white, male slave owners. Kristin Waters argues that Stewart (and her contemporary Anna Julia Cooper) "succeeded in 'fracturing' the conceptions of race and gender while at the same time employing them, obliquely addressing concerns about essentializing that were not even to be officially raised until a century later."[19]

Sojourner Truth

Truth is claimed nearly universally as one of the nineteenth-century touchstones in the history of intersectionality. Work functions centrally to Truth's argument and to the history of intersectional and proto-intersectional theorists who draw on her work and insights.

In particular, Truth was one of the first to call significant attention to the kinds of labor, both productive and reproductive, that were the conditions of enslaved black women, an insight that, as we will see below, became central in the work of Patricia Hill Collins, Deborah King, and Angela Davis, as well as other intersectional theorists. Truth demands:

---

17 | Patricia Hill Collins, *Black Feminist Thought: Knowledge, Consciousness, and the Politics of Empowerment*, 1 edition (New York: Routledge, 2008), chap. 1.
18 | Maria Stewart and Marilyn Richardson, *Maria W. Stewart, America's First Black Woman Political Writer* (Bloomington: Indiana University Press, 1987), 59.
19 | Kristin B. Waters, "Some Core Themes of Nineteenth Century Black Feminism," in *Black Women's Intellectual Traditions: Speaking Their Minds*, ed. Kristin B. Waters and Carol B. Conway (Lebanon, NH: University Press of New England, 2007), 382.

That man over there says that women need to be helped into carriages and lifted over ditches, and to have the best place everywhere. Nobody ever helps me into carriages, or over mud-puddles, or gives me any best place! And ain't I a woman? Look at me! Look at my arm! I could have ploughed and planted, and gathered into barns, and no man could head me! And ain't I a woman? I could work as much and eat as much as a man—when I could get it—and bear the lash as well! And ain't I a woman? I have borne thirteen children, and seen them most all sold off to slavery, and when I cried out with my mother's grief, none but Jesus heard me! And ain't I a woman?[20]

In her speech, Truth exposes a variety of pressing insights that contributed to the development of the intersectional tradition and of Marxist understandings of black women's situation under capitalism. Truth's famous speech is often thought to be indicative of an early analysis of the differential position between black women and white women. It is certainly this, pointing to the racist myopia of white women suffragists who conceived of sexism only on the basis of the norms, standards, and exclusions that they themselves experienced. In this way, Truth is one of the first to recognize that sexism is not constructed uniformly, producing differential shapes of oppression across the color line. She thus exposes by means of personal narrative, the way in which racism and sexism interact through the institution of slavery in order to produce a distinct experience of oppression for black women in comparison to white women. Though she "bore thirteen children", the protection and sanctity of motherhood, often exalted for white women (and, we should remember, also deployed against white women as its own hegemonic expectation and controlling narrative) was continually denied to her. The refrain of her speech "ain't I a woman?" poses the problem of using essentialist understandings of womanhood in order to ground a feminist politics. Her speech also highlights the differences between the treatment and social position of enslaved women and enslaved men. Though she "bear[s] the lash' and 'work[s] as much as a man'," it is still clear that Truth is not actually treated *as a man*; sexist norms still apply to her, making it harder for her to get work, presumably because of the way in which the stereotypical image of women as less efficient workers still applies to her. Thus, Truth precisely and concretely describes the ways in which sexism persists against black women, but it is so intertwined with racism, that her situation is qualitatively different from both white women and enslaved men.

Insofar as this speech addresses white women suffragists, Truth also suggests that the kind of gradual, legal reforms of inclusion into the political system are themselves a rather limited strategy of political change, falling disastrously short of anything that could bear the name of liberation. Addition-

---

20 | Sojourner Truth, *Sojourner Truth: Ain't I a Woman?*, ed. Patricia C. McKissack (Southfield, Mich.: Scholastic Paperbacks, 1994).

ally, Truth focuses extensively on the way in which her labor was central to her position under slavery; slavery, she shows, was predicated on the expropriation of enslaved people's labor. In the case of black women, manual labor—plowing, planting, gathering—was not gender-segregated in the way that white working class women's labor was, at the time, generally (though not exclusively) segregated from white men of the same class. Truth thus highlights not only how an analysis of labor is central to understanding slavery, but also, crucially, that women's labor consists not only in the manual labor on the field, but also in her reproductive labor of bearing thirteen children, each of whom are stolen from her and sold for profit. This emphasis draws attention to the way in which slavery profits from the reproductive labor of enslaved women in a qualitatively different way from that of black men: enslaved women produce enslaved *people*, who are themselves bought and sold. Truth's emphasis on the role of reproduction under slavery not only expands her characterization of the specific position, structurally and experientially, of enslaved women, but has also been enormously influential on studies of women under slavery, as well as more generally in the political fight for black women's reproductive justice.[21] Francis Beal draws on Sojourner Truth's work in order to explain how it is that capitalism distorts the image of black femininity in order to accumulate wealth. bell hooks, whose intersectional anti-capitalism will be discussed below, was so influenced by Truth's words that the latter's famous speech became the title of one of hooks' most famous works: *Ain't I a Woman?*[22]

Ida B. Wells-Barnett

Ida B. Wells-Barnett is a touchstone in black feminist organizing and writing of the late-nineteenth and early-twentieth century. Born in 1862, Wells-Barnett is more often referenced than read carefully, obscuring the critique of capitalism that subtends her analysis. Wells-Barnett is best remembered for her groundbreaking investigative reporting on lynching in the U.S. South. At the time, much of the common discourse around lynching had been steeped in racist and gendered narrative that lynchings were justified punishments for black men's sexual advances towards white women; Angela Davis and

---

21 | Angela Y. Davis, "Reflections on the Black Women's Role in the Community of Slaves," *Black Scholar* 12, no. 6 (1971): 2-15; Dorothy Roberts, *Killing the Black Body: Race, Reproduction, and the Meaning of Liberty* (New York: Vintage, 1998); Danielle L. McGuire, *At the Dark End of the Street: Black Women, Rape, and Resistance—A New History of the Civil Rights Movement from Rosa Parks to the Rise of Black Power*, Reprint (New York: Vintage Books, 2011).
22 | bell hooks, *Ain't I a Woman: Black Women and Feminism* (Boston, Mass.: South End Press, 1999).

others have referred to this as the "Myth of the Black Male Rapist."[23] Wells was one of the first to expose this myth through her systematic reporting on the causes, incidences, and frequency of lynching in the South. After three of her close friends, owners of a successful grocery store in Memphis, were lynched because of white business owners' resentment, Wells-Barnett began investigating lynching as a practice that extended far beyond the narrative of rape; she argued instead that lynching was predominantly a tool of economic control. In 1884, she wrote "Thomas Moss, Calvin McDowell, and Lee Stewart had been lynched... with just as much brutality as other victims of the mob; and they had committed no crime against white women. This is what opened my eyes to what lynching really was. An excuse to get rid of Negroes who were acquiring wealth and property and thus keep the race terrorized and 'keep the nigger down.'"[24] The rape narrative that supposedly justified lynching, was, on Wells-Barnett's account, a specific racial and gendered way of creating a general climate of terror that could continue to foster the continued control of property by a class of white capitalists. Wells-Barnett's account is noteworthy for a variety of reasons: in the first place, her journalistic work was some of the earliest systematic interrogations of lynching, and the data she collected continued to be used in community organizing and legal challenges to lynching for decades. Davies notes that Wells-Barnett was a significant influence on generations of black women journalists, specifically on Claudia Jones, who will be discussed later in this chapter.[25] Secondly, Wells-Barnett linked lynching to the material conditions of life in the South in new ways. Lastly, Wells-Barnett's prescient analysis allowed for new investigations into the complicated nexus of race, gender, and capitalism. Recognizing that racist narratives of sexual violence were being used as ideological cover to ground the continuous operation of impoverishment, her work was some of the first to expose the ways in which white women often contributed to racist violence in specifically gendered ways. As Meghan Ming Francis notes, "*Crusade for Justice* provides a new way to think about black death and its relationship to modern capitalism and white supremacy. According to Wells, the logic of lynching was not criminal; it was economic. Lynching and mob violence were tactics of economic subordina-

---

23 | Angela Y. Davis, "Rape, Racism, and the Myth of the Black Rapist," in *Women, Race, & Class*, 1st Vintage Books ed edition (New York: Vintage, 1983).
24 | Ida B. Wells-Barnett, *On Lynching: Southern Horrors and Other Writings*, ed. Jacqueline Jones Royster (Boston, MA: Bedford/ St. Martin's, 1997), 4.
25 | Carole Boyce Davies, *Left of Karl Marx: The Political Life of Black Communist Claudia Jones* (Durham: Duke University Press, 2008), 69-70.

tion, used to protect white economic power and to ensure a captive black labor force."[26]

It would be a bit too much to claim that Wells-Barnett was herself a Marxist. Rather, it is instructive to see that already in the late nineteenth century, black women such as Wells-Barnett were interpreting the cause of racial violence as structural, economic problems. As we have seen, Wells-Barnett becomes a major inspiration and touchstone for later intersectional thinkers, and her work continues to be used in contemporary intersectional anti-police brutality organizations.

Section Two: Activism and Shared History in the Early-Twentieth Century

When, in this chapter and in this book, I argue that the Marxist and the intersectional traditions share part of their histories, this is ultimately true because of both traditions of theory being deeply committed to activism and street-level politics. We must always remember, as it is too often forgotten by academics, that both Marxism and intersectionality are ways of understanding the world that are irrevocably linked to activism; they both came out of deep, embedded politics among exploited, oppressed, and disenfranchised groups and continue to be mobilized most often in community organizations, coalitions, marches, campaigns, and myriad other forms of real, embodied resistances. While this is not a historiographical project, tracing exactly how and when, through which conversations and chance meetings ideas were shared—though such a project would itself be valuable—ultimately the mutual circuits of influence between the intersectional tradition and the Marxist tradition was born through the significant history of struggle, in national and international organizations, in workplace struggles, in courtroom battles, in marches, strikes, on street corners. For much of the twentieth century, black women organizers were centrally important in several Marxist, socialist, and communist organizations. Moreover, when women of color left communist organizations—often over issues of racism and/or sexism—they took their commitments to anti-capitalism to other groups, organizations, and campaigns. Likewise, women of color continually raised issues of the particular shape of their oppression under capitalism, critiquing, often publicly, the leadership and membership of their own organizations to better conceptualize the relationship between gender, race, sexuality, and capitalism. There is a deep history of interrelation between

---

26 | Megan Ming Francis, "Ida B. Wells and the Economics of Racial Violence," *Items: Insights from the Social Sciences*, January 24, 2017, http://items.ssrc.org/ida-b-wells-and-the-economics-of-racial-violence/.

modes of movement building and organizing that occupies a shared position as historical precursor to contemporary Marxism and intersectionality.

Erik McDuffie's path-breaking study of black women communists in the early-twentieth century traces this history with much more nuance than I will be able to generate in this discussion.[27] Among the figures discussed in this history are: Audley 'Queen Mother' Moore, Louise Thompson Patterson, Thyra Edwards, Bonita Williams, Williana Burroughs, Claudia Jones, Esther Cooper Jackson, Beulah Richardson (who sometimes also went by Beah Richards), Grace P. Campbell, Charlene Mitchell, and Sallye Bell Davis. Black left feminism, a term originally coined by Mary Helen Washington,[28] had been used before McDuffie to name the politics of radical black women after World War II; by tracing black left feminism to black women's vibrant participation in (and critique of) communist and socialist parties in the early-twentieth century, McDuffie argues that one can see not only the influence of Marxism on the development of the black radical feminist tradition, but also how black women's critiques of these parties developed the trajectory of communist organizing in the United States. While there has been extensive study of black women's political agitation in women's clubs, church groups, legislative organizations, and civil rights groups, the memory of black women's leadership in the U.S. Marxist movement has been erased, obscuring the ways in which communism influenced the much better known and studied activism of black women in subsequent decades.[29]

The early-twentieth century saw a massive upsurge in black participation in socialist, communist, and Marxist organizations in the United States, and this was especially true in the case of black women. As Winston James notes, this is largely traceable to the fact that black people "saw the ideology as first

---

27 | McDuffie, *Sojourning for Freedom: Black Women, American Communism, and the Making of Black Left Feminism*.

28 | Mary Helen Washington, "Alice Childress, Lorraine Hansberry, and Claudia Jones: Black Women Write the Popular Front," in *Left of the Color Line: Race, Radicalism, and the Twentieth-Century Literature of the United States*, ed. Bill V. Mullen and James Smethurst (Chapel Hill: University of North Carolina Press, 2003), 183-204.

29 | We should note, however, that McDuffie's understanding of 'intersectionality' and the linkages he makes between it and early black left feminism should be treated with suspicion. He expressly equates the "theory of 'triple oppression'" elaborated by black communist women in the early twentieth century, with what is "now referred to by feminist scholars as intersectionality" (McDuffie, 4). As will be discussed later in this chapter, intersectionality and the 'jeopardy' approach are not in fact synonymous and their equation obscures some of the theoretical specificity of intersectionality. Nevertheless, it is also true that the jeopardy approach was an important precursor to intersectionality.

and foremost a means of solving the race problem," but it is perhaps equally true that black women saw Marxism as way of countering their own experiences of oppositional sexism and racist gendering.[30] And while the story has often been told that Marxist organizers were themselves blind or indifferent to the particular position of black women under capitalism, it is also true that the presence, organizing, and critique of black women in the U.S. significantly influenced the course of communist organizing the world over, especially through the significant focus and attention to race and gender under the Sixth International. In Robin D.G. Kelley's estimation, even the 1928 so-called "Black Belt Thesis" passed by the Sixth International (written by black Chicago-based communist Harry Haywood and Siberian Charles Nasanov) which called for fighting "white chauvinism"' in the party and joining the fights against Jim Crow and lynching itself "essentially precluded a serious theoretical framework that might combine the 'Negro' and 'Woman' questions."[31] Even though the resolution separated these questions, the resolution called black women "the most exploited" population in the American labor force.[32] This is of course not in any way to suggest that Communist organizations were themselves free of racism, sexism, or the particular devaluation, marginalization, or silencing of black women; it is rather to say that an accounting of the history demands a more nuanced understanding, one that can render both the centrality of black women to Communist organizations and the deep limitations of those organizations.

The relationship between the Communist Party (CPUSA) and black communities distinctively changed with the former's involvement in the Scottsboro trial. Louise Thompson, Audley Moore, and Bonita Williams were all centrally involved in these efforts albeit in rather different ways. The labor of these communist women and many others culminated in the "Free the Scottsboro Boys March" which was the first large-scale demonstration for racial equality in the nation's capital, and obviously set the stage for the civil rights movement's use of the tactic. As Audley Moore recounted it was during this period that " [the CPUSA] taught me the science of society", adding that it was in that organization that she "really learned to struggle."[33] Despite this significant history, the relationship between communist parties and black liberation in this period are

---

30 | James Winston, "Being Red and Black in Jim Crow America: Notes on the Ideology and Travails of Afro-America's Socialist Pioneers," *Souls* 1, no. 4 (1999): 54.

31 | Robin D. G. Kelley, *Race Rebels: Culture, Politics, and the Black Working Class* (New York: Free Press, 1994), 114.

32 | Jane Degras, ed., *The Communist International Documents 1919-1943*, vol. 2, 3 vols. (London: Routledge, 2013). See especially the Resolution of 26 October 1928.

33 | Qtd in: McDuffie, *Sojourning for Freedom: Black Women, American Communism, and the Making of Black Left Feminism*, 81.

both complicated and varied. It is true that Communist and Socialist parties were elaborating some of the most radical policies and statements on black liberation of the time period, but it is also true that many black members experienced deeply disturbing racism within the party, that the positions of the national and international organizations changed over time; that there was also a lack of uniformity in just how central black liberation was to different chapters of each organization; and that there were certainly circumstances in which black people and the black liberation struggle were treated merely as means to ends. Harold Cruse's *The Crisis of the Negro Intellectual* (1967) greatly influenced the reception and study of this relationship, by arguing that the communist parties of the period, not caring at all about racial equality, essentially lied about this commitment in order to lure unsuspecting black people into their organization on false pretenses. Though this account has been roundly critiqued, the narrative continues to inform both scholarly works and activist politics.[34]

Black women were also central to labor organizing of the period. In response to the gender-exclusionary policies of many unions, The Working Women's Association (1868), the Women's Trade Union League (1903), and the International Ladies' Garment Workers' Union all advocated for white women, yet often themselves endorsed, explicitly or implicitly, racism against women of color. As King notes, "black women benefited little from unionization efforts among white women"[35] because they were not only disproportionately represented in industries least likely to be unionized (like domestic work and agriculture) but also because white women often actively discouraged or proactively prohibited women of color from joining their unions.

In response to exclusionary policies directed at people of color in the union movement at large, many people of color formed their own caucuses within white-dominated unions or formed associations or unions of their own such as the Urban League's Negro Workers Councils, the National Negro Labor Council, the Dodge Revolutionary Union Movement, the Negro American Labor Council, and the Brotherhood of Sleeping Car Porters. All of these latter

---

34 | Gary Holcomb, *Claude McKay, Code Name Sasha: Queer Black Marxism and the Harlem Renaissance* (Gainsville, FL: University Press of Florida, 2009); Robin D. G. Kelley, *Hammer and Hoe: Alabama Communists During the Great Depression* (Chapel Hill: University of North Carolina Press, 1990); Mark Naison, *Communists in Harlem During the Great Depression* (New York: Grove Press, 1983); Michael C. Dawson, *Blacks In and Out of the Left* (Cambridge, Mass.: Harvard University Press, 2013); Manning Marable and Leith Mullings, *How Capitalism Underdeveloped Black America: Problems in Race, Political Economy, and Society* (Haymarket Books, 2015).

35 | Deborah K. King, "Multiple Jeopardy, Multiple Consciousness: The Context of a Black Feminist Ideology," *Signs* 14, no. 1 (1988): 66.

organizations would become central figures in larger anti-racist organizing and struggle of the period. Some unions actively encouraged an integrated membership, like the Knights of Labor (1886), the Industrial Workers of the World (1905), and the Congress of Industrial Organizations (1938). King argues that black women were centrally important to black men's labor organizing of the period, even though their contributions to these struggles are consistently undervalued:

Black women benefitted indirectly from black men's labor activism and they often supported those efforts by participating on picket lines, providing food and clothing to strikers and their families, and, most important, making financial contributions to the households from their own paid labor. Black women also engaged in labor organizing directly, both through existing predominantly white unions and through their own activism. Black domestics, tobacco workers, garment workers, and others organized strikes and fought for union representation.[36]

But the relationship between black women and communism extended far beyond communist parties and direct labor organizing. Equally important to understand is the way in which black women communists developed an explicitly antiracist, anti-sexist, and anti-capitalist politics beyond the confines of organized socialist organizations, often taking Marxist anti-capitalist politics into organizing not only workplaces, but home communities around issues of segregation, food and housing justice, domestic labor, and many other issues. The Harlem Tenants League (HTL) was one of the organizations run by radical black communist women. The League organized street protests, rent strikes, and blocked evictions. They mobilized against segregation, landlords who ignored housing regulations, and unemployment. In McDuffie's estimation, the women of the HTL "recognized the connections between black women's exploitation, consumption, unemployment, and radical discrimination, thereby challenging Marxist-Leninist notions that the shop floor constituted the key site for producing class consciousness and for initiating transformative change."[37] The HTL and other organizations like the Harlem Women Day Workers League (HWDWL) were some of the first to push for the unionization of black women domestic workers. Fanny Austin, a domestic worker herself and head of the HWDWL, explained that the unionization campaign was crucial because they remained "among the most exploited sections of the working class."[38] In 1932,

---

36 | King, 66.
37 | McDuffie, *Sojourning for Freedom: Black Women, American Communism, and the Making of Black Left Feminism*, 45–46.
38 | Qtd in: Mark Soloman, *The Cry Was Unity: Communists and African Americans 1917-1936* (Jackson: University of Mississippi Press, 1998), 100.

Maude White, a black member of the Communist Party USA, described the way in which even exploited white workers were paid a "psychological wage" due to their socially-conferred superiority over their black comrades; White called attention to the ways in which this both hindered class solidarity across racial lines, but also how this specifically played out in gendered ways.[39] In both their activism and their writing, black women in the socialist and communist parties at this time "recognized... black women's employment as domestics in white women's homes, their subjugation to racialized sexual violence, and the denigration of their bodies and reputation by their oppressors, and the intractable issues facing diasporic communities' very survival."[40]

We can see these linkages not only through the campaigns black women communists ran, but also through their writings in organization and party sponsored publications. The explosion of anti-capitalist organizing among black women produced significantly new and innovative theorizing around the particular socio-historical position that black women held under capitalism, and some of this theorizing would itself prove to be significant in the later development of intersectionality. It should come as no surprise then that just as intersectionality and Marxism share certain aspects of their history in theory, they also share some histories of organizing. Moreover, one cannot be reminded often enough that most of the thinkers under consideration in this book were themselves activists, and hence their contributions to theory were largely generated in constant dialogue with activist movements. Recognizing the ways in which anti-capitalism influenced an entire generation of black women's activism allows us to see the ways in which a "black women's international"[41] was absolutely central to the theorizing and organizing of the period. An exhaustive inventory of all of these radical black women's writings would be impossible in these pages, but as brief examples, it will be helpful to turn to the work of Louise Thompson, Claudia Jones, and W.E.B. Du Bois.

Louise Thompson

Louise Thompson was a black woman member of the Communist Party and contributor to the CPUSA's journal *Woman Today*. In April 1936, she published her most famous work, "Toward a Brighter Dawn," an exposé of what she calls "the Bronx slave market," the market for black women's domestic labor. Drawing evocative comparisons between black women's work in white homes and the system of Southern sharecropping, she reads the continuities

---

39 | Qtd in: McDuffie, *Sojourning for Freedom: Black Women, American Communism, and the Making of Black Left Feminism*, 52.
40 | Ibid, 4.
41 | Ibid, 18.

between slavery and post-Emancipation. She imagines the women sitting in the "slave market" to be saying: "Here we are, for sale for the day. Take our labor. Give us what you will. We must feed our children and pay high rent in Harlem. Ten cents, fifteen cents an hour! That won't feed our families for a day, let alone pay rent. You won't pay more? Well, guess that's better than going back to Harlem after spending your last nickel for carfare..."[42] Her analysis was both striking and influential for a variety of reasons. In the first place, by naming the contemporary domestic labor market a slave market, Thompson is able to highlight the structural and experiential continuities between slavery under capitalism and the exceedingly low wages black women under capitalism receive. Moreover, Thompson gives voice to the black women, explaining the logic at work as they make the decision to continue to sell their labor in this way. Third, Thompson elaborated a concept of *triple exploitation*, which was itself somewhat different from other contemporary and subsequent theories of triple oppression: "The Bronx 'slave market' is a graphic monument to the bitter exploitation of this most exploited section of the American working population—the Negro women. Over this whole land, Negro women meet this triple exploitation—as workers, as women, as Negroes."[43] Thompson explained that this triple exploitation is manifested in a variety of ways: the racial-gendered division of labor that confines black women to domestic or service work, the discrimination against black people in attaining social benefits, and structural conditions that ensure the underfunding and under-provisioning of black neighborhoods. Thompson's account is noteworthy because hers is one of the few extant works to specifically identify racism and sexism *as themselves forms of exploitation* rather than as oppressions used in order to justify or maintain exploitation. Her account was influential on Claudia Jones, who elaborated a new concept of "superexploitation."

Claudia Jones

By far one of the most commonly discussed black women communists was Claudia Jones. Born in Trinidad, Jones migrated to the United States as a child, where she lived until she was eventually deported under the Smith Act for her political organizing. Jones was a member of the Young Communist League in her youth and later served as the secretary for the National Women's Commission of the Communist Party (USA). She was a writer and later editor of the communist newspaper *The Daily Worker*; after her deportation and resettle-

---

42 | Louise Thompson Patterson, "Toward a Brighter Dawn (1936)," *Viewpoint Magazine*, October 31, 2015, https://www.viewpointmag.com/2015/10/31/toward-a-brighter-dawn-1936/.
43 | Ibid.

ment in the UK, she founded London's first major black newspaper, *The West Indian Gazette*. Jones became notable not only for popularizing the concept of "triple oppression", but also for her conceptualization of "superexploitation of black women." One of the leading theoreticians of the CPUSA, Jones was specifically attentive to the role of black women under capitalism, as well as to the larger context of international imperialism in which black women in the U.S. were situated.

Before Jones used the term "superexploitation" to refer specifically to black women's position, the concept had a long history in Marxist theory stretching all the way back to the publication of *Capital, Volume 3* in 1893. In Marx, the term referred to the possibility of wages falling so low that they dip below the value of labor.[44] Lenin revised and expanded the concept of super-exploitation to take stock of the global effects of imperialism in redistributing wealth and resources away from colonized and formerly colonized countries to Europe and the United States. He specifically used it to conceptualize how workers in the Global North could be thought to profit from exploited workers in the Global South. Through the structure of international imperialism, profits of immense proportion are able to be extracted from workers in colonized countries or those under imperial influence.[45] A certain part (though not all) of these super-profits are themselves distributed among the working classes of the imperial nation in the form of higher standards of living, access to new goods and services, access to social safety nets financed through imperial ventures, etc. This gives workers a direct, material stake in the continuation of the imperial, capitalist system, even as it is complicit in their own exploitation.[46]

In the late nineteenth and early twentieth centuries, the term superexploitation was being applied more broadly—to women's work and the labor of people of color, even inside imperial nations. This language became common in some of the work of black left feminists in the United States to conceptualize the status of black women. Jones' most famous article, the 1949 "An End to the Neglect of the Problems of the Negro Woman!" centered a theory of triple oppression and superexploitation. In the 1949 piece, Jones used superexploitation to explain black women's position under capitalism. Jones uses the term superexploitation to conceptualize "uniquely severe, persistence, and dehumanizing forms of capitalist exploitation"[47] that referred to

---

44 | Karl Marx, *Capital, Volume III* (Harmondsworth, England: Penguin Books, 1981), chap. 14.

45 | V.I. Lenin, "Imperialism and the Split in Socialism," *Marxists Internet Archive*, October 1916, https://www.marxists.org/archive/lenin/works/1916/oct/x01.htm.

46 | Ruy Mauro Marini, *Dialéctica de Dependencia* (Mexico: Ediciones Era, 1973).

47 | McDuffie, *Sojourning for Freedom: Black Women, American Communism, and the Making of Black Left Feminism*, 8.

the way in which black women's labor is assumed; the ways they are relegated to service work by all sectors of society, with the complicity of progressive and white women's and labor interests (including those on the Left). It related to their low salary, compared with the level of work they are asked to give in return.[48]

She writes, "Negro women—as workers, as Negroes, and as women—are the most oppressed stratum of the whole population."[49]

In particular, Jones argued that women's role in domestic work was central to "the special oppression [they] face."[50] This social and economic segregation of black women to care-taking work, in Jones' estimation, was not merely confined to the lower pay and higher rate of exploitation black women domestic workers experienced—though it was this too—but also due to "the white chauvinist stereotype as to where [their] place should be," which continued, in the twentieth century to replay the "stereotype of the Negro slave mother," who was "a traditional 'mammy' who puts the care of children and families of others above her own."[51] According to Jones' biographer, Carole Boyce Davies, several aspects of Jones' thinking "advanced Marxist-Leninist positions beyond their apparent limitations" in conceiving the unique position of black women under capitalism.[52] Her use of superexploitation was influential in disseminating the idea that black women's situation under capitalism was *something more* than mere exploitation, which was the dominant interpretation in certain Marxist circles at the time, and indeed, still is. The "super'" of "superexploitation" suggests not only that black women are exploited as workers, often in significantly more precarious positions than their white and male counterparts, but also that their exploitation is structured differently, through the production and maintenance of both a segregated labor market *and* through racist and sexist ideas of their place in society. The accumulated and sedimented histories of the uniquely sexist and racist narratives, stereotypes, and images of black women that derive from their position under slavery continues, according to Jones, to constitute black women's position under capitalism in ways that are simply not reducible to the form of exploitation that is common to all members of the working class. For Jones, black women's position as superexploited people uniquely placed

---

48 | Boyce Davies, *Left of Karl Marx: The Political Life of Black Communist Claudia Jones*, 42.

49 | Claudia Jones, "An End to the Neglect of the Problems of the Negro Woman! (1949)," in *Words of Fire: An Anthology of African-American Feminist Thought*, ed. Beverly Guy-Sheftall (New York: The New Press, 1995), 109.

50 | Ibid, 111.

51 | Ibid, 111.

52 | Boyce Davies, *Left of Karl Marx: The Political Life of Black Communist Claudia Jones*, 2.

them as "the most revolutionary segment of the U.S. working class, thereby challenging orthodox Marxist postulations that industrial (white male) workers represented the [revolutionary] vanguard."[53] As we will see elsewhere, the idea that black women constitute a vanguard social position in the fight against capitalism influenced the development of the intersectional tradition, specifically in the development of the Combahee River Collective's *Statement*.

But Jones' position was itself somewhat different from the full-blown intersectional position that would be developed later. In particular, Jones was quite explicit in rejecting the non-hierarchy of oppressions, which, as we will see in the next chapter, constitutes a central differentiating feature of intersectionality from many of the other formulations of black women's position in the intersectional tradition. As Jones writes,

A developing consciousness on the woman question today[...] must not fail to recognize that the Negro question in the United States is prior to, and not equal to, the woman question; that only to the extent that we fight all chauvinist expressions and actions as regards the Negro people and fight for the full equality of the Negro people, can women as a whole advance their struggle for equal rights. For the progressive women's movement, the Negro woman, who combines in her status the worker, the Negro, and the woman, is the vital link to this heightened political consciousness.[54]

Thus, while Jones' commitment to understanding the unique position of black women under capitalism influenced the intersectional tradition, her argument still differed from the intersectional position that would develop later. Moreover, while Jones saw race, gender, and class as intimately connected, she also embraced the perspective that they were distinct and separable, which would distinguish her position from both intersectionality and unitary Marxist feminist theory.

W. E. B. Du Bois

In some accounts of intersectionality, W.E.B. Du Bois is cited as an 'intellectual forefather' of the tradition.[55] Many intersectional thinkers have drawn on the work of Du Bois, who was an explicit and avowed socialist. Du Bois is perhaps

---

53 | Erik S. McDuffie, "'No Small Amount of Change Could Do': Esther Cooper Jackson and the Making of a Black Feminist Left," in *Want to Start a Revolution? Radical Women in the Black Freedom Struggle*, ed. Dayo Gore, Jeanne Theoharis, and Komozi Woodard (New York: New York University Press, 2009), 34.
54 | Jones, "An End to the Neglect of the Problems of the Negro Woman! (1949)," 120.
55 | Ange-Marie Hancock, "W.E.B. Du Bois: Intellectual Forefather of Intersectionality?," *Souls* 7, no. 3-4 (2005): 74-84.

best known for his work on race in the United States in the Reconstruction period; less well known is the way in which, through nearly all of his writing, Du Bois understands race as a specifically gendered concept that is also sutured directly to capitalism. In contemporary accounts, as Manning Marable argues, Du Bois is most frequently associated with his work with the NAACP and his espousal of Pan Africanism, but all too often his most radical views "as an advocate of women's suffrage, socialism, and peace" are overlooked.[56] While Marxist studies of Du Bois often focus on his debates with his contemporaries about the relevance of race to class, and feminist writings on Du Bois focus often on his writings about gender and race,[57] the intersectional tradition has convincingly argued that, in fact, Du Bois focused on race, gender, and class together as centrally important issues that "mattered simultaneously in most, if not all, political contexts."[58]

There is no doubt that Du Bois was a thinker interested in questions of race, gender, and class; Hancock's question is whether his conceptualization of them was "multiple" or "intersecting."[59] While Hancock stops short of declaring Du Bois a full-fledged intersectional theorist, she argues that three of his claims about race, gender, and sexuality "presage" intersectionality.[60] The three claims are: 1) that black people can be thought of as "outsiders within" American society 2) that race, gender, and class are of "simultaneous significance" 3) and that both an individual and a structural account of oppression is necessary in order to understand it. In addition to these points, it is important to understand 4) that Du Bois argued for the centrality of capitalism as the system that grounded the relations of race, gender, and class as he understands them and 5) that in foregrounding the structural contradictions of capitalism, Du Bois

---

56 | Manning Marable, "Reconstructing the Radical Du Bois," *Souls* 7, no. 3-4 (2005): 2.

57 | We should note however, that Du Bois' feminism is contested, with many arguing that his thought, activism, and personal life complicate this picture. For multiple positions in this debate, see: Hazel Carby, *Race Men* (Cambridge: Harvard University Press, 1998); Farah Jasmine Griffin, "Black Feminists and Du Bois: Respectability, Protection, and Beyond," *Annnals of the American Academy of Political Science*, no. 568 (2000): 28-40; Nellie Y. McKay, "The Souls of Black Women Folk in the Writings of W.E.B. Du Bois," in *Reading Black Reading Feminist: A Critical Anthology*, ed. Henry Louis Gates Jr. (New York: Meridian Books, 1990), 227-43; Katherine Bell Banks and Robert C. Hayden, *W.E.B. Du Bois, Family, and Friendship: Another Side of the Man, Letters, and Memories* (Littleton, MA: Tapestry Press, 2004).

58 | Hancock, "W.E.B. Du Bois: Intellectual Forefather of Intersectionality?," 74.
59 | Hancock, 76.
60 | Ibid.

unlocks a different history of anti-capitalist resistance that centers on black women's agency, a central component of later Marxist and intersectional theory.

First, Du Bois' "outsider within" perspective clearly influenced Patricia Hill Collins' account in *Black Feminist Thought*, where she elaborates an account of the "controlling images" of black women that significantly frame their oppression. Collins wrote extensively on Du Bois, not only naming him as the person who had a preliminary concept of controlling images, but also thinking critically about his relationship to her own discipline of sociology.[61] In another text, Collins writes: "Du Bois saw race, class, and nation not primarily as personal identity categories but as social hierarchies that shaped African American access to status, poverty, and power."[62]

Second, and perhaps most importantly, DuBois argued for the simultaneity of race, class, and gender. As he writes in *Darkwater*

What is today the message of these black women to America and to the world? The uplift of women is, next to the problem of the color line and the peace movement, our greatest modern cause. When, now, two of these movements—woman and color—combine in one, the combination has deep meaning.[63]

Hancock argues that this formulation advances toward intersectionality as Du Bois "locates the problems of 'the color line' and 'uplift of women' next to one other rather than one after the other."[64] Dispensing with the chronological or causal priority that was much more common at that time, Du Bois rather shows that struggles need to combine in order to achieve their ends. Alys Eve Weinbaum calls attention to Du Bois' emphasis on the role of women's reproductive labor and sexual exploitation to the constitution of slavery. While she rejects reading *Black Reconstruction* as an overtly feminist text, Weinbaum does argue that "it performs an explosive, if fleeting, opening up of the question of the gender and sexual politics of slavery and the revolt against it."[65] Angela Davis also specifically calls attention to the ways in which Du Bois thought of gender, race, and class as fundamentally inter-articulated categories: "As a male

---

61 | Patricia Hill Collins, "Du Bois's Contested Legacy," *Ethnic and Racial Studies* 39, no. 8 (2016): 1398-1406.

62 | Patricia Hill Collins, "Gender, Black Feminism, and Political Economy," *The Annals of the American Academy of Political and Social Science* 586 (2000): 41-53.

63 | W.E.B Du Bois, *Darkwater: Voices from Within the Veil* (New York: Prometheus Books, 2003), 187.

64 | Hancock, "W.E.B. Du Bois: Intellectual Forefather of Intersectionality?," 77.

65 | Alys Eve Weinbaum, "Gendering the General Strike: W.E.B. Du Bois's Black Reconstruction and Black Feminism's 'Propaganda of History,'" *South Atlantic Quarterly* 112, no. 3 (2013): 441.

advocate of woman suffrage, W.E.B. Du Bois was peerless among Black and white men alike" for not only championing women's equality, but for doing so without "male supremacist undertones."[66] She argues that his essay "The Damnation of Women" constituted a strong influence on later works that "emphasized the extent to which black working class women's relative economic independence summoned various modes of female consciousness that emphasized strength, resilience and autonomy." Davis does however critique some of Du Bois' account, arguing that his work often assumes a "strictly causal relationship between the economic conditions of slavery... and the gendered consciousness among working-class black women" that is ultimately too reductive.[67]

The third element Hancock identifies as being intersectional is Du Bois' commitment to an analysis of oppression that integrates both structural and individual accounts. Most clearly evidenced in *Darkwater and Dusk of Dawn*, Hancock explains that understanding Du Bois' overall analysis of structures of oppression requires reading these texts' structural account in conjunction with the more personal accounts he gives in other writings, notably in *The Souls of Black Folk*. Distinguishing him from other theorists like Frederick Douglass, Booker T. Washington, or David Walker, Hancock explains that "Du Bois acknowledges the interaction between individual agent and structure in political outcomes, which again predates claims made by intersectionality theorists."[68] In this way, Du Bois embodied the combination of careful analysis and political activism that characterize both intersectionality and Marxism, as domains that boast deep academic engagement as well as extensive street level activism. As Du Bois once wrote about his own call to join active struggles, "one could not be a calm, cool, and detached scientist while Negroes were lynched, murdered, and starved."[69] However, Hancock downplays the centrality of Du Bois' anti-capitalism. While we can see through Hancock, Collins, Davis, and Weinbaum's analysis how Du Bois' ideas were influential on the intersectional tradition, all but Davis leave out Du Bois' commitment to socialism. However, Du Bois' critique of capitalism is precisely one of the ways he influenced the development of the intersectional tradition.

Du Bois had an ambivalent relationship to Marxist politics, if not Marxist theory. He joined the Socialist Party in 1911, but left in 1912 due to the party's

---

66 | Angela Y. Davis, *Women, Race, & Class*, 1st Vintage Books ed edition (New York: Vintage, 1983), 146–47.

67 | Angela Y. Davis, *Blues Legacies and Black Feminism: Gertrude "Ma" Rainey, Bessie Smith, and Billie Holiday*, 1st Vintage Books edition (New York: Vintage, 1999), 46–47.

68 | Hancock, "W.E.B. Du Bois: Intellectual Forefather of Intersectionality?"

69 | W.E.B Du Bois, *The Autobiography of W.E.B. Du Bois: A Sololoquy on Viewing My Life from the Last Decade of Its First Century* (New York: International Publishers, 1968), 222.

inability to combat racism within its own ranks. Later in his life, he joined the Communist Party in 1961. Despite his critique of the Marxist organizations of his time, Du Bois' writings altered the trajectory of Marxist theory and practice in the United States through his insistence on the intertwining of capitalism and racism. As Earl Ofari has noted, *Dusk of Dawn,* "laid out... a comprehensive program for the total economic reconstruction of black America" that was rooted in "socialism rather than capitalism."[70] Du Bois was central to Cedric Robinson's account of the Black Radical Tradition in *Black Marxism,* and the latter claimed that Du Bois' analysis of the relationship between European imperialism, global capitalism, and the racialization of non-white exploited labor "anticipat[ed] Lenin's thesis on imperialism."[71] As Robinson explains, one of the most decisive of Du Bois' contributions was his insistence on the slave as a 'black worker', a move that both drew on and radically reorganized Marxist conceptions of class, struggle, and revolution.[72] Du Bois argued that resistance to slavery expressed not "merely... the desire to stop work", but rather a whole political program; in this way, the whole Civil War "was a strike on a wide basis against the conditions of work."[73] Manning Marable further argues, Du Bois' understanding "of what scholars today describe as structural racism" was "undergirded by a political economy of modern capitalism. The Jim Crow system in the United States was just a subsidiary of that larger global system of racialized exploitation and empire."[74]

Lastly, Du Bois understood the complex dynamics of race, gender, and class to be fundamentally contradictory. In this sense, it is not just, as Hancock notes, that black people are positioned in a contradictory location, but that the system of capitalist slavery itself creates a whole series of contradictory ideologies and practices. He specifically noted the structuring contradictions capitalist slavery required in terms of reproduction: "Human slavery in the South pointed and led in two singularly contradictory and paradoxical directions—toward the deliberate commercial breeding and sale of human labor for profit and toward the intermingling of black and white blood. The slave holders shrank from acknowledging either set of facts but they were clear and

---

70 | Earl Ofari, *The Myth of Black Capitalism* (New York: Monthly Review Press, 1970), 90-91.
71 | Cedric J. Robinson, *Black Movements in America* (New York: Routledge, 1997), 114.
72 | Cedric J. Robinson, *Black Marxism: The Making of the Black Radical Tradition*, 2nd ed. (Chapel Hill: University of North Carolina Press, 2000), 185-240.
73 | W.E.B Du Bois, *Black Reconstruction in America, 1860-1880* (New York: Free Press, 1992), 67.
74 | Marable, "Reconstructing the Radical Du Bois," 19.

undeniable."[75] As Weinbaum interprets this chapter, "when Du Bois goes on to discuss rape in the 'deliberate commercial breeding' of slaves, he emphasizes the instrumental role of sexual violence in the perpetuation of the slave economy."[76] Weinbaum then notes that in Du Bois' discussion of runaways, wherein he argues strenuously for the revolutionary agency of enslaved people, two of the three cases he mentions are of women, signaling that Du Bois conceived of enslaved women as the bearers of resistance, revolt, and revolution. Du Bois, moreover, comments on the ways in which the economy of slavery made particular demands on enslaved women's labor, both in the fields and in their homes, and he pays particular attention to enslaved women's emotional distress and pain at the "raising of slaves... for systematic sale on the commercialized cotton plantations."[77] Du Bois recognizes the multiplicity of techniques that planters used in order to increase their profits, and on this point Du Bois was sensitive to the roles of both productive and reproductive labor to this end, explaining the myriad ways in which "sexual chaos... arose from economic motives."[78]

Weinbaum argues that "Du Bois' main argument in his book's central chapter on planter-slave relations is built out of an account of the sexual and reproductive exploitation that enslaved women were forced to endure at the hands of planters."[79] Through a careful reading of *Black Reconstruction*, Weinbaum argues that recognizing the deep relationship between Du Bois' anti-capitalism and contemporary black feminism lays the foundation for "recogniz[ing] that slave women's protest against the exploitation of their sexual and reproductive labor—against rape and the work of breeding—was as central to the struggle against slavery in the nineteenth century as it might yet be to the struggle against contemporary biocapitalism."[80] In this way, Du Bois conceives not only of black women's position under capitalism as structurally central, but he also reads black women's resistance and agency as historically crucial to anti-racist struggle in ways that frame the multiple shared histories of Marxism and intersectionality.

---

75 | Du Bois, *Black Reconstruction in America, 1860-1880*, 11.
76 | Weinbaum, "Gendering the General Strike: W.E.B. Du Bois's Black Reconstruction and Black Feminism's 'Propaganda of History,'" 442.
77 | Du Bois, *Black Reconstruction in America, 1860-1880*, 41.
78 | Ibid, 44.
79 | Weinbaum, "Gendering the General Strike: W.E.B. Du Bois's Black Reconstruction and Black Feminism's 'Propaganda of History,'" 444.
80 | It is important to note, however, that while a gender-focused analysis is clearly evident in the first few chapters of *Black Reconstruction*, this lens of analysis nearly totally disappears as the book progresses, leading the reader to wonder about the place of enslaved women during the Civil War itself and of women of color generally during Reconstruction. Weinbaum, 440.

Section Three: Marxism and the Intersectional Tradition in the Late Twentieth Century

Despite the backlash against both Marxism and black left feminism, the 1960s-1980s constituted a significant era of new theorizing on the specific relationship between gender, race, and class. Multiple new lexicons were developed in order to give clarity and depth to the specificity of women of color's position and oppression under capitalism during this period. In this section, I consider some of the most influential of these accounts: double/triple/multiple jeopardy, standpoint theory, and sexist racism.

The Jeopardy Approach

The jeopardy approach to conceptualizing black women's social, political, and economic position was a common one in the twentieth century, one that formed an important precursor to intersectonality.[81] The jeopardy approach can be traced to the work of Frances Beal, who was a member of the Third World Women's Alliance, a women of color activist organization specifically aimed at eliminating the intertwined systems of capitalism, imperialism, and the oppression of women of color. The newspaper of the TWWA was called *Triple Jeopardy* to reflect these concerns and this anti-capitalist orientation. After co-founding the Black Women's Liberation Committee of the Student Nonviolent Coordinating Committee (SNCC) in 1968, Beal wrote "Double Jeopardy," a piece which circulated quickly, initially as a pamphlet through SNCC and subsequently printed in volumes edited by Toni Cade Bambara and Robin Morgan. Beal's work did not occur in vacuum however; she cites Sojourner Truth, Harriet Tubman, Ida B. Wells-Barnett, Mary McLeod Bethune, and Fannie Lou Hamer as black women who pioneered the liberation struggle before her.[82] The title of the piece "Double Jeopardy" refers to its subtitle: "To Be Black and Female." Beale attributes the intensity and specificity of Black Women's oppression to the "superexploitation" of the "capitalist system."[83] In this piece, Beal excavates the logic of a system that subordinates, exploits, oppresses, dehu-

---

81 | Carastathis, *Intersectionality*; Patricia Hill Collins and Sirma Bilge, *Intersectionality*, 1 edition (Cambridge, UK ; Malden, MA: Polity, 2016); Patrick R. Grzanka, *Intersectionality: A Foundations and Frontiers Reader*, 1 edition (Boulder, CO: Westview Press, 2014); Hancock, *Intersectionality*; May, *Pursuing Intersectionality, Unsettling Dominant Imaginaries*.
82 | Frances Beal, "Double Jeopardy: To Be Black and Female (1970)," *Meridians: Feminism, Race, Transnationalism* 8, no. 2 (2008): 169.
83 | Frances Beal, "Double Jeopardy: To Be Black and Female," in *Black Woman's Manifesto* (New York: Third World Woman's Alliance, 1970), 19–34.

manizes, and degrades people on the basis of their race and their gender; Beal names this logic "the System of capitalism."[84] Though class does not appear as one of the axes of jeopardy in the title, it is clear through her analysis that class exploitation is an ever-present reality under capitalism and that it affects black women in all aspects of their lives. Beal's analysis of race, gender, and class under capitalism takes multiple forms. She excoriates the gender roles of her time, explaining that the social definitions of "manhood" and "femininity" are defined in terms of capitalism's "own interests," noting also that these images are coded in racialized terms. Specifically, in the case of black women, it is not only race but also class that shapes an image of white femininity that is inaccessible to working-class black women. Beal notes, "though we have been browbeaten with this white image, the reality of the degrading and dehumanizing jobs that were relegated to us quickly dissipated this mirage of 'womanhood.'"[85]

Moreover, Beal argues with zeal against black men ingesting a white, ruling class notion of femininity and projecting it as an expectation on to black women. Noting that many black men see the capitalist "System for what it really is", she also argues that "when it comes to women," black men seem to derive their expectations "from the pages of *Ladies Home Journal*."[86] Rather than blaming black men for their own sexism, however, Beal both recognizes black men's complicity with the devaluation of black women, and argues that ultimate cause and source of black men's sexism is the capitalist system's divide, conquer, and scapegoat strategy; she explains:

The economic System of capitalism finds it expedient to reduce women to a state of enslavement. They oftentimes serve as a scapegoat for the evils of the system. Much in the same way that the poor white cracker of the South, who is equally victimized, looks down upon black and contributes to the oppression of blacks, so by giving to men a false feeling of superiority (at least in their own home or in their relationships with women), the oppression of women acts as an escape valve for capitalism.[87]

There are many important aspects of this passage. First, the idea that racial and gender divides within oppressed populations serves the ultimate end of capital accumulation is an extremely important theory in many contemporary Marxist accounts of race and gender. Theodore Allen and David Roediger, among others, have argued for exactly this same position, decades after Beal's

---

84 | Beal, 166.
85 | Beal, 167.
86 | Beal, 168.
87 | Beal, 170.

insightful articulation,[88] yet Beal is never cited in these accounts. The idea that women act as an "escape valve" for the rage and disempowerment caused by capitalism is itself a central part in many Marxist feminist accounts, especially those that deal with sexual and domestic violence.[89]

But perhaps the most interesting part of this passage is the reference to the "poor white cracker" who is *"equally victimized."* This claim might seem outlandish in 1969, when poor whites from the south were vociferously protesting against even the smallest steps toward racial justice. But Beal here is prefiguring the intersectional axiom of the equality of oppressions. Capitalism does, under her analysis, exploit and victimize poor white people and any sufficient analysis of capitalism, from a race and gender justice perspective, must be able to account for this fact as well; "There are certain comparisons one can make," between various subject positions "simply because we both live under the same exploitative System."[90] From Beal's perspective, hiding or denying the real systematic harm done to impoverished white communities only plays into capitalism's strategy. However, recognizing the injustice done to poor whites does not exonerate or explain away their complicity with racism; on the contrary, the only way to fight for liberation is to understand the ways in which different configurations of oppression and exploitation stem from the same system and to hold people accountable for their complicity in that system. For Beal, complicity and victimization are not counter-posed positions, but rather ones that are constructed in and through one another; this position is another central tenet of intersectionality.

Another important point is Beal's insistence on both the structural and the individual as units of revolutionary transformation. While much of her essay looks at macro, structural-level problems and movements, Beal also explores the necessity of thinking about "how you relate to your wife, your husband, your parents, and your coworkers."[91] Just like many later intersectionality theorists, Beal conceives of the relationships of oppression and exploitation as having real consequences in direct interpersonal relations, consequences that must be

---

88 | An extended discussion of Allen, Roedigger, and the history of Marxist critical whiteness studies can be found in Chapter Four.

89 | Mariarosa Dalla Costa and Selma James, *The Power of Women and the Subversion of the Community, 3rd Edition*, 3rd edition (Bristol: Falling Wall Press, 1975); Giovanna Franca Dalla Costa, *The Work of Love: Unpaid Housework, Poverty & Sexual Violence at the Dawn of the 21st Century*, ed. Mariarosa Dalla Costa, trans. Enda Brophy (Autonomedia, 2008); Maria Mies, *Patriarchy and Accumulation On A World Scale: Women in the International Division of Labour*, 2nd edition (London; Atlantic Highlands, N.J., USA; Atlantic Highlands, N.J.: Zed Books, 1999).

90 | Beal, "Double Jeopardy: To Be Black and Female (1970)," 174.

91 | Beal, 175.

Chapter Zero: The Shared History of the Intersectional and Marxist Traditions

discussed and worked through in order to make real revolutionary change. The personal and the structural are intertwined in Beal's analysis, showing that real change can occur only when both individual people and their structures of life are overhauled to reflect the revolutionary imperative. Though people in all racial and gendered positions are exploited by capitalism, Beal's focus is on the particularities of black women's position and experience in this system. Beal draws a narrative arc of oppression that begins in the work of slavery and continues in the exploitative work of her own time:

Let me state here and now that the black woman in America can justly be described as a "slave of a slave." By reducing the black man in America to such abject oppression, the black woman had no protector and was used, and is still being used in some cases, as the scapegoat for the evils that this horrendous System has perpetrated on black men. Her physical image has been maliciously maligned; she has been sexually molested and abused by the white colonizer; she has suffered the worst kind of economic exploitation, having been forced to serve as the white woman's maid and wet nurse for white offspring while her own children were, more often than not, starving and neglected.[92]

Recognizing that black women's labor is doubly exploited—by her white employers and by her black partner—Beal develops an understanding of exploitation that transcends its traditional location on the factory floor. Drawing earlier black women communists' understanding of the centrality of domestic work to capitalism, Beal locates the dual role of black women's reproductive work as occurring both in their paid place of employment and in their own homes. In many ways, this analysis shares some similarities with other Marxist-feminists of the time, who were writing about women's reproductive labor and running campaigns for wages and unionization. Where Beal's account steps beyond those of her contemporaries (and indeed, many of those that would come in later years) is her recognition that black women's reproductive labor also formed a "surplus labor supply,"[93] which the capitalist class used in order to drive down wages over all. Women's function as "superexploited" surplus labor may have been lost on many of Beal's contemporaries, but it wasn't lost on many of the white, male union leaders, who Beal argues "work in collusion" with the ruling class, continue to support apartheid in South Africa, and generally failed to fight either racism or sexism within their own ranks.[94] Beal connects these issues directly to U.S. imperial expansion and the immiseration of people of color around the world, showing how unions themselves

---

92 | Beal, 168.
93 | Beal, 170.
94 | Beal, 170-71.

have been historically complicit in the system they ostensibly are responsible for fighting.

Beal extends her analysis of imperialism in discussing the sexual and intimate dimensions of black women's exploitation. She explains that black women are often denied any reproductive autonomy, with birth control and sterilization techniques being suggested to her at every turn, and with the illegality and inaccessibility of safe abortions. Beal explicitly links these techniques of birth control and sterlization to the U.S. colonial occupation of Puerto Rico, where the U.S. medical establishment used poor and precarious women of color as medical "guinea pigs," pioneering techniques that are then used to curtail black women's bodily autonomy within the metropole.[95] She explains that black women are often sterilized without their knowledge or consent and that they are forced to accept sterilization in order to maintain access to social services.[96] We know that these practices continue to this day, especially to incarcerated women of color. Beal argues that reproductive justice is a central part of black women's liberation and that attaining this justice will require not only rooting out the specific practices, but also the systems of capitalism, colonialism, and imperialism that make it possible.

It is on the basis of the interconnection of these systems that Beal evaluates the possibility of working in solidarity with white men and women. She concludes that "if the white groups do not realize that they are in fact, fighting capitalism and racism, we do not have common bonds. If they do not realize that the reasons for their condition lie in the System… then we cannot unite with them around common grievances or even discuss these groups in a serious manner, because they are completely irrelevant to the black struggle."[97] Here Beal begins to articulate a notion of solidarity that becomes central to intersectionality: being able to form coalitions that are based on shared enemies rather than on shared experiences. Beal recognizes the deep differences between black women's experiences and those of black men, white men, and white women; without erasing those differences, it is possible and indeed necessary to form coalitions committed to uprooting the violent systems of capitalism, imperialism, and colonialism that create and maintain the differences in power between these groups, and the marked gap between working class people of all of these identities and the ruling class.

Deborah King, who elaborated a concept of multiple jeopardy, critiques Beal for supposedly failing to include class as a central axis of women's oppression; as we can see from the previous discussion of Beal, however, class and capitalism

---

95 | Beal, 172.

96 | For a more in depth account of reproductive injustice done to black women, see: Roberts, *Killing the Black Body*.

97 | Beal, "Double Jeopardy: To Be Black and Female" (1970), 175.

constitute absolutely fundamental dimensions of black women's social, political, and economic subjugation, which makes this particular criticism rather puzzling. Carastathis also mentions the strange nature of this critique, arguing that class and capitalism are suffused with both race and gender at every step.[98] Perhaps Beal's refusal to name class a separate, third axis or 'jeopardy' actually constitutes the most intersectional moment of her thinking. While Beal does suggest that gender and race are somewhat separable categories, perhaps her refusal to separate class signifies the absolute fusion between class and race on the one hand and class and gender on the other. In this interpretation, both race and gender are such heavily class-dependent concepts that neither can be spoken of adequately without understanding capitalism; likewise, capitalism is itself so heavily suffused with race and gender that class just simply cannot be spoken of separately from the dynamics of race and gender. This kind of reading would suggest that Beal's position is perhaps closer to intersectional thinking than is often realized, as the standard narrative suggests Beal's double jeopardy as a more rudimentary form of triple jeopardy which then leads to multiple jeopardy and then to intersectionality. But while Beal's analysis certainly stops short of a full-blown intersectionality position—which would have to recognize the suffusion of gender and race—her work is substantially closer to intersectionality than is often realized. Rather than an omission, Beal's refusal to name capitalism as something separate from race and gender is actually one of the most important theoretical contributions of this text to the shared history of Marxism and intersectionality.

The discourse of double jeopardy spawned a variety of attempts to think about other dimensions of oppression as constituting forms of jeopardy. Famously, the periodical of the Third World Women's Alliance (TWWA) bore the name "Triple Jeopardy", referring to patriarchy, capitalism, and racist imperialism. Beverly Lindsey argued explicitly for class to be seen as a third element of jeopardy.[99] Deborah King interpreted Audre Lorde and Barbara Smith's work on black queer women to mean that they suggested that heterosexism or homophobia constituted a triadic jeopardy structure.[100]

In 1988, the same year that Kimberlé Crenshaw began using the term 'intersectionality' to describe the position of black women,[101] Deborah King

---

98 | Carastathis, *Intersectionality*, 43-44.
99 | Beverly Lindsay, "Minority Women in America: Black American, Native American, Chicana, and Asian American Women," in *The Study of Woman: Enlarging Perspectives of Social Reality*, ed. Eloise C. Snyder (New York: Harper and Row, 1979), 318-63.
100 | King, "Multiple Jeopardy, Multiple Consciousness: The Context of a Black Feminist Ideology," 46.
101 | Crenshaw's first published article using the term 'intersectionality' was released in 1989, but this was an expansion and revision of a presentation she gave in 1988.

published a critique and expansion of Beal's "Double Jeopardy" essay and some of the discussions of triple jeopardy that had continued after its publication. While King is formally in agreement with the motivation of these studies to think about the specificity of oppression faced by black women, King critiques Beal's concept of "double jeopardy" for "not conveying the dynamics of multiple forms of discrimination" and for being "overly simplistic in assuming that the relationships among the various discriminations are merely additive."[102] In contradistinction to the additive model, King argues that "racism, sexism, and classism constitute three, interdependent control systems"[103] that cannot be adequately conceived apart from one another. King argues that the "multiple" in "multiple jeopardy" refers not only to several, simultaneous oppressions but to the multiplicative relationships among them as well."[104] As she speaks of multiplication rather than addition, she supposedly does not fall into the same additive problem that she critiques in others.[105] In so far as it moves beyond the additive model, King's essay is often treated as a kind of bridge between the jeopardy approach and intersectionality.

When discussing the history of black women under slavery, King turns directly to a discussion of capital: "Our reproductive and child-rearing activities served to enhance the quantity and quality of the 'capital' of a slave economy. Our institutionalized exploitation as the concubines, mistresses, and sexual slaves of white males distinguished our experiences from that of white females' sexual oppression because it could only have existed in relation to racist and classist forms of domination."[106] In her estimation, "the legacy of the political economy of slavery under capitalism is the fact that employers and not black women still profit most from black women's labor"; labor, she argues, "whether unpaid and coerced or paid and necessary… has been a distinctive characteristic of black women's social roles."[107] King thus recognizes two important aspects of black women's position under capitalism: in the first place, the racist sexual abuse of slavery forms the historical precondition to the continual exploitation of black women's labor, meaning that there is not only a racial, but a gendered and sexual component to the contemporary operation of exploitation; rape and

---

102 | King, "Multiple Jeopardy, Multiple Consciousness: The Context of a Black Feminist Ideology," 46-47.
103 | Ibid, 47.
104 | Ibid.
105 | Though, as others have noted, multiplication can itself often be expressed as multiple additions, so it is unclear if this mathematical metaphor adequately captures the point King intends.
106 | King, "Multiple Jeopardy, Multiple Consciousness: The Context of a Black Feminist Ideology," 47.
107 | Ibid, 50.

slavery are the conditions for the possibility of black women's differential and disadvantaged position even in the formal labor market, meaning that capitalist exploitation retains the taint of this abuse in its contemporary operation. This insight is central for the development of Marxist-feminism, as we will see in Chapter Three: while a more traditional Marxism would argue that all exploitation is the same—it is 'just' the objective and uniform situation of a worker being paid less for their labor than the value of that labor to the capitalist employer—King here recognizes that actually exploitation itself is constituted differentially for black women. Black women are exploited under capitalism, but they are not exploited just as *all* members of the working class; they are exploited in and through the historical conditions that frame their exploitation, that is through enslavement and systematic sexual violence. These conditions are internal to black women's exploitation rather than an external graft onto it.

Second, King insists on the relationship between exploitation and oppression, exploring the mutually-enabling conditions, both economic and social, that frame black women's position. There is no unilateral determination of position by either oppression or exploitation, but rather a specific synthesis that determines black women's social position. It is this point that Marxists, according to King, have often missed in their analyses. The dogged insistence that exploitation itself is the sole or primary determinant of oppression in each and every case has made the Marxist approach to liberation excessively "monist"; she argues against frameworks of liberation that reduce entire oppressive systems to one single cause. King argues instead that we must attend to the "dialectics" of liberation in order to make visible the "actual victims of racism, sexism, or classism."[108] Instead, King proposes an "interactive model" which would understand that "the relative significance of race, sex or class in determining the conditions of black women's lives is neither fixed nor absolute, but rather, is dependent on the socio-historical context and the social phenomenon under consideration."[109]

It is not hard to see how and why the jeopardy model was foundational to the development of the intersectional tradition and how wedded it was to a Marxist critique of capitalist political economy. However, the jeopardy model itself was critiqued by both Marxists and feminists within the intersectional tradition. As we will see in the next chapter, the full-blown theory of intersectionality roundly rejects this additive model, arguing instead that oppression and categories of identity are best conceived as mutually constructed and integratively maintained, rather than as separate systems that can be added or multiplied together; as Gundrun Axeli Knapp explains, "It is a long way from a fast travelling mantra of 'race-class-gender' to the theoretical challenge of intersectional

---

108 | Ibid, 51-52.
109 | King, 49.

analysis."[110] As we will see in Chapter Three, Marxist feminists also critiqued the jeopardy model on similar grounds, for falling into a dual or triple systems approach to thinking oppression that fails to conceive of their integration under capitalist political economy. From both later Marxist-feminist and intersectional perspectives, the jeopardy approach admitted too much structural separation between race, gender, and class than constituted an adequate theory.

Standpoint Theory

Both the intersectional tradition and the Marxist tradition have been significantly invested in elaborating theories of standpoint epistemologies. Drawing on Marx's understanding of ideas as materially produced,[111] Georg Lukács argued that one's relationship to the process of production specifically framed one's ability to understand exploitation as the basis of class society. As people with a vested political and economic interest in maintaining the capitalist system, the bourgeoisie face self-imposed obstacles to perceiving their wealth as the result of exploitation rather than as the result of hard work, ingenuity, god-given right, or their essential superiority over the lazy and uneducated poor. By contrast, members of the working class both understand their own situation as exploited (since it is the very condition of their life) *and* can understand the ideology of the capitalist class, since the working class lives under the authority, domination, and power of the bourgeoisie. For Lukács, then, the working class has an epistemic privilege in understanding how capitalism operates: forced to understand *both* their own situation and the denial of this reality by the bourgeoisie, the working class world-view affords more clarity, precision, and focus on how the system of capitalism operates than anyone else. This dual vision affords an epistemic advantage to exploited people.[112]

The idea that exploitation affords epistemic privilege was significantly radicalized by a host of feminist theorists, who argue that oppression could also form the basis of a clearer understanding of the operations of the world. Explaining that women inhabit a "bifurcated consciousness," Dorothy Smith

---

110 | Gundrun-Axeli Knapp, "Race, Class, Gender: Reclaiming Baggage in Fast Travelling Theories," *European Journal of Women's Studies* 12, no. 3 (2005): 261.

111 | Marx makes this point clear in a variety of his writings, for example in the Preface to the *Contribution to the Critique of Political Economy* (1859), where he argues "consciousness must rather be explained from the contradictions of material life, from the existing conflict between the social forces of production and the relations of production." Karl Marx, *Contribution to the Critique of Political Economy*, trans. N.I. Stone (Chicago: Charles H. Kerr & Company, 1904), 12.

112 | Georg Lukács, *History and Class Consciousness: Studies in Marxist Dialectics*, trans. Rodney Livingstone (Cambridge: The MIT Press, 1972).

concluded that women also inhabit an epistemic advantage.[113] Marxist-feminist Nancy Hartsock argued that women's position in the sexual division of labor, in which they bear disproportionate responsibility for reproductive labor, grounds both women's differential material position in relationship to men and therefore their epistemic privilege in understanding patriarchal power, systems, and institutions. However, critiquing earlier manifestations of standpoint theory, Hartsock significantly argued that standpoints could not simply be assumed as an ahistorical universal feature of individuals' understanding, but rather that they required active work and engagement in order to achieve. In Hartsock's version, then, one could not posit a feminist standpoint uniformly of all women on the basis of their birth, but this standpoint constituted a potential that could be developed or achieved.[114] Sandra Harding thus contends that all researchers should strive to produce knowledge from the perspective of oppressed people in order to understand the aspects of the world unlocked by these positions, regardless of the social location of the individual researcher.[115] Donna Haraway, another Marxist-feminist, introduced the term "situated knowledges" in order to contest the idea in previous standpoint theory that the oppressed group (the working class for Lukács, women for Smith and Hartsock) necessarily understood the entirety of a system, arguing rather that *all* knowledge is limited and perspectival. Haraway thus suggests that since knowledge is connected to material conditions, the different material conditions of various positions (capitalist, working class, woman, man, etc.) will all produce different perspectives on the world; for Haraway, the differences in situation and therefore in knowledge require actively building relations of solidarity and coalition in order to produce accurate understandings of the world beyond the limitations of each individual's partiality.[116]

As a theoretical body of work, standpoint epistemology charted an important direction. Flipping the script on traditional power relations, it was a kind of analysis that clarified the places in which oppressed and exploited people actually attained a strategic advantage over the systems and structures of power. It provided yet another basis for challenging the hegemony of white,

---

113 | Dorothy E. Smith, "Women's Perspective as a Radical Critique of Sociology," *Sociological Inquiry*, no. 44 (1974): 7-13.
114 | Nancy Hartsock, "The Feminist Standpoint: Developing the Ground for a Specifically Feminist Historical Materialism," in *Discovering Reality: Feminist Perspectives on Epistemology, Metaphysics, Methodology, and the Philosophy of Science*, ed. Sandra Harding and Merrill Hintikka (Dordrecht, Netherlands: D. Reidel, 1983), 283-310.
115 | Sandra Harding, *Whose Science? Whose Knowledge? Thinking from Women's Lives* (Ithaca: Cornell University Press, 1991).
116 | Donna Haraway, "Situated Knowledges: The Science Question in Feminism and the Privilege of Partial Perspective," *Feminist Studies*, no. 14 (1988): 575-99.

middle class leaders in anti-capitalist organizations, as well as in challenging the racial, gendered, and class make-up of the academy, workplaces, and other positions of power. In this way, it rejected the stilted and often implicitly classist traditional Marxist understanding of the working class as so thoroughly dominated by capitalist ideology as to be living, breathing incarnations of false consciousness. It gave theoretical space for a theory of how and why oppressed people knew more about their oppressions than they were ever given credit for, opening the path to examine how and why consciousness raising programs were not a silver bullet in the struggle against structural systems of power: if oppressed and exploited people *already knew* they were oppressed and exploited, then education in this regard could not be seen as the sole mechanism of overcoming the system.

But for all of its advantages, standpoint theory was limited. The Marxist and Marxist-feminist traditions of standpoint theory themselves were heavily critiqued by anti-racist theorists on a variety of grounds. Firstly, by insisting that all members of the working class or all women shared a single standpoint, these rudimentary theories relied on homogenous and often essentializing conceptions of the identities they considered in their analyses. They seemed also to posit a flat, bifurcated understanding of power in which there were those who held power and those who did not, and that one's location in this split was natural and immutable. These theories did not take stock of the way in which intra-group differences were significant in understanding power hierarchies, erasing the complicated ways in which, for example bourgeois white women might contribute to the oppression of black working class women. Standpoint theory seemed also not to be able to account for any oppression that was not tied specifically to a rather reductive understanding of divisions of labor. In Collins' words, many standpoint epistemologies "reflect[ed] in part the isolation of White, middle class women" in their notion of oppression.[117]

Standpoint theorists in the intersectional tradition specifically took aim at these weaknesses in existing theories in order to nuance, complicate, and critique them. While some standpoint epistemologists have focused on how to achieve better knowledge, others have focused more substantially on understanding how ignorance functions to perpetuate and maintain oppression and inequality. Linda Martín Alcoff and Charles Mills have significantly advanced the understanding of "white ignorance" as itself a political tool of domination, oppression, and exploitation.[118] Gloria Anzaldúa explores the way in which her fractured identity as a working class Mestiza lesbian constituted a 'borderland'

---

117 | Collins, *Black Feminist Thought*, 292n1.

118 | Linda Martín Alcoff, "Epistemologies of Ignorance: Three Types," in *Race and Epistemologies of Ignorace*, ed. Shannon Sullivan and Nancy Tuana (Albany: State University of New York Press, 2007), 39–58; Charles W. Mills, "White Ignorance," in *Race*

that allows her to think and understand both her own situation, as well as the operations of patriarchy, colonization, and capitalism.[119] bell hooks elaborated a version of standpoint theory by focusing on the way in which race is itself also constitutive of a standpoint, recalling, "living as we did—on the edge—we developed a particular way of seeing reality. We looked both from the outside in and from the inside out [...] we understood both."[120]

Perhaps the most influential intersectional account of standpoint theory comes from the work of Patricia Hill Collins. Recognizing the value in standpoint theory's ability to explain and mark historically and institutionally constructed group-based experiences, her landmark *Black Feminist Thought* centers on explaining "theories created by African-American women which clarify a Black women's standpoint."[121] Specifically, Collins' focused on the radically participatory, anti-elitist understanding of knowledge production opened up by standpoint theory; rather than focusing her landmark study solely on black feminist academics or published authors, Collins explains that black feminist thought "has been produced by ordinary Black women in their roles as mothers, teachers, musicians, and preachers" in ways that are significant, worthy of attention, and as important to consider as more 'traditional' theory. Collins here completely radicalizes standpoint theory by intertwining a more nuanced, intersectional understanding of the theory of standpoint with the actual words, reflections, and knowledge produced by oppressed groups. While much of Marxist and Marxist-feminist standpoint theory had rendered only a theory of how or why oppressed groups *should* have developed understandings of their own oppression, Collins actually renders the content of those understandings in a way that was nearly entirely absent from previous work.[122]

Collins retains the material basis for her theory of black feminist thought as a modified standpoint epistemology. She writes

---

and Epistemologies of Ignorace, ed. Shannon Sullivan and Nancy Tuana (Albany: State University of New York Press, 2007), 39–58.

119 | Gloria Anzaldúa, *Borderlands/ La Frontera* (San Francisco: Aunt Lute Books, 1987).

120 | bell hooks, *Feminist Theory: From Margin to Center* (Routledge, 2014), vii.

121 | Collins, *Black Feminist Thought*.

122 | Anzaldúa's work is a notable exception. Though the work of French Marxist Jacques Rancière does not explicitly reference the intersectional tradition of standpoint theory nor does he speak nearly at all about race and gender, his *Proletarian Nights* did significantly render nineteenth century proletarian men's understandings of their own situation in a way strongly reminiscent of Collins' approach. Jacques Rancière, *Proletarian Nights: The Workers' Dream in Nineteenth-Century France*, Second Edition (London ; New York: Verso, 2012).

Conditions in the wider political economy simultaneously shape Black women's subordination and foster activism. On some level, people who are oppressed usually know it. For African-American women, the knowledge gained at intersecting oppressions of race, class, and gender provides the stimulus for crafting and passing on the subjugated knowledge of Black women's critical social theory.[123]

In this way, Collins harnesses the explanatory power of material conditions in order to render the specificity of experiences and knowledge of black women in the U.S. Doing so, for Collins, is not merely about beginning to undo the centuries of erasure and marginalization of black women's voices, but also about harnessing their words in order to "explicat[e] how knowledge remains central to maintaining and changing unjust systems of power."[124] Thus, standpoint epistemology as developed by Collins is explanatory in two senses: it both renders visible knowledge that has, in her words, been "subjugated"[125] but it also exposes the way that power operates intersectionally, by producing a specific standpoint for black women that cannot be rendered by class-only, race-only, or gender-only approaches to understanding the relationship between power and knowledge.

Sexist Racism and the Legacy of Latinx Feminism

Latinx and Chicanx communities also found ways of expressing the effects of capitalism on women of color, drawing attention to the interconnection between racism, sexism, and capitalism. Many of these concepts also influenced the intersectional tradition.[126]

One of the most pivotal and under-studied figures in the shared history of the intersectional tradition and the Marxist tradition is Elizabeth "Betita" Martínez. Martínez was a Chicana who was one of only two Latinas to work full time for the Student Nonviolent Coordinating Committee (SNCC). In this capacity, Martínez has significant and direct contact and working relationship with some of the most prominent black feminists of the time and her ideas were circulated in multiple internal education documents for SNCC. She also

---

123 | Collins, *Black Feminist Thought*, 8–9.

124 | Patricia Hill Collins, "Comment on Hekman's 'Truth and Method: Feminist Standpoint Theory Revisted': Where's the Power?," *Signs* 22, no. 2 (1997): 375.

125 | Collins, *Black Feminist Thought*, 291.

126 | For a meticulous history of the convergences and divergences, especially between white, black, and Chicana feminist organizing in the mid-twentieth century, see Roth (2004), where she argues that "in Black and Chicana feminisms of the second wave we find the roots of feminist insights about the *intersectionality* of inequalities in people's lives" (11, emphasis original).

co-founded and edited the newspaper *El Grito del Norte* with Beverly Axelrod, the lawyer for the Black Panther Party. Over the five years that *El Grito* was active, the bilingual paper published some of the most detailed coverage of the Chicanx movement, through a decisively socialist and feminist lens. In 1972, Martínez published an article suggesting three connected "faces of the same enemy"[127] as one way to conceive of the specific system of racist-sexist-capitalist domination with which women of color must contend. Martínez's analysis here perhaps comes the closest to the contemporary intersectional analysis that posits, rather than distinct, autonomous enemies, women of color are oppressed by a single enemy who has "three faces". "For the Chicana," she writes, "all three types of oppression cannot be separated. They are all a part of the same system... They must all be fought with all our courage and our strength."[128] In a workshop on white supremacy for the Catalyst Project, Martínez made explicit the connection between racism and capitalism:

The roots of White Supremacy lie in establishing economic exploitation by theft of resources and human labor. That exploitation has then been justified by a racist ideology affirming the inferiority of its victims—and this continues today. The first application of White Supremacy or racism by the Euroamericans who control U.S. society was against indigenous peoples, whose land was stolen; then Blacks, originally as slaves and later as exploited waged labor; followed by Mexicans when they lost their land holdings and also became wage-slaves. Chinese, Filipino, Japanese, and other Asian/Pacific people also became low-wage workers here, subject to racism. Arab workers have also been exploited in this way. In short, White Supremacy and economic power were born together[...] This is not a coincidence. In this country, as history shows, capitalism and racism go hand in hand.[129]

Martínez elaborats a conceptualization of capitalism that is fundamentally structured in and through racialized regimes of exploitation as a central rather than accidental feature of its constitution. Moreover, she emphasizes how the consequences of racialized exploitation form the basis for a racial ideology that, in constructing narratives of inferiority, have consequences beyond the economic realm.

Yolanda Nava's work built on this insight, developing an analysis of the inseparability of race, gender, and class under contemporary capitalism. Breaking with many theories and organizing strategies of the time that argued

---

127 | Alma García, ed., *Chicana Feminist Thought: The Basic Historical Writings* (New York: Routledge, 1997), 34.
128 | Ibid, 34.
129 | Elizabeth Martínez, "What Is White Supremacy?," *Catalyzing Liberation Toolkit: Anti-Racist Organizing to Build the 99% Movement*, 16–21.

for the priority of one manifestation of oppression over others, Nava paved the way for much of the later intersectional tradition by insisting that it is "unacceptable to separate racial-sexual and economic struggle in a hierarchical list of priorities."[130] Both the use of "racial-sexual" as a compound phrase and the insistence on thinking about racism, sexism, and class as inextricably linked would later influence the work of Anna Nieto-Gómez and others.

In 1974, Anna Nieto-Gómez began writing of "sexist racism" to describe the ways in which American society oppressed and exploited women of Mexican descent. She writes,

As minority women, the Chicanas have had to fight racism, sexism, and sexual racism. Sexist racism is manifested by those who consider and recognize only the needs of the single, Anglo and middle class women. It is also reinforced when Anglo women are compared as more 'politically active, educated,' and in general superior to the non-Anglo women who in turn are viewed as passive, apolitical, and illiterate beings. The Chicana feminist has called attention to how racism, sexism, and sexist racism are used to maintain the Chicana woman's social and economic oppression.[131]

While a major focus of her work is to detail the sexism within the Chicano movement, Nieto-Gómez is also particularly concerned with explaining the ways in which capitalism, colonialism, and race create the "different socio-economic needs... and therefore... different political positions" of white women and Chicana women. It is important to draw out several implications of Nieto-Gómez's formulation. In the first place, her use of the term "sexist racism" and, in other places, "racist sexism" points to the way in which racism and sexism are intermeshed, rather than autonomous and different systems. Moreover, Nieto-Gómez is attentive to the way in which structural conditions create and foster sexist racism toward Chicanas both within their own communities and within white, Anglo-society. The idea that the same system creates the conditions for manifestations of sexist racism is an insight that will be taken up both by later intersectional theorists and by Marxist scholars of race and gender. In explaining the ways in which the same system can produce Chicanx oppression and Chicano chauvinism, Nieto-Gómez illustrates not only how oppression can become internalized, but also how sexist racism, as a single system, can create multiple subject positions simultaneously. Also, in an analysis that predates the establishment of critical masculinity studies by a significant margin, Nieto-Gómez explains how Chicano men's sexism or machismo is itself an expres-

---

130 | Yolanda Nava, "Myths, the Media, Minority Groups, and Women's Liberation: An Overview" (Santa Monica College Women's Week, California, March 21, 1973).
131 | Anna Nieto-Gómez, "La Feminista," *Encuentro Femenil* 1, no. 2 (1974): 34–47.

sion of the system of racist-gendering under colonial or imperialist capitalism. In 1976, she wrote:

Racism-Sexism. Both the Chicano and the Chicana experience are affected by these two ideologies. In fact, both the Chicano and Chicana experience racist-sexism. Colonized men of color are considered as inferior as women since colonized men do not have the power or authority to rule, provide economically and protect the family. Thus racist-sexism considers Mexican males as either effeminate or a 'Macho', overcompensating because of his powerless position in his society.[132]

Drawing attention to the complicated racist histories of sexualization and gendering ushered in by colonial capitalism, Nieto-Gómez thus explores how systems of oppression influence and shape the subjectivities of everyone living in an oppressive society; it is not only women who are effected by sexism, but men are constructed and constrained through living in a sexist society as well, even if the constraints produced by sexism are not organized uniformly for men and women, or indeed, for all women. Indeed, according to Nieto-Gómez, this is precisely how capitalism works: through using a single system to create multiple kinds of subject positions under capitalism. These subject positions, for Nieto-Gómez, have material bases—different socio-economic needs produce different political positions—but the material ground of capitalism could not adequately explain the position of Chicanas through an abstract analysis of the movement of capital alone. For Nieto-Gómez, "the Anglo woman is a product of Protestant and imperialistic Anglo-European capitalism" just as is the Chicana, though they are certainly not *the same* product; having different material positions, different political histories, and different relationships to imperialism, colonization, and capitalism, they inhabit vastly different positions. This insight of Nieto-Gómez's cannot be overstated in its importance in the history of the development of both Marxism and intersectionality.

SECTION FOUR: CLASS AND CAPITALISM IN INTERSECTIONALITY

Until this point, this chapter has examined the way in which the intersectional tradition and the Marxist tradition have influenced one another, looking specifically at the concepts and theories that predated the rise of intersectionality itself. It is useful to remember that Crenshaw introduced the term 'intersectionality' specifically to speak about a labor issue: in Crenshaw's article, intersectionality refers to: "the various way[s] in which race and gender interact

---

132 | Anna Nieto Gómez, "Sexism in the Movimiento," *La Gente de Aztlán* 6, no. 4 (1976): 10.

to shape the multiple dimensions of Black women's employment experiences."[133] While Crenshaw herself does not explicitly speak about capitalism, recognizing the labor roots of intersectionality might help Marxists ground and orient an analysis of it. This last section turns to some of the most prominent intersectionality scholars in order to excavate the way in which Marxism and anti-capitalism form central nodes in the development not only of the precursor concepts, but of intersectionality itself. As Hancock notes

critiques of capitalism and imperialism have previously been part of intersectionality-like thought, but these critiques have dropped out in important ways, as opposed to having been missing in the first place. Importantly, this ebb and flow of attention to certain kinds of categories is generally unaccounted for by scholars who make this critique, perhaps because of the absence of attention to the intellectual history of intersectionality.[134]

The discussions in this section provide a brief overview of the role of capitalism in the work of the Combahee River Collective, Patricia Hill Collins, Angela Davis, bell hooks, and Audre Lorde, with a broader discussion of these thinkers in subsequent chapters; the present survey is intended to highlight the relationship between these thinkers and a Marxist anti-capitalist analysis.

Combahee River Collective

Perhaps the most famous and often-cited example of anti-capitalist intersectionality is the Combahee River Collective's "A Black Feminist Statement". They write, "The most general statement of our politics at the present time would be that we are actively committed to struggling against racial, sexual, heterosexual, and class oppression and see as our particular task the development of integrated analysis and practice based upon the fact that the major systems of oppression are interlocking. The synthesis of these oppressions creates the conditions of our lives."[135] One of the positions that contemporary intersectional theorists associate with the Combahee River Collective is its politics of the "vanguard center." As Benita Roth explains, if "Black women were at the intersection of oppressive structures, they [black women in the

---

133 | Kimberlé Crenshaw, "Demarginalizing the Intersection of Race and Sex: A Black Feminist Critique of Antidiscrimination Doctrine, Feminist Theory, and Antiracist Politics," *University of Chicago Legal Forum*, no. 140 (1989): 139.
134 | Hancock, *Intersectionality*, 56.
135 | Combahee River Collective, "A Black Feminist Statement," 362.

1970s] reasoned that their liberation would mean the liberation of all people."[136] While there is some debate about whether this approach truly accounts for the non-hierarchy of oppressions,[137] it is certainty a position expressed by many intersectional thinkers, and this idea directly derives from black women communists' thinking about triple exploitation and triple oppression.

The Combahee River Collective articulate an analysis of oppression that understands the ways that the race, gender, class, and sexuality can neither be separated in experience nor in structure, arguing that there is "racial-sexual oppression which is neither solely racial nor solely sexual."[138] In order to combat this matrix of domination, the Combahee River Collective specifically embraces a form of socialism that takes not only class, but race, gender, and sexuality as structuring aspects of exploitation and oppression:

We realize that the liberation of all oppressed peoples necessitates the destruction of the political-economic systems of capitalism and imperialism as well as patriarchy. We are socialists because we believe that work must be organized for the collective benefit of those who do the work and create the products, and not for the profit of the bosses. Material resources must be equally distributed among those who create these resources. We are not convinced, however, that a socialist revolution that is not also a feminist and anti-racist revolution will guarantee our liberation. We have arrived at the necessity for developing an understanding of class relationships that takes into account the specific class position of Black women who are generally marginal in the labor force, while at this particular time some of us are temporarily viewed as doubly desirable tokens at white-collar and professional levels. We need to articulate the real class situation of persons who are not merely raceless, sexless workers, but for whom racial and sexual oppression are significant determinants in their working/economic lives. Although we are in essential agreement with Marx's theory as it applied to the very specific economic relationships he analyzed, we know that his analysis must be extended further in order for us to understand our specific economic situation as Black women.[139]

---

136 | Benita Roth, *Separate Roads to Feminism: Black, Chicana, and White Feminist Movements in America's Second Wave* (Cambridge, UK ; New York: Cambridge University Press, 2003), 77.
137 | Carastathis in particular insists that the Combahee River Collective's politics of the vanguard center violates intersectionality's principle of the hierarchy of oppressions, and thus, argues that the CRC's "Statement" is best categorized as a precursor to intersectionality, rather than intersectionality itself. This does not seem to be a widely-held position. Carastathis, *Intersectionality*.
138 | Combahee River Collective, "A Black Feminist Statement," 365.
139 | Combahee River Collective, 366.

In this articulation, the Combahee River Collective explains that traditional Marxist analyses that have ignored, marginalized, or misunderstood the central importance of race, gender, and sexuality to the system of capitalism are insufficient, but they conceive of socialism as a project that can be "extended" in order to adequately conceptualize them. In particular, race, gender, and sexuality cannot be simply "added" to class in this extension as mere epiphenomena of class relations that will be magically solved through thinking about class. Collective member and one of the authors of the "Black Feminist Statement," Beverly Smith argued against a Marxism that conceives of class as ontologically primary in this sense, critiquing "Marxists who say 'Well, when class oppression and racism end, definitely the oppression of women and lesbians will end.'"[140] What is needed is not just a mere conservation of already-existing Marxism with the additions of other forces of oppression, but a full extension of the foundational concepts of Marxism to think about the ways in which race, gender, and sexuality permeate all moments of capitalist exploitation. In this sense, the Combahee River Collective's statement should be read both as a contribution to Marxism and as a critique of many dominant trends of Marxism.

Patricia Hill Collins

While Patricia Hill Collins' focus has not exclusively been on capitalism or class, it is important to remember that her analysis is completely suffused with an analysis of both. In *Black Feminist Thought*, Collins continually refers "economic exploitation" and black women's status as "economically exploited workers."[141] In particular, she also notes Marxist Angela Davis' *Women, Race, and Class*, the Combahee River Collective's "A Black Feminist Statement" and Audre Lorde's *Sister/Outsider*, all staunchly anti-capitalist texts, as "groundbreaking" works that influenced her own thinking.[142] In her analysis of slavery, Collins writes that the consequence of black women's "forced incorporation into a capitalist political economy" had the effect of establishing a more general "racial division of labor" based both in economic exploitation and in political disenfranchisement.[143]

Moreover, "African-American women's experiences as mothers have been shaped by the dominant group's efforts to harness Black women's sexuality

---

140 | Barbara Smith and Beverly Smith, "Across the Kitchen Table: A Sister-to-Sister Dialogue," in *This Bridge Called My Back: Writings by Radical Women of Color*, ed. Cherrie Moraga and Gloria Anzaldúa, 2nd ed. (New York: Kitchen Table Press, 1983), 122-23.
141 | Collins, *Black Feminist Thought*.
142 | Ibid, 18.
143 | Ibid, 50.

and fertility to a system of capitalist exploitation."[144] In explaining the way in which the matrix of domination impacts black women, Collins writes, "Controlling Black women's reproduction was essential to the creation and perpetuation of capitalist class relations."[145] As we explored in the discussion of Collins' approach to standpoint epistemology, her entire concept of black women as a group that holds a standpoint is itself rooted in an analysis of material conditions, specifically those of class.

Angela Davis

Angela Davis, author of over a dozen books and countless articles, is another thinker who is foundational to both Marxism and intersectionality. While much of Davis' early work does not use the term intersectionality, she has more recently explained that she views her own work as being intersectional, and as contributing to the tradition of intersectionality.[146] She highlights the Third World Women's Alliance and its newspaper *Triple Jeopardy* as one of the theoretical anchors in her conceptualization of intersectionality and of her own work and in speaking about the history of her own work, Davis comments, "I think that the whole notion of intersectionality that has characterized the kind of feminisms we're talking about, that we cannot simply look at gender in isolation from race, from class, from sexuality, from nationality, from ability, from a whole range of other issues."[147] While many of Davis' most important texts—like *Women, Race and Class*,[148] *Are Prisons Obsolete?*,[149] and *Blues Legacies and Black Feminism*[150]—do not use the term intersectionality, and thus have been often left out of many genealogies of intersectionality, Davis' comments here and her constant attention to the interwoven dynamics of race, gender, class and sexuality, reveal her work to be touchstones of both intersectional and Marxist traditions.

After a question in which she is called "a pioneer" of intersectionality, Davis responds:

---

144 | Ibid.
145 | Ibid, 51.
146 | Angela Y. Davis and Cornel West, *Freedom Is a Constant Struggle: Ferguson, Palestine, and the Foundations of a Movement*, ed. Frank Barat (Chicago: Haymarket Books, 2016), 38.
147 | Davis and West, 65-66.
148 | Davis, *Women, Race, & Class*.
149 | Angela Davis, *Are Prisons Obsolete?* (New York: Seven Stories Press, 2003).
150 | Davis, *Blues Legacies and Black Feminism*.

Of course intersectionality—or efforts to think, analyze, organize as we recognize the interconnections of race, class, gender, sexuality—has evolved a great deal over the last decades. I see my work as reflecting not an individual analysis, but rather a sense within movements and collectives that it was not possible to separate issues of race from issues of class and issues of gender.[151]

Davis notes the "rich history of struggle" that informs intersectionality, remarking, "There were those of us who by virtue of our experience, not so much by virtue of academic analyses, recognized that we had to figure out a way to bring these issues together. They weren't separate in our bodies, but also they are not separate in terms of struggles." Highlighting the level of political intersectionality, Davis argues that the most interesting aspect of intersectionality for the contemporary moment "is the conceptualization of the intersectionality of struggles. Initially intersectionality was about bodies and experiences. But now, how do we talk about bringing various social justice struggles together, across national borders?"[152] In fact, Davis notes that it was the introduction of an intersectionality perspective into feminism that made her identify as a feminist in the first place, especially an intersectionality that foregrounded "the struggles of working-class women of all racial and ethnic backgrounds" that took a "transnational" approach to both theory and practice.[153]

Thus, despite much of Davis' most cited work not using the term 'intersectionality' explicitly, it is clear that, in retrospect, her work on race, gender, class, and more recently on nationality and sexuality should be seen as foundational in the intersectional tradition and doubly foundational for any project of integrating Marxism and intersectionality.

bell hooks

bell hooks is another important intersectionality theorist who explicitly names the matrix of domination the "white supremacist capitalist patriarchy" throughout her work.[154] In explaining her continued use of the term, hooks explains, that the term highlights "the interlocking systems of domination" that must be taken as a synthetic whole.[155] Because of this synthetic whole,

---

151 | Davis and West, *Freedom Is a Constant Struggle*, 38.
152 | Davis and West, 39.
153 | Angela Y. Davis and Robin D. G. Kelley, *The Meaning of Freedom: And Other Difficult Dialogues* (San Francisco, Calif.: City Lights Publishers, 2012), 281.
154 | bell hooks, *The Will to Change: Men, Masculinity, and Love* (New York: Atria Books, 2004), 17; hooks, *Ain't I a Woman*; hooks, *Feminist Theory*.
155 | bell hooks, Media Education Foundation Interview, 1997, http://www.mediaed.org/transcripts/Bell-Hooks-Transcript.pdf.

hooks argues that a gender analysis is crucial to ending capitalism, just as an anti-capitalist orientation is central to ending gender oppression: "we will never destroy patriarchy without questioning, critiquing, and challenging capitalism, and I don't think challenging capitalism alone will mean a better world for women."[156] For her, this means that "a class rooted analysis" is central in developing a conceptual apparatus that can speak to the domination of black women, an analysis she argues is rooted in Marx. In explaining why multiple strands of the feminist movement have failed to develop an anti-capitalist politics, hooks elsewhere argues, "had poor women set the agenda for the feminist movement, they might have decided that class struggle would be a central feminist issue."[157]

Audre Lorde

In her article "Age, Race, Class, and Sex: Women Redefining Difference" Audre Lorde draws attention to the "white male heterosexual capitalist" structure of the world.[158] She explains that part of the way in which age, race, and sex, are connected to capitalism by using the language of surplus population—a term that Marx used and many contemporary Marxists have used in order to describe how race and gender organize and are organized by capitalism on a structural level. For Lorde, "a society where the good is defined in terms of profit rather than in terms of human need" produces populations that are "surplus," which she argues refers both to their economic status and to a more general sense of dehumanization.[159] In expanding the concept of 'surplus populations' beyond its traditional Marxist use, Lorde points to the ways in which structural economic relations effect social positions, but she also insists that the social effects spill over far beyond the economic realm, to social discourses and internalized senses of value and worth. She continues, "Institutionalized rejection of difference is an absolute necessity in a profit economy which needs outsiders as surplus people."[160] She once described herself as a "Black lesbian feminist socialist mother warrior poet." Some have argued that it makes the most sense to describe Lorde's project as a "Queer Black Marxism."[161]

---

156 | bell hooks, Challenging Capitalism & Patriarchy: An Interview By Third World Viewpoint, accessed August 1, 2017, http://soaw.org/component/content/article/110-gender-sexuality/910?format=pdf.
157 | Ibid.
158 | Audre Lorde, "Age, Race, Class, and Sex: Women Redefining Difference," in *Sister/Outsider* (Berkeley: Crossing, n.d.).
159 | Lorde, 114.
160 | Lorde, 115.
161 | Gary Holcomb, "A New Spelling of Her Name: Audre Lorde's Queer Black Marxism" (Annual Meeting of the American Studies Association, Washington, DC, 2014).

Conclusion

This brief and partial survey demonstrates that far from intersectionality theorists conceiving of themselves as universally opposed to Marxism, many of the key thinkers of intersectionality have themselves identified as Marxists, socialists, and anti-capitalists, arguing for the centrality of class and capitalism in the intersectional tradition. It is on this basis that attempts to think the Marxist tradition and the intersectional tradition together should be based: in the long, heterogenous, powerful tradition of thinkers and activists who have sought for nearly two hundred years to think about these systems together. Rather than bringing together two completely exogamous traditions, bringing intersectionality and Marxism together does justice to the deep history of these traditions interweaving. While there are multiple places in which these traditions diverge—and these divergences will be the focus of subsequent chapters—it is necessary to remember what these traditions share.

Part Two: Debates

Chapter One: The Intersectional Tradition

The variety of theories that influenced the development of intersectionality are quite different from a full-blown theory of intersectionality as it develops in the 1980s-the present. In order to differentiate them from one another, as well as to dispel many of the mischaracterizations of intersectionality that persist, especially within Marxist circles, this chapter is devoted to answering the question: *what is intersectionality?* In its broadest formulation, intersectionality is a term that brings together a variety of positions on the relationships between modes of oppression and identity in the contemporary world. Primarily developed by black women and women of color who found a variety of anti-racist, feminist, and anti-capitalist theories and activist organizations insufficient to explain or respond to their oppression, intersectionality as a theory is based in the analyses, experiences, activism, and identities of women of color. As such, intersectionality is itself an internally varied set of engagements. Intersectionality has been called variously a "buzzword,"[1] has been portrayed as holding theoretical hegemony,[2] and the "most important theoretical contribution that women's studies has made."[3] But for all its ubiquity, intersectionality seems to be little understood, or understood only in the vaguest and broadest sense. All of the major book-length projects on the history and theory of intersection-

---

1 | Kathy Davis, "Intersectionality as Buzzword," *Feminist Theory* 9, no. 1 (2008): 67-85.

2 | Susan Archer Mann, *Doing Feminist Theory: From Modernity to Postmodernity*, 1 edition (Oxford ; New York, NY: Oxford University Press, 2012), 60.

3 | Leslie McCall, "The Complexity of Intersectionality," Signs: Journal of Women in Culture & Society 30, no. 3 (2005): 1771. Whether or not intersectionality can rightly be claimed by "Women's Studies" as a discipline and a field is the subject of dispute in intersectionality literature, both because it localizes intersectionality's development to the academy and not in activist circles and because many of the recognized foundational theorists of intersectionality like Patricia Hill Collins, Kimberlé Crenshaw, and other key thinkers of intersectionality were trained and made their careers in other disciplines.

ality remark that for all of the widespread familiarity with intersectionality, its central arguments, debates, and conceptual innovations remain misrepresented and misunderstood, when they are not completely ignored.[4] In the words of Cho, Crenshaw, and McCall, the bulk of "what circulates as critical debate about what intersectionality is or does reflects a lack of engagement with both originating and contemporary literatures on intersectionality."[5] It is thus important not to conflate widespread awareness of the term with an adequate conceptualization of its meaning.

In order to understand intersectionality, it is particularly important to take stock of the central debates and disagreements that inform it. As a vast and varied field, understanding the central debates in intersectionality are crucial to parsing its various uses, abuses, analytic power, as well as to framing potential critiques on firm and generous ground. There is some debate about what exactly intersectionality is: some argue that it is a full blown theory of oppression,[6] that it is a theory of representation,[7] that it is a critique of representation,[8] that it is a field of study,[9] that it is a methodology,[10] that it is an 'analytical and political orientation,"[11] "a provisional concept,"[12] an "analytical framework,"[13]

---

4 | Carastathis, *Intersectionality*; Collins and Bilge, *Intersectionality*; Hancock, *Intersectionality*; May, *Pursuing Intersectionality, Unsettling Dominant Imaginaries*.

5 | Sumi K. Cho, Kimberlé Crenshaw, and Leslie McCall, "Toward a Field of Intersectionality Studies: Theory, Applications, and Praxis," *Signs: Journal of Women in Culture & Society* 38, no. 4 (2013): 788.

6 | Sumi K. Cho, "Post-Intersectionality: The Curious Reception of Intersectionality in Legal Scholarship," *Du Bois Review* 10, no. 2 (2013): 385-404.

7 | Evelien Geerts and Iris van der Tuin, "From Intersectionality to Interference: Feminist Onto-Epistemological Reflections on the Politics of Representation," *Women's Studies International Forum* 41, no. 3 (2013): 171-78; Eline Severs, Karen Celis, and Silvia Erzeel, "Power, Privilege, and Disadvantage: Intersectionality Theory and Political Representation," *Politics* 36, no. 4 (2016): 346-54.

8 | Carastathis, *Intersectionality*, 117-20.

9 | Cho, Crenshaw, and McCall, "Toward a Field of Intersectionality Studies: Theory, Applications, and Praxis."

10 | McCall, "The Complexity of Intersectionality"; Cho, "Post-Intersectionality: The Curious Reception of Intersectionality in Legal Scholarship," 385.

11 | May, *Pursuing Intersectionality, Unsettling Dominant Imaginaries*, 3.

12 | Carastathis, *Intersectionality*; Kimberlé Crenshaw, "Mapping the Margins: Intersectionality, Identity Politics, and Violence Against Women of Color," *Stanford Law Review* 43, no. 6 (1991): 1244-5n9.

13 | Julia S. Jordan-Zachary, "Am I a Black Woman or a Woman Who Is Black? A Few Thoughts on the Meaning of Intersectionality," *Politics & Gender* 3, no. 2 (2007): 255.

and that it is both an "ontology" and an "epistemology."[14] Sometimes, over the course of even a particular author's work, multiple definitions might be used, and it should be noted that some conceive of these different registers of intersectionality as complementary rather than mutually exclusive.

The history of intersectionality is one that is also debated and contested. While there is broad consensus that the term was first used by critical legal scholar Kimberlé Crenshaw, the metaphor of intersections to describe the operation and experiences of multiple modalities of oppression had been circulating in U.S. women of color feminisms for at least a decade prior to Crenshaw's articulation.[15] Crenshaw herself first used it in a presentation at the Chicago Legal Symposium in 1988; her talk was published in 1989. The language of intersection was used by Gloría Anzaldúa and Cherrie Moraga in 1980, when they sent the following interview question to Barbara and Beverly Smith: "How do race and class intersect in the women's movement?"[16] Bonnie Thornton Dill used the phrase "intersecting structures of race, gender, and class" in her 1979 dissertation and in an article in 1983.[17] Patricia Hill Collins is widely credited with having developed a theory of what would later be called intersectionality in her landmark 1990 text *Black Feminist Thought*[18] even though Collins uses the term "matrix of oppressions" rather than "intersections" to name her conceptualization of the interaction between race, gender, class, and sexuality.[19] In order

---

14 | Hancock, *Intersectionality*.

15 | As Carastathis writes, "By the mid-1980s, the language of 'intersections'—if not the metaphor and concept of intersectionality as Crenshaw would, in a few years time, elaborate them—had already been circulating in antiracist feminist thought" (17). Despite her acknowledgement of the widespread nature of the metaphor of intersections, Carastathis insists that Crenshaw's analysis is quite different from all other iterations and that Crenshaw's should be treated as the foundational one, though exactly why is unclear.

16 | Hancock, *Intersectionality*, 97. Anzaldúa and Morraga's *This Bridge Called My Back* is itself often cited as one of the foundational texts of intersectionality. Barbara and Beverly Smith were two members of the Combahee River Collective, and with Demita Frazer, were responsible for drafting the majority of the influential "A Black Feminist Statement", also considered a founding text of intersectionality.

17 | Bonnie Thornton Dill, "Race, Class, and Gender: Prospects for an All-Inclusive Sisterhood," *Feminist Studies* 9, no. 1 (1983): 130-50.

18 | Hancock thus argues that we should understand "that Crenshaw and Collins simultaneously (but not collaboratively) founded intersectionality" (9).

19 | In the preface to the 1990 edition of *Black Feminist Thought*, Collins uses the term "intersection" to describe the interaction between "individual and collective, personal and political" and her "unique biography with the larger meaning of [her] historical times" in the argument and perspective offered in that text (vi). In the revised and

to illustrate this expanded genealogy, Jennifer Nash argues that, rather than dating intersectionality's beginning exclusively to Crenshaw's articulation, it is more apt to think about a three phase genealogy: the "early era" of 1968-87, the "watershed years" of 1988-1990, and the contemporary moment of 1999-present.[20] Looking back farther into intersectionality's history, many intersectional theorists locate the its roots in the writings and speeches of Black women going back to the nineteenth century. While each theorist draws upon a slightly different historical legacy, Sojourner Truth, Ida B. Wells, Anna Julia Cooper, and Claudia Jones are often named in this legacy.[21] In these analyses, intersectionality is positioned as building on, expanding, but also fundamentally challenging and changing earlier understandings of the relationships between race, gender, class, and sexuality in particular.

Because intersectionality is a heterogenous term, the discussion that follows seeks to elucidate some broad principles of alignment about what constitutes it, recognizing that these principles of alignment are neither universal nor exhaustive. In order to generate this list, I have drawn on a number of leading intersectionality scholars'[22] understandings of what the term refers to, keeping in mind both that these definitions are contested and the subject of many contemporary interventions and that, as Patricia Hill Collins notes, "definitions constitute starting points for investigation rather than end points of analysis."[23] This chapter thus proceeds in three sections. The first section looks at the definitions of intersectionality as offered by five foundational thinkers: Kimberlé Crenshaw, Patricia Hill Collins, Leslie McCall and historiographers of intersectionality, Ange-Marie Hancock and Vivian May. Given the widespread nature of intersectional theorizing, the five thinkers covered in this section are not exhaustive, but nor is the choice of them wholly arbitrary. Crenshaw, Collins, and McCall are all widely cited as foundational thinkers of intersectionality, even though I think this claim in the case of McCall is empirically false—McCall's account is doubtlessly influential, but to claim her as the 'orignator' of intersectionality is both historically wrong and engages in a potentially dan-

---

updated 2000 edition of the text, Collins uses "intersections" and "intersectionality" frequently.

20 | Nash, "Home Truths on Intersectionality." Nash's genealogy is helpful, but inexplicably erases any contributions to intersectionality made between 1990 and 1999.

21 | Nash; Combahee River Collective, "A Black Feminist Statement"; Hancock, *Intersectionality*; May, *Pursuing Intersectionality, Unsettling Dominant Imaginaries*.

22 | This list is illustrative, rather than exhaustive. It by no means seeks to cover all of the existing definitions of intersectionality, but rather to cull and highlight some of the important, foundational, and expansive notions of the concept.

23 | Patricia Hill Collins, "Intersectionality's Definitional Dilemmas," *Annual Review of Sociology*, no. 41 (2015): 3.

gerous politics of citation. The three thinkers, moreover, demonstrate three profoundly different definitions of intersectionality, so I have selected them both on the basis of their prominence and due to their disagreements with one another. In addition to considering the perspectives of founational thinkers of intersectionality, I thought it important to include the work of two authors who write on intersectionality as a cohesive tradition, over and above the differences between each foundational theorist individually. I thus look also at the work of Hancock and May, who have written two of the most circulated histories of intersectionality as a theory. But as historiographers with somewhat different perspectives on intersectionality, and different disciplinary trainings, it is helpful to place them in conversation with one another. Each of their definitions is quite different; meditating on the differences between the respective definitions instructively demonstrates the internal heterogeneity of intersectionality, exposing the limitations of accounts that reduce intersectionality to one single position or set of positions.

In the second section, I argue that despite the differences and internal debates, there are still certain positions shared by most if not all intersectionality theorists. I develop a series of six shared propositions that have, in large part, come to define intersectionality and to distinguish it from other accounts of the relationship between race, gender, class, and other axes of oppression. The last section revisits the positions explored in the previous chapter in order to distinguish them from intersectionality. While jeopardy, multiple oppression, sexist racism, and other formulations should be clearly located in the long tradition of intersectionality-like thinking, it is important to form clear analytical distinctions between these positions and intersectionality as explored in this chapter. Doing so will be crucial for examining the debates between intersectionality and Marxism that constitute Chapters Two and Four.

SECTION ONE: FIVE DEFINITIONS

Often cited as the founder or originator of intersectionality, Kimberlé Crenshaw offers the following definition of intersectionality: "the various way[s] in which race and gender interact to shape the multiple dimensions of Black women's employment experiences."[24] In her original usage, intersectionality was about the relationship between race, gender, and work, though both she and others have expanded, reformulated, and reconceptualized it. In a subsequent article, Crenshaw distinguishes between three kinds of intersectionality; a "structural intersectionality," a "political intersectionality," and a "representational inter-

---

24 | Crenshaw, "Demarginalizing the Intersection of Race and Sex: A Black Feminist Critique of Antidiscrimination Doctrine, Feminist Theory, and Antiracist Politics," 139.

sectionality."[25] For Crenshaw, structural intersectionality refers to the ways in which the structures of race and gender (and, she is very clear, class and sexuality, and potentially other factors as well) come together to produce a qualitatively different modality of oppression than those who face oppression on the basis of only one factor. Political intersectionality refers to the failures of social movements such as the feminist and anti-racist movements, to adequately conceptualize the oppressions they fight in terms that are representative of the experiences of women of color. In other words, political intersectionality highlights the failures of the anti-racist movement to think of gender as central to its project, and of the feminist movement to think of race as central to its project. Representational intersectionality refers to the tropes, stereotypes, and images of women of color that contribute to their exclusion, marginalization, and disempowerment. It is interesting that Crenshaw emphasizes that intersectionality is not "some new, totalizing theory of identity"[26] even though others have taken intersectionality to mean just this.

A second conceptual definition comes from Leslie McCall, who develops a triadic conceptualization of the multiple approaches to intersectionality: the 'intercategorial', the 'intracategorial' and the 'anti-categorial.'[27] For McCall, the intercategorial approach focuses on inequalities between "already constituted social groups,"[28] for example, looking at differences in access to resources, opportunities, social legibility, and power between white men and black women. The intracategorial approach focuses on the complexities and differences of lived realities inside a particular social group, calling attention to in-group differentiations that are caused by the ways in which multiple kinds of institutions and social structures intersect within them. An approach of this kind would be interested in looking at differences between Latinx women on the basis of class or sexuality. The anti-categorial approach specifically deconstructs the social categories often under discussion in intersectional theories, categories like race, gender, sexuality, and others. This kind of approach calls attention to the internal contradictions, inconsistencies, and limitations of "fixed categories" in explaining complex social realities.[29] In doing so, it would be concerned with noting the limitations of categories themselves in explaining the phenomena they supposedly refer to. For example, the anti-categorial approach might deconstruct the term 'queer'—which is often used to refer to a wide spectrum of non-heterosexual sexualty—by calling attention to the fact that 'queerness', and

---

25 | Crenshaw, "Mapping the Margins: Intersectionality, Identity Politics, and Violence Against Women of Color."
26 | Crenshaw, 1244.
27 | McCall, "The Complexity of Intersectionality."
28 | McCall, 1785.
29 | McCall, 1773.

the practices and identities associated with it, is already suffused with elements of racialization and gendering, among other factors. McCall's account is helpful because it directly thematizes three rather distinct ways of conceiving of both identity and relationships between structurally constituted identity groups. We should note that McCall's account thinks about intersectionality as related to identity, which differs from the definition offered by Crenshaw. Employment practices are nowhere to be found in McCall's definition, nor, it is important to note, are black women. Rather, for McCall, intersectionality is broadly applicable theory, with insights for multiple spheres of life, and with implications for diagnosing inequality and identity *generally* rather than of black women *specifically*.

Patricia Hill Collins offers a third, rather different understanding of intersectionality than either Crenshaw or McCall. In her estimation, "the term intersectionality references the critical insight that race, class, gender, sexuality, ethnicity, nation, ability, and age operate not as unitary, mutually exclusive entities, but as reciprocally constructing phenomena that in turn shape complex social inequalities."[30] Here Collins focuses neither on the experiences that are central to Crenshaw's account nor on the relationship between identity and inequality that frame McCall's intervention. Rather, for Collins, intersectionality is a theory about how the very categories, structures, or identities at issue *themselves* have a mutually constructing and reciprocally determining relationship. This claim is quite important in the development of the intersectional tradition: for Collins, intersectionality represents the insight, not that black women experience race and gender as simultaneous oppressions (though this is also true), but that the structures of race and gender are themselves related, that is, race is always already a gendered category (and a classed, sexualized, nationalized, etc. one) and gender is always already a raced (and classed, sexualized, etc.) category. The focus is neither on the experience or identity of those who inhabit the intersection, nor on the inequalities (inter-group and intra-group) that exist in the world, but rather, for Collins, intersectionality is a claim about how social, political, economic, and interpersonal inequalities are shaped, produced, and maintained. This is an ontological claim of a fundamentally different order than the definitions offered by McCall and Crenshaw.

In addition to being an ontological diagnosis, for Collins, intersectionality is also an epistemology, a "broad-based knowledge project" that has three "interdependent sets of concerns": "a) intersectionality as a field of study, e.g. its history, themes, boundaries, debates, and direction; b) intersectionality as an analytical strategy, e.g. how intersectional frameworks provide new angles of vision on social institutions, practices, social problems, and other social phenomena associated with social inequality; and c) intersectionality as critical

---

30 | Collins, "Intersectionality's Definitional Dilemmas," 2.

praxis, e.g. how social actors use intersectionality for social justice projects."[31] The epistemological project and the ontological project, for Collins, entail one another; it is because the world is structured through intersectionally-produced inequalities that the epistemological claims of intersectionality represent the most appropriate for thinking the world. Additionally, the use of an intersectional epistemology is also, for Collins, directly necessitated by the political project of countering the marginalization, invisibility, and domination that these inequalities produce and maintain.

In the original 1990 version of *Black Feminist Thought*, Collins used the term "matrix of domination" rather than intersectionality to discuss the particular situation of black women. In the revised and updated version, Collins explains the relationship between these terms:

> Intersectionality refers to particular forms of intersecting oppressions, for example, intersections of race and gender, or of sexuality and nation. Intersectional paradigms remind us that oppression cannot be reduced to one fundamental type, that oppressions work together in producing injustice. In contrast, the matrix of domination refers to how these oppressions are actually organized. Regardless of the particular intersections involved, structural, disciplinary, hegemonic, and interpersonal domains of power reappear across quite different forms of oppression.[32]

For Collins, then, the matrix of domination is the name for the world as it is, the structure that produces intersectional oppressions. Rather than being reducible to any one particular system—capitalism, imperialism, patriarchy, racism, heterosexism—the matrix of domination refers to the relations and interarticulations between all of these systems, the way in which each one of these systems relies on all of the others, in both their historical constitution and their contemporary operation. But crucially, for Collins, these systems exist *as a matrix*, in which, because of their structural and historical interwovenness, none of these systems can be adequately conceived as the sole cause, master term, or ultimate foundation. As becomes apparent in the next section, one of the shared contentions of intersectionality is the fundamental equi-primordiality of oppressions that refuses a politics of ranking them. For Collins, the matrix is thus the model of conceiving the non-hierarchical interpenetration of systems of domination that produce intersectionally-structured inequalities.

Historiographers of intersectionality Ange-Marie Hancock and Vivian May have both attempted to synthesize the vast and varied writings on intersectionality to produce definitions that are not specific to any one thinker of intersectionality, but holistically integrative of the multiple approaches, divergences,

---

31 | Ibid, 3.
32 | Collins, *Black Feminist Thought*, 18.

and internal debates within the intersectional tradition. From this perspective, Ange Marie Hancock, offering a fourth approach, argues that

intersectionality's intellectual project is thus twofold: an analytical approach to understanding between-category relationships and a project to render visible and remediable previously invisible, unaddressed material effects of the sociopolitical location of Black women or women of color.[33]

For Hancock, then, intersectionality constitutes both a general analytic that thematizes the relationships between race, gender, sexuality, class, nation, ethnicity, age, and ability in order to explain relationships between multiple sites of oppression and a particular political commitment to counter intersectional oppression by specifically focusing on the ideas, experiences, and disadvantages experienced by women of color. Here Hancock insists on intersectionality as both a general approach to thinking categories of experience, identity, and oppression that could be taken to any site—including, for example, straight, white, cisgender men—and a tool that has particular salience for women of color in combatting their own marginalization, exclusion, and oppression. Hence, Hancock attempts to integrate debates about who constitutes the subject of intersectionality by arguing that it is both true that everyone is this subject and that women of color are its exceptional subjects. This political commitment is centrally important to Hancock's account; without it, intersectionality can become a de-politicized, wholly academic enterprise that simply considers identity or social position differently without the direct commitment to unsettling the practices, discourses, and institutions that create and perpetuate intersectional oppression. In order to make good on intersectionality's potential, Hancock contends that the analytical commitments of intersectionality must thus be connected to its politics of challenging oppression. In order to do this, Hancock explains that intersectionality operates at multiple levels: intersectionality "identifies the hegemonic (ideas, cultures, and ideologies), structural (social institutions), disciplinary (bureaucratic hierarchies and administrative practices), and interpersonal (routinized interactions among individuals) playing fields upon which race, gender, class, and other categories or traditions of difference interact to produce society."[34] Hancock here explains that intersectionality's object, insofar as it is committed to the dual project of analysis and political challenge, must take aim at the material organizations of the matrix of domination that produce the experiences of intersectional oppression on these

---

33 | Hancock, *Intersectionality*, 33.
34 | Ange-Marie Hancock, "When Multiplication Doesn't Equal Quick Addition: Examining Intersectionality as a Research Paradigm," *Perspectives on Politics* 5, no. 1 (2007): 74.

four levels. We should note, importantly, that the interpersonal is only one of these levels, even though, as we will see in subsequent chapters, intersectionality is often accused of only focusing on this level.

Vivian May offers a fifth definition, one that also foregrounds the relationship between analysis and a politics of insubordination in her definition of intersectionality:

> Intersectionality is an analytical and political orientation that brings together a number of insights and practices developed largely in the context of Black feminist and women of color theoretical and political traditions. First, it approaches lived identities as interlaced and systems of oppression as enmeshed and mutually reinforcing: one aspect of identity and/or form of inequality is not treated as separable or as superordinate. This "matrix" worldview contests "single-axis" forms of thinking about subjectivity and power and rejects hierarchies of identity or oppression. An intersectional justice orientation is thus wide in scope and inclusive: it repudiates additive notions of identity, assimilationist models of civil rights, and one-dimensional views of power.[35]

In this definition, May focuses on the non-hierarchical nature of oppressions, contending that no one aspect can be treated as superordinate because they are interlaced on the structural level. She draws out the particular implication that additive notions of identity as well as uni-causal ones are by definition not intersectional. May continues,

> Intersectionality is an epistemological project that contests dominant mindsets; an ontological approach that accounts for complex subjectivity and offers different notions of agency; a radical political orientation grounded in solidarity, rather than sameness, as an organizing principle; and a resistant imaginary useful for intervening in conventional historical memory and prevailing social imaginaries.[36]

In addition to the ontological, epistemological, and political projects of intersectionality that Collins and Hancock identify, May contends that central to intersectionality is a "resistant imaginary," a mode not only of critiquing the world as it is currently constructed, but also an avenue for thinking the world as it could be constructed otherwise. It is therefore not only a project of negative critique, but also a project of positive critique, one that furnishes the coordinates for thinking an emancipated society by radically re-evaluating what liberation would mean and what it would entail.

---

35 | May, *Pursuing Intersectionality, Unsettling Dominant Imaginaries*, 3.
36 | May, 12.

SECTION TWO: SIX POSTULATES OF INTERSECTIONAL THINKING

Though the previous section explored many of the differences in some of the dominant trends of conceptualizing intersectionality, this section argues that, despite all of the differences and debates within intersectionality, some themes and positions remain constant between all or nearly all intersectionality theorists. Every theoretical tradition contains both its internal debates as well as its core principles of alignment, and intersectionality is, in this regard, no different.

In the first place, intersectionality emphasizes the inseparability of oppressions and critiques accounts that embrace 'single-axis' thinking. One of the key components of intersectionality is of the mutually constructed character of oppressions. In the words of Hancock, one of the key contentions of intersectionality is

the idea that analytical categories like 'race', 'gender', 'class' and the hegemonic practices associated with them (racism, sexism, classism, to which imperialism and homophobia certainly could be added) are mutually constitutive, not conceptually distinct.[37]

In the tenth anniversary edition of *Black Feminist Thought*, Patricia Hill Collins explains that intersectionality is an "analysis claiming that systems of race, social class, gender, sexuality, ethnicity, and age form mutually constructing features of social organization which shape Black women's experiences and in turn are shaped by Black women."[38] According to Alison Bailey,

Race and gender should be conceptualized not as 'race+gender', instead they should be thought of in terms of 'gendered racism' or 'how gender is racialized'. It makes sense to talk about capitalist patriarchies rather than capitalism and patriarchy.[39]

Vivian May argues that "intersectionality also is not a cumulative or arithmetical identity formula (race + gender + class + sexuality + disability + citizenship status, and so on, as if these were sequential, separate factors)."[40] According to Nira Yuval-Davis, from an intersectional perspective, "social divisions [are] constituted by each other in concrete ways, enmeshed in each other,

---

37 | Hancock, *Intersectionality*, 71.
38 | Collins, *Black Feminist Thought*, 299.
39 | Alison Bailey, "On Intersectionality, Empathy, and Feminist Solidarity: A Reply to Naomi Zack," *Journal of Peace and Justice Studies* 18, no. 2 (2009): 17.
40 | May, *Pursuing Intersectionality, Unsettling Dominant Imaginaries*, 22.

although they [...] are also irreducible to each other."[41] Crenshaw explains that "by tracing... categories to their intersections, I hope to suggest a methodology that will ultimately disrupt the tendency to see race and gender as exclusive or separable."[42]

Secondly, another key component of intersectionality is the claim that oppressions cannot be ranked. Audre Lorde called this approach the "hierarchy of oppressions"[43] and Elizabeth Martínez named it "Oppression Olympics."[44] In this sense, intersectionality rejects theories of oppression and identity that situate one (or more) axes of oppression or categories of experience as primary. The rejection of primacy entails two claims: no one oppression is *more important* (ontologically, experientially, politically) than the others, and no one oppression *unilaterally causes* the others. While oppressions are conceived as interlocking and mutually constituting, none are conceived as epiphenomenal of the others. This claim means politically, for both theory and activism, that solving the problems of oppression, exploitation, marginalization, or exclusion in one axis will not magically solve the others, and moreover, combined with the non-additive conceptualization described above, means specifically that no particular kind of oppression can be solved without solving all of the others. This claim is predicated on two additional claims: a) that oppressions are experienced as compounding and inseparable and b) that oppressions are ontologically constructed in relation to one another.

Thirdly, in many of the accounts above, intersectionality requires thinking multiple registers of oppression simultaneously and in conjunction with one another. While intersectionality is often portrayed as an analysis located exclusively or primarily at the level of individual identity, theorists of intersectionality argue that it is important to conceptualize oppression not only at the individual level, but also at the structural, representational, and discursive levels as well. Crenshaw, McCall, and Collins in particular highlight the ways in which intersectional thinking is necessary in multiple registers, including the individual, structural, familial, political, and community levels. Often overlooked, however, is that intersectionality not only operates on each of these levels, it also

---

41 | Kathleen Guidroz and Michele Tracy Berger, eds., "A Conversation with Founding Scholars of Intersectionality: Kimberlé Crenshaw, Nira Yuval-Davis, and Michelle Fine," in *The Intersectional Approach: Transforming the Academy through Race, Class, and Gender* (Chapel Hill: University of North Carolina Press, 2009), 65.

42 | Crenshaw, "Mapping the Margins: Intersectionality, Identity Politics, and Violence Against Women of Color," 1244n9.

43 | Audre Lorde, *Zami: A New Spelling of My Name - A Biomythography*, First edition (Berkeley, Calif.: The Crossing Press, 1982).

44 | Elizabeth Martínez, "Beyond Black/White: The Racisms of Our Time," *Social Justice*, no. 20 (1993): 22-34.

insists on thinking the ways in which these levels or domains themselves influence, constitute, and interact with one another in producing the social field.

Fourth, intersectionality takes identity as an important aspect in political organizing and theorizing. While many have caricatured identity politics, intersectionality theorists conceive of identity as multi-pronged, group-based, historically-constituted, and heterogenous. Nikol Alexander-Floyd explains that in intersectionality, "identity politics [is] centered on complex, negotiated understandings of group interests" rather than on individual identities.[45] These negotiated conceptions of group-based identity politics signify the shifting, historically situated nature of oppressions, precisely the opposite of the ahistoricism and naturalization of identity of which intersectionality theorists are accused. As Vivian May attests, this gross misreading of intersectionality is itself embroiled in a politics of knowledge production, one that ignores the theoretical sensitivity and nuance that these theories elaborate:

Pitting context versus identity ignores how intersectionality posits identity as located within, navigating across, and shaped by social structures. A more thorough reading of the literature, in any period of intersectionality's genealogy, substantiates that a 'both/and' approach to (multiple) identities contextualized within myriad social structures and cognizant of relational power dynamics within and between groups is a basic premise of intersectionality.[46]

An important corollary of this argument rejects a simplified, 'pure' notion of identity politics.[47] Theorists of intersectionality are particularly concerned with understanding identity and oppression in ways that accounted for the multiplicity of social locations one inhabits and accounting for heterogeneity within groups. For example, Patricia Hill Collins' *Black Feminist Thought* is concerned with understanding and highlighting the multiplicity of responses, theories, and experiences of black women. Many other such examples of the anti-categorial approach to intersectionality argue that because of the complexity of social life, there are neither "pure victims" nor "pure oppressors", but rather a "permeability of the binary between oppressed and oppressor."[48] May thus argues that a politics of coalition is integral to the definition of intersectionality, which she defines as encompassing "a radical political orientation grounded

---

45 | Nikol Alexander-Floyd, "Disappearing Acts: Reclaiming Intersectionality in the Social Sciences in a Post-Black Feminist Era," *Feminist Formations* 24, no. 1 (2012): 11.
46 | Vivian May, "'Speaking into the Void?: Intersectionality Critiques and Epistemic Backlash," *Hypatia* 28, no. 1 (2014): 103.
47 | Hancock, *Intersectionality*, 140–46.
48 | Hancock, 114.

in solidarity, rather than sameness."[49] It is in this sense that Crenshaw and Carastathis argue that identities should themselves be conceived as coalitions.[50]

Indeed, working in coalition is one of the key themes of intersectionality.[51] According to Cole, intersectional coalitions should be organized on the basis of "shared interests rather than shared identity."[52] While many intersectionality theorists critique so-called coalitions that require de-emphasizing differences in position, power, and experiences, they emphasize that working in true coalitions—ones that honor, foreground, and learn from these differences as a source of power—is a central theme of intersectionality scholarship. Recognizing that forming coalitions based in honoring difference is a difficult political praxis, Chandra Mohanty emphasizes that intersectional coalitions are "always an achievement, the result of active struggle."[53] When and where intersectionality theorists have advocated for a certain kind of separatist politics, those who do conceive of this separatism as a temporally-bounded, strategic tactic intended to help members of oppressed groups find community, identify demands, and think more lucidly about their experiences *in order to then re-integrate in larger coalitional projects of social justice*.[54]

Fifth, intersectionality is indeed a theoretical orientation, but it is indexed to thinking about power within social movements and activist spaces. Intersectionality developed not only as a theory in academic spaces, but also in and through activism and organizing. Many of the texts that formed the intellectual inheritance of intersectionality were first composed and circulated through newsletters, zines, and conferences that were associated with national, regional, and local activist organizations like the Third World Women's Alliance, the National Black Women's Organization, the National Domestic Worker's Alliance, the Black Women's Alliance, the National Black Feminist Organization, the National Alliance of Black Feminists, and feminist groups within other organizations, like the Student Nonviolent Coordinating Committee.[55]

---

49 | May, *Pursuing Intersectionality, Unsettling Dominant Imaginaries*, 12.
50 | Crenshaw, "Mapping the Margins: Intersectionality, Identity Politics, and Violence Against Women of Color"; Carastathis, *Intersectionality*.
51 | María Lugones, *Pilgrimages = Peregrinajes: Theorizing Coalition against Multiple Oppressions* (Lanham, Md.: Rowman & Littlefield, 2003); Smith and Smith, "Across the Kitchen Table: A Sister-to-Sister Dialogue," 126; Hancock, *Intersectionality*, 152-58.
52 | Elizabeth Cole, "Coalitions as a Model for Intersectionality: From Practice to Theory," *Sex Roles* 59, no. 5-6 (2008): 447.
53 | Chandra Talpade Mohanty, *Feminism without Borders: Decolonizing Theory, Practicing Solidarity* (Durham: Duke University Press, 2003), 78.
54 | Bailey, "On Intersectionality, Empathy, and Feminist Solidarity: A Reply to Naomi Zack."
55 | This list is illustrative, not exhaustive.

Moreover, many of the writers of these texts who were themselves academics worked out the theories through conversations, questions, and problems they encountered in their organizing. Crenshaw specifically notes that her understanding of intersectionality came out of her activist work. Many intersectionality theorists were themselves in a variety of struggles, including but not limited to those about "sterilization abuse, abortion rights, battered women, rape, and health care."[56]

Sixth, intersectionality is both an account of power and a critique of power. This is the sense in which intersectionality is an ontology: it explains how power operates in the contemporary world; intersectionality illuminates "the workings of power, which is understood as both pervasive and oppressive... at all levels of social relations."[57] But it is not a neutral, disinterested account of that power; rather, it is also a critique of the way that power operates. It is thus both descriptive and normative, offering an account of the world and a critique of the world as it exists. Sumi Cho explains, "Intersectionality theory suggests a methodological approach and epistemological stance vis-à-vis combating multiple forms of subordination within and through various movements for social change."[58] In the words of Joy James, intersectionality and other Black feminist liberation perspectives are oriented against the prevailing order of the world, confronting "state power by addressing class exploitation, racism, nationalism, and sexual violence with critiques of and activist confrontations with corporate-state policies."[59] In this sense, intersectionality is both descriptive and normative.

SECTION THREE: INTERSECTIONALITY'S DIFFERENCE FROM OTHER ACCOUNTS

Having developed a clearer understanding of what constitutes intersectionality's core, we are now in a position to consider the differences between intersectionality and the concepts discussed in the previous chapter. Recognizing the distinctions between intersectionality and alternative ways of conceiving the relationship between race, gender, and class under capitalism is important for

---

56 | Combahee River Collective, "A Black Feminist Statement," 371.

57 | Bonnie Thornton Dill and Ruth Enid Zambrana, eds., *Emerging Intersections: Race, Class, and Gender in Theory, Policy, and Practice*, Edition Unstated edition (New Brunswick, N.J: Rutgers University Press, 2009), 11.

58 | Cho, "Post-Intersectionality: The Curious Reception of Intersectionality in Legal Scholarship," 385.

59 | Joy James, *Seeking the Beloved Community: A Feminist Race Reader* (SUNY Press, 2013), 57.

a number of reasons: in the first place, to understand the theoretical advances made by intersectionality on its own terms, over and above the other conceptions that influenced its development; secondly, to parse some rather fine distinctions that will become important in subsequent chapters in order to consider some of the critiques of intersectionality. Some (though not all) of the critiques of intersectionality misidentify it as one of the other theories; differentiating intersectionality from them will thus be key in distinguishing between fair and misplaced critiques, and especially, in explaining some of the divergences, misapprehensions, and confusions in the debates between Marxism and intersectionality as approaches to liberation.

Intersectionality is most often conflated with the jeopardy approach; the two differ significantly, however, in that intersectionality rejects the additive approach. In the jeopardy and double/triple oppression literature, the very language of 'double' and 'triple' suggests both a separability of race, gender, and class, and that the particular positions of women of color are produced through the addition of multiple oppressions together. But this fails to conceive of the ways in which categories are fundamentally, structurally and experientially interarticulated and mutually constructing. When intersectionality is critiqued for 'adding' an endless string of identities together, the true object of such a critique is the jeopardy approach.

Jones' conception of superexploitation, while helpful, remains a conceptualization distinct from intersectionality. In a similar vein to triple oppression, superexploitation seems to suggest an additivity of race, gender, and class: the "super" suggests that gender, race, and class exist as compounded, additive intensifiers of one another, but that they are in principle separable. Superexploitation, in contrast to intersectionality, seems to locate oppression in only one sphere, that of labor. While it is true that Crenshaw first used 'intersectionality' to explain black women's experiences in employment, and thus the concepts are deeply connected to one another, intersectionality is committed to a multi-level, multi-valent analysis that extends far beyond labor practices and practices of exploitation (though these spheres are still fundamental to it). Jones also argues that capitalism is the sole cause of black women's oppression, which directly contradicts intersectionality's understanding of the matrix of oppression, which insists on the non-reducibility of systems to one another. Thus, from an intersectional perspective, while superexploitation might constitute an intersectional understanding of exploitation, it falls short of conceiving how oppression works generally and systematically beyond relations of exploitation.

Intersectionality also, in some contexts, crucially draws on standpoint epistemology, but is not synonymous with it. One of the most enduring critiques of standpoint theory is its reliance on a dichotomy between the center and the margin: in Marx and Lukács, that dichotomy is figured as capitalist-proletariat, in much feminist standpoint theory, as men-women, in anti-racist standpoint theory as white-of color. In explaining intersectionality's critique of standpoint theory, Hancock argues that standpoint theory merely furnishes "diverse" perspectives on the world, doing nothing to "eradicate the existence of a margin or a periphery." "Diversification of the center" is itself a different project than intersectionality, though the two are often conflated.[60] Because standpoint theory relies heavily on a binaristic center/margin or center/periphery model, it is helpful to explore intersectionality's critique of this paradigm in order to better understand its difference from standpoint theory.

The margin-center approach takes its point of departure from a post-colonial and U.S. Third World women's perspective that conceives of oppression as organized through the fundamental distinction between the margin and the center. The margin and center, in these accounts is both empirical and theoretical. In the more empirical accounts, the center is conceived as the Euro-American capitalist and imperialist counties that produce the rest of the world, its bodies of knowledge, practices, cultures, and economies as marginal or peripheral. In this version, the center or the core is conceived as the locus of power in a hegemonic sense, while the margin or the periphery is uniformly portrayed as oppressed, repressed, and powerless. Within U.S. Third World feminism, the margin-center discourse, famously articulated by bell hooks, explains the way in which white, capitalist, heterosexual masculinity is the center of politics, economics, and social institutions.[61] The fundamental institutions, narratives, and perspectives of social, political, and economic life are hence constructed in the interests of those who inhabit the center; the world is created in their image. This leads to the marginalization of all those who do not fit this position: women, queer people, people of color, poor people, disabled people, immigrants etc. Those who inhabit these identities are *marginalized*, meaning that their ideas, experiences, feelings, and material conditions are constructed as insignificant, and they are often repressed and silenced. Intersectionality has critiqued the margin-center perspective as being too reductive, too flat, and too binary to account for the multiplicity of power relations in the world. As Collins explains, despite the intention of the margin-center distinction to critique existing power hierarchies, it often functioned "a yet another ahistorical 'universal' construct" that could not adequately conceptualize differences.[62] For example, the margin-center metaphor homogenizes all places in the margin, suggesting that all places in the margin are constituted in the same way; it thus is not a particularly helpful framework in distinguishing between, for example, the settler-colonial extraction of resources on Indigenous land

---

60 | Hancock, *Intersectionality*, 85.
61 | hooks, *Feminist Theory*.
62 | Patricia Hill Collins, *Fighting Words: Black Women and the Search for Justice* (Minneapolis: University of Minnesota Press, 1998), 129.

in the United States and the politics of extraction of Euro-American corporations in Latin America.[63] In this binary conception, it is difficult to explain the differential power relations between Chicano men and Chicana women, or between U.S.-born Chicanas and Mexican-born Chicanas, as Anzaldúa argues is essential for understanding mestiza experience in Texas.[64] It is also nearly impossible to adequately conceive multiple, divergent strategies of racialization between, for example, black and indigenous people within the United States. Moreover, Collins worries that rather than "talk of tops and bottoms, long associated with hierarchy," the margin-center metaphor tends to "recast [power relations] as flattened geographies" in ways that obscure or inhibit the real, actually existing hierarchies that must be critiqued.[65]

All of these critiques of the center/margin or core/periphery models of oppression are operative in intersectionality's critique of standpoint theory as a wholly adequate theory of oppression. While some intersectionality theorists, like Collins, have significantly adapted standpoint theory beyond its initial articulations in ways that may overcome its limitations, it is still important to differentiate most standpoint theory from intersectionality. Moreover, while intersectional theorists may use reformulations of standpoint theory, they do so in the *service* of producing an intersectional analysis; because intersectionality is much more than a theory of epistemology, standpoint theory and intersectionality operate on fundamentally different domains and scales.

While the theory of sexist racism elaborated by Nieto-Gómez, Yolanda Nava, and others seems rather close to intersectionality, there is an important difference. Sexist racism adequately and sensitively renders one of intersectionality's key contentions: that forms of oppression are totally and completely suffused with one another. The formulation of racist sexism highlights the way in which race is gendered and gender is raced in ways that very presciently presage intersectionality. However, this formulation falls somewhat short of intersectionality's understanding of *all* oppressions being constituted in such a way: sexist racism, for Nieto-Gómez, Nava, and Martínez, is deeply interlinked with capitalism and thus can perhaps speak of class, but it does not seem to be able to render the way in which nationality, immigration status, ability, age, or

---

63 | For an account of the role natural resources play in the settler colonial imaginary in the U.S. and Canada see Iyko Day's book. For an analysis of a different set of neo-imperial conditions in Latin America, see Gómez-Barris' excellent discussion. Macarena Gómez-Barris, *The Extractive Zone: Social Ecologies and Decolonial Perspectives* (Durham and London: Duke University Press, 2017); Iyko Day, *Alien Capital: Asian Racialization and the Logic of Settler Colonial Capitalism* (Durham: Duke University Press Books, 2016).

64 | Anzaldúa, *Borderlands/ La Frontera*.

65 | Collins, *Fighting Words: Black Women and the Search for Justice*, 129.

sexuality are as central to understanding race as gender is. In this sense, sexist racism contains the seed of one of intersectionality's most important contributions, but without its complete or full articulation. It is important to note, however, that in many contemporary usages and appropriations of intersectionality, it is taken to mean sexist racism (and racist sexism) in ways that obscure intersectionality's commitment to a much larger and nuanced matrix of domination, and, for this reason, it is important to clearly distinguish between these conceptions.

Lastly, there is some debate about whether the Combahee River Collective's understanding of oppression is strictly consonant with a full-blown theory of intersectionality. This is hotly debated because the Combahee River Collective Statement is often seen as one of intersectionality's foundational texts. As many intersectionality scholars have noted, one of the notions that the Combahee River Collective shares with other black feminist politics, like that of the Third World Women's Alliance, was an embrace a politics of "the vanguard center"; as Benita Roth parses it, this conception relied on an idea of "Black women constituting a 'vanguard center' whose liberation would mean the liberation of all."[66] McDuffie also associates the position that black women were "the vanguard of social change" with Claudia Jones' thesis on superexploitation.[67] The idea latent in the politics of the vanguard center is that by focusing on black women's oppression, *all* oppressions could be undone, precisely because black women sit at the intersection of gender, race, and often class. The politics of the vanguard center and the assertion that if black women were free, all people would be free, seems to position black women as the most oppressed within society, seemingly violating the non-hierarchy of oppressions postulate.[68] In addition, it would seem that focusing on the intersection of race, gender, and class could leave open the possibility of leaving intact oppressions on other bases: sexuality, age, ability, and nation. In this way, the framing of the vanguard center could potentially contribute to marginalizing the ways in which gender, race, and class, are *themselves*, constituted in and through these other axes. Moreover, the assertion of black women as the vanguard center potentially obscures power differentials *between* black women and may not adequately account for the different ways in which black women and other women of color experience intersectional oppression.

---

66 | Roth, *Separate Roads to Feminism*, 91.
67 | Erik S. McDuffie, *Sojourning for Freedom: Black Women, American Communism, and the Making of Black Left Feminism* (Durham: Duke University Press, 2011), 116.
68 | Carastathis in particular takes this approach, arguing that the Combahee River Collective's Statement is thus better conceived as an antecedent to intersectionality rather than part of intersectionality itself.

CONCLUSION

In many ways, the theory of intersectionality developed in this chapter constitutes one of the trajectories that develops out of the shared history sketched in the previous chapter. While many (but certainly not all, or even, perhaps, a majority) of the texts, perspectives, and ideas that intersectionality draws on are part of this shared history, and thus bear a historical relationship to Marxist anti-capitalism, it is clear that intersectionality is not itself *essentially* Marxist, developing in conversation with other thinkers, texts, and considerations, and drawing significantly on non-Marxist theories of race, gender, sexuality, and other axes of oppression. The next chapter probes some of the most common Marxist critiques of intersectionality; we will see in that chapter some key examples of scholars and activists misunderstanding and misapprehending intersectionality in many of the ways discussed in this chapter.

Chapter Two: Marxist Critiques of Intersectionality

Despite the shared genealogy of Marxism and intersectionality, much of the scholarship of both traditions have positioned these bodies of work as opposed to one another, rather than as sharing vital commitments, textual bases, and critical analyses. In this chapter and Chapter Four, I sketch some of the dominant points of contention and critique between contemporary manifestations of the two traditions. Understanding the debates and divergences between these frameworks is central to any project of thinking the possibilities of bring them together, as Part Three of this book attempts. Unfortunately, as will become clear, many of the critiques levied between traditions, indeed especially some of the most commonly-repeated accusations, have little basis in the actual texts of the traditions at hand. This is of course, not uniformly true. The project of these two chapters is not to "save" either tradition from the critiques of the other, but rather to understand more fully the substance of their divergence.

This chapter focuses on some of the most common Marxist critiques of intersectionality. In particular, I focus on the following claims about intersectionality: that its conception of identity politics is individualistic and bourgeois, that intersectionality is postmodern, that it is essentially reformist and/or liberal, that it misunderstands the fundamental nature of class, that it lacks a causal explanation of oppression, and that intersectionality is a poor metaphor for understanding oppression. Many of these criticisms are misplaced, generated from a failure to engage substantively with intersectionality as a vibrant body of scholarship and activism."

Identity Politics[1]

Perhaps the most commonly critiqued (and poorly understood) aspect of intersectionality hinges on its conception of identity politics. In a widely read and distributed pamphlet, Eve Mitchell alleges that the focus of intersectionality on identity politics constitutes a reinforcement of capitalist ideas of individuality. Responding specifically to bell hooks' iteration of the critique of the homogeneity of experience so frequent in non-intersectional analyses, Mitchell writes,

> hooks is correct to say that basing an entire politics on one particular experience, or a set of particular differences, under capitalism is problematic. However, intersectionality theory replicates this problem by simply adding particular moments, or determinant points; hooks goes on to argue for race and class inclusion in a feminist analysis. Similarly, theories of an 'interlocking matrix of oppressions,' simply create a list of naturalized identities, abstracted from their material and historical context. This methodology is just as ahistorical and antisocial as Betty Friedan's.[2]

This selection highlights two related but slightly different criticisms. In the first place, Mitchell's critique is representative of a frequent criticism of additive or multiplicative approaches to explain the position of working class women of color who experience class, gender, and race-based oppressions.[3] While there are certainly some intersectional theorists who deploy this framework, many intersectional theorists themselves have argued against additive and multiplicative models for their failure to highlight the mutual constitution of the structures of domination. Chapter One addressed the ways in which intersection-

---

[1] | I will return to an extended discussion of identity politics, especially in relation to solidarity, coalition work, and movement building in Chapter Seven.

[2] | Eve Mitchell, "I Am a Women and a Human: A Marxist Feminist Critique of Intersectionality Theory," *Libcom.Com*, 2014, https://libcom.org/library/i-am-woman-human-marxist-feminist-critique-intersectionality-theory-eve-mitchell.

[3] | It is important to note here that while Mitchell does not simultaneously criticize the tradition of Marxist feminism, the mathematical model of oppression has also been frequent in this tradition. Many marxist feminists used the language of 'double jeopardy' to describe the duality of class and gender oppressions. The refusal to recognize the roots of this mathematical model in the very tradition that Mitchell defends is itself a form of epistemic domination, one in which the voices and theories of women of color are the only voices criticized for a more general tendency in theory. While I agree with Mitchell that mathematical models of oppression are not the most helpful metaphors for explaining the relationships between various instantiations of social domination, we should be wary of the power dynamics at play in accusing only intersectionality and not other frameworks of this problem.

ality specifically rejects the additive or mathematical approach to conceiving oppression. As this same intervention is made by many other intersectionality theorists, Mitchell's (and others') identification of intersectionality with these mathematical models constitutes a straw-person argument, one that refuses to seriously engage with the vast intersectional literature critiquing the very position Mitchell attributes to this framework.

The second but related criticism Mitchell levies concerns the nature of identity as it is discussed by intersectionality. Mitchell worries that identities are conceived as "natural," "ahistorical," and later in the same essay, "idealistic" and "bourgeois." Mitchell's worry about identity politics is rooted in a long history of Marxist criticism. Marxism, as a perspective grounded in historical materialism, generally views identities as effects of structural, material, and historical processes. Hence, accounts of identity that are only descriptive and do not speak about the structures enframing, creating, policing, and maintaining these identities lack, from a Marxist perspective, the crucial and necessary explanatory element of theory that would be grounded in a historical perspective of the power of structures and institutions. Politics of identity that center *only* on describing one's social location are seen as overly self-congratulatory and, potentially, reaffirming of the social cleavages created by dominating structures. Certain iterations of identity politics ground themselves in purely individual terms and reduce politics solely to an issue of claiming a position within a social totality. Some Marxists argue that identity politics is essentially bourgeois because capitalism depends on the fabrication of a social order of discrete, atomistic, competitive individualism; hence, because of its (supposed) reliance on the ideology of individualism, Mitchell and other Marxists have maligned identity politics as essentially compatible with capitalism, and hence, as bourgeois. Critics of identity politics, especially those who are engaged not only in theory but also in movement-based activist work, also worry that grounding a politics in identity can have the effect of limiting the possibilities for cross-group coalition building and solidarity.[4] Because of the above enumerated worries, Mitchell accuses intersectionality as reconfirming a certain kind of bourgeois politics: "Since identity politics, and therefore intersectionality theory, are a bourgeois politics, the possibilities for struggle are also bourgeois. Identity politics reproduces the appearance of an alienated individual under capitalism and so struggle takes the form of equality among groups at best, or individualized forms of struggle at worse."[5]

---

4 | It is interesting to note that these kinds of arguments were precisely those made by many mainstream marxists *against* the development of Marxist feminism. We will return to the possibilities of coalitions and solidarity in Chapter Seven.
5 | Mitchell, "I Am a Women and a Human: A Marxist Feminist Critique of Inter-sectionality Theory."

While the Marxist critiques offered above adequately respond to certain strands of identity politics, they critique a fundamentally different understanding of identity politics than that held by the majority of developed intersectionality theories. Take, for example, the explanation of identity politics offered by the Combahee River Collective: "this focusing upon our own oppression is embodied in the concept of identity politics. We believe that the most profound and potentially most radical politics come directly out of our own identity, as opposed to working to end someone else's oppression."[6] But what exactly do these theorists mean by the term identity politics? Do they use it to signify an endless, congratulatory string of individual identifications, disconnected from structures and histories? Even a cursory reading of intersectionality would demonstrate that this is clearly not the case. Rather, intersectionality theorists frequently critique this tendency in post-structural feminisms with which intersectionality is often confused.

In her article on the relationship between intersectionality and postmodernism, Susan Archer Mann mobilizes Patricia Hill Collins' grounding of intersectionality inside historically-dependent, group-based identities against the postmodern position of the irreducible difference and uniqueness of each individual and hence the absolute untranslatability of every experience to another. She explains that in postmodern accounts of differences and identity, "differences are infinite and each individual is potentially unique." In contrast, for Collins and other intersectionality theorists, identities are based in "groups who have shared histories because of their shared location in relations of unequal power and privilege. They are neither groups based simply on identities chosen by individuals nor groups analytically created by demographers, bureaucrats or scholars."[7]

It is not only Patricia Hill Collins who argues against this version of identity politics. Nikol Alexander-Floyd explains that "women of color feminists generally support identity politics centered on complex, negotiated understandings of group interests" rather than on individual identities.[8] These "negotiated" conceptions of group-based identity politics signify the shifting, historically situated nature of oppressions, precisely the opposite of the ahistoricism and naturalization of which intersectionality theorists are accused. As Vivian May argues, this gross misreading of intersectionality is itself embroiled in a politics of knowledge production, one that ignores the theoretical sensitivity and nuance that these theories elaborate:

---

6 | Combahee River Collective, "A Black Feminist Statement."
7 | Susan Archer Mann, "Third Wave Feminism's Unhappy Marriage of Poststructuralism and Intersectionality Theory," *Journal of Feminist Scholarship*, no. 4 (2013): 64.
8 | Alexander-Floyd, "Disappearing Acts: Reclaiming Intersectionality in the Social Sciences in a Post-Black Feminist Era," 11.

Pitting context versus identity ignores how intersectionality posits identity as located within, navigating across, and shaped by social structures. A more thorough reading of the literature, in any period of intersectionality's genealogy, substantiates that a 'both/and' approach to (multiple) identities contextualized within myriad social structures and cognizant of relational power dynamics within and between groups is a basic premise of intersectionality.[9]

Mitchell's accusation can only seem ludicrous in this context. The Combahee River Collective, for example, mobilize their experiences of the simultaneity of oppressions rather as a starting place—not the end goal—of theory and praxis, as a window into the structures of domination from which to speak, interrogate, analyze, and explain. And while it may be true that eliminating the structures of oppression is not *per se* about any one person's experience of these oppressions, ultimately, eliminating oppression and exploitation are political urgencies *because* of their maleffects on the lives and experiences of really existing human beings.

Certainly, this was Marx's position. He argues that historical materialism is a necessary philosophical commitment because of its focus on real, historical individuals and the violence they face. Without this insight, theory and political organizing fall back into the idealist trap of German metaphysics. He writes in *The Germany Ideology*, using problematically androcentric language:

In direct contrast to German philosophy which descends from heaven to earth, here we ascend from earth to heaven. That is to say, we do not set out from what men say, imagine, conceive, nor from men as narrated, thought of, imagined, conceived, in order to arrive at men in the flesh. We set out from real, active men, and on the basis of their real life-process we demonstrate the development of the ideological reflexes and echoes of this life-process [...] Life is not determined by consciousness, but consciousness by life. In the first method of approach the starting-point is consciousness taken as the living individual; in the second method, which conforms to real life, it is the real living individuals themselves, and consciousness is considered solely as their consciousness.[10]

Thus, it may be that intersectionality's commitment to theorizing experience as the starting place for structural analysis is more in line with historical materialism than is Mitchell's critique.

But identity politics in the intersectional tradition is not only a theoretical position, but an actual politics, with a developed understanding of strategic

---

9 | May, "'Speaking into the Void?: Intersectionality Critiques and Epistemic Backlash," 103.

10 | Marx, *The German Ideology*, Chap 1, sec. 4.

objectives. Kimberlé Crenshaw argues that defending group rather than individual identity politics constitutes an important political tactic: "At this point in history, a strong case can be made that the most critical resistance strategy for disempowered groups is to occupy and defend a politics of social location rather than to vacate and destroy it." Crenshaw here points to the distinction between theory as a political strategy and theory as a supposedly value-free inquiry aimed at establishing a form of everlasting or universal truth. The argument is not that group-based identity politics forms a political truth *tout court*, but that inside the *particular* historical context of the exclusion and marginalization of women of color from both mainstream theory and political practice, the act of recentering analysis on these groups itself constitutes an intervention into sedimented structures of domination. This notion of identity and identity politics in intersectionality thus greatly differs from the version often attributed to it. Rather, intersectionality and its conception of identity politics is all-too-often confused with a post-modern approach.

Postmodernism

One of the most common critiques of intersectionality from a Marxist position alleges that intersectionality is primarily a post-modern theory. While often in these critiques "postmodern" is neither specifically defined nor is it precisely articulated why post-modernism is an inherently flawed position, these critiques often seem to hinge on two charges: that postmodernism is committed to a notion of radical individualism and that it is a fundamentally idealist position. Insofar as these critiques of post-modernism are applied to intersectionality, this charge seems levied at intersectionality's supposed focus *only* on the individual and experiential elements of oppression and its alleged neglect of structures and institutions. While it is true that many intersectional theorists have critiqued a singular focus on structures and a complete neglect of individual identities and lived realities, the key texts of intersectionality seek to intervene in discussions of oppression by thinking the multiplicity of ways in which oppression functions at *both* the personal and the structural levels; as covered in the last chapter, this multi-level, multi-valent analysis is a central unifying component of intersectionality.

In addition to the focus on individuality, Marxists often critique post-structuralism (and therefore, wrongly, intersectionality) for its focus on language and discourse at the expense of structural power relations. From this perspective, Marxists often worry that the post-structural focus on language seeks to solve real, historical problems of oppression and exploitation in the realm of thought or speech alone, leaving the sedimented histories of institutional practices largely undisturbed. Given that Marxists—rightly or wrongly—tend to equate post-modernism with a decisively anti-materialist discourse, the charge that intersectionality is a fundamentally post-modern idea is often a veiled way of alleging that it lacks an account of matter, materiality, and a materialist analysis.[11] One particularly scathing example of such an accusation comes from Delia Aguilar, who contends that in the theoretical transition from triple jeopardy to intersectionality, the "material anchor" of capitalism is irrevocably lost, leaving intersectionality to be confined to the fundamentally liberal "realm of discourse."[12] This critique is particularly ironic, given the way in which the post-structuralist tradition has developed to critique its own reliance on language.

As explored in Chapter One, many intersectional theorists specifically embrace a material, structural, historical, and group-based approach to thinking about oppression and identity. In this regard, many intersectionality theorists specifically differentiate intersectionality from post-modernism. Cho in particular argues that postmodern understandings of intersectionality significantly distort its key principles.[13] The sharp differentiation between postmodernism and intersectionality is widely shared among scholars of intersectionality.[14] Hancock argues that the conflation of intersectionality with postmodernism serves a particularly nefarious purpose: by subsuming intersectionality under the aegis of (largely) white Euro-American postmodern theorists, women of color and the content of their writings are effectively de-centered from intersectionality scholarship, a practice Sirma Bilge has called the "whitening of intersectionality."[15] It is important to note that Bilge's understanding of 'whitening intersectionality' is not synonymous with 'white people reading/writing/ using intersectional scholarship'; rather, 'whitening intersectionality' names a strategy of power whereby women of color are alienated and marginalized from the sites of their own intellectual production. Insights and accomplishments of women of color are wrongly cast as derivative of white men's ideas, race in

---

11 | Whether or not this equivalence is a helpful or analytically correct one is far beyond the scope of the present investigation. Regardless of the accuracy of this assertion, it is present in these debates and needs thus to be unpacked.

12 | For a discussion of this tendency in post-structuralism and post-post structuralism, see Puar (2012), 57-9. Delia Aguilar, "Tracing the Roots of Intersectionality," *Monthly Review Zine*, April 12, 2012.

13 | Cho, "Post-Intersectionality: The Curious Reception of Intersectionality in Legal Scholarship."

14 | May, "'Speaking into the Void?: Intersectionality Critiques and Epistemic Backlash"; May, *Pursuing Intersectionality, Unsettling Dominant Imaginaries*; Hancock, *Intersectionality*; Mann, *Doing Feminist Theory*; Collins, "Intersectionality's Definitional Dilemmas."

15 | Bilge, "Whitening Intersectionality"; Hancock, *Intersectionality*, 2; Nina Lykke, *Feminist Studies: A Guide to Intersectional Theory, Methodology, and Writing* (New York: Routledge, 2010).

particular is erased as a central component of intersectional scholarship, a poor politics of citation allows for the publication of articles with a nearly all white bibliography, etc. Thus 'whitening intersectionality' is not about the identity of the people writing about intersectionality, but about whether and when practices that sustain white supremacy are evident in the particular use of intersectionality.

The genealogy (even as a contested one) of intersectionality derives much more from women of color feminisms than from the theories of Foucault, Butler or other post-structuralist theories. However, it is important to note that in "Mapping the Margins," Crenshaw, "consider[s] intersectionality a provisional concept linking contemporary politics to postmodern theory," even though what exactly Crenshaw means by 'postmodern theory' and the exact nature of this linkage remains unexplored in her article. Collins does indeed cite Foucault's concept of 'subjugated knowledges' in order to radically reformulate the concept, but as Hancock argues, this is a rather weak linkage to then declare Collins' work post-structural or *essentially* Foucauldian in any way—as it would be rather ludicrous to claim that a single footnote in a 500 page book is sufficient evidence for such a proclamation. [16]

That intersectionality and post-structuralism are not synonymous is recognized not only by intersectionality theorists, but also by post-structuralists. For example, Jasbir Puar critiques intersectionality for *not being post-structural enough*; Puar suggests synthesizing intersectionality with post-structuralism, specifically of the Massumi-Deleuze assemblage theory vein, in order to counter the limitations of intersectionality.[17] While it would be beyond the scope of the present project to consider the validity and voluminous literature on Marxists critiques of post-structuralism, it is clear that the charges here simply do not apply, because intersectionality is not itself a post-structuralist theory.

Reformist/Liberalism

One trenchant critique of intersectionality is the ways in which it has been mobilized in service of a reformist project of inclusion under the aegis of multicultural liberalism. In particular Jasbir Puar has been an outspoken critic of intersectionality as merely "a way to manage difference in ways that reinforce 'liberal multiculturalism.'"[18] While it is certainly true that intersectionality has been used as a tool of reforming institutions rather than subverting them, it

---

16 | Crenshaw, "Mapping the Margins: Intersectionality, Identity Politics, and Violence Against Women of Color," 1244n9; Collins, *Black Feminist Thought*, chap. 1; Hancock, *Intersectionality*, Introduction.
17 | Jasbir Puar, "I Would Rather Be a Cyborg than a Goddess: Becoming-Intersectional in Assemblage Theory," *Philosophia* 2, no. 1 (2012): 49-66.
18 | Puar, 53.

is important to note that intersectionality theorists both insist on the radical, revolutionary potential of intersectionality *and* critique its (mis)use and (mis)appropriation when it is not aimed at a total reordering of society. In 1989, Crenshaw clearly argued that "problems of exclusion cannot be solved simply by including Black women within an already established analytical structure" precisely because the structures and institutions of modern life are predicated on the exclusion and oppression of black women in particular and women of color in general.[19] As Vivian May contends,

That some have used or understood intersectionality in ways that align with liberal multiculturalism, reinforce and rationalize state surveillance, further settler colonial logics, or ignore the coloniality of gender, doing so undermines its antisubordination impetus and ignores its long-standing focus on the (settler) state's founding brutalities and ongoing abuses.[20]

It may be important to critique liberal, multicultural appropriations of intersectionality, but these misuses should not be construed to faithfully represent the theoretical aims or political orientation of intersectionality itself.

In some iterations of this argument, the fact that Crenshaw—taken in these accounts to be the unproblematic and undisputed originator of intersectionality—is a lawyer allows a positioning of intersectionality and its roots in Critical Race Theory and Critical Legal Studies as uniformly reformist, beholden to the boundaries and problems of the law.[21] Crenshaw's response to this kind of objection counters that these traditions of thought rather use the "law's apparent intimacy with prevailing racial order" to critique it as a structure by staging "an intellectual sit in."[22] Elsewhere, Crenshaw has argued that intersectionality and critical race theory clearly understood that "law was obviously a discourse of domination, but at the same time, it constituted an arena through which the rules of racial subordination might be engaged" in order to subvert them.[23] It is profoundly ironic that Crenshaw's version of intersection-

---

19 | Crenshaw, "Demarginalizing the Intersection of Race and Sex: A Black Feminist Critique of Antidiscrimination Doctrine, Feminist Theory, and Antiracist Politics," 140.
20 | May, *Pursuing Intersectionality, Unsettling Dominant Imaginaries*, 231.
21 | Joanne Conaghan, "Intersectionality and the Feminist Project in Law," in *Intersectionality and Beyond: Law, Power, and the Politics of Location*, ed. Emily Grabham et al. (Abingdon, UK: Routledge Cavendish, 2009).
22 | Kimberlé Crenshaw, "Twenty Years of Critical Race Theory: Looking Back to Move Forward," *Connecticut Law Review* 43, no. 5 (2011): 1310.
23 | Kimberlé Crenshaw, "Postscript," in *Framing Intersectionality: Debates on a Multi-Faceted Concept in Gender Studies*, ed. Helma Lutz, Maria Theresa Herrera Vivar, and Linda Supik (Farnham, UK: Ashgate, 2011), 227.

ality is taken to signal intersectionality's complicity with the law, when the term was invented in order to highlight *the insufficiency* of the law in addressing the particular situation black women face in employment. Only a careless reading could conflate a theory that exposes the structural insufficiency of law to be an endorsement of it.

That is not to say that intersectionality has not been used or appropriated in the service of liberalist projects of inclusion, neoliberal diversity, and multiculturalist management. It clearly has been, just as radical theory of every stripe and position has been used and appropriated, in domesticated form, in order to evacuate it of its radical commitments and revolutionary potential. While it is perfectly appropriate for Marxists to critique liberal appropriations of intersectionality, it is important to note that intersectionality theorists also critique them; the true object of Marxist critiques of liberal appropriations of intersectionality is liberalism, not intersectionality.

Class, Classism, and Capitalism

Perhaps unsurprisingly, one of the most frequent Marxist critiques of intersectionality alleges that the latter has an underdeveloped analysis of class as a fundamental axis of oppression. This critique takes multiple forms. In the first place, intersectionality is often critiqued for simply adding class to the end of a list of qualifiers without any particular developed class analysis. Jean Ait Belkhir argues that: "despite its place in the now familiar list of race, class, and gender—class is often the last addressed of these issues" in contemporary feminist theory.[24] As Martha Gimenez explains this problem, fear of class reductionism has lead intersectional analyses to overcorrect, nearly leaving out class entirely:

the flattening or erasure of the qualitative difference between class, race and gender in the RGC [Race, Gender and Class] perspective is the foundation for the recognition that it is important to deal with 'basic relations of domination and subordination' which now appear disembodied, outside class relations. In the effort to reject 'class reductionism,' by postulating the equivalence between class and other forms of oppression, the RGC perspective both negates the fundamental importance of class but it is forced to acknowledge its importance by postulating some other 'basic' structures of domination.[25]

---

24 | Belkhir, Jean Ait, "Marxism Without Apologies: Integrating Race, Gender, Class; A Working Class Approach," *Race, Gender & Class* , 8, no 2 (2001): 160.
25 | Martha Gimenez, "Marxism and Class, Gender and Race: Rethinking the Trilogy," *Race, Gender and Class* 8, no. 2 (2001): 24.

Chapter Two: Marxist Critiques of Intersectionality 111

In another way, Gimenez's critique goes farther than the underdevelopment of class; rather, Gimenez argues, intersectional analyses often have the effect of misapprehending the nature of class itself, postulating a qualitative equivalence between it and other forms of oppression where none exists. Gimenez argues that there is something distinctive about the organization of class oppression that makes it different in kind from either race or gender. Another enduring criticism of intersectionality is the persistence of the term "classism" in intersectionality, which is used in some intersectional work in place of capitalism or exploitation. Theorists like Martha Gimenez take this to denote a variant of class-based elitism that, for them, does not fully grasp the systematic nature of class relations as a fundamental, material cleavage that organizes society. She writes, "Class is not simply another ideology legitimating oppression; it denotes exploitative relations between people mediated by their relations to the means of production."[26] It is from this perspective that Gimenez and others resist equating class with other forms of oppression like those of race, gender, or sexuality. From this perspective class is fundamentally organized in a different way than the others. A variant of this perspective maintains that oppression and exploitation are themselves different structures and require different analyses. Martha Gimenez continues, "To argue, then, that class is fundamental is not to 'reduce' gender or racial oppression to class, but to acknowledge that the underlying basic and 'nameless' power *at the root* of what happens in social interactions grounded in 'intersectionality' is class power."[27] We will return to this concept of the root in the next section.

While it is certainly true that not all texts within the intersectional tradition embrace an anti-capitalist politics, many of them name capitalism as a central structural determinant of intersectional oppression. Hancock notes that Francis Beale, Anna Nieto-Gómez, Chela Sandoval and Nawal El Sadaawi "all produce incisive critiques of capitalism." Indeed, she continues, this critique derives from an "absence of significant attention to the intellectual history of intersectionality."[28]

This position is echoed by May, who explains that it is common in the Marxist tradition to "overlook its [intersectionality's] long-standing critiques of material forces and structural power, particularly capitalism, setter colonial, and (neo)liberal forms of exploitation and extraction."[29]

Moreover, intersectionality scholars have argued that these accounts replay the very formations and theoretical commitments that intersectionality was invented to critique. Irene Gedalof explains the problem with class-first under-

---
26 | Ibid.
27 | Ibid. Emphasis mine.
28 | Hancock, *Intersectionality*, 56.
29 | May, *Pursuing Intersectionality, Unsettling Dominant Imaginaries*, 132.

standings of power, inequality and oppression as having two different, but related problems:

> this hierarchizing of entitlement claims effectively pits class against the 'equality strands', in two related ways. It defines class as something we all have, while gender, race, ethnicity and sexuality are reduced to 'the politics of identity', a kind of special pleading. And it undoes the possibility of any kind of intersectional understanding of these categories of difference, by de-linking the socio-economic from the gendered, sexualized and racialized ways in which socio-economic positioning is lived, and situating it solely in the undifferentiated space of 'class'. Class then becomes a way of stabilizing sameness.[30]

In this way, Gedalof argues that actually understanding the contemporary and historical operations of class *requires* an intersectional approach that can understand intra-class distinctions, hierarchies and inequalities. In other words, in thinking about class as something separable from race, sexuality, or gender, we are offering an impoverished and incomplete class analysis.

Linda Martín Alcoff argues that there are never "pure" class issues that do not intersect with race, gender, sexuality. She explains, "there are demands of skilled or unskilled workers, of the trades or the service professions, of migrant workers, of women workers, of immigrant workers, and so on." Even class demands are particular, generated out of the specific experiences and organizations of harm within a discrete time and place within capitalism's accumulation. It is, of course, possible for various workers to "make common cause" across these differences, "but the very project of doing so will require a clear understanding of how identities mediate class relations to produce specific workplace hierarchies and conflicts of interest."[31] In this sense, part of intersectionality's argument is that in order to be doing good, careful, deep class analysis, an intersectional frame is required.

Causation and Intersectionality

As we saw in the previous section, Gimenez's and other Marxist critiques of intersectionality frequently hinge on what *causes* oppression and exploitation. In critiques such as these, intersectionality provides a fine descriptive account of the world, but flounders when providing a causal one. Broadly, this is the critique most often offered by Marxists who conceive of Marxism and intersec-

---

30 | Irene Gedalof, "Sameness and Difference in Government Equality Talk," *Ethnic and Racial Studies* 36, no. 1 (2013): 129.
31 | Linda Martín Alcoff, "An Epistemology for the Next Revolution," *Transmodernity* 1, no. 2 (2011): 74.

tionality to be complementary approaches and who see immense (but circumscribed) value of intersectionality. In one example of this argument, Sharon Smith argues that because intersectionality (supposedly) has no account of exploitation or the genesis of oppression, it "needs" Marxism[32] as it is inadequate on its own to ground this account of how and why oppression and exploitation happen.[33] A similar criticism is levied by Martha Gimenez, who argues that intersectionality has "taken for granted categories of analysis whose meaning apparently remains invariant in all theoretical frameworks and contexts" rather than providing a causal, structural, or historical account of these categories.[34] McNally and Ferguson expand this critique, arguing that intersectionality lacks "any coherent explanation of how and why" intersections are organized in some ways rather than others.[35]

It would take us too far afield here to reconstruct in detail all of the various intersectional histories and histories of intersectional oppression that have been written. However, intersectionality is not merely a theory of the contemporary, but is also a perspective that has produced its own historical scholarship, looking to answer precisely the question of how intersectional oppression has been produced.[36] It is important to note that in many of these accounts,

---

32 | Sharon Smith, "A Marxist Case for Intersectionality," *Socialist Worker*, August 1, 2017, https://socialistworker.org/2017/08/01/a-marxist-case-for-intersectionality.

33 | While Smith does not explicitly call race, gender, or sexuality epiphenomenal on class exploitation, in a flowery turn of phrase, she suggests that racism, homophobia, and sexism can disappear "in a matter of days" when workers join together in a strike, suggesting that she conceives of fighting class exploitation sufficient to tackle gender, race, and sexuality-based oppressions, something that as we saw above, was clearly rejected by intersectionality theorists.

34 | Gimenez, "Marxism and Class, Gender and Race: Rethinking the Trilogy," 21.

35 | David McNally and Sue Ferguson, Social Reproduction Beyond Intersectionality: An Interview, Viewpoint Magazine, October 31, 2015, https://www.viewpointmag.com/2015/10/31/social-reproduction-beyond-intersectionality-an-interview-with-sue-ferguson-and-david-mcnally/.

36 | While it is true that many scholars of intersectionality focus on the contemporary, it is a grave error to assert that no work is being done on intersectional history. For just a few of the many works focusing on the historical genesis of the particular matrix of domination in which we live, see, among others: María Lugones, "Heterosexualism and the Colonial / Modern Gender System," *Hypatia* 22, no. 1 (2007): 186–209; Anne Mcclintock, *Imperial Leather: Race, Gender, and Sexuality in the Colonial Contest*, 1st edition (New York: Routledge, 1995); Ladelle McWhorter, *Racism and Sexual Oppression in Anglo-America: A Genealogy* (Bloomington: Indiana University Press, 2009); C Riley Snorton, *Black on Both Sides: A Racial History of Trans Identity* (Minneapolis: University of Minnesota Press, 2017); Lisa Lowe, *The Intimacies of Four Continents* (Chapel

capitalism plays an important, structural role, even if it does not play a unilateral or universal role, as colonization, Christian supremacy, pre-existing gender and sexual ideologies, organized resistances, diseases, technologies, and non-European ideas, histories, religions, and customs also exert causal force in these histories. Far from historical explanations being 'non-existent' in intersectionality, it is rather that intersectional histories refuse to name a singular cause for the multi-dimensional, contradictory, internally variant, and historically-dependent relations between the various forces in matrices of domination. As above in Gimenez's work, many strands of Marxism assert that there is a singular root cause of the contemporary configuration of oppression: material relations of re/production (and the struggle against it). As we saw in the previous chapter, to what extent capitalism's status as the root of oppression can be read to mean that oppression is epiphenomenal on class relations is the subject of significant debate, with many theorists arguing that capitalism's causal status does not entail a class-primary or class-reductionist approach to thinking racism, hetero/sexism, disability, or imperialism. However, what Smith, Gimenez, McNally, and Ferguson assert as a lack of causal explanation is rather better rendered as a different account of the historical formation of the current matrix of oppression. And, it is important to note, in none of these works do these thinkers offer an argument for the superiority of Marxist version(s) of this historical narrative—or even precisely specify which Marxist version of the emergence of capitalism they endorse.[37]

It is not wrong to suggest, however, that intersectionality's strength and its most developed areas of interrogation are located in the twentieth and twenty-first centuries. However, the relative under-development of intersectional history relative to other areas of intersectional scholarship and activism, hardly represents the deep conceptual limitation that Smith, Gimenez, McNally, and Ferguson suggest it might be. This critique assumes that intersectionality as an analysis or a theory is incapable of producing this history, which seems untenable given the numerous accounts cited above. In any case, arguing for the superiority of Marxist history over intersectionality because (supposedly) the latter lacks a historical account is simply not the same as actually reading intersectional history, understanding its commitments and operations, and then arguing for a Marxist account on the basis of a deep understanding of the different approaches and their stakes.

Hill: Duke University Press, 2015); Siobhan B. Somerville, *Queering the Color Line: Race and the Invention of Homosexuality in American Culture* (Chapel Hill: Duke University Press, 2000); Kim F. Hall, *Things of Darkness: Economies of Race and Gender in Early Modern England*, 1 edition (Ithaca: Cornell University Press, 1995).

37 | McNally is the exception here. David McNally, *Political Economy and the Rise of Capitalism* (Berkeley and Los Angeles: University of California Press, 1988).

Scope and Limitations

As a corollary to the causation objection, some Marxists, notably Sharon Smith, have argued that intersectionality on its own constitutes an excellent theory, but one that is so fundamentally limited as to need other analyses to support, subtend, or buttress it. This is a different position from McNally and Ferguson, who argue not for the integration of Marxism and intersectionality, but for the replacement of intersectionality by social reproduction theory.[38] Smith has consistently argued for the integration of Marxism and intersectionality, arguing that the latter "does not merely complement" the former, but that intersectionality "strengthens Marxist theory and practice." Calling intersectionality "an additive to Marxist theory" Smith asserts that

> intersectionality leads the way toward a much higher level of understanding of the character of oppression than that developed by classical Marxists, enabling the further development of the ways in which *solidarity* can be built between all those who suffer oppression and exploitation under capitalism to forge a unified movement.[39]

In this piece, Smith adequately portrays intersectionality as the product of black feminism, not postmodernism, and recognizes that intersectionality is not an additive theory of multiple oppression. Smith also recognizes that intersectionality is not only a theory of individual identity, but is also concerned with structural and institutional hierarchies and inequalities.[40] And yet, Smith repeats a series of assertions here that are neither fully defended nor seem particularly defensible: 1) that intersectionality is "a concept, not a theory" 2) that intersectionality has no account of exploitation 3) that Marxism is a theory of the "connection between exploitation and oppression"[41] and 4) that intersectionality "needs" Marxism because it is inadequate on its own.[42] As we have seen in

---

[38] | McNally and Ferguson, Social Reproduction Beyond Intersectionality: An Interview.

[39] | Sharon Smith, "Black Feminism and Intersectionality," *International Socialist Review*, no. 91 (Winter -2014 2013), http://isreview.org/issue/91/black-feminism-and-intersectionality.

[40] | Sharon Smith, "A Marxist Case for Intersectionality," *Socialist Worker*, August 1, 2017, https://socialistworker.org/2017/08/01/a-marxist-case-for-intersectionality.

[41] | What exactly this connection is or who has theorized it remain a mystery in this piece.

[42] | Smith continues, "But intersectionality is a concept for understanding *oppression*, *not exploitation*... So the concept of intersectionality needs Marxist theory to realize the kind of unified movement that is capable of ending all forms of oppression. At the same time, Marxism can only benefit from integrating left-wing Black feminism into our own

Chapter One, whether intersectionality is a concept, a theory, a methodology, or a number of other things, is clearly a debate *within* intersectionality, a debate that Smith completely ignores in her account. She also gives no argument for why we should conceive of intersectionality as a concept over and above any of the other ways that intersectionality scholars have described their work. From the analysis in the previous section, the idea that intersectionality has no account of exploitation is demonstrably false. It is interesting to note that Smith insists that intersectionality "needs" Marxism, but Marxism is "strengthened" by intersectionality. It is clear that Smith's account, intersectionality is subordinate to Marxism.

In another version of the objection to intersectionality's scope, many critics, Marxist and non-Marxist alike, have objected that intersectionality lends undue focus to certain organizations of oppression and systematically overlooks others. While there is some criticism that intersectionality focuses primarily on race, gender, and class as the paradigmatic oppressions to be investigated, many scholars of intersectionality have called for and developed theories that focus specifically on ability,[43] national origin, particularly in respect to colonialism and imperialism,[44] incarceration status,[45] immigration status,[46] religion[47] and others. Indeed, Crenshaw herself, who focused on race and gender, notes that this is not meant to suggest that they are the only relevant ones; rather that

politics and practice." Note the way in which Marxism and 'left wing Black feminism' are counterposed, erasing the history of Marxism that was itself coextensive with left-wing black feminism.

43 | Nirmala Erevelles and Andrea Minear, "Unspeakable Offenses: Untangling Race and Disability in Discourses of Intersectionality," *Journal of Literary & Cultural Disability Studies* 4, no. 2 (2010): 127–45.

44 | Lugones, *Pilgrimages = Peregrinajes*.

45 | Tanya Golash-Boza, "The Parallels between Mass Incarceration and Mass Deportation: An Intersectional Analysis of State Repression," *Journal of World-Systems Research* 22, no. 2 (2016): 484–509; Priscilla A. Ocen, "Unshackling Intersectionality," *Du Bois Review* 10, no. 2 (2013): 471–83.

46 | Mary Romero, "The Inclusion of Citizenship Status in Intersectionality: What Immigration Raids Tell Us about Mixed-Status Families, the State, and Assimilation," *International Journal of Sociology of the Family* 34, no. 2 (2008): 131–52; Ramón Grosfoguel, Laura Oso, and Anastasia Christou, "'Racism', Intersectionality and Migration Studies: Framing Some Theoretical Reflections," *Identities* 22, no. 6 (2015): 635–52.

47 | Nancy Wadsworth, "Fractured Believers: Race and Religion as Intersectional Aspects of United States Political Development," in *Race and U.S. Political Development*, ed. Joseph Lowndes, Julie Novkov, and Dorian Warren (New York: Routledge, 2008), 312–36; Jakeet Singh, "Religious Agency and the Limits of Intersectionality," *Hypatia* 30, no. 4 (2015): 657–74.

the factors she addresses "only in part or not at all, such as class or sexuality", are often as critical to intersectional analyses. Her "focus on race and gender only highlights the need to account for multiple grounds of identity when considering how the social world is constructed."[48] While in certain accounts of intersectionality, sexuality has dropped out of many analyses as a primary node of consideration,[49] sexuality was an important aspect of early intersectionality theory.[50] As we saw in Chapter One, intersectionality has also been accused of omitting class as a field of investigation, even if this accusation is largely unfounded.

As these objections operate on multiple levels, it is helpful to disentangle them. One set of objections argues that intersectionality, in under-theorizing certain axes of domination, fails to live up to its own intersectional promise: in this sense, the critique is that intersectionality needs to produce work that is *more* intersectional. I think these critiques are rather well taken and contemporary intersectional scholarship is exploding in some of these areas, producing insightful critique, exposing previous lacunae, and revising elements of the intersectional tradition constantly. These critiques are thus absolutely vital.

Smith's critique, however, is of a rather different nature. She argues that intersectionality fails to explain capitalism, something that is not its immediate object. But intersectionality is not a theory of everything, nor should it be; no one claims that intersectionality could tell us how to build a bridge or confirm historically whether or not Caesar crossed the Rubicon.[51] Nor do intersectional theorists claim that intersectionality is a structural analysis of the operations of capitalism. This is just simply not its intellectual project. In this sense all theories are limited, partial, and take account only of the problems they are trying to explain. Neither Marxism nor intersectionality can explain the whole world and every micro-occurrence within it. It is far more accurate to say that the strongest versions of intersectionality are the ones that can explain how

---

48 | Crenshaw, "Mapping the Margins: Intersectionality, Identity Politics, and Violence Against Women of Color," 1244-45.
49 | Nash, "Home Truths on Intersectionality."
50 | Smith and Smith, "Across the Kitchen Table: A Sister-to-Sister Dialogue"; Combahee River Collective, "A Black Feminist Statement"; María Lugones, "Hispaneando y Lesbiando: On Sarah Hoagland's 'Lesbian Ethics,'" *Hypatia* 5, no. 3 (1990): 138-46.
51 | Though it could certainly tell us a lot about the geopolitics of building a bridge in this or that particular place, who needs to be displaced or inconvenienced in the process of its building, whose plans for the bridge are seen as credible, who has access to the educational institutions that that certify bridge builders. It could certainly tell us something about why Anglophones and white people in general are so obsessed with the Roman Empire—an imperialistic, militaristic slave society—that Caesar is an object of common knowledge such that he could be deployed in a throw-away example.

capitalism functions in and through the matrix of domination and vice versa; it is equally accurate to say that the strongest and clearest versions of Marxism are ones that take their point of departure from the complex, multi-faceted interactions between and among race, gender, class, sexuality, ability, and nationality under capitalism. It is just bizarre to critique intersectionality for not being Marxism; a much more interesting conversation is to ask how and in what ways might these approaches strengthen each other, how and in what ways they may have shared histories, how and in what ways their different objects of analysis might lead them to use different kinds of tools and produce different lenses on the same situation. One kind of response to these questions is to argue for a synthesis of Marxism and intersectionality, but that kind of position is quite different from arguing that intersectionality is limited because it isn't already Marxism, especially without arguing for the obverse position.

Intersectionality is a Bad Metaphor[52]

One reason intersectionality is often misconstrued is certainly the mainstreaming of intersectionality; while the widespread availability of intersectionality as a framework certainly in some ways constitutes a great advantage to thinking intersectionally, it also, like any theory, becomes easily liable to misreadings, misuses, and misappropriations. But beyond this, the image of intersections itself might be productive of certain misunderstandings. As many theorists have remarked, the metaphor of intersections may in certain ways contribute to the mistaken idea that intersectionality theorists conceive of oppressions as separate structures or entities that intersect *somewhere*, it would be a mistake to allow this interpretation of the metaphor to substitute for theorists' actual explanations of their projects. In Crenshaw's explanation of the metaphor, she describes a physical intersection, with traffic flowing in all directions; if there is an accident in the intersection, it is not always easy to reconstruct precisely which party was at fault. While this metaphor does indeed explain the experience of intersectional oppression in a certain way—black women often experience a combination of sexism and anti-black racism simultaneously—it does seem to suggest that there are different 'streets' or flows of traffic that only occasionally 'cross' in an intersection. However, as we saw in Chapter One, most intersectionality theorists have roundly rejected this

---

52 | I have always found this objection to be particularly silly coming from the mouths and pens of Marxists, whose whole intellectual project hinges on producing theory that *Marx himself did not already produce*. If one objects to the theoretical content of intersectionality on the basis that its name is not *completely* reflective of the content of the theory itself, Marxists should not be surprised when non-Marxists object *tout court* to Marxism because of an error of arithmetic Marx made in the nineteenth century.

view that oppressions are fundamentally separable axes that cross only in individuals; rather they argue that the structures or axes are themselves fundamentally and irrevocably inseparable in ways that cannot be adequately rendered by the image of a traffic intersection.

Some intersectionality scholars have themselves conceded that the image of a traffic intersection might not be the most capacious image for rendering the theory proposed by intersectionality. As Carasthatis reminds us, in the same article in which Crenshaw uses the intersection metaphor, she also uses another metaphor of a basement to describe the way in which oppression is fundamentally an experience of hierarchy; Carastathis seems to express a preference for the basement metaphor over the metaphor of intersections precisely because of the ways in which it avoids precisely the misunderstandings that intersections can produce.[53] María Lugones also recognizes the limitations of the metaphor of intersections, but argues for the retention of the concept of intersectionality anyway. She writes, "the image of interlocking [oppressions] is of two entirely discreet things, like two pieces of a jigsaw puzzle. I am not ready to give up the term because it is used by other women of color theorists who write in a liberatory vein about enmeshed oppressions. I think interwoven or intermeshed or enmeshed may provide better images." What Lugones explains here is that rendering the limitations of the image of intersections does not really itself constitute a substantive critique of the theory behind the metaphor. It may be true that other images may furnish other, helpful, productive ways of understanding the operations, dynamics, histories, and institutions explored by intersectionality, but a critique of the image cannot be substituted for a critique of the theory. Moreover, Lugones articulates an independently important reason to retain the term intersectionality: in order to engage in a politics of citation that shows intellectual debt, influence, and lineage, that foregrounds and highlights the nuanced theoretical contributions of women of color to understanding how oppression is constituted and how it operates.

Solidarity, Separatism, and Sectarianism

One of the dominant criticisms of intersectionality, from Marxists and liberals alike, is what Alison Bailey has called the 'parsimony objection,'[54] that intersectionality multiplies (or divides) identities into segregated, sectarian groups that makes solidarity, coalition, and work across differences impossible. This kind of criticism is exemplified by Kevin Anderson, who writes:

---

53 | Anna Carastathis, *Intersectionality: Origins, Contestations, Horizons* (Lincoln: University of Nebraska Press, 2016).
54 | Bailey, "On Intersectionality, Empathy, and Feminist Solidarity: A Reply to Naomi Zack," 24.

In the late twentieth century, a theoretical discourse of intersectionality became almost hegemonic in many sectors of radical intellectual life. In this discourse, which concerned social issues and movements around race, gender, class, sexuality and other forms of oppression, it was often said we should avoid any kind of class reductionism or essentialism in which gender and race are subsumed under the category of class. At most, it was said, movements around race, gender, sexuality, or class can intersect with each other, but cannot easily coalesce into a single movement against the power structure and the capitalist system that, according to Marxists, stands behind it. Thus, the actual intersectionality of these social movements—as opposed to their separateness—was usually seen as rather limited, both as reality and as possibility. Saying otherwise ran the danger of falling into the abyss of reductionism or essentialism.[55]

Anderson's critique is a common one of intersectionality, and indeed, of many theories of social justice grounded in experiences or theories that critique universalization as the ground of political struggle. Anderson then turns back to Marx, arguing that Marx wrote significantly about race and gender in relationship to capital, which as we've already seen, many intersectionality theorists already know.

While it is true that some intersectionality theorists like Angela Davis speak about the intersection of movements, it is strange that Anderson asserts (without any references) that intersectionality theorists insist that movements themselves cannot coalesce, especially given that working in coalition is an explicit and central part of intersectionality's commitment to social justice organizing. Here, Anderson seems to conflate the arguments against reductionism (which takes aim at those who want to fold multiple movements together under the banner of one issue's superiority) and essentialism (which takes aim at the severability of categories of identity and systems of oppression) with an injunction against coalition building. While many intersectionality theorists have analyzed the dangers of coalition building across power differentials, according to those theorists, these critiques are meant to strengthen the possibility of coalition building, not reject it.[56] Anderson also seems to conflate the fact that Marx described (at certain points) relationships between gender and capital and race and capital—though not between race, gender, and capital—with the central insights of intersectionality. Intersectionality is much more than the simple pronouncement that race, gender, and class might relate. Anderson and other theorists who levy similar criticisms say nothing about the long history

---

[55] | Kevin B. Anderson, "Karl Marx and Intersectionality," *Logos: A Journal of Modern Culture and Society* 15, no. 2-3, accessed January 10, 2017, http://logosjournal.com/2015/anderson-marx/.

[56] | Chela Sandoval, *Methodology of the Oppressed* (Minneapolis: University of Minnesota Press, 2000); Lugones, *Pilgrimages = Peregrinajes*.

of intersectionality theorizing that is specifically about coalition, solidarity, and inter-issue connections that was explored above as a central tenet of intersectionality.

Moreover, this kind of critique blames intersectionality for the recognition of very real issues and histories confronting and dividing people, rather than blaming the structures that sow division and distrust between people. As Bailey explains, "Intersectionality *reveals* relations of subordination in homogenizing, falsely universal feminist politics: it does not *produce* this 'fragmentation.'"[57] The fact is, our experiences *already are* different; our positions in relationship to social, political, and economic institutions *already are* different. Many of these differences are the result of centuries of institutional and structural hierarchies and inequalities. Refusing to recognize these differences does not make them melt away, nor does taking them seriously create or reinforce them. Rather, if we are to actually think, expansively, sensitively, and concretely about the actual organization of really existing capitalism, revealing relations of domination and subordination must be the beginning point of analyzing and militating against these systems.

These differences produce the necessity of working in coalitional contexts.[58] Combahee River Collective member Barbara Smith has responded to criticisms like this one by saying:

I have often wished I could spread the word that a movement committed to fighting sexual, racial, economic and heterosexist oppression, not to mention one that opposes imperialism, anti-Semitism, the oppressions visited upon the physically disabled, the old and the young, at the same time that it challenges militarism and imminent nuclear destruction is the very opposite of narrow.[59]

In order to build broad coalitions across differences, Audre Lorde suggests that it is important to reconceptualize how coalitions and organizing are often assumed to rest upon finding a solid base of sameness from which to organize:

Being women together was not enough. We were different. Being gay-girls together was not enough. We were different... Being Black dykes together was not enough. We were different.... It was a while before we came to realize that our place was the very house of difference rather than any one particular difference.[60]

---

57 | Carastathis, *Intersectionality*, 165.
58 | Sandoval, *Methodology of the Oppressed*; Lugones, *Pilgrimages = Peregrinajes*.
59 | Barbara Smith, "Introduction to Home Girls: A Black Feminist Anthology," in *Identity Politics in the Women's Movement*, ed. Barbara Ryan (New York & London: New York University Press, 2001), 150.
60 | Lorde, *Zami*, 226.

From Lorde's perspective, and from many intersectional theorists' perspectives, coalition is indeed difficult and potentially impossible if coalitions are imagined as the lowest common denominator between groups; intersectionality's work on coalition-building argues that we should approach them not from sameness, but from solidarity, foregrounding as centrally important the ways in which systems of oppression and exploitation work precisely by working differentially, that is, by not impacting all groups in the same way. In this sense, coalitions are necessary and important by intersectional standards in order to organize against the various, differential ways in which oppression and exploitation are organized, rather than denying that those differences exist. From an intersectional perspective, understanding the differential operations and organizations of oppression is the foundation of all effective coalitions and effective activism rather than the condition of their impossibility.

Conclusion

Many of the criticisms of intersectionality and Marxism of one another are the results of multiple failures in communication. Intersectionality's criticisms of many Marxist positions are themselves also held by Marxist feminists and have been incorporated into contemporary scholarship. Marxist feminists' worries about identity politics seem rather better directed toward other traditions of feminist scholarship, which, while they might discuss multiple kinds of oppression, do not share a framework with the majority of the hallmark texts of intersectionality theories.

Other contentions, however, remain to be worked through. As many Marxists contend, capitalism forms one of the root causes of a network of oppressive social, political, economic, and cultural relations in the contemporary world; exactly how capitalism relates to oppression requires additional unpacking. As intersectionality theorists claim, many treatments of capitalism have amounted at worst to vulgar class reductionism and at best to simple under-theorization of the complex racial, gendered, and sexual dynamics of power operative in the world in which we live. The next chapter focuses on Marxist accounts of capitalism that seek to remedy this problem.

Chapter Three: Queer, Feminist, Anti-Racist, and Anti-Imperialist Marxisms

"Socialist-feminists see class as central to women's lives, yet at the same time, none would reduce sex or race oppression to economic exploitation. And all of us see these aspects of our lives as inseparably and systematically related; in other words, class is always gendered and raced."
- Nancy Holstrom[1]

"In every social space there is a normalized and experiential as well as ideological knowledge about whose labor counts the least. The actual realization process of capital cannot be outside a given social and cultural form or mode. There is no capital that is a universal abstraction. Capital is always a practice, a determinate set of social relations and a cultural one at that. Thus 'race', gender, and patriarchy are inseparable from class, as any social organizations rests on inter-subjective relations of bodies and minds marked with socially constructed difference on the terrain of private property and capital."
- Himani Bannerji[2]

This chapter is slightly more circumscribed than its title might suggest. It is certainly not an exhaustive inventory of the entire literatures of feminist, queer, anti-imperialist, and anti-racist marxisms, as this task would prove to be a man-

---

[1] | Nancy Holstrom, "Introduction," in *The Socialist Feminism Project: A Contemporary Reader in Theory and Politics*, ed. Nancy Holstrom (New York: Monthly Review Press, 2003), 2.
[2] | Himani Bannerji, "Building from Marx: Reflections on Class and Race," *Social Justice* 32, no. 4 (2005): 149.

uscript, perhaps more than one, all on its own. Rather, the aim of this chapter is twofold: on the one hand, it explains the trajectory of Marxist theorizing of gender, race, sexuality, and nationality that continued rather than ceased after the divergence between the Marxist and the intersectional tradition described in Chapter 0. In doing so, it shows that totalizing claims about Marxisms' disinterest in questions of oppression are false, even if many of the approaches contained within these sub-traditions of Marxism have not always been understood or adopted by more mainstream Marxist theory and activism. The second aim of this chapter is to explain and develop the critical Marxist vocabulary that will be deployed in subsequent chapters. While these Marxist traditions themselves have limitations (many of those limitations are ones that the intersectional tradition has identified), these Marxist literatures represent some of the clearest and most developed theories about the relationship between oppression and capitalism and for that reason are indispensable.

Much contemporary intersectional theory caricatures Marxism as reliant either on economic reductionism or on a theory of dual or triple oppression. This narrative significantly distorts the debates, questions, and writings of Marxists on questions of race, gender, sexuality, gender identity, and nationality since the 1970s. While it is true that arguing for a synthetic or unitary theory has been a *debate*—which implies resistance, sometimes dogged resistance to the elaboration of a non-additive theory of oppression and exploitation—there has been a significant amount of work done in this regard.[3] The purpose of this chapter is to trace some of the theoretical elaborations, debates, and questions within Marxism that have developed as the outcome of the shared history examined in Chapter 0.

In order to illustrate the state of contemporary Marxist thinking about race, gender, sexuality, and nationality, I want to start first with what we might call the 'Orthodox Story' of how capitalism operates from a Marxist perspective.[4] By the 'Orthodox Story' I mean the reductive, 15-minute summary of Marx and Marxism repeated both in theory classes and activist meetings that understands Marxism as a fundamentally class-oriented, economically-reductionist, teleological theory of waged factory labor. This story is both familiar and in

---

3 | To do an exhaustive review of such debates would be impossible, and this chapter does not pretend to accomplish such a feat.

4 | The Orthodox Story is, I think, both real and somewhat of a caricature. I capitalize it because this narrative is treated often as a kind of reified abstraction. I do not associate it with any one thinker or activist tendency in particular, because I think it is often a kind of Marxist bogeyman. I do not think about the Orthodox Story as being synonymous with Marx's own thinking, nor as being localizable to a particular period in the development of Marxism. Elements of the Orthodox Story do appear, however, in a variety of Marxist writings, both historical and contemporary.

many ways, patently false, but it is worth exploring what is usually meant by 'Marxism' in order to understand how contemporary Marxism significantly critiques and diverges from this view.

In the Orthodox Story, capitalism works something like this: a worker goes to a factory in order to work because they do not independently have enough money or wealth to sustain themselves without working. That is, without working and receiving a wage for that labor, the worker would not be able to pay for all of the necessities of life that allow them to keep breathing: food, clothing, shelter, etc. Because of this necessity, the worker signs an employment contract in which they agree to receive a certain wage in exchange for their work. Notice how the choice that the worker is offered—participate in capitalism or starve—is a choice of duress, rather than anything resembling a free choice.

The worker indeed goes to work, makes widgets or flips burgers or teaches philosophy, and then goes home, receiving a paycheck at the end of the week or month. However, in order for the system to be profitable, the owner of the business must make more money on each widget/burger/student than the worker has been paid to produce it. In fact, the capitalist must make more money on each widget than not only the workers wage alone, but the worker's wage, plus the raw materials, rent on the factory, the costs of advertising, transport, distribution, utilities, taxes, etc. The only way for business to remain profitable is then for the worker to be paid significantly less than the value of that labor to the boss. The difference between what the worker is paid and the true value of that labor is what Marxists call 'surplus value.' Capitalism is a system that seeks always to increase the amount of surplus value extracted from the worker, that is, to make a profit by by paying the worker less than the value of that labor. Not only are workers exploited in this way, but they are also systematically denied any power or autonomy over their work: they have no choice about whether or not to work in the first place, and once they are employed, they have no power to determine how goods will be produced, how remuneration will be organized, what hours they will work, how profits will be spent, what changes in technology will be adopted, whether or not more workers will be hired, or really, anything else. The capitalist workplace is the most sacred autocracy. Those who extract surplus value, who profit off of the undervaluation of the labor of others, are called the bourgeoisie, and those whose labor is stolen from them, the proletariat.

The critical perspective Marx offers on this process explains that this system as a whole leads a) to increasing stratification between the poor and the rich b) that the repeatability and continuity of this system over time (its 'societal reproduction') will inevitably intensify this stratification, pooling an ever-larger group of people into poverty and and ever-smaller group in obscene and profligate wealth c) that those who are already more vulnerable in society will be forced to accept the lowest wages (Marx was particularly interested in women and children in this regard) and d) that in order to sustain this system of economic exploitation, a whole series of ideas, perspectives, discourses, legal structures, and institutions will be invented in order to sustain it. The state, the police, the schools, the law—all of these will work together in order to make the proletariat more easily exploitable. All of the institutions of society will coalesce to insure that all forms of institutionalized power are concentrated in the hands of the exploiting class, giving proletarian workers little or no possibility of using existing institutional mechanisms to change their position.

According to Iris Marion Young, this understanding of capitalism allows us to see how and why Marxists conceive of the fundamental injustice of capitalism:

The injustice of capitalist society consists in the fact that some people exercise their capacities under the control, according to the purposes, and for the benefit of other people. Through private ownership of the means of production, and through markets that allocate labor and the ability to buy goods, capitalism systematically transfers the powers of some persons to others, thereby augmenting the power of the latter[...] Not only are powers transferred from workers to capitalists, but also the power of workers diminish by more than the amount of transfer because workers suffer material depravation and a loss of control, and hence are deprived of important elements of self-respect.[5]

This story is, I think, common enough, that most people who engage with critiques of capitalism are familiar with it. It is, in much condensed and simplified form, the outline of the argument that Marx gives in the opening chapters of *Capital, Volume I*.

It is easy to see, from this skeleton, how and why Marxism is accused of being essentially blind to race, gender, and sexuality, as well as to complex issues of experience, identity, difference, and a whole host of other important issues raised by considering not just exploitation, but oppression as well. This critique is, however, not only levied from outside the Marxist tradition, but also from within it, and whole traditions of feminist, queer, anti-racist, anti-colonial marxisms have emerged in order to understand how capitalism produces, maintains, shapes, and frames gender, race, sexuality, and coloniality. Rather than explore these workings and expansions of Marxism under each of these headings separately, this chapter proceeds instead by looking the various fundamental presumptions of the 'Orthodox' account. While it would be impossible to detail every critique of the Orthodox Story offered by every queer, trans, anti-racist, and/or decolonial Marxist, the major questions and revisions can be grouped into a few key areas of challenge and debate:

---

5 | Young, *Justice and the Politics of Difference*, 49.

1. Who labors and how is labor organized under capitalism?
2. Is all labor waged under capitalism?
3. Where does labor happen?
4. How did capitalism emerge historically?
5. Does capitalism have only one form?
6. What besides labor is necessary to maintain capitalism?
7. How is exploitation related to other forms of violence under capitalism?

This chapter thus proceeds by asking each one of these questions, specifically through highlighting many of the ways that feminist, queer, and anti-racist Marxists have begun to sketch the answers to each of these. It is important to remember that Marxism, like intersectionality, is not a monolithic tradition, and that many of the issues under consideration in this chapter are the subject of ongoing interrogation, debate, and clarification. These sections should hence be taken as provisional and illustrative rather than exhaustive.

Who Labors and How is Labor Organized?

From the perspective of the Orthodox Story, capitalist labor has a particular shape: factory labor. And while Marx and Engels were actually specifically concerned with the way in which industrial factory production effected women and children, as well as in the connections between Europe and the rest of the world, these facts are often obscured or treated as secondary by the Orthodox Story and its proponents. As Lise Vogel reminds us, "Marx and Engels had a great deal to say, even if it was, nonetheless, nowhere near enough."[6] As I wrote in the introduction to this book, my project here is not an inventory of the works of Marx and Engels; rather, I look here to the ways in which queer, feminist, anti-racist, and anti-colonial Marxists have taken the theoretical armature of Marxism and deployed it to stretch, expand, critique, and revise the fundamental principles and limitations of both Marx's own work *and* the Orthodox Story (though these two should in no way be collapsed).[7]

One of the ways that Marxists have stretched the question what labor looks like is to consider a variety of divisions of labor. The idea of a division of labor explores the ways in which certain groups of people are marked out, in advance, for particular kinds of labor. Divisions of labor are in one sense, a sociological

---

6 | Vogel, *Marxism and the Oppression of Women*, 38.
7 | Indeed, though it is beyond the scope of the current project to reconstruct these debates and arguments, there are flourishing traditions of Marxism, including from feminist/queer/anti-racist/anti-colonial perspectives that specifically look at how the Orthodox Story significantly misrepresents and misinterprets Marx's own writing and thought.

category—they note the ways in which certain sectors of work are disproportionately performed by oppressed and marginalized groups. But more than this, the analysis of divisions of labor also illuminates something more than a quantifiable distribution—it also highlights the ways in which people become defined by the work they do and that work becomes valued on the basis of who performs it. Because capitalist societies are defined so significantly by labor, one's social position, one's value, indeed one's moral and social *worth* is often configured on the basis of what *kind of labor* one engages in. In this sense, the fact that nursing (for one example) is a profession that is disproportionately undertaken by women is not a neutral sociological fact; rather, the feminization of nursing is linked to a whole series of social ideas about gender and femininity. We can, thus, learn a significant amount about both work and about social ideas of gender by looking at the gendered division of labor. This is the fundamental insight of analyses that take the division of labor as its object: there are social systems of valuation under capitalism that contribute to and produce the social and monetary value that people can derive from their positions of employment. While much of the writing in the 1960s-1980s about the gendered division of labor spoke instead of a 'sex division of labor,' Marxist feminists who understand these divisions to be the product of social arrangement rather than biological destiny speak rather of the gender or gendered division of labor.[8] Lise Vogel, drawing on the work of Lourdes Benería,[9] insists that a significant sleight of hand has been introduced when we speak of *a* gender division of labor and uses the plural instead: "I use the plural—sex divisions of labor—because in most societies there are, in fact, distinct divisions of labor according to sex in different areas of work and for different classes, age groups, and so forth. While the singular term—the sex division of labor—can be taken to include these variations, it tends also to merge them into an abstract unity."[10]

Notions of gender also influence the very conditions of work, and the kind of 'attitude' one is expected to have while at work. Increasingly, the dictates of neoliberal capitalism demand a certain affective comportment in completing waged work to standards of customer satisfaction.[11] As Hardt and Negri explain, "Affective labor, then, is labor that produces or manipulates affects[...]. One can recognize affective labor, for example, in the work of legal assistants,

---

8 | Some accounts of the gendered division of labor begin to veer into trans-exclusionary radical feminist territory in their assumption that all those who give birth are women. For an example of this kind of equivalence, see: Shulamith Firestone.

9 | Lourdes Benería, "Reproduction, Production, and the Sexual Division of Labour," *Cambridge Journal of Economics*, no. 3 (1979): 203-25.

10 | Vogel, *Marxism and the Oppression of Women*, 7n5.

11 | Michael Betancourt, "Immaterial Value and Scarcity in Digital Capitalism," *CTheory*, 2010, http://www.ctheory.net/articles.aspx?id=652.

flight attendants, and fast food workers (service with a smile)...A worker with a good attitude and social skills is another way of saying a worker is adept at affective labor."[12] It is not incidental that the examples Hardt and Negri refer to—flight attendants, legal assistants, and fast food workers—are all industries that predominantly employ women.

But the gendered divisions of labor are not the only way that work is divided along identity categories. Racial, racist, and ethnic divisions of labor are all terms that Marxists use in order to mark the way in which the *kinds* of work are inflected with ideas of race.[13] Racialized chattel slavery is only one of the most prominent examples of a historical incidence of a racial division of labor that segments not only the activity of work open to or indeed forced upon racial groups, but it also highlights the ways in which the very conditions of work are often radically different for various racial groups under capitalism. The confinement of various racialized groups to particular sectors of work or to particular conditions of labor has been frequent under capitalism, and here we could highlight a variety of cases: immigrant Chinese workers on the railroad system, immigrant Latinx workers in agricultural labor, the sharecropping system of the Jim Crow South, the continued confinement of many racialized groups to low income, precarious, and service sector industries in the contemporary world. Racial and ethnic divisions of labor themselves hold a variety of consequences: racialized groups of people not only receive disproportionately low remuneration for their work, but they tend also to be the industries that are least likely to be unionized, to carry benefits like healthcare, or to have contract conditions that provide for advancement, long-term stability, overtime pay, or avenues for grievance redress. These industries are rife with wage theft and employer intimidation. Women of color often experience segmentation into positions at the intersection of the racial and gendered divisions of labor, in industries like childcare, cleaning, and service work, that carry their own dangers when they work in other peoples' homes, especially of sexual assault and harassment.

All of these conditions contribute to the overall impoverishment of communities of color under contemporary capitalism, which itself has wide-ranging effects. Lack of employer-provisioned health care means that the racial division of labor systematically contributes to a racialized system of medical neglect. Because of practices like redlining and predatory loan-sharking, racialized

---

12 | Michael Hardt and Antonio Negri, *Multitude: War and Democracy in the Age of Empire*, Reprint edition (New York: Penguin Books, 2005), 108.

13 | Evelyn Nakano Glenn, "From Servitude to Service Work: Historical Continuities in the Racial Division of Paid Reproductive Work," *Signs: Journal of Women in Culture & Society* 18, no. 1 (1992): 1-43; V. Parks and D. Warren, "Contesting the Racial Division of Labor from Below: Representation and Union Organizing among African American and Immigrant Workers," *Du Bois Review* 9, no. 2 (2012): 395-417.

communities often continue to experience de facto segregation. Since access to public education is structured through neighborhood-based taxation, schools in low-income areas have fewer resources for their students, often lacking even basic infrastructure like teachers, books, and classroom supplies. When neoliberal austerity programs cut access to social services like transit, education, welfare, public housing, and public clinics, it is most often communities of color whose access is restricted to the already-paltry avenues for meeting basic needs.

Attempting to bring together the gendered divisions of labor and racial divisions of labor, Maria Mies and Mariarosa Dalla Costa have spoken of the International Division of Labor, which specifically links practices of racialization, imperialism, and sexism under capitalism to produce the precarity of non-Western women of color in particular.[14] International divisions of labor, themselves highly influenced through neocolonial systems of accumulation, often move industrial, factory, and resource extraction industries onto racialized populations of the Global South as one mechanism of maintaining Euro-American capitalist accumulation. Additionally, global economic intervention through international regulatory agencies such as the World Bank and the International Monetary Fund often require that recipients of international loans institute austerity measures and Structural Adjustment programs that marketize national industries and dismantle need-based social services like welfare, education, and healthcare. Thus, even though the poverty of much of the Global South is a direct consequence of Euro-American colonization, Global North countries can continue to profit on the systematic poverty they have themselves produced. As Silvia Federici notes, in addition to the international division of labor that accompanied epochs of direct colonization, the neo-imperial era of globalization has introduced a new international division of labor, one in which women of the Global South are significantly responsible for the labor of reproducing not only middle class lifestyles of the Global North, but also, significantly, the very structure of capitalism itself. In her recent study of migration, social reproduction, and care work, Sara Farris has shown the ways in which racialized Muslim women immigrants to Europe fill roles necessary to the reproduction of white supremacist capitalism at the very same time that Islamophobia and anti-Arab racism has become more and more prominent in recent years and decades.[15]

These multiple divisions of labor are one mode of marking how race and gender are central facets to the operation of capitalism. The analysis shows us,

---

14 | Mies, *Patriarchy and Accumulation On A World Scale*; Mariarosa Dalla Costa, *Women, Development, and Labor of Reproduction: Struggles and Movements*, ed. Giovanna F. Dalla Costa (Trenton, NJ: Africa World Press, 1999).

15 | Sara Farris, *In the Name of Women's Rights: The Rise of Femonationalism* (Durham: Duke University Press, 2017).

in the first place, how race and gender are completely constitutive of the kinds of work—and hence the kind of exploitation—open to various subject positions. It thus illuminates how, on a global level, capitalism's working classes are overwhelmingly women and overwhelmingly people of color. By tracing the consequences of the accumulation of impoverishment in those classes, it is possible to see how conditions of labor have direct impacts on seemingly non-work related areas of life like education, healthcare, and access to social services. It thus explains how, if we are to generate a truly representative analysis of capitalism, we must wrestle with its imbrication in systems of racialization and gendering; classes are hence constituted in and through race and gender.

Is All Work Waged under Capitalism?

Divisions of labor are not the only way that contemporary Marxisms thematize the race, gender, and sexual politics of labor under capitalism; it is not only who performs what *paid* labor, but also a question of what kinds of labor are conceived of *as labor* and which kinds of activities are seen worthy of pay at all. While the Orthodox Story posits the wage as a central and defining feature of capitalism, social reproduction theory critiques this analysis. The wage relation, while definitive for white European men, is only one part of the story of capitalism. Indeed, the Orthodox Story explains how *commodities* are produced under capitalism, which is surely a significant component; however, it says nothing about how *workers* are produced and reproduced under capitalism. As Brenner explains, a feminist historical materialism is based in the recognition of "the socially necessary and socially organized labor through which humans reproduce themselves—not only the production of things but the work involved in using those things to renew life."[16]

The production of workers covers a wide variety of activities: bearing and rearing of children, elder care, cooking, cleaning, subsistence farming, laundry, emotional labor—all the aspects of unwaged work that are necessary in order for workers to continue their waged work. Social reproduction theorists have argued that this (often) unwaged and/or significantly undercompensated labor, undertaken primarily by women, forms a structural necessity under capitalism, for it allows the capitalist to glean the benefits of reproductive labor necessary for the waged worker to enter the formal economy without paying for it; they argue that if all of this labor were paid, it would make the capitalist system itself insolvent.[17] This structural dependence on the unwaged labor of

---

[16] | Johanna Brenner, *Women and the Politics of Class* (New York: Monthly Review Press, 2000), 76-77.

[17] | Elements of this argument have been made by a wide variety of feminist theorists, including Silvia Federici, Maria Mies, Giovanna Franca Dalla Costa (2008), Selma

women leads Maria Mies to deem social reproduction a position of 'structurally necessary super-exploitation' to which women are generally subjected and which affects women of color and women from the Global South in particularly violent ways.[18]

Socially reproductive labor comes with its own set of workplace conditions. Often this work is not paid, and when it is, it is remunerated at low wages. Multiple studies have shown that domestic workers are subject to uniquely coercive conditions, including the expectation of unlimited availability, having passports confiscated by employers, being forced to take birth control, being subjected to rampant sexual violence, facing restrictions on movement and communication, as well as experiencing a variety of racist and sexist micro-aggressions in their workplaces.

This analysis is not merely sociological, meaning, it is not simply an argument about the distribution of labor. Rather, as Grace Kyungwon Hong explains, differences within the distributions and organizations of labor attest to logics of value that stretch far beyond labor, employment, and work: "the devaluation of black women's lives points to the devaluation of racialized women, as global capital fixes on racialized women as the cheapest and most vulnerable form of labor."[19] This relationship is not unidirectional or unilateral, but rather, these dynamics form a sort of feedback loop: people who are confined to forms of undervalued labor themselves become undervalued in social, cultural, and political contexts, and this undervaluation itself continues to frame conditions of precarity and vulnerability that confine people into undervalued labor in order to survive. It is not only women, immigrants, and people of color who are affected by this feedback loop, though they are affected in particularly acute ways; the general vampiric nature of capital, which targets the most vulnerable, feeds back into the general cycles, structures, and conditions of capitalism. The fact that women are often more vulnerable, are inculcated to expect and accept lower wages and more precarious working conditions, and often need to provide not only for themselves but also children and kin, has been used to capital's advantage to "deskill productive sectors and lower labor costs, to worsen working conditions and implement the casualization of work" not only for women, but as a general trend in the labor market more generally.[20]

James and Mariarosa Dalla Costa (1973), Kathi Weeks (2011), Nancy Fraser (2013), Lise Vogel (1983) and innumerable others.

18 | See Maria Mies (1986).

19 | Grace Kyungwon Hong, *The Ruptures of American Capital: Women of Color Feminism and the Immigrant Culture of Labor* (Minneapolis: University of Minnesota Press, 2006), xvii.

20 | Cinzia Arruzza, *Dangerous Liaisons: The Marriages and Divorces of Marxism and Feminism* (Pontypool, Wales; London: Merlin Press, 2013), 126.

Social reproduction theory remapped the ways in which Marxists discussed labor in a variety of ways: in the first place, it reminded Marxists that not all labor under capitalism was paid. This raised significant questions about the concentration on waged labor under capitalism, suggesting rather that unwaged relationships were just as central to understanding capitalist logic. Second, it insisted on the question of the production and reproduction of workers themselves, in all of their complexities, needs, and differences. Investment in the question of the production of workers opened up a whole terrain of thinking differentially about the constitution of the working classes, rather than assuming a shared history or shared experience of class formation.

Moreover, it began to ground conversations about gender in ways that significantly extended beyond the realm of work, whether paid or unpaid, to question the construction of femininity as a concept, as a social narrative, as a set of coercive expectations, and as a naturalized position. The way in which labor becomes feminized and hence naturalized, and so the ways in which the very structure of femininity in its socially constructed, historically variable meaning is significantly framed in and through the dictates of capitalist accumulation. From a social reproduction perspective, we can see the ways in which social positions exceed a direct correspondence to labor. While in the Orthodox Story, it seems as though workers are positioned solely on the basis of the work they *actually* engage in, social reproduction analysis allows us to see the ways in which social *expectations* of labor are just as important in determining social position. Whether or not any particular woman under capitalism actually *engages* in the labor of child-bearing or child-rearing, that this labor is *expected* of women as a function of femininity itself significantly determines their social position. When femininity is constructed as the *naturalized* capacity for and expectation of social reproductive labor, it explains the ways in which women are expected to smile, to be sexually available, to be caring and nurturing, to value others at the cost of self-negation, to act as mediators in their workplace and home relations, etc. The gendered division of labor persists outside of the realm of waged employment as well. Because all of these activities most often occur within a domestic sphere that is linked through a variety of discourses and practices to femininity, labor inside the home is undertaken disproportionately by women, even when they work outside the home, comprising what has often been called a 'second shift' of work. The feminization of reproductive labor also comprises what has been called 'emotional' or 'affective' labor in which not only the physical, biological needs of workers are undertaken, but so too their emotional and psychological health. Workers must find some way of dealing with their emotions, often of rage, inadequacy, and alienation, but also of their desire, imagination, and fulfillment, in order to continue life in the face of workplace exigencies. In this sense, as Silvia Federici explains, "Capitalism has made money out of our cooking, smiling, fucking"—even when those activities are themselves unwaged.²¹ Because contemporary capitalism is structured in and through gendered notions of affect and emotion, women are disproportionately responsible for affective labor.

But women's work in the home was not the only form of unwaged labor on which capitalism depends. As Domenico Losurdo, Sidney Mintz, and Eric Williams have all convincingly argued, capitalism would not have been possible without the invention of the distinctive brand of trans-Atlantic chattel slavery that formed the basis of European economies through the nineteenth century.²² Dorothy Roberts, Angela Davis, and bell hooks have further clarified the specific role of enslaved women in the accumulative regime of capitalism, as their bodies were violently used as a means to birth new slaves and perpetuate the regime of slavery-based capitalism.²³ Many enduring racializing and gendered stereotypes that still hold power in the contemporary world were generated in order to secure this means of reproducing the institution of slavery; the hypersexualization of racialized bodies served to legitimate the mass rape of enslaved women and later, to enforce the terror of lynching when slavery became no longer a viable social form. All of these theorists have contextualized the emergence of race in the rise of colonial capitalism and the persistence of anti-black racism as direct consequences to slavery.

Capitalism also would not have been possible or successful without a sustained regime of colonization. Andrea Smith, Anne McClintock, and Iyko Day argue that the dispossession of indigenous peoples' lands in the Americas formed a necessary historical condition for the concretion of capitalism.²⁴ As Quijano explains, "The vast Indian genocide of the first decades of colonization was not caused, in the main, by the violence of the conquest, nor by the diseases that the conquerors carried. Rather, it was due to the fact that the Indians were used as throwaway labor, forced to work till death."²⁵ While Marx does not have a systematic theory of *race*, he does recognize that colonization and slavery were the historical fulcra of capitalist development: "The discovery

---

21 | Silvia Federici, *Revolution at Point Zero: Housework, Reproduction, and Feminist Struggle*, 1 edition (Oakland, CA : Brooklyn, NY : London: PM Press, 2012), 19.
22 | Domenico Losurdo, *Liberalism: A Counter-History*, trans. Gregory Elliott (London ; New York: Verso, 2014); Sidney W. Mintz, *Sweetness and Power: The Place of Sugar in Modern History*, Reprint edition (New York: Penguin Books, 1986); Eric Williams, *Capitalism and Slavery*, 1 edition (Chapel Hill: The University of North Carolina Press, 1994).
23 | Roberts, *Killing the Black Body*; Davis, "Reflections on the Black Women's Role in the Community of Slaves."
24 | Andrea Smith, *Conquest: Sexual Violence and American Indian Genocide* (Chapel Hill: Duke University Press, 2015); Mcclintock, *Imperial Leather*; Day, *Alien Capital*.
25 | Aníbal Quijano, "Coloniality of Power, Eurocentrism, and Latin America," trans. Michael Ennis, *Nepantla: Views from South* 1, no. 3 (2000): 533–80.

of gold and silver in America, the extirpation, enslavement and entombment in mines of the aboriginal population, the beginning of the conquest and looting of the East Indies, the turning of Africa into a ward for the commercial hunting of black-skins, signalized the rosy dawn of the era of capitalist production."[26]

It might be easy to assume (as some Marxists have) that capitalism's reliance on unwaged work is a relic of the past, which has been overturned by capitalism's supposed 'real subsumption.' But capitalism depends logically on the continued direct appropriation of unwaged labor. Rosa Luxembourg critiques Marx for supposedly restricting primitive accumulation to the conditions for the historical emergence of capital, and for assuming (as does, Luxembourg alleges, the entire tradition of political economy which predates him, including Ricardo, Sismondi, and Smith) that capitalism is a relation solely between workers and capitalists[27]; Luxembourg notes that because "real life has never known a self-sufficient capitalist society under the exclusive domination of the capitalist mode of production," it follows that "capitalism in fact also depends on means of production organized under non-capitalist principles."[28] She continues, "capitalism in its full maturity depends in all respects on non-capitalist strata and social organizations existing side by side with it"[29] in the form of "a market for its surplus value, as a source of supply for its means of production, and as a reservoir of labour power for its wage system."[30] Not only, then, does capital demand the increasing exploitation of its waged labor force, but it also demands the extraction of surplus value from the non-waged. This was precisely Marx's analysis, who argues:

---

26 | Karl Marx, *Capital: Volume 1: A Critique of Political Economy*, trans. Ben Fowkes, Reprint edition (London ; New York, N.Y: Penguin Classics, 1992), 915.

27 | Levying this argument as a criticism of Marx depends on reading the chapter on 'ursprüngliche Akkumulation' as a historically-bounded temporal account of the 'days before capitalism.' In other words, it requires that one read Marx as here inventing an origin story akin to a mythical, ahistorical fiction of the state of nature. This seems inconsistent with Marx's own criticisms of myth, origin stories, the state of nature, and political ideology. So while Luxembourg, and for that matter, many contemporary Marxist feminist scholars like Silvia Federici (2006), Maria Mies (1999), and Mariarosa Dalla Costa (1978), consider this point to be critical of Marx's position, I understand this to be *precisely* the point Marx is trying to make in this section, and hence, as an extremely helpful clarification and not a refutation of his text.

28 | Rosa Luxemburg, *The Accumulation of Capital*, 2 edition (London ; New York: Routledge, 2003), 328.

29 | Luxemburg, 345.

30 | Luxemburg, 348-49.

> Direct slavery is just as much the pivot of bourgeois industry as machinery, credits, etc. Without slavery you have no cotton; without cotton you have no modern industry. It is slavery that has given the colonies their value; it is the colonies that have created world trade, and it is world trade that is the pre-condition of large-scale industry. Thus slavery is an economic category of the greatest importance.[31]

Thinking about slavery as a central component of the historical development of capitalism, and further, thinking about colonizing countries as dependent on their colonies rather than vice versa opened a variety of important nodal points for Marxist analysis. In the first place, it injected into the Orthodox Story some significant revisions: the story that capitalism is primarily organized through factory labor or through wages must be revised and reworked to see, rather, that capitalism was historically constructed through the relationship between the wage labor and formations that are not even hinted at in this narrative. It engendered a need, thus, to think about how and why cleavages within working populations were created, maintained, how they changed over time, how and when these differences could be refused, and how and when workers themselves seemed to be complicit in reinforcing these distinctions.

Reversing the script on dependency and colonialism, moreover, opened up an entire realm of critique of the developmentalist narrative of which Marx and Marxists are often accused. It becomes clear, through Marx's understanding, that rather than the dominant liberal narrative that colonized countries are 'dependent' on colonizing ones, the relationship is quite the reverse: all of the wealth, resources, access, social services, power, opportunities, amenities, power of the Global North is totally dependent on the exploitation, domination, and dispossession of the Global South. Just as the bourgeoisie is parasitic on the work of the proletariat, so too the global dominating powers prey on the the labor and resources of the Global South as the source of its wealth.

In another sense though, it opened up an entire field of thinking about the relationship between capitalism and *other* forms of unwaged labor. Marxist analyses of how capitalism is inextricably linked to prison labor (and to the entire edifice of the prison-industrial complex as a whole), to students' work, and a variety of other realms of unwaged labor have been influential in rethinking how and why labor under capitalism functions as it does. Analyses of unemployment have also blossomed here, exploring the ways in which capitalism requires for its continued exploitation of the waged workforce, a group of unwaged individuals, who are constructed as 'waiting to fill the jobs' that workers currently have in order to depress wages and create a climate of fear around organizing for better working conditions.

---

31 | Karl Marx, *The Poverty of Philosophy: A Reply to M. Proudhon's Philosophy of Poverty* (New York), 94.

Thus, rather than focus exclusively on the realm of waged work as the Orthodox Story does, contemporary Marxisms have specifically interrogated the centrally important function of unwaged work, and indeed, of those who do not work, as structural to capitalist logic. In expanding our understanding of the role of labor under capitalism, contemporary Marxisms have specifically thematized the dynamics interrelation of gender and race as the very condition of the possibility of capitalist accumulation itself.

Where Does Labor Happen?

Marxists' interests in non-waged work has lead many Marxists to rethink what the 'workplace' actually means under capitalism. As analyses of slavery and prison labor make clear, the prison and the plantation are perhaps archetypal sites of capitalist production, even when, and indeed especially when, these do not conform to the traditional principles of factory production.

From analyses of social reproduction, it is clear that labor also happens in the home and inside the family. As Michel Foucault argued, a whole series of social and political institutions—like the school, the army, the psychiatric institution, and the prison—are themselves organized in order to institute norms of capitalist work discipline, molding 'errant' and pathologized subjects into those who not only acquiesce to the organization of responsibility, self-sufficiency, and orderliness that capitalism requires, but that reshape themselves completely in conformity with these principles, finding purpose, meaning, and joy in their subjection.[32] In this way, many Marxist theorists have followed Mario Tronti, who argues that under capitalism, "the whole of society lives as a function of the factory and the factory extends its exclusive domination to the whole of society."[33] In reshaping multiple institutions of social and political life along the exigencies of capitalist accumulation, Tronti and others have helpfully thematized these institutions as comprising a "social factory," in which multiple sites, including the intimate and the familial, become folded into capitalism by inculcating the norms, discourses, and practices that sustain the necessary conditions of capitalism far beyond the workplace gates.

Perhaps nowhere has this thesis been more extensively explored than in queer and feminist Marxists' understanding of the role of the family. Peggy Morton, a Marxist feminist, published an important article on the relationship between the family and capitalism in 1971. Morton argues that the family is "a unit whose function is the maintenance and reproduction of labor-power"; she specifies that "the task of the family is to maintain the present work force

---

32 | Michel Foucault, *Discipline & Punish: The Birth of the Prison*, trans. Alan Sheridan, 2nd edition (New York: Vintage Books, 1995).

33 | Mario Tronti, *Arbeiter Und Kapital* (Frankfurt: Verlag Neue Kritik, 1962), 31.

and provides the next generation of workers, fitted with the skills and values necessary for them to be productive members of the work force."[34] While it is certainly helpful to consider the ways in which our intimate and familial relations occur inside capitalism, and in relation to it, pronouncements such as these have been critiqued, both within and beyond Marxist feminism, for reproducing a kind of economic determinism that suggests that families are reducible to this function and/or that family holds the same position in all social formations under capitalism.

It is important to mark distinctions between the capitalist use of the family (or rather of some families) and the working class' uses of its own families. Not marking this distinction can only produce a diagnosis of false consciousness, which is both painfully inadequate and dismissive. It is certainly true that capitalism makes use of the family, that it might even suggest, normalize, and accommodate certain kinds of families more readily than others, and it is certainly true that part of the way that power under capitalism works is by hiding itself in plain sight, by dissimulating, by erasing and obfuscating its logic.[35] To say that capitalism, or power more generally, functions often through hiding itself is not to say that the working class or any one else is a mere dupe, but rather to highlight the ways in which some of the most successful strategies of domination and control take hold in and through our affective and material attachments to them.[36]

This point is related to, yet distinct from an important insight of Vogel's: that the structural function of the family under capitalism is rather different between the exploiting class and the working class. Critiquing and revising Engels' argument in *The Origin of the Family, Private Property, and the State*, Vogel argues that while Engels was right to see that in the ruling class, the family serves the central function of consolidating and transmitting property,

---

34 | Peggy Morton, "A Woman's Work Is Never Done, or: The Production, Maintenance and Reproduction of Labor Power," in *From Feminism to Liberation*, ed. Edith Altbach (Cambridge: Schenkman Books, 1971), 211-27.

35 | Michel Foucault, *The History of Sexuality, Vol. 1: An Introduction*, trans. Robert Hurley, Reissue edition (Vintage, 1990).

36 | While the subject and focus of privilege discourse is somewhat different, we can see a kind of affinity between these perspectives. Fundamentally, and in its most useful iterations, privilege names the ways in which inhabiting structures of power produces a kind of structural ignorance of its own constitution. White privilege, for example, refers often to the ways in which white people can remain blissfully unaware of the extent to which racism structures the contemporary world. Privilege also gestures toward the affective and material investment in structures of domination when it seeks to explain how and why white people, for instance, remain largely hostile to programs of racial justice, reparation, and redistribution, often in ways they cannot fully articulate.

his argument posits the same function for the working class family; this, of course, makes no sense, as for Marx and Engels, the working class is precisely defined by its lack of transmissible property—the working class is composed of those who have nothing to sell but their own labor.[37]

Working class people enter into (and leave) families—biological and chosen—for a variety of reasons, many of which are directly material. Many enter families to pool limited resources to re-appropriate, in the tiniest but most vital ways, the principle of economies of scale so often used against them in their workplaces. Some marry for access to health care, citizenship or residency papers, to make visitation in hospital rooms and prisons slightly less bureaucratic. Some refuse to enter into marriages in order retain the paltry state benefits that haven't yet been chipped away by neoliberal austerity. And none of this analysis touches on the way in which desire at multiple levels—romantic, sexual, platonic—or ideas about love, home, and family enter into this calculus.[38]

Even when Marxist-feminists have attempted to recognize the historical contingency and variability of forms of the family, they have often, perhaps despite themselves, fallen back on to unitary conceptions of the family. Despite Vogel's insightful critique of Engels' tendency to treat the family and patriarchy as a flat, ahistorical invariant, Vogel's text repeats this error, referring constantly to '*the* oppression of women' and '*the* relationship of *the* family', "*the* position of women," throughout the text, treating each of these as singular unities, with a coherent, internally consistent relationship to capitalism. This is rather strange because Vogel herself draws on Marx, who argues that 'one cannot speak of the family *as such*' because "families have widely varying places within the social structure."[39]

---

37 | Vogel, *Marxism and the Oppression of Women*, chap. 6.

38 | There seems to be a certain tendency in contemporary Marxism to neglect desire, fantasy, and ideas as themselves too 'idealistic' for inclusion in a material analysis. This is ironic, considering Marx himself argued both that immaterial needs were as central to his analysis as biological ones, and developed a theory of ideas and discourses as rooted in material conditions. Historical materialism is not and should not be about the circumscription of phenomena to be studied; it is rather a perspective or a heuristic than can be used to understand phenomena—even ideal ones (indeed, even idealism itself). Notable exceptions to the Marxish aversion to these kinds of studies include: Rosemary Hennessy, *Profit and Pleasure: Sexual Identities in Late Capitalism* (New York: Routledge, 2000); Kevin Floyd, *The Reification of Desire: Toward a Queer Marxism* (Minneapolis: Univ Of Minnesota Press, 2009); Judith Butler, *The Psychic Life of Power: Theories in Subjection* (Stanford University Press, 1997).

39 | Quoted in Vogel, *Marxism and the Oppression of Women*, 135.

But of course, there is no singular family and no singular oppression of women (or of queers or racialized subjects or of any other identity category). As early as 1896, Clara Zetkin, the leader of the German Social Democratic Party's women's movement already posed the question of structural sexism's relationship to capitalism in differential terms. She outlines the way in which women of the working class, the middle class, and the ruling class or 'Upper Ten Thousand' as she calls it, live under different material configurations of life, and hence, have different interests and ideas about their own liberation. For women of the upper class, property relations rather than work constitute the central power struggle with men of their own class, as these women employ working class women in order to accomplish nearly all of their required social reproduction. For women of the middle class, the primary issue concerns equality of wage and condition; if we were to think about these concerns in contemporary terms, we might use terms like 'mommy tracking', 'the glass ceiling', and 'equal pay for equal work' to describe these concerns. For Zetkin, the primary contestation for women of the working class is not parity with their male counterparts, but the system of capitalism itself that exploits them, condemns them to immiseration, and prevents "the possibility of living a full life as an individual."[40] There are numerous problems with Zetkin's analysis—she only considers gender and class and she severely downplays (to the point of near-omission) the sexism of men in the working class.[41] However, there is something instructive in her analysis that, over a century later, can still clarify a certain part of the present situation: the formulation of how and what constitutes liberation and equality is in large part framed by the material conditions of one's life, and we should *expect* that these formulations would vary in accordance to class.

Holly Lewis formulates this insight in another way in regards to the contemporary queer movement. In much of the contemporary queer left discourse, there is outrage at the the disinterest and active opposition of rich queer people to the needs and situation of queer working class people, especially queer and trans people of color. This outrage, Lewis argues, is based on a notion of the queer community as sharing in some sort of shared oppression that *should* produce a shared standpoint, a vision Lewis calls "queer nationalism."[42] But just as there is no essential woman, there is no essential queer. Lewis' point is that because of the material falsity of queer nationalism, we actually *should*

---

40 | Quoted in Hal Draper and Anne G. Lipow, "Marxist Women versus Bourgeois Feminism," *Socialist Register*, 1976, 176.

41 | For a sustained critique and rescue of Zetkin, see: Vogel, *Marxism and the Oppression of Women*, 111-20.

42 | Holly Lewis, *The Politics of Everybody: Feminism, Queer Theory and Marxism at the Intersection* (Zed Books, 2016).

not expect that bourgeois queer people (or women or people of color) advocate a politics that is in the interest of working class oppressed people.

These critiques are well-worn. Angela Davis raised several objections about Marxist-feminist accounts of social reproduction nearly immediately after they were articulated.[43] Much of the watershed era of Marxist-feminist theorizing and work on social reproduction assumed a heterosexual, cisgender, married couple in which the husband worked and the wife served as a working class housewife. The issue with this move, we should be clear, is not in its analysis of this particular social location—if we are to generate an analysis of capitalism's functioning, we will need analyses of many social locations. Rather, the theoretical problem with this body of literature is the way in which is assumes (and sometimes explicitly argues for) the universal generalizability of this position as the basis for the development of a theory of social reproduction generally. This can be seen in, for example, Dalla Costa and Mies' analysis of the "housewifization" of all women that for them, constitutes the basis of all women's oppression under capitalism. There is some important truth about this argument: it foregrounds that, in general, women, whether or not they work outside the home, whether or not they are partnered, whether or not their partners are cismen, tend to be disproportionately responsible for socially reproductive labor and that expectations of women's supposedly 'natural' inclinations to caretaking migrates into many aspects of their lives outside the home. We can see this in the expectation that women smile on the street, that they bear disproportionate responsibilities for customer service, and many other moments in which femininity has become partially fixed to a notion of reproductive and affective labor as a generalized and gendered expectation.

But this paradigm, for all of its insights, also contains significant limitations. It contains all of the limitations of any theory that pinpoints one social location and uses it as the basis of generalizability. Lewis points to this limitation in recognizing that capitalism is able to rely on multiple forms of domestic arrangements as the basis for the extraction of surplus value. She points specifically to the resurgence of sex-segregated dormitories that prevent the formation of nuclear families. And, it is important to recognize, this invention is not new: there is a whole history of capitalist profit predicated on the break-up and prevention of nuclear families. While Lewis does not explicitly refer to this long history, there are multiple historical examples we could point to here: the prevention of enslaved people entering into marriages at all, as well as the systematic break up of nuclear families through selling members of families to various plantations, often over great distances; the sex-segregation of early

---

43 | Angela Y. Davis, "The Approaching Obsolescence of Housework: A Working Class Perspective," in *The Angela Y Davis Reader* (Oxford: Blackwell Publishing, 1998), 193-209.

modern work-houses and mental health facilities that forcibly split up working class and impoverished families; the forced sterilization campaigns of women of color and disabled people, often without even the illusion of informed medical consent; a rampantly growing prison industrial complex that not only places some family members in physical cages, but also takes children away from their non-incarcerated parents or caregivers; a social order that penalizes houselessness by taking children away from parents rather than furnishing precarious families with safe and stable housing and an often-sex segregated shelter system that prevents families from staying together, even if they want to; the continued policing and deportation regime of immigration police, who are all to happy to force children and parents to live on opposite sides of heavily policed borders; the restrictions, until rather recently, on queer couples' ability to adopt or raise their own children, with queerness and gender non-conformity being cited in custody battles to attest to the 'unfit' status of people to be parents at all; the long-standing history of non-related live-in workers like cleaners, nannies, cooks, and groundskeepers to perform social reproduction tasks (often to 'free' upper class women from the burden of performing such labor themselves), to name just a few examples. Lewis is only one of a whole new generation of social reproduction theorists who have challenged the paradigm of social reproduction to stretch itself toward accounting for the diversity of real lived experience and locations of its arrangement under capitalism.[44]

How did Capitalism Emerge Historically?

In the Orthodox version, capitalism is usually posited as a completely European affair: at some point in the late medieval period, the previously existing social order—feudalism—began to unravel in numerous places in what is now Western Europe, and this was particularly true in England. In response to this (and debates abound as to its precise cause), landowners in England shifted their strategies of control of the peasant population, through both legal and practical reorganizations, in a shift that created the first 'properly' capitalist system. Accounts of peasant resistance to encroaching capitalism are often part

---

44 | Tithi Bhattacharya, ed., *Social Reproduction Theory: Remapping Class, Recentering Oppression* (London: Pluto Press, 2017); Sue Ferguson, "Intersectionality and Social-Reproduction Feminisms: Toward an Integrative Ontology," *Historical Materialism* 24, no. 2 (2016): 38–60; Kathi Weeks, *The Problem with Work: Feminism, Marxism, Antiwork Politics, and Postwork Imaginaries* (Durham: Duke University Press Books, 2011); J.K. Gibson-Graham, *The End Of Capitalism (As We Knew It): A Feminist Critique of Political Economy,* 2006 edition (Minneapolis: Univ Of Minnesota Press, 2006); Kate Bezanson and Meg Luxton, *Social Reproduction: Feminist Political Economy Challenges Neoliberalism* (Montreal and Kingston: McGill-Queen's University Press, 2006).

of this account, though of course, debates rage about their precise effects. In the Orthodox story, capitalism then spread, through Europe and through European colonial ventures, well beyond that small corner of the globe.

Numerous Marxist accounts have interrupted, contested, and revised this account of capitalism's history. Silvia Federici demonstrates in her landmark *Caliban and the Witch*, that the full-scale imposition of patriarchal relations onto the peasantry was a necessary condition of capitalism's development, notably through the invention of a distinction between productive and reproductive labor.[45] Arguing that pre-capitalist peasant relations in Europe had been marked by significantly more equal gender relations, for Federici, the introduction of the wage for some kinds of work (specifically the production of goods and services for exchange) but not for others (like the production of goods and services for direct consumption, especially internal to the family unit) created widespread conditions of male economic, political, and social power over women in new ways. From Federici's perspective, capitalism must be conceived as an *essentially* sexist structure, and this, she argues, is partially seen through revising the historical account of capitalism's genesis; if patriarchal authority was constitutive of the transition to capitalism historically, then gender cannot be conceived as a subsidiary epiphenomenon.

Capitalism also emerged through a regime of colonization, genocide, war, and slavery, and this too is often overlooked in the Orthodox story. As Anievas and Nisancioglu, explain, "capitalist modernity is generally understood as a *sui generis* development unique to Europe. Where non-European societies do figure, they are typically relegated to the status of a passive bystander, at the receiving end of Europe's colonial whip, or a comparative foil—an Other—against which the specificity and superiority of Europe is defined. In short, the history of capitalism's origins is an unmistakably *Eurocentric* history."[46] Unseating this Eurocentric history, Anievas and Nisancioglu meticulously trace the wide variety of historical factors around the globe that made capitalism possible, generating a non-Eurocentric account of the birth and expansion of capitalism. As Irfan Habib explains, the "[s]ubjugation of other economies was crucial to the formation of industrial capital within it. In other words, colonialism, in its harshest forms, was not a mere attendant process to the rise of capitalism, it was one of its basic, inescapable premises."[47] This perspective, that the emergence of capitalism was contingent on global systems of accumulation, dispossession, territorial expansion, and colonization, has thus opened up lines of argument and inquiry within Marxist circles that take white supremacy, settler colonization,

---

45 | Federici, *Caliban and the Witch*.
46 | Anievas and Nisancioglu, *How the West Came to Rule: The Geopolitical Origins of Capitalism*, 4.
47 | Irfan Habib, "Capitalism in History," *Social Scientist* 23, no. 7/9 (1995): 23.

imperial domination, and what Neil Gotanda calls the invention of 'historical race'[48] as fundamental, irreducible, and structural features of capitalism.

In many ways, this tradition has been most vibrant in Marxist traditions located outside of the Global North. While in many leftist circles, Marxism is caricatured as an essentially white and Eurocentric perspective, this characterization systematically neglects the generations of anti-colonial revolutionaries who considered a Marxist critique of capitalism to be central to any liberation project. This is true not only in countries that adopted socialism as the form of their national governments, but also of multiple revolutionary organizations and movements in Latin America,[49] the Caribbean,[50] Africa,[51] and Asia.[52] It is

---

48 | Neil Gotanda, "A Critique of 'Our Constitution Is Color-Blind,'" *Stanford Law Review* 44, no. 1 (1991): 1-68.

49 | Quijano, "Coloniality of Power, Eurocentrism, and Latin America"; Enrique Dussel, *The Invention of the Americas: Eclipse of "the Other" and the Myth of Modernity*, trans. Michael D. Barber (New York: Continuum Publishing Company, 1995); José Aricó, *Marx and Latin America* (Chicago: Haymarket Books, 2014); Bruno Bosteels, *Marx and Freud in Latin America: Politics, Psychoanalysis and Religion in Times of Terror* (London ; New York: Verso, 2012); Sheldon B. Liss, *Marxist Thought in Latin America* (Berkeley and Los Angeles: University of California Press, 1984).

50 | Paget Henry, "Caribbean Marxism Adter the Neoliberal and Linguistic Turn," in *New Caribbean Thought: A Reader* (Kingston: University of the West Indies Press, 2001); Anthony P. Maingot, *Race, Ideology, and the Decline of Caribbean Marxism* (University Press of Florida, 2015); Trevor Munroe, *Jamaican Politics: A Marxist Perspective in Transition* (Kingston: Heinemann and Boulder, 1990); C. L. R. James, *The Black Jacobins: Toussaint L'Ouverture and the San Domingo Revolution*, 2 edition (New York: Vintage, 1989); Aime Cesaire, *Discourse on Colonialism* (New York: Monthly Review Press, 1973).

51 | Abdoulaye Ly, *Les Masses Africaines et l'actuelle Condition Humaine* (Éditions Présence Africaine, 1956); William H. Crawford and Carl G. Rosberg, *African Socialism* (Palo Alto, California: Stanford University Press, 1964); Adam Mayer, *Naija Marxisms: Revolutionary Thought in Nigeria* (London: Pluto Press, 2016); Thomas Sankara, *Thomas Sankara Speaks* (Pathfinder Press, 2007); Walter Rodney, "Marxism and African Liberation," in *Yes to Marxism* (Georgetown, Guyana: People's Progressive Party, 1975); Amilcar Cabral, *Resistance and Decolonization*, trans. Dan Wood (London: Rowman & Littlefield, 2016).

52 | Petrus Liu, *Queer Marxism in Two Chinas* (Durham ; London: Duke University Press Books, 2015); Amiya Kumar Bagchi and Amita Chatterjee, *Marxism: With and Beyond Marx* (Delhi: Routledge India, 2014); Tania Barlow, *New Asian Marxisms* (Durham: Duke University Press, 2002); Bidyut Chakrabarty, *Left Radicalism in India* (London: Routledge, 2014); Kamran Asdar Ali, *Communism in Pakistan: Politics and Class Activism 1947-1972* (I.B. Tauris, 2015); Vivek Chibber, *Postcolonial Theory and the Specter of*

precisely because of capitalism's deep structural imbrication in colonialism, imperialism, and war that Marxist critique has been so powerful within movements for national liberation, and why some of the strongest, best organized, and longest lasting communist parties have been located inside the Global South. While it is true that this element of capitalism's emergence is, in some Euro-American Marxists, downplayed, much of the Marxist left the world over understands that "any serious materialist critique... [cannot] bypass the colonial encounter, because it is constitutive of the historical development of modern society and capitalism."[53]

Does Capitalism Have Only One Form?

On the basis of many Marxist insights from the Global South, Marxism has often debated the question of whether or not capitalism is a single or unified system, with a single or unified logic. Since capitalism has taken many different forms historically, has interacted with a variety of social, political, and material conditions, and has produced a wide away of structures, the question persists as to what, if anything, allows us to bring these multiple formulations and organizations under the same conceptual heading. From this perspective, the Orthodox Story seems to have yet another defect: it posits a largely uniform story of how capitalism is organized, without significant deviation (or, in some cases, positing deviation as defect). However, if one does the real, empirical work, both historical and contemporary, one encounters a dizzying set of capitalist arrangements, some of which we have only just gestured toward in the preceding discussion. The historical record evidences a wide variety of capitalist responses to impediments, unlikely alliances, painful compromises, orientations toward politics, social practices, family arrangements, racial hierarchies, gender systems, and nearly any other facet of social, political, or economic life. One of the most important realizations that Marxists over the last two centuries have had to grapple with is accommodating theoretically the empirical diversity of capitalist arrangements.

As Dipesh Chakrabarty explains this problem,

There are various ways of thinking about the fact that global capitalism exhibits some common characteristics, even though every instance of capitalist development has

---

Capital, 1 edition (London: Verso, 2013); Sudeep Chakravarti, *Red Sun: Travels in Naxalite Country* (London and New Delhi: Penguin Books, 2008); Li Onesto, *Dispatches from the People's War in Nepal* (London: Pluto Press, 2005).
53 | Shaun Grech, "Disability and the Majority World: A Neocolonial Approach," in *Disability and Social Theory: New Developments and Directions*, ed. Dan Goodley, Bill Hughes, and Lennard Davis (New York: Palgrave, 2012), 53.

a unique history. One can, for one, see these differences among histories as invariably overcome by capital in the long run. The thesis of uneven development, on the other hand, sees these differences as negotiated and contained—though not always overcome—*within* the structure of capital[...] One can visualize capital itself as producing and proliferating differences.[54]

Marxists have taken multiple different approaches to explaining these differences and of conceptualizing the relationship between historical differences and capitalism as a logic and a system.

One such approach, the theory of combined and uneven development, seeks to thematize both the contingent, irreducible differences between multiple historical and national instantiations of capitalism, *and* specifically, to look at the transnational and translocational relationships between these forms. Anievas and Nisancioglu further explain this principle by elaborating three different levels at which this theory operates. In the first place, this theory embraces an approach to "ontology" that "incorporate[es] non-identity and multiplicity—unevenness—into its premises." This discloses the second feature that requires a deep, sensitive, empirical analysis of precisely how capitalism has been organized in multiple ways. Lastly, they argue that in order to raise these empirical difference to the level of theory, one must link "more abstract categories to more concrete, determinant, historically significant ones"; by insisting on the "inseparability of theory and history," uneven and combined development provides a theoretical apparatus for negotiating the differences that constitute capitalism as a world system.[55] Those who embrace this theory argue for a view of social and economic development under capitalism is is "ineluctably *multilinear, causally polycentric*, and *co-constitutive* by virtue of its very interconnectedness,"[56] hence disrupting the unhelpful and ahistorical assumption that "'real' capitalism means 'real' subsumption" or the condition of Euro-American economies.[57]

The insights generated from traditions of Marxism that look at the different regional developments of capitalism have themselves profoundly influenced contemporary Marxist accounts of difference within and across these formations. Radicalizing the insight that capitalism as a structure has multiple organizations on a global level, Marxists in queer, feminist, and anti-racist traditions have thus developed ways of understanding differential social posi-

---

54 | Dipesh Chakrabarty, *Provincializing Europe: Postcolonial Thought and Historical Difference* (Princeton, N.J.: Princeton University Press, 2007), 46.
55 | Anievas and Nisancioglu, *How the West Came to Rule: The Geopolitical Origins of Capitalism*, 63.
56 | Anievas and Nisancioglu, 46.
57 | Chakrabarty, *Provincializing Europe*, 50.

tions along the same lines. Peter Drucker in particular has used the term 'combined and uneven social construction' to name the multiplicity of ways that capitalism interacts with gender, sexuality, nationality and race. By this, he means that: "the idea of combined and uneven social construction... can help us understand how different indigenous starting points, different relationships to the world economy, and different cultural and political contexts can combine to produce very different results—while still producing identifiable common elements."[58] Rather than rely on Orthodox versions of capitalism that seem to posit a single, univocal position for all proletarians, the thesis of combined and uneven social construction allows us to see how, at one and the same time, capitalism is committed to and profits from differentiating social positions. It is from a similar position that Cedric Robinson understood the necessity and the specificity of a Black Marxism, not as "a variant of Western radicalism whose proponents happen to be black", but rather as "a specifically African response to an oppression emergent from the immediate determinants of European development in the modern era."[59] Neither capitalism nor anti-capitalist responses to its horrors should be conflated or sublated into a single narrative, and there are vibrant traditions of Marxism that take this principle of differentiation to be constitutive of the very concept and structure of capitalism itself.

What Besides Labor is Necessary to Maintain Capitalism?

While Marxism is often portrayed as a body of work concerned specifically and chiefly with labor, it is important to remember that even for Marx himself, capitalism relied on two "original sources"[60]: both land and labor. While Marx's analysis of land was rather thin, in *Capital* as well as in other places, Marx explained that integral to capitalism's history was European colonization, which was, on his account, specifically a coordinated, bloody, violent intervention aimed at expanding European territory; capitalism, according to Marx could not have occurred without colonization, which was a regime constituted *both* by new regimes of labor exploitation—slavery, *encomiendas*, tribute labor, indentures, etc.—*and* by the actual conquest of land and territory. Marx refers to this process as *'ursprüngliche Akkumulation'* which has been translated into English as 'primitive accumulation', but more directly means 'original accumulation.'[61] While above we explored the use and expansion of the frame of

---

58 | Peter Drucker, *Warped: Gay Normality and Queer Anti-Capitalism* (Historical Materialism, 2015), 63.
59 | Robinson, *Black Marxism*, 73.
60 | Marx, *Capital*, 638.
61 | Indeed, the term 'primitive' here might suggest to some readers that, especially given its reference to indigenous lands that the term is somehow pejorative, but the term

'primitive accumulation' to speak about ongoing profit on unwaged labor, primitive accumulation, for Marx, and for many Marxist and Marxish thinkers, is one important way to think about the constitution of colonialism and settler colonialism as structuring aspects of capitalism. It is not only labor, but land, that was seized in Marx's analysis of primitive accumulation, and thinking about ongoing primitive accumulation in the form of the continual seizure of indigenous land, structures of settler colonialism, and general disregard for the ecological structure of the world has proved a fecund ground to continue to interrogate the status of land under capitalism.

As Glen Sean Coulthard explains, the primitive accumulation analysis allows us to understand the absolute interpenetration of capitalism and settler colonialism as historical and contemporary structures of the world—a point that is also common in many Latin American Marxist writings.[62] As Coulthard explains the relevance of Marx to indigenous struggles, "these formative acts of violent dispossession set the stage for the emergence of capitalist accumulation and the reproduction of capitalist relations of production by tearing Indigenous societies, peasants, and other small-scale, self-sufficient agricultural producers from the source of their livelihood—the land."[63]

Coulthard finds primitive accumulation a helpful point of connection between indigenous people and Marxism and argues that, with revision, Marxism might help ground anti-capitalist and anti-settler colonial politics at one and the same time. Coulthard explains that not only in the realm of labor, but also in issues of land, settler colonialism demands an analysis of primitive accumulation as a continuing, contemporary phenomenon that is built into the

---

'Ursprung' in German simply lacks the racialized connotations that 'primitive' holds in English. In fact, Marx's use of the term was simply his translation into German of what, in English, Adam Smith had called 'original accumulation' in his own work. 'Primitive accumulation' is just a bad translation; it is however, the accepted term in Anglo-speaking circles and is used nearly universally, including by indigenous scholars, so I continue to use it here. I retain the English word 'primitive' despite this unfortunately bad translation because it has become standard in Marx translations and thus in the vast and rich literature explaining, expanding, and critiquing the concept, including the feminist analysis of 'ongoing primitive accumulation' discussed below.

62 | Dussel, *The Invention of the Americas: Eclipse of "the Other" and the Myth of Modernity*; Anibal Quijano, "Coloniality and Modernity/ Rationality.," *Cultural Studies* 21, no. 2/3 (2007): 168-78; Anibal Quijano, "Colonialidad de Poder y Clasificación Social," *Journal of World-Systems Research* 1, no. 2 (Summer/Fall 2000): 342-86.

63 | Glen Sean Coulthard, *Red Skin White Masks: Rejecting the Colonial Politics of Recognition* (Minneapolis: University of Minnesota Press, 2014), 7.

structure of contemporary life, specifically in Canada, but also in other settler colonies.[64]

From another perspective, land and the environment have been central to thinking about the complex relationships between gendering, racialization, and global capital. In *Alien Capital,* Iyko Day argues that the discourse of "romantic anti-capitalism" can explain the ways in which white, male frustrations with industrialization and capitalism can and have been expressed through racialized practices of rejuvenation that often entail pernicious practices of Native erasure.[65] In Day's analysis, the strictures of capitalism can be used to understand *both* how and why workers might experience capitalism as alienating *and* how their avenues of dealing with this alienation might contribute to the reinforcement rather than dismantling of racist and settler colonial structures. All of this takes place, of course, inside a capitalist system that views land primarily as a commodity, to be bought, sold, and exploited for the sole purpose of accumulation, a point that Marxists concerned with nature and the environment have repeatedly explored.[66]

Expanding the analysis of capitalism to think about both land and labor is only one way in which Marxists have begun to think beyond labor in understanding capitalism. While labor in both its productive and reproductive forms are absolutely central in understanding capitalism as a structure of accumulation and dispossession, capitalism can not be reduced *merely* to a system of production. In order to maintain and perpetuate capitalism, a whole host of structures which are neither reducible to labor nor land are required. Ideology,

---

64 | It is important to note that Coulthard argues that the colonial relation, not the capital relation is the central feature of contemporary life and hence the emphasis in investigation should fall to the former rather than the latter, a claim that many Marxists will argue should preclude his inclusion as a Marxist in these pages. However, as I explained in the introduction, I am interested here in the Marxish, and Coulthard's analysis not only of primitive accumulation, but also of Fanon's understanding of the relationship between capitalism, colonialism, recognition, and resistance, certainly qualifies in this regard as a helpful critique and substantive engagement with Marxist work.

65 | Day, *Alien Capital.*

66 | Fred Magdoff and John Bellamy Foster, *What Every Environmentalist Needs to Know about Capitalism* (Monthly Review Press, 2011); John Molyneux, "Marxism and the Environmental Crisis," *Climate & Capitalism*, November 25, 2011, http://climateandcapitalism.com/2011/11/25/marxism-and-the-environmental-crisis/; K.D. Shifferd, "Karl Marx and the Environment," *Journal of Environmental Education* 3, no. 4 (1972): 39-42; Jason W. Moore, *Capitalism in the Web of Life: Ecology and the Accumulation of Capital* (London: Verso, 2015); Andreas Malm, *Fossil Capital: The Rise of Steam Power and the Roots of Global Warming* (London: Verso, 2016); Michael Löwy, *Ecosocialism: A Radical Alternative to Capitalist Catastrophe* (Chicago: Haymarket Books, 2015).

psychology, social narratives: all of these are necessary to capitalism. They are, of course, necessary, because they provide the social scaffolding necessary in order to maintain and justify exploitation and its resultant inequality, but social practices, narratives, and norms coalesce in ways that have impacts on human life far beyond the economic sphere.

It is from this perspective that deep and thorough understanding of the social is central to Marxist accounts of capitalism. As Tithi Bhattacharya explains in her close reading of what Marx means by 'the economy', rather than a reductive analysis of a specific sphere of exchange or production, "he is inviting us to see the 'economic' as a social relation: one that involves domination and coercion, even if juridical forms and political institutions seek to obscure that." She thus argues that Marxism makes three specific and fundamental claims about the economy:

One, that the economy as we see it is, according to Marx, a surface appearance; two, that the appearance, which is steeped in a rhetoric of equality and freedom, conceals a 'hidden abode' where domination and coercion reign, and those relations form the pivot of capitalism; hence, three, that the economic is also a social relation, in that the power that is necessary to run this hidden abode—to submit the worker to modes of domination—is also by necessity a political power.[67]

While inside capitalism, the economic *seems* to be a separate, specific sphere of action, one that neither constitutes the 'public' realm of political action nor the 'private' realm of the home, the fact is that society is never so neatly divided. It is rather that economic relations are wholly suffused with the political, the social, and the intimate in ways that cannot be separated from one another. Capitalism relies on the reproduction of this narrative of false separation; it is only through this false split that capitalism in liberal democracies can, for instance, insist on enfranchisement and (an always anemic form of) democracy, while insisting that workplace relations should be run through absolute authoritarian hierarchy. It also relies, as we have seen above, on the continued exploitation of unwaged labor in the so-called private sphere, as the condition of the possibility of its reproduction. But the interpenetration of the economic, the political, and the social go even deeper: in capitalist societies, access to a whole host of resources, activities, opportunities, and needs is constituted through one's ability to pay, and hence the economic is present at every turn: every time we are sick and need medicine, every time we must make the decision between keeping the lights on and buying food, every time we must forgo education in

---

67 | Bhattacharya, *Social Reproduction Theory: Remapping Class, Recentering Oppression*, 71.

order to work, every time an arts program is cut in a public school, every time a cop arrests a houseless person for sleeping on the street.

It goes further even still: in order to maintain this widely unequal system, social narratives and ideologies must continually reinforce the naturalness, the ahistoricity, and the justice of leaving many to scrimp, save, and die. Capitalism is thus deeply connected to social ideas of responsibility, work ethic, deservingness, success, equality, and justice. It is, likewise, deeply entrenched in narratives about punishment and poverty, which suggest that those who end up in physical cages or confined to unlivable conditions must somehow deserve their lot. Indeed, it is even complicit with ideas of representation, of vulnerability, of an entire 'distribution of the sensible'[68] in which those who live precarious lives often cannot even enter into the social sphere of legibility, whose cries and pain can be disregarded or denied. Capitalism is thus entirely complicit and productive of a system of both biopolitical and necropolitical power in which some people, some communities, are constructed as those worth saving and others are constructed as disposable, exposed to death, violence, and destruction at every turn.[69] It influences who amongst us we will even be able to mourn and to grieve.[70]

When the Marxist linkage between the economic and the social is engaged, it is often done on the basis of a reductive understanding of what is called the base and superstructure model. In Orthodox versions of this understanding, it is assumed that a material or economic 'base' somehow uniquely and unilaterally determines a social, cultural, and political 'superstructure' as mere functional output of capitalism. Though this is a rather common way of understanding this relation in the non-Marxist left, it could not be further from what Marxists typically mean by it. Rather than a simple, one-way determination, the relationship between economics and social life, is conceived dialectically, which is to say, as mutually constructing, wholly interpenetrated areas of life in which influence runs constantly in all directions.[71] This influence is a multi-directional "dynamic process" in which a socialized understanding of the economic and a political, social, and intimate realm wholly suffused with capitalist relations, continue to "reconstitute" each other in a "potentially interminable" process.[72] It is from this perspective that many Marxists like Himani

---

68 | Jacques Rancière, *The Politics of Aesthetics*, trans. Gabriel Rockhill, Pbk. Ed edition (London ; New York: Bloomsbury Academic, 2006).

69 | Achille Mbembe, "Necropolitics," trans. Libby Meintjes, *Public Culture* 15, no. 1 (n.d.): 11–40; Michel Foucault, *The Birth of Biopolitics: Lectures at the Collège de France, 1978-1979*, Reprint edition (Basingstoke England; New York: Picador, 2010).

70 | Judith Butler, *Frames of War: When Is Life Grievable?* (London: Verso, 2016).

71 | We will return to questions of dialectics in Chapter 6.

72 | Jameson, *Valences of the Dialectic*, 44, 47.

Bannerji argue that neither economic reductionism nor cultural reductionism can generate the complex understanding of society generated by a Marxist critique of capitalism: "we need to venture into a more complex reading of the social, where every aspect or moment of it can be shown to reflect others, where each little piece of it contains the macrocosm in its microcosm."[73] Given this understanding of the complex, multifocal relationship between the economic, the social, the political, and the intimate, we can now turn more specifically to the question how violence at all of these levels might be connected to capitalism as a system.

What is the Relationship between Exploitation and other Forms of Violence?

One of the pervasive effects of the Orthodox Story is the way in which it suggests that capitalism is an economic structure only, that has little to say about the ways in which violence, prejudice, and oppression structure life beyond work generally. However, as we have seen, contemporary Marxist analyses stretch far beyond the traditional 'workplace' as sites of urgent investigation into the structure, logic, and effects of capitalism. In particular, it is blatant that the relationship between capitalism and slavery hinged on race and racialization and the the relationship between capitalism and social reproduction hinges squarely on gender and sexuality. Though the relationship between these realms has often been underthematized, numerous Marxist theorists have been precisely interested in the ways that racialization, gender, sexuality, and class coalesce into systems of oppression under capitalism. Exactly *what* the relationship between capitalism and larger systems of domination and oppression is, is itself a subject of ongoing debate within Marxist circles. A deeper discussion of these perspectives is discussed in Chapter 5.

In some of the most widely-accepted answers to this question, Marxists have given what we might call 'the functionalist answer.' By functionalist, here, I mean that from this Marxist perspective, race, gender, sexuality, and other oppressions are primarily related to capitalism through *their function* under capitalism, that is, the *use* to which these distinctions are put under the system of capitalism. Common functionalist answers to how and why oppression continues to be structured into capitalism include: a) that oppressions based on differences allow for artificial divisions between members of the working class to prevent unified uprisings b) that differences serve a psychological function, as a kind of consolation prize for the 'privileged dispossessed' that can in some situations assuage the feelings of powerlessness that comes from living under capitalism. These approaches' insights have advanced Marxist thought signifi-

---

73 | Bannerji, "Building from Marx: Reflections on Class and Race," 146.

cantly. In particular, they are really helpful at thinking about how systematic violence is ultimately *in the interests* of capitalist accumulation. These accounts can furnish us with an analysis of *who benefits* and why from widespread, structural acts of violence and erasure in ways that significantly more compelling that many other analyses.

But functionalist answers are not the only ones that Marxists have offered in their understandings of capitalism; rather, there is a deep multiplicity of ways that Marxism can think the interrelation between oppression and capitalism. I could not ever hope to detail or inventory all of them here. An analysis of any individual instance of violence would be required to unpack the relationship between capitalism, normativity, and violence in all of its depth and nuance. However, there are a few grounding and guiding lines of interrogation that Marxists have often used in understanding and marking these relations:

A. Who benefits from this violence?
For all of his faults (and there are many!) early modern philosopher Thomas Hobbes once framed the question of politics under the question of *cui bono*—to whose benefit. Many Marxists approach the question of the relationship between capitalism and violence through asking this question. Who ultimately benefits from this systematic violence? Who profits from it? In what ways are those who already hold power in capitalist society assuaged, empowered, and enriched by this violence? This question has been particularly prominent in Marxist analyses of the prison industrial complex for example, in which we find the profitability of this violence manifested in a variety of ways: private prisons, corporations who contract to provide 'services', the intense mark-up of items in commissaries and per minute prices of phone calls to the outside, the use of prison labor at far below even the already depressed minimum wage, police uses of asset forfeiture, uses of monetary bail to profit off of pre-trial detention, payments to privatized security forces like G4S in and around prisons and immigrant detention facilities—all of these evidence a deep connection that the owners of industries profit immensely from the structural violence of incarceration; Marxist thus argue that part of the endemic and indeed, increasing, deployment of this kind of violence can be directly traced to a profit-motive.

B. How does this violence relate to the general production of group-based precariousness?
As we saw in an earlier chapter, Ida B. Wells-Barnett was one of the first to draw a linkage between a general climate of fear and terror caused by lynching and the general precariousness, both economic and social, that black populations faced. Drawing on this line of analysis, many Marxists have sought to thematize the ways in which structural and constant deployments of violence, both in and far beyond the workplace, contribute to

creating a climate of fear that feeds into and reproduces the precarity of oppressed and marginalized groups. Inside a climate of terror, individuals are less likely to report instances of abuse like wage theft or sexual assault on the job if they have no guarantee that they will not be fired or indeed, as in the case of many immigrant domestic workers, if their visas are tied to their place of employment. This violence thus contributes to the ability of individual capitalists to continue to extract value even far above what the law allows. In another way, the violences inherent in lack of access to education, healthcare, clean food, safe water, and other vital needs, are ways that society is structured in order to inculcate the idea that life is only possible through work on the capitalist market. The violences done to houseless and hungry people thus promote integration within capitalism by acting as a brutal and deranged threat of what refusing to be a 'good worker' will bring.

C. In what ways does violence contribute to more general structures of disempowerment?

It is a common position among Marxists that those who already face the most disempowerment in political and social spheres are more easily exploitable. Generalized violence may inhibit or prohibit people from coming forward, from exercising political rights, from organizing in public ways against their condition. When, for example, social scripts deride and devalue people and their lives, it becomes much more possible to subject them to derision and devaluation in their workplaces. In the cases of pieces of harmful legislation like 'bathroom bills', the violence of refusing to recognize peoples' gender identities and their biological needs, social narratives suggest that transpeople are less than human, and they do not need to be treated as such. Those who are systematically marked outside of a given community can be more easily treated as disposable, and prejudice at many levels will constitute further barriers for the redress of any grievances. The more and more access to politics, the media, education, and other sources of social power and authority are restricted, the more vulnerable populations become in general.

D. What norms, narratives, and ideologies overlap between this instance of violence and capitalist discipline?

As we explored above, a Marxist understanding of capitalism is tethered to understanding social norms, narratives, and ideology, as they provide the justification for capitalism's continued process of accumulation. Moreover, social narratives that confirm and reaffirm that poverty, hardship, or lack of access to vital social services are somehow the outcome of individual failure themselves deeply conform to capitalism's reliance on a notion of individual responsibility and anti-collectivism that frame the entire project of capitalist accumulation. Moreover, the idea that people can be segmented into deserving and undeserving populations, notions about the fairness or equality of opportunity of capitalism serve only to mask and justify the profoundly structural inequalities that form capitalism's basis, and the idea that fulfillment, comfort, stability, and safety should be offered only to those who can afford to pay for it.

It is helpful here to mark ways that normativity and respectability politics often emerge within oppressed and marginalized communities, creating conditions in which entrance into and success within capitalism is refigured as the goal and vision of emancipation. The dominant model of gay subjectivity as upper class assumes that gay subjectivity under capitalism is essentially "a queer liberal one, invested in consumption, property ownership, stable sexual relationships, relying on an archaic formulation of public/private divides."[74] In this way, images of what it means to *be* queer, for example, are rather hegemonic, finding sites for capital to reappropriate inclusion and proffer diversity as one of its core values. This hence specifically contributes to the re-marginalization and disempowerment of the most vulnerable sections of oppressed populations, now not only from outside, but from within marginalized communities themselves.

E. How does this violence suggest that capitalism can solve the problem of violence or oppression?

Particularly in the post-Civil Rights Era, it has become a common strategy for those of marginalized and oppressed positions to push for legal protections. These have often come in the form of anti-discrimination laws and legal reforms for everything from non-heterosexual marriages, marijuana use, sex work, and pathways to citizenship for undocumented people. While many Marxists actively and vocally support such measures because of their immediate harm-reduction aspect, they also interject the necessity of remaining critical toward legal solutions. Relying only or wholly on the law engenders a series of effects, not the least of which is the idea that capitalist political institutions are the guarantor and protector of freedom, when precisely the opposite is true, only further entrenches the idea that liberal capitalist politics is the only option for safety, even as this system relies so heavily on the very violences it pretends to redress.[75]

F. How does the denial of ongoing, systemic violence contribute to capitalism's ability to reproduce itself?

Lastly, another way that Marxist theorists have thematized the relationship between capitalism and oppression is in and through the ways that capitalism denies its own violence and oppression, allowing it to continue to

---

74 | Puar, *Terrorist Assemblages: Homonationalism in Queer Times* (Durham: Duke University Press Books, 2007), xxxvi.

75 | Dean Spade, *Normal Life: Administrative Violence, Critical Trans Politics, and the Limits of Law* (Chapel Hill: Duke University Press, 2015).

proffer the idea that capitalism, equality, and freedom are synonymous. This line of inquiry has been particularly insightful in critiquing Western and Euro-American supremacist narratives that in particular, a kind of openness toward gender and sexuality diversity is best procured and protected through neoliberal capitalism. We might call this the pinkwashing and rainbow-washing effect of capitalism, though others have used femonationalism[76] and homonationalism to mark this structure. As Jasbir Puar explains,

> The use of gender equality as a marker of an economic and regulatory modernity marks the subject of gender equality as Western, capitalist, and democratic, and the West, capitalism and democracy themselves as sites that create the possibility of, and reproduce, rather than hinder, gender equality. Critically, they position the objects of gender equality as non-Western or post-socialist[...] as creating and perpetuating traditional gender inequalities not part of the modern world. A gender agenda is thus consistently harnessed to cultural or economic difference from Western subjects and sites.[77]

In this way, systematic violence operates in two directions at once: it justifies and even demands continued neocolonial and militaristic intervention into non-Western countries, and erases the continued violence to which women, transpeople, gender non-conforming people, and queer folks are subjected to inside Western societies. It thus both contributes to the ideological linkage between capitalism and equality at the same time that it provides narratological cover for ongoing projects of accumulation and dispossession in the Global South.

These are general lines of inquiry and should not be conceived exhaustively, nor should these answers be taken as final. It would be impossible to, in the span of a chapter, detail every answer to these question for every case of racialized, gendered, sexuated, or class-based violence that Marxists have analyzed, around the world and over hundreds of years of history. These questions are thus markers of ways of engagement, lines of alliance between capitalism and thinking through the multi-faceted operation and constitution of oppression, marginalization, and precarity.

---

76 | Farris, *In the Name of Women's Rights: The Rise of Femonationalism*.
77 | Clare Hemmings, *Why Stories Matter: The Political Grammar of Feminist Theory* (Durham, NC: Duke University Press, 2011), 9.

CONCLUSION

Far from the Orthodox Story with which Marxism as a whole is conflated, feminist, queer, anti-colonial, and anti-racist Marxisms form vibrant and compelling traditions in their own right. Despite all of their differences, these varied positions and heterogeneous modes of inquiry all speak to the necessity of retaining capitalism as a central feature of contemporary modes of domination, exploitation, and oppression; indeed, capitalism as a structure is highly dependent on many forms of exclusion, marginalization, domination, and disempowerment. If we are to take one lesson from these discussions, it should be that no account of race, gender, sexuality, imperialism, or colonization could ever hope to be complete without a systematic understanding of how capitalism operates, not only as an economic system, but as a structuring field of life with ramifications far beyond the workplace.

However, in spite of all of the insight generated by these thinkers, there have been numerous articulations within each of these strands that necessitate further explanation and critique. It is to intersectionality's critique of Marxism that we now turn.

Chapter Four: Intersectional Critiques of Marxism

This chapter looks at critiques of Marxism from an intersectional perspective. I focus on four charges in particular: that Marxism is economically reductive, holding critical purchase only in the realm of work or the economy; that it necessarily treats all other forms of oppression as mere epiphenomena of the 'true' oppression of class; that Marxism is inherently a male, Eurocentric form of analysis that can therefore never speak to the oppression of women, people of color, and people from the Global South; that a Marxist understanding of exploitation is founded on the binary opposition of capitalist and proletarian, making it incapable of thinking through the complex and nuanced organizations of exploitation and oppression. I argue that, while many of these critiques are valid against certain Marxist authors, they are frequently caricatures. However, there are a variety of places in which Marxism, even queer, antiracist, and feminist marxisms continue to reproduce features critiqued by the intersectional tradition.

Economic Reductionism

One of the most enduring critiques of Marxism on the left, from intersectional and non-intersectional theorists alike, remains an association of Marxism with economic reductionism. Economic reductionism, in these accounts, is the position that all areas of life—especially politics and social relations—are directly determined, unicausally, by economic factors. Because Marx and Engels argued for a material basis of ideas, ideology, and social practices,[1] many

---

1 | Take, for example, the following passage from *The Communist Manifesto:* "Your very ideas are but the outgrowth of conditions of your bourgeois production and bourgeois property, just as your jurisprudence is but the will of your class, made into law for all, a will whose essential character and direction are determined by the economic conditions of the existence of your class."

(including some Marxists) have taken this claim to mean that economic life is the sole, univocal, mechanistically determining force in history.[2] Despite generations of Marxist scholars explicitly and vociferously rejecting economic reductionism as a form of 'vulgar Marxism', this idea continues to produce skepticism among leftist academics and activists alike.

In the context of intersectionality, the critique of economic reductionism takes on a particular form. Economic reductionism is seen, from an intersectional perspective, to directly or implicitly undermine the equality of oppressions that is so central to intersectionality's distinctive approach to oppression. In positing that oppression is caused specifically, uniquely, and directly by capitalism—in conjunction with the position that class is the only or most fundamental structuring cleavage under capitalism—Marxism seems to suggest that class relations cause or are in some other way more primary than other oppressions. I discuss the response to class primacy below, but it is important to note that this position is directly linked to economic reductionism.

But moreover, economic reductionism seems unable to capture the multiplicity and diversity of the organizations of oppression or to generate deep analyses of the differences (of experiences, identities, choices, narratives, and traumas) between individuals who share economic positions under capitalism. As we will return to later in the chapter, it also seems unable to thematize the multiple modes of resistances to hegemonic forces of capitalism within movements.

It is true that some Marxists, even those fundamentally sympathetic to intersectionality, have often fallen back on economically reductive accounts of capitalism and oppression, even despite their own best intentions. Take, for example, this passage by Sharon Smith, which seems to suggest that recognition of shared economic position is sufficient to overcome deep and entrenched histories of oppression: "When workers go on strike, confronting capital and its agents of repression (the police), the class nature of society becomes suddenly clarified. Racist, sexist, or homophobic ideas cultivated over a lifetime can disappear within a matter of days in a mass strike wave."[3] In response to flippant lines such as these, we might counterpose the Combahee River Collective's

---

2 | Marx's use of the terms 'base' and 'superstructure'—which, since Marx's own writings, have taken on a life of their own—have seemed to complicate matters here, giving the illusion that Marx believed the economic 'base' independently, unilaterally, and uni-directionally causes the political and social 'superstructure.' Though this interpretation is indeed ubiquitous, it is rather far from Marx's own conception of this relation. For an extended discussion of this history, see: Dileep Edara, *Biography of a Blunder: Base and Superstructure in Marx and Later* (Cambridge: Cambridge Scholars Publishing, 2016).

3 | Smith, "Black Feminism and Intersectionality."

assessment, which is that "as black feminists we are made constantly and painfully aware of how little effort white women have made to understand and combat their racism, which requires among other things, that they have a more than superficial comprehension of race, color, and black history and culture."[4] Are we really to believe that walking a picket line for a few days is really sufficient to impart 'more than a superficial comprehension of race, color, black history and culture' in addition to gender, sexuality, gender identity, citizenship status, incarceration status, and ability? Does walking a strike line outside of a factory in the settler colonial US adequately grapple with the questions of indigenous rights and the anti-colonial claim to the land on which the strike operates? It is this kind of dismissiveness of the trenchant nature of prejudice and of the difficulty of genuine unlearning that explains many intersectional theorists' antipathy toward certain strains of Marxism; it treats a picket line as a magical panacea for deep structures, refusing to grapple with the ways in which oppressive power relations replay themselves in activist spaces.

However, it would be a mistake to read all Marxist theory as economic reductionism, or even to assert that Marxism is *essentially* a reductionist theory, even if some Marxist accounts might be guilty of this charge. As Rosemary Hennessey has explained, many Marxists, especially those whose work is principally concerned with oppression, specifically reject the logic of "expressive causality" in which a society is wholly explainable as "emanate[ing] from one central cause."[5]

Consider the following passage from a letter Engels wrote to J. Bloch in 1890:

According to the materialist conception of history, the ultimately determining element in history is the production and reproduction of real life. Other than this neither Marx nor I have ever asserted. Hence *if somebody twists this into saying that the economic element is the only determining one, he transforms that proposition into a meaningless, abstract, senseless phrase*[...]Various elements of the superstructure — political forms of the class struggle and its results, to wit: constitutions established by the victorious class after a successful battle, etc., juridical forms, and even the reflexes of all these actual struggles in the brains of the participants, political, juristic, philosophical theories, religious views and their further development into systems of dogmas — also exercise their influence upon the course of the historical struggles and *in many cases preponderate in determining their form*. There is an interaction of all these elements in which, amid all the endless host of accidents (that is, of things and events whose inner interconnection is so remote or so impossible of proof that we can regard it as non-existent, as negligible), the economic movement finally asserts itself as necessary.

---

4 | Combahee River Collective, "A Black Feminist Statement," 371.
5 | Hennessy, *Profit and Pleasure: Sexual Identities in Late Capitalism*, 26.

Otherwise the application of the theory to any period of history would be easier than the solution of a simple equation of the first degree.[6]

There are two elements of this passage the deserve unpacking. In the first place, Engels does indeed assert that material life—how individuals meet their basic, material needs—will determine, in the broad sense, the path of their lives. This should not itself be a particularly controversial statement, but as a central feature of much Marxism, deserves an explanation. Marx and Engels argued that meeting material needs—food, shelter, clothing, emotional needs necessary for survival and satisfaction—will significantly frame the choices people make. That is to say that where people live and more importantly, how they live, is significantly embedded in these conditions. Where one lives, whether healthy food is available in those places, whether those places are heavily policed or not, whether or not one is subjected to segregation or redlining, with whom one comes into contact, the extent to which contact with bureaucracies and government administrations exert disciplinary power over individuals, what kinds of health risks or environmental pollutants exist near one's home, what kinds of consumer goods one has access to, what kinds of schools one attends, whether one can attend school at all, whether one decides to get married or have children, whether one can access necessary health care—all of these and more are significantly rooted, under capitalism, in one's ability to pay for services, and hence in one's class position. This does not mean that material needs are *the only* factors that affect one's life trajectory, opportunities, and circumstances, but it does mean that material needs are *relevant* and often *revealing* in understanding the choices—often impossible and unfree choices—that human beings make under capitalism. Material needs can also help us decipher whether and when people are liable to join or oppose revolutionary movements for change, as the calculus of what is to be gained, lost, and risked by participating in those movements is often bound up in whether the demands will significantly increase or decrease one's ability to meet those needs; relevant also is an analysis of how and whether repression against those movements will influence one's ability to meet the material needs of oneself and one's family (biological and/or chosen), kin, and dependents.

But second, Engels is rather clear that what both he and Marx mean by 'determining' is rather less than often supposed; Engels is quite clear that 'determining' in this context does not mean *sole determinant*, or even *the most important factor*. Engels readily and explicitly explains that assuming an understanding of the economy in such a reductive, deterministic way is both wrong and meaningless. Determining does not mean deterministic. But moreover,

---

6 | Karl Marx, Friedrich Engels, and V.I. Lenin, *On Historical Materialism: A Collection* (Moscow: Progress Publishers, 1972), 294. Emphasis mine.

Engels explains that in a variety of situations, a whole host of factors—economic, social, religious, individual, political, ideological—could be the *preponderant* cause in any situation. If Marx and Engels, and a whole tradition of Marxists after them, nevertheless argue for a material understanding of society, what then could this 'determining factor' mean?

It means nothing more and nothing less than that the form of economy under which one lives—in this case, capitalism—sets certain 'rules of the game' in relation to which lives unfold. The rules of the game do not determine who will win necessarily in advance (though to be sure the rules favor some rather than others), nor does it determine what numbers will come up on the dice, nor who will cheat the rules (and who will be caught and who not, who pardoned and who punished, punished in what way). As Marx wrote in the *Eighteenth Brumaire*, "human beings make their own history, but they do not make it just as they please; they do not make it under circumstances chosen by themselves, but under circumstances existing already."[7] It is these already existing conditions—economic, institutional, bureaucratic, political, social, and structural—that Marx and Engels understand as the material forces that significantly shape the choices, actions, thoughts, opportunities, and sacrifices made by people. Agency is real and important; it is just not the only thing that matters. Capitalism, in this sense, is *relevant* to all analyses but it cannot alone *explain* or *cause* them.

In a certain way, this kind of analysis is rather similar to intersectionality's account of any point in the matrix of domination. Since race is itself wholly constructed in and through its relationship to gender, sexuality, ability, class, and nationality, race is *always relevant*—to whatever phenomenon one could investigate. This is precisely what it means for race to be 'structural'; it is part of the fundamental constitution of the contemporary shape of the world—there is no phenomenon that could be wholly, completely, or totally explained without reference to race.[8] But it would also be absurd to argue that *all phenomena* could be explained *solely* in reference to race. The same, of course, from an intersectional perspective could be said of any node in the matrix of domination: as structural, each node is *always* relevant (though not always relevant in the same ways across time and circumstance).

---

7 | Karl Marx, *The Eighteenth Brumaire of Louis Bonaparte*, 6th ed. (Moscow: Progress Publishers, 1972), 10. Translation modified by me.

8 | This is, I would argue, even true of contemporary investigations of phenomena that precede the historical invention of race, because of the way in which the contemporary investigation is enframed by the conditions of the present.

Class Primacy

Related but not reducible to the charge of economic determinism is the critique of Marxism as a theory of oppression that is significantly or essentially a class-primary account. By 'class primacy', I mean the position that, despite whatever other oppressions may indeed exist in the world as important dynamics, class remains the dominant, structuring, most important or causal substrate of other oppressions. Class primacy has constituted a significant and consistent critique of Marxism from the intersectional tradition.[9] Some Marxist theorists do in fact omit any significant discussions of race, gender, or sexuality from their work, explaining the processes of capital accumulation, crises, and dispossession in gender and race-blind terms (or discussing axes of oppression but only as epiphenomena of class).[10] This erasure of race, gender, and sexuality as relevant terms in the discussion of oppression is one tendency that intersectionality theorists, as well as feminists generally, have identified as a serious limitation of the tradition of Marxism.[11]

From an intersectional perspective, there are multiple issues with the postulate of class primacy. In the first place, class primacy often generates reduc-

---

9 | For example, take the following claim by Beverly Smith of the Combahee River Collective: there are "people who are Marxists who say 'Well, when class oppression and racism end, definitely the oppression of women and lesbians will end.'" Smith was herself a Marxist and an intersectional thinker who repeatedly critiqued a class reductionist trend in Marxist organizing.Smith and Smith, "Across the Kitchen Table: A Sister-to-Sister Dialogue," 122. See also: Gedalof, "Sameness and Difference in Government Equality Talk"; Alcoff, "An Epistemology for the Next Revolution."

10 | For a particularly unabashed example of such a position see: Walter Benn Michaels, *The Trouble with Diversity: How We Learned to Love Identity and Ignore Inequality* (New York: Holt, 2006).

11 | While this criticism is certainly valid of many Marxist theorists, as we saw in the previous chapter, it would be misleading to erase the long history of Marxists who spoke extensively of gender, race, and colonialism. Some of the major theorists of the Marxist tradition, among them Karl Marx himself as well as Friedrich Engels discussed imperialism, colonialism, and slavery and in Engels' case, patriarchy. It is true that Marx's discussions of slavery and imperialism do not themselves constitute a theory of race, or at all reference the gendered dimensions of these structures. Indeed, it may be particularly problematic to give an account of colonization and slavery that does not center race and gender. It is true that many who wrote in the tradition of Marx and Engels ignored these dimensions in their analysis. For an analysis of Marx's stances on slavery, imperialism, and colonialism, see Kevin B. Anderson, *Marx at the Margins: On Nationalism, Ethnicity, and Non-Western Societies* (Chicago: University Of Chicago Press, 2010).

tive, static, and homogeneous notions of oppressions that can only be conceptualized in their relationship to class, but not in relation to each other. This has often led to investigations into oppressions that consider class and gender *or* class and race *or* class and sexuality, but not to accounts that understand the deep connections, historical and structural, between gender, race, and sexuality themselves. Much of the nineteenth and twentieth century attempts to think about Marxism and oppression followed this model. While these theories of oppression and capitalism certainly developed resources that can and have been mobilized to understand the intersections, they still fall prey to the problem of treating race, sexuality, and gender as fundamentally separable from each other, ignoring the deep and foundational ways in which each of these formations is constructed and influenced precisely in and through their conjunction. For example, Jean Ait Belkher, engaging with but ultimately rejecting intersectionality from a Marxist perspective, declared that "despite the warning to scholars not to isolate race, class, or gender, this is a necessary step...in the end."[12] This approach to thinking about capitalism and oppression, whether undertaken explicitly or implicitly, often manifested itself in homogenizing the categories of race, gender, and sexuality themselves in ways that, for example, took white working class women as the default or privileged subjects of the analysis of gender and capitalism, or of taking black men as the default or privileged subjects of the analysis of race and capitalism, replaying rather than subverting the fundamental problems highlighting by intersectional critique. This not only has the effect of marginalizing those who live at the intersections, but also refuses to see the necessary, structural, and historical interconnections of various social locations.

One of the central contentions of intersectionality as a framework is the necessity of embracing "the working hypothesis of the equivalency between oppressions."[13] This working hypothesis, as Collins puts it, has often been misunderstood by Marxism as an ontological claim, but Collins understands it as a strategic claim. In other words, one of the central insights of intersectionality is precisely that hierarchalizing oppressions itself perpetuates the marginalization of those who are often invested with the least social power. In this way, single systems theories that discuss gender (and occasionally race), only as secondary after-effects of capital relations, cannot adequately account for the specific forms of oppression faced by women of color, working-class queers, or gender non-conforming people. These theories seem still to take white,

---

12 | Jean Ait Belkhir and Berenice McNair Barnett, "Race, Gender, and Class Intersectionality," *Race, Gender and Class* 8, no. 3 (2001): 163-64.
13 | Patricia Hill Collins, "On West and Fenstermaker's 'Doing Difference,'" in *Women, Men, and Gender: Ongoing Debates*, ed. Mary Roth Walsh (New Haven: Yale University Press, 1997), 74.

employed, married, white, heterosexual men (and their wives) as the only subjects of inquiry. In this way, intersectional theorists have critiqued Marxist accounts of oppression for ignoring multiplicity, diversity, and heterogeneity within their discussions of marginalized groups.

Moreover, class-first accounts of oppression tend to reify the concept of class. As Vivian May explains, many of these approaches "present class as universal, suggesting other factors, like race, gender, or sexuality, are secondary or particular: not only are identities atomized, but so are the structural and material processes that inform them."[14] The presentation of class as 'that which we all share' while gender, race, and sexuality are particular attributes only of certain populations, re-entrenches a version of universality that is persistently mobilized against marginalized groups in order to undercut the urgency and seriousness of their situations, problems, and demands. Linda Martín Alcoff argues that there are never "pure" class issues that do not intersect with race, gender, sexuality. She explains, "Class reductionists argue here that conflicts will dissolve if we can only wean ourselves from our identity attachments. It is in just this way that the left colludes with the right in portraying ethnic group politics today as special interest agendas with opportunistic leaders who never take into account the common good."[15]

It thus, as May and Alcoff suggest, generates a theoretically impoverished understanding of how class actually functions, which is, in reality, heterogeneously, differentially, and unevenly. In class primary accounts, we lose the richness and sensitivity of a deep and thorough understanding of *class itself*, in addition to misunderstanding the multiple and multi-valent operations of various oppressions in conjunction with each other and with capitalism.

This is not to say that all Marxist accounts of oppression fall prey to class primacy. In fact, it was due to the long history of the occlusion of women's work, lives, and experiences of violence and exploitation that Marxist feminists critiqued more mainstream discussions of capitalist economy and culture. In this sense, the criticism of mainstream or hegemonic Marxism as race and gender-blind is a criticism shared by both intersectionality theorists and a whole series of feminists, queer folks, people of color, disabled people, and people from the Global South who locate themselves in the Marxist tradition.

---

14 | Vivian May, *Pursuing Intersectionality, Unsettling Dominant Imaginaries* (New York: Routledge, 2015), 174.
15 | Alcoff, "An Epistemology for the Next Revolution," 74.

Eurocentrism, Androcentrism, and the Limitations of Production

A whole set of criticisms of Marxism focus on the conditions of its initial development. There are two dominant versions of this critique, one I call the 'Identity Version' and one the 'Conditions Version.'

The Identity Version of this critique dismisses Marxism because of the identity of Karl Marx himself or aspects of his biography; as a White, European, heterosexual, married, cisgender man of the nineteenth century, his work can hold nothing of value for people who do not fit these identity categories to think about their own liberation. In some versions of this argument, the claim is less about Marx's identity, and more about the limitations of his own work; it is alleged that Marx himself had nothing to say (or not enough to say) about race, gender, or sexuality, and this is taken to be proof that Marxism has nothing productive to contribute to an analysis of these formations. There are multiple issues here to be disentangled. While it is certainly true that Marx did not have a theory of race, gender, or sexuality, this does not mean that he did not write about the ways in which capitalism specifically effected women, children, colonized people, and enslaved people; multiple points in Marx's own writings, both journalistic and academic, evidence a deep and life-long interest in these questions, even if we might now find his answers unsatisfactory. It is also true that writing about women is not the same as having a theory of gender, just as writing about the status of racialized slavery is not the same as having a theory of race or racism. We must hold these apart and refuse to collapse them.

In yet another tendency within this argument, what Marx did say on these issues is taken as evidence of his actual racism, sexism, and/or Eurocentrism. In this version, Marx's comments, especially in his early writings on India and China, are evidence of his Eurocentric, modernist, and progressivist stance. His tone is indeed derisory toward many non-Western formations, and multiple pieces of his empirical analysis have been challenged for accuracy. It is not only his explicit writings that certainly evidence Orientalism and Eurocentrism in multiple places, but also his general commitment to the idea of a linear and progressive model of overcoming capitalism that are used as evidence of his Eurocentrism.

I am not particularly interested in 'saving' Marx from these critiques or in explaining these comments away. There have been multiple scholarly accounts that contextualize, refine, and explain what Marx actually meant in these comments,[16] and some, like Glen Coulthard, argue that many of these beliefs

---

16 | Crystal Batrlovich and Neil Lazarus, eds., *Marxism, Modernity and Postcolonial Studies* (Cambridge, UK ; New York: Cambridge University Press, 2002); Anderson, *Marx at the Margins*.

changed and shifted over Marx's own lifetime.[17] Projects that seek to clarify Marx's own stance are interesting and helpful in their own way, but my own work is focused elsewhere, on thinking about what the potential limitations of Marx's own work mean for the development of Marxism as a perspective and a politics nearly two centuries on. That is to say, there is a certain way in which the Identity Version of this critique does expose real and prescient problems that contemporary Marxists need to confront rather than dismiss. Marx was a product of his own position, his own time, and his own circumstances, as are we all. And, as multiple stands of feminist, critical race, queer, and disability theory have shown us, our vision and understanding is always limited by those circumstances; no one observes from a god's-eye perspective. Marxism has, in certain circles, become Marxology, a kind of fetishistic obsession with *what Marx said* as if he were an oracle rather than a man, as if Marxism were gospel rather than critical tools to be used and deployed in strategic and situated ways. I am more interested in the question: to what extent can texts, authors, ideas, strategies, and tools be useful, even when, perhaps especially when, they were developed under problematic conditions and with aims, language, or methods we would not endorse? To what extent does all Marxism inherit the conceptual problems in Marx, even when they specifically critique those problems, identify alternative modes of conceptualization, and revise Marx's theories?

In the second version, what I call the 'Conditions Version', the focus is less on *Marx* as an individual, but on the way that *Marxism* has developed. In this version of the critique, Marxism was a theory developed in order to explain the particular operation of waged work in nineteenth century factory production, undertaken primarily (though not exclusively) by white men. The argument goes that while Marxism is well-disposed to critique contemporary variations on this formation, it essentially has nothing to say about other arrangements: slavery, racialization, neocolonialism, settler colonialism, etc. That is to say, that the conditions of Marxism's initial development continue to constrain its possibilities for addressing a whole host of pressing problems of oppression, and even constrain its potential for recognizing the existence of problems that are not easily assimilable under this framework. In this sense, Marxists are often accused of (and may indeed sometimes be guity of) subtly re-inscribing white supremacy, Eurocentrism, and androcentrism, by taking European men

---

17 | Coulthard's analysis is particularly instructive on "the normative develop-mentalism that problematically underscored" much of Marx's writing, including his work on colonization. Coulthard argues that "Marx began to reformulate this teleological aspect of his thought in the last decade of his life, and this reformulation has important implications with respect to how we ought to conceptualize the struggles of non-Western societies against the violence that has defined our encounter with colonial modernity." Coulthard, *Red Skin White Masks: Rejecting the Colonial Politics of Recognition*, 9.

as the conceptual anchor, the base of an analogy to which all other positions might differ in degree, but not enough to alter the fundamental appropriateness of using it as the model. In this way, the situations of women, people of color, non-European people, and others are not treated as equally universalizable. No Marxist I know of—or at least, no Marxist in the North—grounds their analysis in, say, the position of Bolivian women, using their situation, the development of capital in Bolivia, its specificities over and against other countries in the Global South, as the base situation from which an analysis of white, European, working class men could be derived, albeit with slight tweaks. It is this asymmetry of universalizability that allows Euro-American-ness, whiteness, masculinity, etc. to continue to masquerade as the standard, the universal, the default in theory, while implicitly conceiving of all the 'others' as excessively 'particular' situations.

Marxist feminism is not wholly immune from this kind of critique. Much of social reproduction feminism, especially in the 1970s and 1980s tended to assume women's confinement to the home as 'housewife', a situation that applied to very few women of color. Social reproduction feminism also took heterosexual coupling, and child-bearing to be hallmarks of 'women's' experience, assuming monogamy, heterosexuality, and reproduction as essential pieces of proletarian femininity in ways that either ignored or marginalized queer, non-monogamous, and non-parent persons. In many versions, both dual system and single systems accounts alike, the problem was not only one of representation, but also one of essentialism; in many of these accounts womanhood was conflated with holding these positions, often specifically with the reproductive capacity to bear children.[18] While this has begun to change somewhat in the recent wave of social reproductive feminism, much earlier theory lacked a thorough analysis of the interracial dynamics between women, especially when women of color are increasingly the caretakers of the families of white women.

In both iterations, the Marxist-feminist and the Eurocentric, the intersectional critique runs deeper than a mere critique of visibility or inclusion. The problem is not only that the assumptions of both models are exclusive or exclusionary (though this too is certainly a problem). Rather, the intersectional critique is focused on the *perspective of enunciation*, that is, that the assumptions, often implicit, one makes about the universalizability of one's theory betray a very particular kind of racial, gendered, and sexualized politics. When, for example, Maria Mies proclaims that 'the housewife is the universal', the intersectional critique is not just that a statement like this marginalizes the

---

18 | For a particularly committed version of biologically-reductive Marxist feminism, see: Shulamith Firestone, *The Dialectic of Sex: The Case for Feminist Revolution* (New York: Farrar, Straus and Giroux, 2003).

experiences of those who actually are not housewives, treating them as ancillary, secondary, or epiphenomenal. The intersectional critique locates itself rather as an intervention into *whose perspective is seen as universalizable* and whose is seen as irreducibly *particular*. The function of statements like this, and of broader trends in Marxist-feminism, is the continuation of the assumption of white working class families as the default, the norm, the unspoken model from which conceptual resources, theories, and analyses are generated, and then applied, stretched, tweaked, or revised in order to account for queer, non-monogamous, non-white, non-family based domestic arrangements. The intersectional critique alerts us to the hidden presumptions of universality and normality that pervade our analyses. The fact is that white, heterosexual, monogamous, nuclear families are themselves *also particular*, just as particular as any other arrangement. This, I think, most social reproduction theorists would readily admit. But intersectionality finds this insight insufficiently digested in much Marxist-feminism.

The intersectional tradition heavily critiques those Marxist accounts that import pre-existing Marxist understandings of the world and merely apply them to 'new' phenomena like gender or race.[19] As Hancock explains, there are

---

19 | Or indeed, to 'new' frameworks, like intersectionality. In one particularly pointed example of this kind of move, David McNally and Sue Ferguson suggest that intersectionality can be absorbed into Marxist social reproduction theory. Arguing that intersectionality contains key insights that Marxism, and specifically social reproduction theory can learn from, they argue that intersectionality provides a convincing image of a "messy experiential world" "that sustain[s] patriarchal, racialized, and settler colonial relations to name but a few." They also credit intersectionality with the insight "that it is impossible to isolate any particular set of oppressive relations from the other." They then argue that in essence, social reproduction theory can replace intersectionality by conserving all of its insights and jettisoning all of its insufficiencies. In this narrative, social reproduction contained the seed of a correct theory of race, gender, class, sexuality, age, nation, and ability (and all of their interconnections), needing only to think more broadly, beyond the narrow phenomena of its initial consideration: the situation of the working class housewife. McNally and Ferguson conclude, "While intersectionality theory has raised important questions, and generated important insights, it tends to flounder at explaining *why* these multiple oppressions exist and are reproduced throughout late capitalism, and at accounting for the *how* of their interaction. Because its approach is holistic and unitary, social reproduction theory is, we think, potentially better equipped in these areas." McNally and Ferguson seem to suggest that the same categories, relations, and theories initially developed to respond to white, working-class, heterosexual, married, cisgender, able-bodied, women (social reproduction theory) can remain essentially unchanged, and respond productively, sensitively, and profoundly to the situation of people who fit none of these social locations. This strategy has been

fundamentally two paths that Marxist understandings of gender have taken: those that seek to "include" a gender perspective within Marx's analysis by applying existing categories to an analysis of gender, and a "second approach, embraced by Black Feminists, Chicana feminists, and feminists not based in the United States, us[ing] historical materialism pioneered by Marx in conjunction with consciousness raising and other methods to reconceputalize the relation between the 'oppressed' and 'oppressor' as multivalent and contingent."[20] For Hancock, Sandra Harding and Nancy Hartsock's versions of feminist standpoint epistemology[21] are indicative of the first path of Marxist feminism, diversifying the identities included within the Marxist critique, but fundamentally failing to jettison them in favor of a conceptual apparatus built in and through a feminist, anti-racist analysis. From Hancock's perspective, the second path is that taken by the Combahee River Collective who do not "seek to merely replicate Marx's methodology on another question (gender equality) or population (Black women), because they seek not to *replace* a class analysis with a race or gender analysis, but instead to *reformulate* the analysis itself."[22] Just as mere inclusion into liberal capitalism is insufficient to generate real emancipation, that mere inclusion of gender, race, sexuality, ability, nationality, immigration status, age, and other axes of oppression into a pre-existing Marxist analysis is also insufficient to overcome the residue of exclusion. I return to this point in Part Three of this book.

The Homogenization of the Proletariat

Intersectionality has also critiqued Marxism's reliance on an overly simplistic characterizations of oppression, grounded in a binary understanding of class relations. A Marxist analysis of capitalism identifies the distinction between capitalists and proletarians, and understands the latter to be exploited (and, in some versions, also oppressed) on this basis. There is an important reason why Marxists do so: ultimately, even when white workers, for example, receive material advantages—increased pay, access to credit, the 'psychological wage'

---

one that intersectionality, as well as many other critical social theories of oppression, have critiqued heavily in Marxism—the idea that context and history is only secondarily, epiphenomenally, or incidentally important to theory. McNally and Ferguson, "Social Reproduction Beyond Intersectionality: An Interview."
20 | Ange-Marie Hancock, *Intersectionality: An Intellectual History*, 1 edition (New York, NY: Oxford University Press, 2016), 87.
21 | Harding, *Whose Science? Whose Knowledge? Thinking from Women's Lives*; Hartsock, "The Feminist Standpoint: Developing the Ground for a Specifically Feminist Historical Materialism."
22 | Hancock, *Intersectionality*, 86.

of which Du Bois spoke, etc.—white supremacy is ultimately not a system designed to benefit poor whites, but rather in order to benefit white capitalists. The ultimate benefit to white capitalists by preventing cross-racial working class solidarity certainly dwarfs the comparatively tiny material advantages white people have in many aspects of their lives. The Marxist analysis, interested in discovering causes and macro-logics, has often emphasized the way in which systems that confer material advantage on parts of the working class do so *only insofar as* they benefit the capitalist class, and do so in exponentially greater terms. Many Marxists worry that by focusing too much on the ways in which working class white people benefit from white supremacy, we will lose the important thread that identifies the 'real' enemy and the real historical reason for white supremacy's invention: the maintenance and reproduction of capitalism.[23]

However, from an intersectional perspective, this is only part of the story. For intersectional theorists, the binary conceptualization of class has too often led Marxists to deny or minimize the ways in which members of the working class themselves participate in and/or materially benefit from systems of oppression, neglecting an analysis of the complicated and contradictory position of working class people as inhabiting both oppressed and oppressive positions within capitalism. As Barbara Smith explains, "As women of color, ... it's often hard for us to believe that we can be both oppressed and oppressive at the same time."[24] One of the central contentions of intersectionality is that each person inhabits this contradiction, and this contradiction itself necessitates its own analysis, as well as its own forms of mobilization and accountability in order to ground truly revolutionary praxis. Recognizing working class complicity in oppression is thus central for the possibilities of organizing effective tools for combatting capitalism.

Intersectionality has also critiqued the binary understanding of class for being too reductive of the diversity of actual, material life situations of proletarianized populations. While it may be true that all proletarianized people live off of their own labor, what this means in terms of life opportunities, dangers, stressors, institutional access and organizations of precarity varies widely

---

23 | Marxists also tend to worry about the way in which engaging in these discussions can muddy the conceptual waters about what *exactly* constitutes a class in the Marxist sense. In many left conversations, the concept is either ill-defined or wrongly conceived. In many cases, class is seen as a sociological category, definable by one's income or wealth, rather than one's position in relation to the means of production. Thinking about class in this way is limited, taking the entire, complex and internally differentiated nature of class relations to be a mere cipher for poverty.

24 | Barbara Smith, ed., *Home Girls: A Black Feminist Anthology* (New York: Kitchen Table Press, 1983), xliii–xliv.

across groups within the working class. For example, Patricia Hill Collins understands the differences in what she calls "social class", which encompasses a variety of other factors and determinants than simply whether or not one owns the means of production: the general character of the relative in/stability of one's life, access to education and the quality of it, access to a variety of consumer choices about housing, food, etc.[25] From many Marxist perspectives, these distinctions are irrelevant to an overall analysis of capitalism. Moreover, it is historically true that these kinds of distinctions (between the poor, the working class, the middle class) have been used as wedges by the ruling elite to undermine solidarity within the proletariat, and there seems to be a trepidation about granting any substance to distinctions that may be used against the 99% in organizing and recognizing common cause. But one should remember here that Collins' insight is not about drawing distinctions at a structural level, but about drawing relative distinctions about the *experiences* and *material realities* of class, especially in times in which these realities have become highly differentiated. This argument is important because it mirrors the work that Collins is doing around race and gender: the black working class experience is not the same as the white working class experience, but naming that difference is actually the fundamental pretext of coalitional politics and solidarity rather than its condition of undoing.

One of the clearest ways to see this dynamic is in the way that, in some left circles, the 'middle class' has become the incarnation of the enemy of liberation. In many of these narratives, it is 'middle class values' that act as the agent of oppression and immiseration of the poor, and 'middle class' itself tends to stand in for a variety of other logics of domination—racism, patriarchy, settler colonialism. The discourse of the middle class in this way is intended, in its best moments, to attest to the ways in which individuals who attain some level of comfort and temporary economic stability can and do enact and reinforce prevailing ideologies of capitalism. It is often people of the sociological middle class that most immediately present themselves as the managers of working class people, as the administrators who control multiple aspects of peoples lives, as the figures of interpersonal power that the most marginalized are likely to come into contact with. There is something important about holding on to this insight: the vast majority of marginalized people simply do not, in their day to day, come into direct contact with the actual bourgeoisie, or the owners of the means of the production; rather, they experience the petty tyrants of the middle class who enforce rules, norms, wage negotiations, hirings and firings, administrative procedures, billing departments, and large array of pencil-pushing and keystroke-entering decisions that have very real, detrimental effects on people's lives. This truth is what is trying to be articulated when *'bourgie'* is

---

25 | Collins, *Black Feminist Thought*.

used as a derogatory description of middle class consumptive habits and most often used to describe people who would not fit the technical description of the bourgeoisie. While there is an important truth moment here, ultimately, this kind of perspective, which blames the 'middle class' for the actions, decisions, and accumulation of the actual bourgeoisie, ultimately hinders a clear and helpful analysis of class itself, misrecognizing the important role of capitalism in perpetuating both exploitation and oppression.

This is not to say that middle class people do not act in ways that perpetuate, maintain, or reinforce oppression—of course they do. So too do working class people, unemployed people, oppressed people, and marginalized people. It is also true that by virtue of serving as a professional class of mediators between the bourgeoisie and the most precarious populations that middle class professionals often have direct power, often highly discretionary, to act according to their own individual biases and prejudice. It is thus important to note that the middle class does then have power to perpetuate prejudice in ways that more precarious people do not. It is also not surprising that the middle class, on the basis of this power, and on the basis of their proximity to precarious people, would be seen to itself be the cause of the norms, structures, and marginalization they enforce. Because middle class professionals often use their own discretion to do so, it is also not surprising that calls for justice and accountability would be directed at them.

However, to argue that middle class people should be held accountable—whatever accountability means in this instance—and to argue that middle class people are themselves the individual or collective architects of the system in which they hold power are rather different propositions. The former perspective, one seen most often in the discourse of the non-Marxist left, has the effect of misattributing the root causes of the structures of exploitation and oppression. It also has the effect of operating at the level of moral and individual discourse ('it's *bourgie* to buy/eat/use/want/etc that'; 'my boss is oppressive') what would more accurately be understood at level of structures of power that the middle class does not ultimately control in the macropolitical sense.

It rather makes more sense to think about the power and discrimination of the middle class as part of the complicated, multifaceted, internally contradictory politics within the working class itself. Doing so allows us to mobilize concepts like Du Bois' 'psychological wage' or Roedigger's 'wages of whiteness' to see how one of capitalism's most constant strategies is the division of the working class, pitting individuals against one another, incentivizing the ideology of competition and zero-sum mentality among them. This is precisely what many analyses of contemporary movement dynamics show us: current immigration reform proponents seek to draw distinctions between 'good' and 'bad' immigrants, 'worthy' or 'unworthy' ones. Feminists have often explained the complicated dynamics, often saturated with class, race, sexuality, and gender-presentation dynamics, that constitute the distinction between 'perfect victims' and the real diversity of experiences and social locations of the real survivors of sexual assault and harassment.

While Marxist analysis has not often mediated on the complex differentiations within the working class in such a way, neither does this kind of analysis strike me as wholly outside the Marxist tradition. It seems to me to be that contemporary Marxist desires to name new subsections of the working class, like the 'precariat', is precisely trying to navigate this same terrain: drawing certain kinds of important distinctions about lived, material realities within the working class. We should also note that this kind of thinking is not entirely foreign to Marxist thinking, as certain distinctions within the working class, like the *lumpenproletariat* and the industrial reserve army, have always been parts of Marxist analysis. What intersectionality demands of class analysis is thus, not the erasure of the very real, structural distinctions between capitalist and proletarian, but rather a concerted, clarified, and more nuanced discussion of the way in which proletarianization is experienced and lived in a variety of ways, often in ways that give certain sectors of the proletariat power and privilege over other parts—and of the way in which that power and privilege is often exercised in petty and oppressive ways.

But moreover, there is a certain tradition of Marxism that is precisely grounded in the understanding that the working class divided, in ways that specifically lead certain elements of the working class to be invested in oppression. That tradition is what might be called the 'Whiteness Studies' group of Marxists. David Roediger's account of race and class takes aim at "activists and labor history scholars whose 'class first' claims reduce social divisions so profoundly as to miss both the gravity of race-based inequality and the reality that much social motion responds to that inequality not because of manipulation by 'middle class' activists, but because of a history of struggles and a present shaped by old and new incarnations of white supremacy."[26] The fact is that "US capitalist management both exploited and reproduced racial division as part of processes of expansion, production, and accumulation"[27] just as much as it has both exploited and reproduced structures of sexism and heteropatriarchy. The history of critical whiteness studies and indeed the formation of the discourse of white privilege itself has a thoroughly Marxist history. Drawing on the insights of many black socialists like Du Bois, C.L.R. James, and James Baldwin, many of the foundational texts of 'whiteness studies' were themselves either explicitly Marxist or at least grounded in a historical materialist project.[28]

---

26 | David R. Roediger, *Class, Race, and Marxism* (London: Verso, 2017), 6.
27 | Roediger, 29.
28 | Theodore W. Allen, *The Invention of the White Race, Volume 1: Racial Oppression and Social Control*, Second Edition edition (London ; New York: Verso, 2012); Theodore

Whiteness Studies' "emergence as an historical materialist project, and partly in the specific context of the Black freedom movement, also warrants elaboration because there is some tendency among academic critics to imagine that the critical study of whiteness issues from postmodernism... even in opposition to Marxism."[29] In the 1960s Theodore Allen began writing about 'white privilege,' which he conceptualized, drawing on Du Bois' account of the "psychological wage", to refer to the many small moments of psychological and material resources offered to white working-class people in order to break their bonds of solidarity with poor and working class black people. In this account, and in contradistinction to many contemporary accounts of white privilege, whiteness here is conceived both as absolutely based in the exploitative system of capitalism *and* therefore offers an account by which poor whites can be properly distinguished from a 'ruling class' who *really* benefits the most from this system and for whom it was created. This Marxist account of white privilege (or, as others like Roediger prefer, 'white advantage'[30]) is able at once to both mark the *complicity* of white working class people in the system of racism without identifying them as *the source* of racial oppression.

This differs from other, more widespread, conceptualizations of white privilege, like those offered by McIntosh and others[31] in a few ways. In the first place, Marxist analyses of privilege evidence a more nuanced analysis of power, holding simultaneously that working class people may indeed hold both material advantages and deep psychological investments in oppression, but they are ultimately neither the cause nor the greatest beneficiaries of systematic oppression. Rather, the capitalist class who benefits from the exploitation of

---

W. Allen, *The Invention of the White Race, Volume 2: The Origin of Racial Oppression in Anglo-America*, Second Edition edition (London ; New York: Verso, 2012); Karen Brodkin, *How Jews Became White Folks and What That Says about Race in America* (New Brunswick, N.J: Rutgers University Press, 1998); Noel Ignatiev, *How the Irish Became White* (New York: Routledge, 2008); George Lipsitz, *The Possessive Investment in Whiteness* (Philadelphia: Temple University Press, 1998); Nell Irvin Painter, *The History of White People* (New York: W. W. Norton & Company, 2010). Saxton was active in the Communist movement of the 1930s in Chicago and was active in labor struggles that specifically affected Asian-Americans. Allen was a member of the Communist Party in West Virginia, where he was also a delegate to the CIO and a labor organizer among miners. Ignatiev, born Ignatin, was a member of Students for a Democratic Society, and then went on to be a central figure in the Sojourner Truth Organization, which positioned itself as a synthesis of Leninism and the work of CLR James.

29 | Roediger, *Class, Race, and Marxism*, 50.
30 | Ibid., 20.
31 | Peggy McIntosh, "White Privilege: Unpacking the Invisible Knapsack," *Independent School* 49, no. 2 (Winter 1990): 31–37.

both white workers and workers of color, moreover benefits from the wedge that racialization places between them. White privilege and white racism are themselves profitable for capitalism, leading both to the further precarity of workers of color and preventing, or at least making more difficult, cross-racial working class alliances. But second, the critical Marxist analysis of whiteness and white privilege levies such an analysis into a particular politics, one grounded in the idea that in order to change the white working class, we must fundamentally alter and ultimately abolish the system of capitalism that incentivizes racism. While it is not representative of intersectionality as a whole, there are certain deployments of 'privilege theory' and 'privilege checking' that suggest that the best we can hope for is a generalized awareness of our social locations. While this awareness is, indeed, deeply necessary, awareness is, from a Marxist perspective, insufficient to counter the structural and hegemonic conditions that produce and reproduce white racism, white ignorance, and white solipsism.

One of the ways in which Marxist accounts of whiteness have often failed is through their separation of race from gender and sexuality, especially in the early years of this line of inquiry. This did, in many ways, contribute to the very problems that intersectionality—and other strands of women of color feminism and queer theory—sought to thematize as crucial to a deep and thorough accounting of these relations. However, a significant body of contemporary Marxism has sought to remedy this problem, revising and critiquing earlier Marxist understandings of racialization to highlight the highly gendered and sexuated dimensions of capitalism's operation. It is also true that many of these Marxist discussions of race have reified a binary of race that takes black-white relations as its founding relation or indeed, sometimes its only manifestation. These are indeed, real and helpful critiques, exposing the places in which Marxist theories of race and racialization have yet to fulfill their nascent potential, and providing the grounding questions through which many of these analyses demand to be reconsidered, altered, and reconceived.

The Politics of Citation

Intersectionality also critiques Marxism's appropriation without recognition of the former's insights. In the best moments, Marxist scholars have sometimes recognized the shared history between the Marxist tradition and the intersectional tradition that I argued for in Chapter 0. However, rather than recognizing that figures are shared between these traditions, that their insights were derived from multiple sites and not only Marxism alone, some Marxist scholars treat everything of value within the intersectional tradition to be an endogamous derivation from the precepts of *Capital*, without any recognition of the variety of influences, experiences, conversations, and organizing spaces that influenced these thinkers. In the worst versions of these politics of citation, black women and women of color are completely absent from some Marxist accounts of intersectionality or their work and insights are mistakenly attributed to white feminist thinkers. For example, in their introduction to a published version of conference proceedings, Lutz, Vivar, and Supik posit Barrett and McIntosh's *The Antisocial Family* as a founding text of intersectionality.[32] Nina Lykke credits Judith Butler with the creation of intersectionality in a variety of texts as well.[33]

In fact, Marxists' persistent association of intersectionality with post-structuralism may itself be part and parcel of what Sirma Bilge calls the "whitening" of intersectionality in which the theory is severed from its founding context of women of color contesting the specific shape of their positions, and posited as the outcome or accomplishment of theories that do not meaningfully center race.[34] In the words of Leslie McCall, "writings by feminists of color... [are] often assimilated into and then associated with the writings of feminist post-structuralists" in ways that attribute the theoretical insights and novelty of the former to the latter.[35] This is one of the ways in which "paradoxically, recognition [of intersectionality] can entail avoidance, even suppression of black women's knowledge, even as it may seem to signal engagement."[36]

Hancock contends that if one is clearly attentive to the actual genealogy of intersectionality, one that locates the intersectional tradition as emerging out of women of color feminisms of the long twentieth century, then the form of power that intersectionality analyzes predates the post-structural turn,

---

32 | Helma Lutz, Maria Theresa Herrera Vivar, and Linda Supik, *Framing Inter-sectionality* (Farnham, UK: Ashgate, 2011), 2.

33 | Lykke, *Feminist Studies: A Guide to Intersectional Theory, Methodology, and Writing*; Nina Lykke, "Intersectional Analysis: Black Box or Useful Critical Feminist Thinking Technology?," in *Framing Intersectionality: Debates on A Multi-Faceted Concept in Gender Studies*, ed. Helma Lutz, Maria Theresa Herrera Vivar, and Linda Supik (Farnham, UK: Ashgate, 2011), 207-21. In perhaps the strangest account of intersectionality's genealogy, Lykke (2010, 128) argues that it is actually Thomas Kuhn and Paul Feyerabend who are responsible for some of the grounding principles of intersectional epistemology.

34 | Sirma Bilge, "Whitening Intersectionality: Evanescence of Race in Intersectionality Scholarship," in *Racism and Sociology: Racism Analysis Yearbook 5-2014*, ed. Wulf D. Hund and Alana Lentin (Berlin: Lit Verlag/Routledge, 2014), 175-205.

35 | McCall, "The Complexity of Intersectionality," 1776.

36 | May, "'Speaking into the Void?: Intersectionality Critiques and Epistemic Backlash," 94.

and many of the concepts of the hallmark theorists of post-structuralism—Foucault, Derrida, Butler, Deleuze, and others.[37]

This is also evident in Marxist accounts that do not meaningfully center race in usages of intersectionality. On Tomlinson's estimation,

> many European social scientists and philosophers [...] appear to find valuable a 'purified' intersectionality, quarantined from its exposure to race. Establishing the Black feminist scholars who originated intersectionality as 'unworthy', parochial, 'race-bound', incapable of 'theorizing' justifies extracting from them the valuable tool of intersectionality. Such justification also reinforces the self-conceptions of racial Europeanization and its construction of its own innocence with regard to its colonial histories and contemporary racism.[38]

While this is most often seen in European appropriations of intersectionality in the academy, it is by no means exclusively bound to that context. Accusations that intersectionality is insufficiently theoretical—often, either explicitly or by implication *because* the theory is centered on black women's experience and identity—also participate in this kind of analysis. Self-styled 'Marxist-realist' Lena Gunnarsson, for example, claims that intersectionality is inherently anti-theoretical, reductive, and naïve because of its "empiricist fixation with physical appearances [read: race] and directly accessible identities."[39]

But Marxists' citational politics can be seen not only in discussions of intersectionality's genealogy, but in broader reconstructions of intersectionality in general. Many of the positions central to intersectionality are often ignored, misread, or not consulted in Marxist work that makes broad, sweeping generalizations about an internally heterogeneous body of theoretical work. What the ubiquitous misreadings suggest to intersectionality scholars is not a merely intellectual problem—it is a political one. As Holly Lewis writes, "Learning about the language an debates inside queer, trans, and feminist political

---

37 | Hancock, *Intersectionality*, 164. The analysis of intersectionality's temporal priority in this regard is contingent on locating the emergence of intersectionality much earlier than the oft-cited 1988-1991 chronology, which is itself a contentious claim within intersectional theorists themselves. May, for example, argues that embracing Hancock's timeline has the effect of diminishing Crenshaw's particular articulation and theorization to a mere 'coining' of the term, which, on her account, walks dangerously close to willfully misrecognizing or suppressing the ingenuity and importance of her contribution.

38 | Barbara Tomlinson, "Colonizing Intersectionality: Replicating Racial Hierarchy in Feminist Academic Arguments," *Social Identities* 19, no. 2 (2013): 266.

39 | Lena Gunnarsson, "A Defense of the Category 'Women,'" *Feminist Theory* 12, no. 1 (2011): 27.

movement is... the *concrete* practice of solidarity," the basic and minimal gesture that the positions, experiences, ideas, and insights of oppressed people are important and valued, theoretically and politically.[40] In this sense, the often abysmal citational politics of Marxist engagements with intersectionality evidence a political disinterest or instrumentalization of women of color in not only the theoretical approach to understanding capitalism, but also the political strategy inherent in such an approach.[41]

None of this should suggest that an accurate historical genealogy of the intersectional tradition should omit Marxist texts or those written by white scholars altogether; indeed, it is a central contention of this book that there was far more dialogue, overlap, and cross-pollination between the intersectional tradition and many other theories of liberation than is often acknowledged. Rather, it is to say that narratives of intellectual inheritance are not only theoretical questions, but political ones. This is what many intersectional scholars call "the politics of citation." In erasing or diminishing the contributions of women of color to intersectionality, by decentering race from the theory and its applications, and by supposing that all of the insights of the intersectional tradition were simply waiting *in nuce* in Marxism, many of the Marxist scholars writing about the intersectional tradition have participated in a subtle and insidious form of undermining the position of women of color—and calling this 'solidarity'. It is this kind of move and theoretical posturing that often makes intersectional theorists skeptical of Marxism: intersectional scholars see their work and the work of women of color generally being co-opted or diluted, being turned into straw-person versions of itself, and they (unsurprisingly) wonder about the 'real' commitments of not just the individual scholars engaging in these practices, but also about the theoretical framework in whose name bad citational politics are ostensibly mobilized.

---

40 | Lewis, *The Politics of Everybody*, 24.

41 | By this I do not mean to suggest that Marxists with poor citational politics *are the same as* those who create and maintain the structures that devalue, marginalize, oppress, and exploit women of color. Between the structural enactment of violence and the failure to recognize all of its subtle and quotidian arrangements, there can be no equivalence. While in some left spaces, there is the tendency to equate these, I think this is a mistake. While I see and understand the logic of such equivalence—the reproduction of oppression is central to its structure and hence not easily or cleanly separable—I think we must insist on the qualitative difference between the active fabrication and profit from systematic oppression and the failure to live up to the highest vision of dismantling that oppression.

CONCLUSION

This chapter has looked at some of the most common intersectional critiques of Marxism. In it, as in Chapter Two, which looked at Marxist critiques of intersectionality, I focused on the philosophical and theoretical divergences, misunderstandings, and disalignments between the perspectives. In both of these chapters, I have spoken rather little of disagreements over organizing, strategy, and resistance, though the intersectional tradition and the Marxist tradition approach agitation and organizing often also in divergent ways. In particular, intersectional thinkers have also argued that Marxist conceptions of resistance are overly rigid for inadequately thinking about the myriad ways oppressed people respond to, challenge, and undermine their own oppression; in this way, intersectionality argues that it "provid[es] an important corrective to Marxist constructions of power that underestimate the value of everyday acts of resistance."[42] While there is certainly a tendency within especially Marxist organizing to conceive of resistance in only one way—as collective, visible agitation, often specifically into communist and/or socialist parties and workplace unions—the last chapter of this text seeks to think about what organizing in a truly Marxist and intersectional way might look like.

In order to build up to thinking about organizing in this way, all of the chapters of Part Three seek to harness the insights of both the Marxist and the intersectional traditions in order to think beyond the current debates. As we have seen in the previous chapters, many of the debates rage on shifting terrain, as contemporary work is being done constantly and all the time to bring the projects of intersectionality and Marxism into real conversation, not only around their differences, but about what they could contribute in real, loving conversation.

---

42 | Hancock, *Intersectionality*, 116.

Part Three: Possibilities

Chapter Five: Oppression and Exploitation Beyond Reductions

Thinking productively about Marxism and intersectionality together requires a deep and thoughtful investigation of how oppression and exploitation relate to one another. As demonstrated in earlier chapters, both traditions evidence helpful insights in constituting this relation, but these insights must be synthesized in order to chart a full and robust theory of how capitalism *actually works* and how contemporary theories might be mobilized to intervene and unseat it.

One of the perennial problems in understanding the relationship between exploitation and oppression is the tendency to reify both, treating each category as internally unified. As previous chapters have clarified, however, exploitation is constituted in a variety of irreducibly different ways, as is oppression. In this sense, theorizing the relationship between exploitation and oppression must be thought as explaining the relation between internally heterogeneous categories. In speaking about exploitation and oppression in this chapter, I do not mean at all to suggest that all oppressions are constituted in the same way nor that all structures of exploitation are. Rather, as we will see in the conclusion to this chapter, oppression and exploitation take on a variety of structures, forms, and histories; giving a general understanding of the relationship between these forms should not be taken as an attempt to define in advance any of those arrangements or to detract from the absolutely necessary empirical and historical work that tracing any particular conjunction between oppression and exploitation requires. As Iris Marion Young argues, beyond a general assertion that oppressed groups are structurally consigned to some form of domination, "in any specific sense, it is not possible to define a single set of criteria that describe the condition of oppression" of various groups.[1] Likewise, exploitation names an internally heterogeneous category; while all exploited people suffer from the condition of having their labor and its products stolen from them, this can occur in multiple configurations, under a variety of conditions, buoyed

---

1 | Young, 40.

by a diverse set of institutions, narratives of justification, and social practices. The complexities of both exploitation and oppression, while often beautifully rendered in discussions of each concept alone, are rarely conserved in theories of their relation. What often passes for robust theories unwittingly reproduces each term as singular. But generating a deep and expansive understanding of capitalism requires discussing the relationship between these sets of differences. Part Two of this book explored the dangers of erasing the differential constitution of exploitation and oppression separately. This chapter seeks to articulate a mode of conceiving the relation of exploitation and oppression that holds each in the complexity earlier chapters exposed as necessary. In this sense, it may be helpful to ground this discussion in Glen Sean Coulthard's notion that structures of domination are not "things" with stable identities, but are rather "the sum[s] of interlocking oppressive social relations that constitute [them]."[2]

Thinking about both exploitation and oppression as names for wide sets of social relations exposes the insufficiency of multiple previous attempts, from both the Marxist and the intersectional traditions, to think their relation. This chapter focuses on debates around how to conceive of this relation. In order to do so, this chapter has three sections. The first section examines three different ways that their relationship has been discussed or understood. This section ultimately argues for two positions: first, that exploitation and oppression refer to different kinds of phenomena and second, that both exploitation and oppression are necessary analytics in order to adequately understand the operations of race, gender, sexuality, and class under contemporary capitalism. The second section traces the outline of a provisional theory that might do justice to this perspective. Drawing on and clarifying the intersectional postulate of the non-hierarchy of oppressions, I argue that we should apply this principle to the relationship between oppression and exploitation. The third section returns to the concept of class, explaining why reconceiving class as *both* an exploitation and an oppression clarifies both how class works and how it is imbricated in the workings of gender, race, and sexuality.

SECTION ONE: TRACING THE RELATIONSHIP BETWEEN EXPLOITATION AND OPPRESSION

In order to clarify the relationship of exploitation and oppression, it is helpful to broadly explain three different paradigms that Marxism and/or intersectionality have offered. While ultimately each of the following three positions prove insufficient to render the complicated relays of oppression and exploita-

---

2 | Coulthard, *Red Skin, White Masks*, 15.

tion under contemporary capitalism, understanding the limitations discloses what a fuller theory would require, a theory developed in a later section in the chapter.

Exploitation Produces Oppression

One of the most common Marxist frameworks for thinking about the relationship of exploitation and oppression is that, either historically or logically (or both), exploitation *produces* oppression. In this conceptualization, it is the ultimate interests of those with material resources and power that create, perpetuate, and maintain oppression. The capitalist class requires racism and hetero/sexism in order to continue to produce some populations as disposable, and therefore more vulnerable to ever-more exploitable conditions. There are two related but nonetheless distinct versions of this argument.

Version A posits oppression as a tool that capitalism uses, but argues that exploitation is fundamental to the logic of capitalism, whereas oppression is not; rather, oppression is a tool of convenience under capitalism, which may be historically important, but it ultimately only holds empirical rather than structural significance. David Harvey has marked a distinction between "capitalism" and "capital" that has framed much of his work in relationship to gender, race, and class. Harvey readily acknowledges that multiple forms of oppression are absolutely central, constitutive features of capitalism, the historically existing politico-economic structure. However, he argues that capital is a certain kind of logic, which is essentially and at its core, independent of race, gender, and sexuality, but not class. In his response to Alex Dubilet, he argues on this basis that "none of these other struggles should transcend or supercede that against capital and its contradictions," by which he means struggles against forms of oppression.[3] This is a similar position to the one taken by Ellen Meiksins Wood, who argues that "class exploitation is *constitutive* of capitalism whereas gender or racial inequality are not."[4]

This distinction is intended to mark out historical contingencies of internal logics. In one sense, marking these distinctions are actually quite useful for looking at the ways in which capitalism has manifested differently throughout

---

3 | David Harvey, "Response to Alex Dubilet," *Syndicate*, April 1, 2015, https://syndicate.network/symposia/theology/seventeen-contradictions-and-the-end-of-capitalism/; David Harvey, *Seventeen Contradictions at the End of Capitalism* (Oxford and New York: Oxford University Press, 2015).

4 | Ellen Meiksins Wood, "The Uses and Abuses of Civil Society," in *The Retreat of the Intellectuals: Socialist Register 1990*, ed. Ralph Miliband and Leo Panitch (London: Merlin Press, 1990), 76; Ellen Meiksins Wood, "Capitalism and Human Emancipation," *New Left Review*, no. 167 (February 1988).

history or in different ways at the same time: it is the logic rather than the contingency that allows us to see that there is something called 'capitalism' which does not have to follow a single path, but that can be flexible in response to local conditions, the swerve of history, and a variety of conditions. The important insight here is one that is worth noting and holding on to, namely, it comes directly out of an impulse to be able to attend to historical and regional specificity and variability, in other words, to be able to think capitalism more expansively and in a way that does not erase the differences of custom, circumstance, and contingency that characterize certain more rigid forms of Marxist theory. I disagree with the way Harvey affiliates oppression to capitalism rather than capital, but I do agree that a distinction between capitalism and capital has its use.

Meiksins Wood and Harvey's argument that capital's logic is oppression-neutral perpetuates two distinct errors. First, it presumes that it is possible to separate history and logic, material and theory. This premise reifies the idea that capitalism is wholly constituted in and through the appropriation of surplus value, but, of course, this is the very question to be answered. As Cinzia Arruzza has recently shown through a close reading of Meiksins Wood, ultimately this position makes use of the very distinctions it must disavow.[5] On its own terms, this position cannot account for how it decides which features of actually-existing capitalisms belong to the contingencies of history and which belong to the essential logic or structure of capital. This answer classically begs the question. If the question on the table is whether oppression is central to capitalism, to say 'no, because capital is, by my definition, not about oppression' answers very little. But this is not only or even primarily a logical or semantic problem. There has never been a capitalist society that has not relied on gender, race, and sexuality as central structures of exploitation, dispossession, accumulation, and violence. If a distinction between capital and capitalism intends to give us tools to understand the historical variation of capitalist forms, it is strange that one of its most common features is dubbed "merely empirical," without any significance for thinking the logic of capital beyond its historical contingency.

But moreover, the idea that the logic of capitalism is somehow only about exploitation is precisely the principle of class reductionism, in the sense that exploitation is seen not only as the root historical cause of oppression, but also as its only or primary animus for its perpetuation. In some thinkers and activists, this leads to the conclusion that simply eliminating exploitation would naturally, indeed magically, eliminate all oppressions in their various forms by uprooting its ultimate cause or justification. This position thus seems incapable of thematizing the ways in which oppression is organized over and

---

5 | Arruzza, "Remarks on Gender."

beyond market mechanisms or how, indeed, oppression can, at times, function to disrupt the accumulation of capital. The problem with this approach, in assuming the universal and direct causal provenance of economic structures of exploitation, are well documented in the variety of critiques of class reductionism that we examined in earlier chapters. A non-reductionist reading of what capitalism might look like is outlined in the concluding section to this chapter.

Version B of this position is more nuanced and complicated. It locates the logic of oppression, historically and/or theoretically in the interests of capitalist accumulation, but in a way that cannot exactly be reduced to exploitation. I take the 'production of difference' approach, as exemplified by Roediger, Esche, and Lowe to be paradigmatic of this kind of approach.[6] In Lowe's understanding, the fundamental relationship between exploitation and oppression is constituted through capitalism's manufacture of difference in order to increase its ability to accumulate. She explains, "In the history of the United States, capital has maximized its profits …precisely through the social productions of 'difference.'"[7] This position is also taken up by Guyanese activist and academic Walter Rodney. In his explanation of the source of racial oppression, he argues:

It can be affirmed without reservations that the white racism which came to pervade the world was an integral part of the capitalist mode of production[…] European planters and miners enslaved Africans for *economic* reasons, so that their labor power could be exploited[…] Europeans at home and abroad found it necessary to rationalize that exploitation in racist terms as well. Oppression follows logically from exploitation so as to guarantee the latter. Oppression of African people on purely racial grounds accompanied, strengthened, and became indistinguishable from oppression for economic reasons.[8]

In Rodney's account, which is in some ways similar to Roediger, Esche, and Lowe's, oppression emerges as a tool of capitalist exploitation. Rodney's helpfully highlights how oppression strengthens exploitation not only in a material sense, but also as an ideological tool, guaranteeing the possibility of reproducing and justifying practices of exploitation over time. Rodney's analysis also specifically foregrounds the eventual indistinction of these systems as they

---

6 | David R. Roediger and Elizabeth D. Esch, *The Production of Difference: Race and the Management of Labor in U.S. History* (Oxford University Press, 2012); Lisa Lowe, *Immigrant Acts: On Asian American Cultural Politics* (Durham, NC: Duke University Press, 1996).

7 | Lowe, *Immigrant Acts: On Asian American Cultural Politics*, 27.

8 | Walter Rodney, *How Europe Underdeveloped Africa* (Washington, D.C.: Howard University Press, 1982), 223-35.

become totally intermeshed over time. However, as much as experientially or even structurally in the contemporary world, oppression and exploitation for Rodney are totally enmeshed, Rodney's analysis evidences a position based in the clear causal and historical priority of exploitation as the ground and condition of oppression.

That capitalism makes use of oppression as a tool of accumulation can hardly be in doubt. In this sense, Rodney, Lowe, and others who emphasize this relationship bring to light a centrally important way that oppression and exploitation relate. However, this explanation is only a partial one, bringing into relief only one of the many ways in which exploitation and oppression are related under contemporary capitalism. In this way, the "production of difference" approach does not constitute an adequate analysis of the relationship between exploitation and oppression in all of its forms, though it does provide invaluable insight into one aspect of their linkage. In order to illustrate the limitations of this analysis for adequately conceiving of the relationship between exploitation and oppression, I highlight three other ways in which this relation occurs *in addition* to the production of difference.

Firstly, the production of difference is inadequate to explain moments in which the logic of oppression and the logic of exploitation can diverge. In thinking about the contemporary politics of migration and border policing, the racist and neocolonial panic around undocumented immigration has led to increased fear in migrant communities of incarceration and deportation. In one sense, the produced vulnerability of undocumented workers certainly bolsters the ability of capital to exploit social disempowerment to offer even lower pay, with higher productivity quotas, under worse conditions; it creates the conditions in which increased levels of exploitation are even less likely to be contested and fought against, as insecurity on the part of undocumented communities grows. However, amid heightened regimes of policing, multiple industries that disproportionately rely on undocumented labor have been reporting massive losses: in the agricultural industry, ripe Californian crops lay rotting in the fields because levels of anti-immigrant policy have reached such heights that many undocumented people have stopped working to harvest them. In this sense, the oppressive obsession with documentation, increased xenophobia, and racist hyper-policing have become in some cases so great as to undercut and prevent the exploitative labor relation. The oppression of undocumented immigrants both actively constructs their vulnerability to capitalist exploitation and in some cases prevents that very exploitation, inhibiting the accumulation of profit. The production of difference approach may be able to helpfully render the first phenomenon, but it is inadequate to explain social and political commitments to oppression that come at financial losses to the capitalist class.

Secondly, the production of difference approach cannot generate an adequate account of the relations between capitalism and oppression that are not reducible to exploitation in the classical sense. As Coulthard and other theorists of settler colonization argue, exploitation simply cannot capture the specific shape of indigenous peoples' domination under capitalism. As Coulthard explains, "the history and experience of dispossession, not proletarianization, has been the dominant" experience of capitalism for indigenous peoples in settler colonial states.[9] When considering the various forms of contemporary oppression to which indigenous people are subjected, the production of difference approach elides the connections that oppressions may have to capitalism that are not immediately or most prominently related to exploitation. Of course, this does not suggest that exploitation has been absent in the history of settler colonization; it only insists that exploitation is not the total or complete framework to understand the continued and ongoing oppression of indigenous people. The case of indigenous dispossession is an illustrative example of the ways in which exploitation may not be sufficient to capture the multiplicity of ways that oppression relates to capitalism, but it is far from the only such site.[10]

Lastly, if oppression is a mere tool of exploitation, this suggests that one cannot be oppressed without being exploited, or at least, that *a group* cannot be oppressed without also being exploited. This position presents difficulties when trying to think adequately about individuals from oppressed groups who are part of the capitalist class. For example, how are we to understand the oppression of racialized business owners or postcolonial elites? How are we to understand heterosexism in the lives of women and queer capitalists, especially when they are neither subject to workplace exploitation or to the exploitation of their socially reproductive labor (when, for example, they live alone, pay others to do this labor, and/or have partners who perform this labor)? In order to interpret these scenarios, there seem to be a few avenues that one could take. In the first place, one could argue that on a structural level, racism and heterosexism are based in exploitation, even when the individual experiencing oppression is not exploited. In other words, one might say that the widespread nature of rape culture is based in the entitlement men have to women's bodies, which is necessary in order to perpetuate the expectation that women do socially repro-

---

9 | Coulthard, *Red Skin, White Masks*, 13.
10 | Contemporary debates about 'informality' also bring this question into relief, where relations of domination are not always modeled precisely on capitalist modes of exploitation and yet is structurally produced in and through capitalism. Another site that might expose this problem comes through what Sayak Valencia has called 'gore capitalism', in which capitalism is committed to the continued production of death and dismemberment in ways that cannot be easily subsumed under the exigencies of exploitation.

ductive labor; if women of the capitalist class are also raped, beaten, harassed, told to smile, or subject to sexist micro-aggressions, this is ultimately a kind of spill over or collateral damage effect of the supposedly real logic of oppression. This is the kind of analysis offered, for example, by Maria Mies, who argues that, on the basis of the sexual, racist, and international divisions of labor, all women, regardless of their empirical class position, become treated *as if* they were subjected to the exploitation of their reproductive labor, whether or not they individually hold such a position in their households.[11] Likewise, one might argue that if racialized capitalists are still subjected to police brutality or to racist micro-aggressions, this is ultimately because all racialized subjects become treated *as if* they held exploited positions, due to the way in which the images, narratives, and social scripts of racialization have sedimented the idea that to hold an exploitable position is what it means to be a person of color.

While there are merits to this position, and configurations in which it might prove a useful or fruitful mode of analysis, intersectional theorists have long warned about the dangers of analogizing various organizations of oppression, of modeling analyses of some social positions on others. In doing so, analogical theories occlude the differential ways in which oppression is produced, organized, lived, and experienced, obscuring the multiplicity of (potentially contradictory) ways in which oppression constitutes contemporary capitalism. By wholly subsuming oppression within the capitalist class under the model of oppression within the working class, we lose the ability to truly meditate on the fundamental contradictions that capitalism produces, minimizing the specificities, differences, and nuances of the way that capitalism is constructed. This understanding has been reflected in certain Marxist feminist analyses as well, who have long recognized that the working class family serves different functions under capitalism than does the ruling class family; analyzing oppression in one case as the model for others covers over the specific conjunctions that constitute the multiple ways capitalism depends on oppression. For reasons returned to in Chapter 6, the deepest understanding of capitalism, and indeed one most faithful to the insights of both the intersectional and the Marxist traditions, must take the moments of rupture, complication, counter-intuitive linkage, and contradiction as paradigmatic rather than accidental moments of capitalism; indeed, it is through probing the moments of contradiction that the structure of capitalism is most effectively unlocked, a possibility foreclosed by the position that exploitation ultimately structures the logic of oppression under capitalism.

---

11 | Mies, *Patriarchy and Accumulation On A World Scale*.

Exploitation is a Form of Oppression

By contrast, intersectional theorists often view exploitation as a kind of oppression or as an instrument of oppression. Exploitation emerges as just one of many mechanisms that those with power use in order to conserve their wealth, power, and authority in all spheres of life. Broadly, this position is implied by accounts that treat class as an oppression, which is true of many intersectional approaches. We can see this in Patricia Hill Collins' definition of oppression:

> Oppression describes any unjust situation where, systematically and over a long period of time, one group denies another group access to the resources of society. Race, class, gender, sexuality, nation, age and ethnicity among others constitute major forms of oppression in the United States.[12]

While in this particular passage, Collins does not name exploitation specifically, she does use the term consistently in *Black Feminist Thought* in order to name one of the key mechanisms and structures that produce both class oppression and poverty more generally. What is clear in Collins' definition, and more generally in her approach, is that oppression is the key term or the genus, of which exploitation is one mode, one strategy, one situation, one organization, among a whole host of others.

It is, however, interesting to note that there are some, if few, Marxists who embrace this position as well. This position is perhaps best exemplified by Erik Olin Wright and Iris Marion Young.[13] In *Justice and the Politics of Difference*, Young argues that oppression is constituted through five "faces" of oppression, that are empirically and experientially interwoven, yet analytically distinct.[14]

---

12 | Collins, *Black Feminist Thought*, 4.
13 | Erik Olin Wright, *Interogating Inequality* (London: Verso, 1994); Erik Olin Wright, *Class Counts* (London: Verso, 1997).
14 | Young, *Justice and the Politics of Difference*, chap. 2. It is important to note that exploitation is not the only face of oppression for Young that specifically relates to capitalism. On her account marginalization is specifically a labor process; marginality names "people the system of labor cannot or will not use" specifically including the elderly, the disabled, and some racialized groups, especially of racialized young men (Young 53). In more technical Marxist vocabulary, 'marginalization' might be called a 'surplus population', a 'reserve army of labor', or the 'lumpenproletariat.' The third face of oppression, powerlessness, is specifically related to the ways in which social assignation of authority, worth, and access to decision-making power is distributed under capitalism through one's position in the labor market; through both the actual structure of the working conditions of the 'professional class' and the social signifiers of wealth, power, education and authority that comes from being a member of that class, one has

She contends that a social group is oppressed if, with some consistency and systematicity, members of that group are subjected to one or more of the following processes: exploitation, marginalization, powerlessness, cultural imperialism, and violence. After a reconstruction of Marx's account of exploitation, Young explains that exploitation is a kind of oppression because it "enacts a structural relation between social groups...about what work is, who does what for whom, how work is compensated, and the social process by which the results of work are appropriated operate to enact relations of power and inequality."[15] For Erik Olin Wright, exploitation is likewise a particular form of oppression. Exploitation, he argues, is indeed one form of economic oppression (though by far, not the only one); however, non-exploitative oppression, which for Wright is characteristic of settler colonial society's genocidal treatment of indigenous people, must also be recognized: "In the case of non-exploitative oppression, the oppressors would be happy if the oppressed simply disappeared...Genocide is thus always a potential strategy for non-exploitative oppressors."[16] As this passage points towards, the general structure of power distribution is rather different between exploitation and oppression. Under exploitation, power is distributed such that, in the ultimate calculus, it is the workers who have the power, even if they may not feel it, experience it, or understand it to be true. It is ultimately the bourgeoisie that is dependent on the proletariat for all of the work: the common strike slogan 'You don't need the boss; the boss needs you!' is simply another way of rendering this central aspect of the relation of exploitation. By contrast, oppression does not necessarily imply the same form of dependency of oppressor on oppressed, though this may occur in some configurations.

The idea that oppression either causes exploitation or that oppression is the genus for which exploitation is the species had a variety of benefits. In the first place, it avoids the problems of economic reductionism explored in some of the other approaches to thinking this relationship. It is thus better poised to examine modes of oppression that seemed far removed from economic factors. For Young, for example, cultural imperialism and violence refer to modes of

---

access to both formal and informal channels of relative autonomy, input into collective decision making, and often, individualized power over employees, contractors, service providers, or service-users. In this sense, it should not be alleged that Young's account is in any way not tethered to the material configuration of life under capitalism or that her account ignores class relations. Rather, "these three categories refer to structural and institutional relations that delimit people's material lives, including but not restricted to the resources they have access to and the concrete opportunities they have or do not have to develop and exercise their capacities" (Young 58).
15 | Young, 50.
16 | Wright, *Interrogating Inequality*, 40.

oppression that are not reducible to employment, income, class, or position in a society's organization of production. One of the key difficulties of Marxist accounts of oppression is often how to think about elements of oppression that are not immediately or apparently linked to issues of class exploitation. This is not to say that Marxists cannot or do not account for non-economic forms of oppression, only that these accounts are relatively less frequent than discussions of oppression that have a clear and direct tie to work, employment, poverty, or a variety of other 'economic' factors. This approach seems also able to sensitively intertwine the personal and the political, giving due attention not only to the structures of oppression, but also to the ways that oppression is experienced, personally, intimately, psychologically, and on a very human level.

However, by placing exploitation as either the outcome of oppression or as a subset of oppression, we are liable to lose the specific explanatory potential of exploitation as a unique structure. Exploitation clarifies a particular organization of force and power within capitalist society in which the vast majority of human beings produce the wealth in society but do not benefit from this wealth. Given that nearly every area of social life is market-mediated under capitalism, systematic exploitation uniquely effects all areas of life: health, education, art, cultural life, religion, and recreation in addition to fundamental questions about food, housing, and social reproduction. Under capitalism, exploitation performs a particularly insidious function: it makes relationships of inequality *appear* as though an equal exchange has taken place. Because a worker receives a wage and has 'consented' to work in exchange for this wage, it seems as though working relationships are fair, even as they are structured under hierarchical relationships. However, because it is the capitalist that benefits from this exchange in the form of profit, waged relationships systematically hide the ways in which workers produce value for which they remain uncompensated. Exploitation thus explains two things uniquely: on the one hand, it explains how wealth is actually created within capitalist society, something that analyses of oppression might gesture toward but do not systematically explain. On the other hand, an understanding of exploitation acts as a theoretical lever to understand how notions of equality continue to perpetuate unequal relationships, one of the key contradictions of capitalist society.[17]

Oppression and Exploitation are Completely Different

Another framework for approaching the relationship between oppression and exploitation posits that these are fundamentally different structures. In forms such as these, exploitation is primarily a phenomenon in and about work

---

17 | The centrality of contradiction to capitalist society will explored more thoroughly in Chapter Six.

(whether waged or unwaged), while oppression refers to the vast interconnected systems of social and political power, legibility, visibility, and violence to which some groups are subjected. Versions of this argument can be found in both intersectional scholarship and in Marxist work. From a Marxist perspective, this position is most often taken by those who espouse dual, triple, or multiple systems theories.[18] These approaches argue that capitalism is a system rooted in economic exploitation and that it interacts with other systems of oppression, like racism or heteropatriarchy, but that these latter are fundamentally distinct from the logic of capitalism (and, indeed, in multiple versions, distinct from one another). Multiple systems theory did have the benefit of not reducing oppression to exploitation or vice versa, and of being able to conceptualize the ways in which multiple modes of oppression predated the rise of capitalism. However, multiple systems theory has been critiqued for many of the same reasons that the double, triple, and multiple jeopardy approach also has: in separating these systems, it becomes difficult if not impossible to see their co-constitution. Indeed, for many theorists of both Marxist and intersectional varieties, these approaches fundamentally elide the ways in which race, gender, sexuality, and class are tied together. Marxist thinkers in particular have criticized multiple systems theory for endorsing a view of capitalism that treats racism, sexism, and homophobia as inessential to the logic of capital accumulation.

Section Two: The Equiprimordiality of Oppression and Exploitation

Rather than fall back onto any of the positions sketched above, integrating the insights of Marxism and intersectionality calls for an altogether different understanding of the relationship between exploitation and oppression in order to understanding how gender, race, sexuality, and class are constituted under capitalism. In this section, I unpack the various meanings of intersectionality's refusal to rank oppressions in order to explain a mode of relation that falls prey neither to reductionism nor to opposition. While intersectional theorists do not use this mode of relation, what I call "equiprimordiality," to thematize the relationship between exploitation and oppression, I argue that it most adequately reflects the constitution of capitalism.

As discussed in Chapter One, one of the essential differences between intersectionality and many other theories of oppression is the insistence on irreducible and equal importance of race, class, gender, and sexuality. This

---

18 | Sylvia Walby, *Gender Segregation at Work* (Open University Press, 1988); Heidi Hartman, "The Unhappy Marriage of Marxism and Feminism," in *Women and Revolution*, ed. Lydia Sargent (Boston: South End Press, 1981).

insight marked a radical departure from previous theories that had sought to rank or hierarchize forms of marginalization which were common, even in many theories that foregrounded the importance of multiple axes of oppression. While this position is widely shared among intersectional theorists, there is considerable difference in how and why intersectional scholars reject what Audre Lorde calls the "hierarchy of oppressions"[19] and what Elizabeth Martínez terms the "Oppression Olympics."[20] In some versions of this argument, the equality of oppressions is an "ontological" statement[21]; it is a description of how the world functions. Some defend this descriptive equality on the basis that pain or oppression cannot be 'measured' in any reliable way, that because oppressions are mutually constitutive, it would be impossible to pull them apart such that, for example, a woman of color could rank whether she is oppressed worse or more often by race or gender.[22]

In another version, the equality of oppressions is a *strategic* argument. It holds that ranking oppressions as a political and intellectual project contributes to counterproductive arguments that shift the emphasis away from understanding how oppressions are co-constituted and how multiple groups of people are oppressed (in different ways) by the same structures of power, instead contributing to internal factionalization and marginalization within social movements. If we spend all of our time trying to develop criteria for which oppressions are worst or which are most fundamental, we will, at the end of the day, have done very little to advance the struggle for justice, solidarity, and the transformation of the conditions that produce, maintain, and perpetuate oppression. As Martínez writes, "Pursuing some hierarchy of competing oppressions leads us down dead-end streets where we will never find the linkage between oppressions or how to overcome them." It is not, she continues, "an effective strategy."[23] In this sense, the refusal to rank oppressions operates more as a heuristic or an axiom than a description; as an intellectual commitment, its ultimate fidelity is to *what best builds power* among oppressed people.

In both versions, the rejection of ranking oppressions is based in understanding inter-group and inter-positional relationships as being based in a form of difference that does not necessitate, and indeed militates against, subsuming variation under modes of primacy. As Angela Davis reminds us, "There are

---

19 | Lorde, *Zami*.
20 | Angela Y. Davis and Elizabeth Martínez, "Coalition Building Among People of Color," *Inscriptions* 7 (1994), https://culturalstudies.ucsc.edu/inscriptions/volume-7/angela-y-davis-elizabeth-martinez/.
21 | Ange-Marie Hancock, *Intersectionality: An Intellectual History*, 1 edition (New York, NY: Oxford University Press, 2016), 97.
22 | Smith and Smith, "Across the Kitchen Table: A Sister-to-Sister Dialogue," 116.
23 | Martínez, "Beyond Black/White: The Racisms of Our Time," 22.

more options than sameness, opposition, or hierarchical relations."[24] One of these options is precisely what intersectionality shows is possible through what is often called the "equality of oppressions," but what in this analysis I call "equiprimordiality." Though it is more common in the literature and in activist spaces to use the term equality of oppressions, this terminology seems to imply that all oppressions are *equal* in a more robust sense than equally important or equally relevant, suggesting they might be *equal* in the sense of resembling one another or being constituted in equivalent ways. "Equality" tends to generate the impression of a sense of sameness that runs counter to intersectionality's important understanding of how oppressions are organized in non-analogous ways.

Moreover, there have also been some ways in which the equality of oppressions has produced some confusion around how to read moments in which certain relations appear to be more dominant than others. When Eric Garner was killed by New York Police, it is evident that race and racism are some of the most important factors in that story, in ways that class or sexuality might not seem to be. In this sense, equality of oppressions should not be construed to mean that in every instance, every axis of oppression is equally present. However, the interconnectedness of race with gender, sexuality, and class means that even though, in this particular instance, race has an important emphasis, a full or complete picture of Eric Garner's death would not be complete without understanding the gendered, sexual, and class politics of his murder by NYPD. Garner was approached while selling cigarettes on the street; class is surely important in explaining how and why he was engaged in that activity; class is also important in understanding while NYPD care more about a man selling cigarettes than they ever have about crimes committed by the capitalist class and in explaining how police departments in the US have been rapidly shifting toward policing so-called "lifestyle" crimes that are both racialized and classed. We might also draw attention to the gender politics of Garner's case, how black masculinity in particular has been constructed as predatory and violent, and how those dynamics inflect police use of lethal force. All of this is to say that it is both true that race has an especially important role to play in understanding this particular case, and that, because of the way that race is structured through gender, class, and sexuality, all of these factors are all also relevant, though not exactly relevant in the same way.

Given some of these complications with the term equality, I prefer to think of the relationship between oppression and exploitation as 'equiprimordial.' Primordial here has the sense of being fundamental, of being of or related to the root or structure. Rather than saying that oppressions are 'equal', it is more accurate to say that they are equally fundamental, equally deep-rooted, and

---

24 | Davis and Martínez, "Coalition Building Among People of Color."

Chapter Five: Oppression and Exploitation Beyond Reductions   199

equally anchoring of the contemporary world. Equiprimordiality can render the deep, complex, and multi-directional relations between exploitation and oppression in ways that refuse the reductive moments of other approaches. To trace what the analytic of equiprimordiality might offer, it might be helpful to look at a particular historical example, that of racialized chattel slavery.

As many have argued, it is impossible to generate an analysis of slavery without an economic component that places the exploitation of labor for the purpose of extracting profit at the center; in other words, racialized exploitation is absolutely central to this analysis.[25] Indeed, the entire rationale, the motivating impetus of racialized chattel slavery, was that labor could be commandeered for free, massively increasing the profits that colonial slave holders could extract. In order for this practice to be sustainable at a time when European societies were firmly convinced that human beings had rights, including some rudimentary labor rights, the only way to reconcile such a profit-machine was to declare that enslaved people were not human beings and thus not bearers of such rights. In this way, the entire edifice of racialized slavery and all of its attendant policies codifying race were inextricably linked to the capitalist profit motive. But likewise, one cannot explain slavery without an analysis of racial oppression, as the mechanism of surplus value extraction is simply insufficient to capture what Orlando Patterson has called the position of "social death" that characterizes this position.[26] In other words, the designation of racialized people as sub-human, the amount of direct, personal violence enslaved people encountered, and the entire edifice of racist ideologies that emerged in relation to slavery all far outstrip any direct reduction to a profit logic.

Moreover, the profit-logic narrative systematically overlooks any of the deeply urgent issues that oppression can help bring into relief: what kinds of thoughts, feelings, social relations, complexes, traumas, etc. emerged in implementation of these policies. The profit analysis centers on the reasons capitalists had for the decisions they made but leaves out any substantive discussion of slavery from the perspective or position of enslaved people themselves. It also tends to gloss over the ways in which even the shrewdest capitalist plantation owner does not always act as a machine of self-interest, with multiple historical examples of, for example, colonists inflamed with such racist hate that they killed or maimed enslaved people, even at what was considered a financial loss in the system they inhabited. Both the exploitation and the oppression characteristic of chattel slavery were completely suffused with gender and sexual dynamics as well. There was both a specific shape of the exploitation of

---

25 | Williams, *Capitalism and Slavery*; Edmund Morgan, *American Slavery, American Freedom*, Reissue edition (New York: W. W. Norton & Company, 2003).
26 | Orlando Patterson, *Slavery and Social Death: A Comparative Study*, 1st edition (Cambridge, Mass.: Harvard University Press, 1982).

enslaved women, through the use of mass rape to extract value (incarnated in a new generation of enslaved people), and also a specific shape of racial oppression for racialized women, who were constructed as 'rape-able' (or, expressing the same sentiment, as un-rape-able, as both law ans social discourse denied that sexual assault of black women was a crime at all) in ways that continue to shape and enframe controlling images of black women's sexuality in the contemporary world.

The point is less that chattel slavery is a particularly acute instance of the intersection of race, class, gender, sexuality, and capitalism (though surely it is this as well), and more that neither exploitation nor oppression can separately capture the phenomenon; it is rather the dynamic interplay between exploitation and oppression that create the particular topography of chattel slavery. The relationship between forms of oppression charted by the intersectional tradition is itself a helpful model in thinking the relationship between exploitation and oppression, and hence, the relationship between the Marxist and the intersectional traditions. This approach is particularly helpful at taking a non-causal approach to the relationship between exploitation and oppression. It is able to recognize what we might call, following Walter Benjamin and Theodor Adorno, an "elective affinity" between exploitation and oppression, a kind of consonance or amenability between the two structures, without necessarily reducing one to the other. It is able to show the profit motive pulsing through many structures of oppression in ways that are deeply linked to but not reducible wholly to exploitation. As we can see from this example, it is indeed possible to think about exploitation and oppression as different, yet related structures without reverting to a dual systems analysis. Thinking of race, gender, sexuality, and class as equiprimordial does not mean that we should think about them separately; rather, the refusal to name one of these relations as more foundational than the other, in insisting on their shared foundation is the logical consequence of thinking about oppression and exploitation as different, unranked, mutually constituting, and part of the same system. To say that exploitation and oppression are not reducible to one another is not the same as to say that capitalism, racism, and heterosexism are part of different systems. Quite the opposite: capitalism is a structure in which both exploitation and oppression are necessary.

SECTION THREE: CLASS AND EQUIPRIMORDIALITY

Under an equiprimordial analysis, even class must be reconceived as constituted through both oppression and exploitation. Many Marxists balk at even the mere intimation that class might be an oppression, and this is evidenced by the derision aimed at the term 'classism' in many Marxist circles. The term 'classism' seems to suggest that the problems of capitalism and exploitation can be reduced to questions of bias or elitist attitude toward the poor. Conceiving of class wholly as an issue of oppression, without recourse to a structural understanding of exploitation, does indeed obscure the fundamental structures of capitalist accumulation, as a fundamental aspect of its logic. However, class cannot be reduced exploitation alone. A full understanding of how class functions under capitalism requires understanding how exploitation and oppression function equiprimordially. Through a discussion of class in this section, I hope to show both why a concrete and vibrant analysis of class requires *both* exploitation and oppression as equiprimordial features.

A rigorous account of class dynamics necessitates a thorough understanding of exploitation. The logic of exploitation animates the polarization of society into a small group of capitalist owners and a large group of exploited workers. It is impossible to grasp how and why such a structure continues and accelerates with such tenacity without an account of the accumulation of surplus value that causes labor to be the structural source of continual impoverishment for most human beings on the planet. While exploitation is an incredibly potent analytic to understand the operation of surplus value extraction, the question of exploitation is insufficient to explain how social power is constituted beyond the workplace. In a real, material, and strategic sense, part of the reason that capitalism is reproducible has to do with the ways in which exploited people are disadvantaged or often barred altogether from the various institutions of social and political power that might otherwise serve the interests of the working classes. In this sense, it is because of decreasing access to institutions, resources, power, and modes of contestation that the capitalist class can continue to maintain and reproduce relations of exploitation over time. This is why, for example, exploited groups are systematically denied access to healthcare, education, political power, influence over the media, and generally to decision-making power and authority over everything from legislative policy to the distribution of social resources to the production of academic knowledge. Exploited people hold almost no influence in the political sphere, and no access to what Dean Spade has called 'administrative power'—policy and bureaucratic power located in the various state, local, and federal agencies that frame the material organization of many poor folks' lives.[27] All of these considerations constitute relations of oppression, not of exploitation. But these relations of exploitation and oppression feed off and play into one another as mutually reinforcing and co-constituting aspects of the organization of capitalist society. In this way, both oppression and exploitation are fundamentally material catego-

---

27 | Spade, *Normal Life: Administrative Violence, Critical Trans Politics, and the Limits of Law.*

ries, that refer to the ways in which resources, opportunities, and institutions structure the possibilities of life.

Given this understanding of class as constituted through both exploitation and oppression it is possible then to understand how notions of classism both speak to something real about the nature of class and yet also do not render it completely. Rita Mae Brown explains how class itself becomes a kind of identity, in a way that is simply not reducible to exploitation alone:

> Class is much more than Marx's definition of relationship to the means of production. Class involves your behavior, your basic assumptions about life[...]how you are taught to behave, what you expect from yourself and from others, your concept of a future, how you understand problems and solve them, how you think, feel, act. It is these behavioral patterns that middle class women resist recognizing although they may be perfectly willing to accept class in Marxist terms, a neat trick that helps them avoid really dealing with class behavior and changing that behavior in themselves.[28]

It is these aspects of class that is often most clearly and faithfully rendered by those who think about class as a form of oppression. Generating a complex and accurate understanding of the layered, complicated, and contradictory constitution of class can thus only be accomplished by integrating exploitation and oppression in our understandings of class.

This may seem a bitter pill to swallow to many Marxists, who have for so long based their theories of capitalism specifically and primarily on exploitation, with oppression serving a subsidiary or intensifying role. But, in reality, most Marxists recognize some version of the argument here, even if they do not articulate it explicitly or in these terms. From a Marxist perspective, capitalism is a world system, encompassing much more than simply a workplace relation; capitalism is the frame, the grammar, of not only economics, but politics, the family, media, cultural movements, artistic expression, science, narratives of history, social institutions, education, and more. In these analyses, exploitation is never the single fulcrum of the system, though it is necessary to it. As Val Plumwood explains, "The material and the cultural spheres both do the work of domination and may be thought of as mutually selecting one another, just as particular technologies are both selected by certain social and political arrangements and select them, helping to maintain, strengthen and prepare the ground for certain types of social structures."[29] Exploitation in the strict sense alone is certainly insufficient to explain capitalism, if one conceives of it as the multivalent, dynamic, shifting, proliferating regime that it is.

---

28 | Rita Mae Brown, "The Last Straw," in *Class and Feminism* (Diana Press, 1974).
29 | Val Plumwood, *Feminism and the Mastery of Nature* (London and New York: Routledge, 1993), 42.

If Marxists are truly interested in the material conditions of life, it is immediately apparent that for the vast majority of people on the planet, oppression and exploitation are co-constituted material conditions, and that many of the most grueling, devastating, and gut-wrenching material conditions that frame people's lives have to do with conditions that may be related to their working lives but are not exhausted by them. Because social, economic, political, and interpersonal systems are themselves deeply interpenetrated, one can only adequately conceive of oppression and exploitation together. Just as we saw in the intersectional tradition that speaking of any '-ism' alone was itself misleading, speaking of oppression or exploitation alone, without the buttressing power and historical co-constitution of the other is conceptually inadequate and politically dangerous.

Conclusion: A Non-Reductionist Reading of Capitalism

Rendering the deep structural complexities of capitalism in all of its forms requires a vibrant theoretical apparatus, one that can chart the multiple flows and conjunctions of oppression and exploitation, that can think capaciously and differentially about their constitution. Developing an adequate theory of capital requires rapt attention to the multiplicity of formations that constitute it, revealing complicated and contradictory relations. Without such a view of capitalism, the depth, complexity, and resiliency of capitalism will be missed. Conceiving oppression and exploitation as equiprimordial generates a more complete rendering of capitalism's proliferating multiplicities, producing a non-reductionist reading of capitalism.

Equiprimordiality avoids two common forms of reductionisms within contemporary theories of capitalism: class reductionism and exploitation reductionism. In both intersectional and Marxist work, these two distinct operations are collapsed. Class reductionism should be understood as reducing the operations or mechanisms of capitalism to *only* the interplay of class dynamics. Class reductionism can be economistic, though it need not necessarily be.

Exploitation reductionism, on the other hand, is something rather different; rather than assuming that capitalism operates only or fundamentally through *class*, this position argues that it operates only or fundamentally through *exploitation*. Many (though not all) queer, feminist, or anti-racist Marxisms, when read carefully, are much more committed to an exploitation reductionism than a class reductionism. In these accounts, it is certainly not only class that is central, foundational, or constitutive for capitalism; race, gender, sexuality, and/or (post)colonial status often emerge as pivotal or structural features of capitalism. Under these accounts, however, what makes race, gender, sexuality, or national origin is the *differential modes of exploitation* to which members of those groups are subject. Under such a conception, race, for example, is an ideological and material practice of a specific kind of exploitation (like slavery, or the *encomienda*, or more general racial divisions of labor), that itself produces oppression in other areas of life besides strictly economic ones; but this oppression is ultimately reducible to the need of capital to accumulate and exploit. Both of these forms of reductionism fundamentally constitute capitalism as an economistic system, a position that both intersectionality theorists and single-systems Marxist feminists reject. As Cinzia Arruzza explains, "To try to explain what capitalist society is only in terms of surplus-value extraction is like trying to explain the anatomy of the human body by explaining only how the heart works."[30]

In order to understand capitalism in a way that integrates both Marxist and intersectional insights, we will need to avoid both kinds of reductions, insisting on equiprimordiality in multiple ways. The outline of such a theory must be committed to the following four positions:

1. Capitalism cannot be reduced to exploitation alone.
2. Capitalism cannot be reduced to class alone.
3. Class cannot be reduced to exploitation alone.
4. Race, gender, sexuality cannot be reduced to oppression alone.

These are merely condensed versions of the arguments of this chapter. Committing to an understanding of capitalism that refuses all four of these common reductions furnishes us with a conception of capitalism that is dynamic, complicated, and based equi-primordially in oppression and exploitation. Capitalism is a central determinant in the constitution of not only class, but also race, gender, and sexuality in the contemporary world. While I do privilege 'capitalism' as the name of the system dominating us all, I do not hold that class, as an isolatable economic or social determination, gives us a privileged understanding of capitalism, or at least, it does not do so any more than race, gender, or sexuality. Slavery, colonialism, heteropatriarchy, white supremacy–all these were developed in and through capitalism, at least in their modern and contemporary forms. So when I argue that capitalism structures the "matrix of domination", this should not mean that economic determinations are privileged in this analysis; on the contrary, while a critique of capitalism must include a political-economic critique, any analysis that avoids interrogating the social, cultural, familial, psychological, and intimate domains will lose the ability to track some of the most important formations of capitalist modernity.

For this reason, a full, non-reductionist reading of capitalism must take the equiprimordiality of oppression and exploitation in both its strategic and onto-

---

30 | Arruzza, "Remarks on Gender."

logical senses. Certainly, the refusal to take questions of identity and oppression seriously have been debilitating for anti-capitalist left organizing, alienating many would-be socialists and reproducing the same forms of domination and exclusion in organizing spaces that are central to capitalist logic. Seeing capitalism as a wholly economic system occludes the ways in which capitalism as a system operates far beyond the workplace, preventing strategic anti-capitalist organizing in the wide variety of social, cultural, and political sites where it could be decidedly useful. Recognizing the centrality of oppression to capitalism centers the structures of colonization, dispossession, heteropatriarchy, ableism, and imperialism in ways that could prove strategic in widening the scope of anti-capitalist organizing.

But the non-reductionist reading is also committed to equiprimordiality on the ontological level. It argues, not that we should act *as if* capitalism were structured through oppression; it argues that it *is*. Equiprimordiality in this stronger sense highlights the ways in which capitalism is itself a system that is and has always been structured through oppression and exploitation; in all of its historical variations across time and place, capitalism evidences a structural and logical commitment to both exploitation and oppression as fundamental modes of its constitution. Recognizing its co-constitution is thus the condition of the possibility of knowing and seeing what capitalism is in its deepest structures.

Chapter Six: Dialectics of Difference

> "Today we are more fragmented than ever, which is terrible, which is beautiful."
> - Ruben Martínez[1]

> "Do I contradict myself?
> Very well then, I contradict myself.
> (I am large, I contain multitudes)"
> - Walt Whitman

Capitalism is structured through contradiction, and dialectics is a strategy of reading these contradictions. Few conceptual figures of Marxism have been as disparaged in the non-Marxist left as dialectics. In many accounts, dialectics, or often *the* dialectic, is understood as the centrally problematic commitment of Marxism, which, we are told, commits it to a notion of reductive binary oppositions, teleological determinism, and the erasure of the difference. We might be surprised then, by the frequency with which dialectics and contradiction figure into various intersectional theories. In the intersectional tradition, dialectics is often understood as dynamic, creative, and exuberant, as the force that erupts in the space of difference, divergence, and lived contradiction. Indeed, contradiction and dialectics figure centrally in multiple intersectional accounts of difference.

As a mode of reading capitalist contradictions, dialectics can provide helpful understandings of the ways in which capitalism is structured through both exploitation and oppression. Mobilizing both intersectional and Marxist accounts of dialectics can clarify the relationship between capitalist contradiction and the variety of ways in which capital appears historically. In order to understand how dialectics might figure into the non-reductive reading of capitalism offered in the previous chapter, this chapter proceeds in three parts. The first section explores what contradiction and dialectics mean for the Marxist tradition, specifically drawing out the ways in which Marx utilized dialectics

---

1 | Qtd in Marcial Gonzáles, "Postmodernism, Historical Materialism, and Chicana/o Cultural Studies," *Science and Society* 68, no. 2 (2004): 161-86.

as a way of reading contradiction in the world; he did so in ways that radically diverge from the way that contradiction is usually understood in logic and the history of Western philosophy. The second section probes the meanings of dialectics and contradiction in the intersectional tradition, highlighting especially those moments that offer helpful correctives to orthodox Marxist understandings of the term. In the last section, I integrate Marxist and intersectional understandings in order to explore the term "dialectic of difference" that emerges in both traditions. Dialectics of difference should be central to understanding capitalism as a structure and a logic, and it is a helpful method that can be mobilized toward understanding capitalism in a non-reductive way.

Section One: Marxist Dialectics

In the Marxist tradition, there are few concepts as poorly understood as dialectics. At its core, dialectics is a way of naming and of interpreting the real contradictions of the material world under capitalism. In this sense, dialectics is both a descriptive term and a methodological one; it explains both how the world is constituted and how we should approach reading and understanding that world, what Marxists refer to as the real contradictions of capitalism as they are produced systemically and systematically. In its most potent form, dialectics figures the non-resolution of these really existing contradictions, the impossibility of their resolution. As George Ciccariello-Maher notes, critiquing many of the uses to which the concept has been deployed, "For too long, however, *dialectics* has not served to denote such moments of combative division that give its name, but instead the opposite: a harmonious closure often announced but rarely experienced."[2] Rather than referring to the resolution of contradictions, dialectics in its truest form for Marx refers to "the dynamic movement of conflictive opposites"[3] that frames the contradictions of life under capitalism. It is, thus, the very opposite of the resolution into unity with which it is often conflated.

Real Contradictions

In order to understand the widespread misapprehension of dialectics, we must first turn to the concept of real contradiction which undergirds it. Real contradiction is often conflated with logical contradiction, even though the concept of real contradiction in many ways rejects the vision of the world offered by logical

---

[2] | George Ciccariello-Maher, *Decolonizing Dialectics* (Durham and London: Duke University Press, 2017), 1.
[3] | Ciccariello-Maher, 2.

contradiction. Logical contradiction holds that contradictions are themselves *actually impossible*, that A and not-A, by definition can never exist at the same time. Many philosophers trace this aspect of logic back to Aristotle, and in this tradition, logical contradiction is based in two different but related principles. The first is called the Law of Non-Contradiction and Aristotle explains it thus: "It is impossible that the same thing can at the same time both belong and not belong to the same object and in the same respect, and all other specifications that might be made, let them be added to meet local objections."[4] In other words, it is impossible that contradictory opposites can exist; this is why, in traditional logic, a contradiction is always false. By contrast, real contradiction specifically focuses on how contradictions *do in fact exist* under capitalism, everywhere and all the time. Capitalism, according to Marx, is a structure that specifically *produces* real contradictions. In other words, rather than endorsing Aristotle's Law of Non-Contradiction, Marxist understandings of capitalism specifically rejects it.

An example might clarify. Perhaps the most basic real contradiction of capitalism is the way in which it produces *both* enormous wealth *and* abject poverty at one and the same time, as necessary consequences of the system of exploitation. When one small group of people (the capitalist class) accumulates wealth by paying workers only a small fraction of the value of their labor, the same interaction (waged work) produces both wealth and poverty. This is one of the key real contradictions of capitalism, that its logic necessitates the accumulation of previously unimaginable wealth and the dispossession into previously unimaginable poverty at one and the same time. We can see this real contradiction play out, not only in economic terms, but also in political forms. As many Marxists note, in order for laborers to enter into contractual labor relations, it was necessary to think about workers as full, free, legal persons; one cannot, under most liberal legal systems, enter into contractual relations with unfree persons or non-persons. This reconceptualization of workers as full, free persons generated the historical conditions of universal suffrage; at the same time however, this notion of freedom—the freedom to contract— produces only ever deeper subjection and subservience to the power of the capitalist class. Capitalism produced something like democracy, and yet it did so only in order to ensure that one of the most fundamental pieces of life—the economic realm—would be permanently sealed off from democratic control, that the freedom of workers to contract, to choose their jobs or their location of employment, is put to the service of employment practices in which workers have no power, no choice, no say, and no vote. Workers under capitalism do not set their pay, their hours, their duties, or determine what is to be done with

---

4 | Aristotle, *Metaphysics* (Bloomington: Indiana University Press, 1966), II. 1005b19-23.

their products or the profits; their supposed legal freedom is the condition of the possibility of their unfreedom. The contradiction here is that freedom and domination are inseparable under the demands of capitalism; the more 'free' contracts one enters into, the less free the conditions of actual life.

Many Marxists have also noted the ways in which gender, race, and sexuality are also structured in and through the contradictions of capitalism. Peter Drucker, for example, commenting on the contemporary structure of capitalism, argues that neoliberalism has reformulated the contradictory structures of gendering: "The family has traditionally served as a mechanism both for inculcating hierarchical and authoritarian social relations and for reproducing the workforce through women's unpaid labour[...] However, neoliberalism in many ways undermines the direct and obvious domination of wives and daughters by husbands and fathers"[5] by, for example, expanding the number of financially independent women, who have become themselves capitalists, without the need for reliance on the male breadwinner model that dominated many earlier organizations of capital. One of the real contradictions of gender relations under neoliberal capitalism is that it *both* empowers women in many spheres of life (social, political, economic) *and* systematically relies on sexist norms, heterosexist understandings of femininity and gendered (and racialized) social reproductive labor. In this sense, the 'freedom' or 'autonomy' of a class of women from direct patriarchal control is constitutively dependent on the continued, and indeed often deepened, conditions of hierarchal and authoritarian control over racialized women's labor. It goes without saying that the 'lean in' feminism of the upper classes has done nothing to alleviate the deep structures of sexism in our society, often rather inoculating them from further interrogation.

We can see the real contradictions of capitalism play out in regard to racialized and immigrant labor as well. There is a real contradiction in a society and an economy that relies so heavily on the value of racialized labor and contributes so continually to the devaluation of black and brown lives. On February 16, 2017, a coalition of immigrants' rights groups organized a national 'Day without an Immigrant' protest that sought to thematize precisely this contradiction; in withdrawing immigrant labor from businesses around the country, the protest sought to dramatize the contradiction between the reliance on and value of immigrant work and the rising tide of xenophobia, immigration restrictions, and deportation that centers on the devaluation of immigrant life.

These are but a few examples of how capitalism is organized in order to produce real contradictions. Far from the Aristotelian tradition of logical con-

---

5 | Drucker, *Warped*, 224.

tradiction, Marxist dialectics focus on these moments of contradiction, what Grace Hong calls "the ruptures of capital."[6]

Because contradictions are really existing, materially organized, and structurally produced in and through capitalism, non-dialectical methods in both academic and activist circles fail to capture the complexity of the world. Resorting to reductive causal explanations, unidirectional, or unicausal accounts of the world, cannot adequately thematize the contradictions of contemporary life.

A Philosophy of the Included Middles

I mentioned above that Marxist dialectics repudiates *two* central facets of logical contradiction. The second, after rejecting the Law of Non-Contradiction, is what is often called the Law of the Excluded Middle. Aristotle explains the excluded middle as follows: "Of any one subject, one thing must be either asserted or denied."[7] In other words, the world is structured according to a series of binaries, according to Aristotle, that A and not-A are the only two options of a given phenomenon; there is no middle ground (hence the law's name). Logical contradiction is thus based in the idea that binaries are really existing, and moreover, that all truth can be reduced to binary conceptualizations. It is no wonder that leftist social thought has been skeptical of the concept of contradiction and a dialectical mode of interpretation, given the obvious limitations of binaries, especially when thinking about identity and social position.[8] There are indeed a whole host of issues with how binaries are used, how they often limit our thinking, and how they erase the diversity and vibrancy of human life. In recent decades, it has become quite fashionable in intellectual circles to

---

6 | Hong, *The Ruptures of American Capital: Women of Color Feminism and the Immigrant Culture of Labor*.

7 | Aristotle, *Metaphysics*, I. 1011b24.

8 | Some people have read the term 'contradiction' to be too closely linked to the binary in Marx's use of it, and of Marxists' subsequent deployment of it. However, when Marx speaks of the contradictions of capitalist society, he doesn't ever seem to suggest that there are two manifestations and only two; rather, he suggests that the actual, really existing diversity of individual moments of capitalism can be read as multiple attempts by—politicians, lawmakers, business owners, inventors, etc.—to find solutions to the contradictions that capitalism inevitable produces. In this sense, then, the real diversity of capitalist strategies is the myriad, highly differentiated responses to structurally produced contradictions, not a denial of this real diversity. Contradictions here describe how ideologies and social practices are organized to produce materially organized binaries of modern society. This is certainly not to ascent to those binaries, only a method of understanding how and why the tensions at the heart of capitalism manifest in and through binary logics in deep and intractable ways.

'deconstruct' the binary in left activist circles. Of course, when the binary to be constructed is one that is harmful – the gender binary, for instance, a binary conception of race, etc. – we can and should deconstruct the binary as much as possible.

The problems with binary thinking are well documented. In the first place, reducing many phenomena in the world to 2-and-only-2 possibilities occludes the real diversity in the world; there are multiple genders, multiple sexes, multiple races, multiple relations to disability, etc. Binary thinking thus not only perpetuates severe reductions, it actively perpetuates the logics that continue to oppress, malign, or deny the very existence of a variety of really existing human beings. Moreover, binary thinking often entails oppositional thinking, wherein the two terms in the binary are not simply 'different' but antagonistic to one another. Even further still, this opposition is often figured, not neutrally, but normatively, with one pole of the binary figured as superior, natural, rational, or universal and the other figured as inferior, unnatural, irrational, or particular. In this sense, binary thinking perpetuates not only erasure of non-binary positions, but also actively contributes to the domination of those who fall on one side of any of these binaries conceptualizations. For all of these reasons, Val Plumwood has called binary thinking "an alienated form of differentiation" that works to undermine liberatory projects grounded in a full, creative, affirmative notion of difference.[9] As Heather Love writes, radicalism is "not only about making a new future, it is also about making space for what is,"[10] and it is undeniable that binary conceptions, especially of identity, close off that space; any radical analysis of human beings must clear the ground for a full, exuberant affirmation of multiplicity.

Often, it is assumed that by virtue of recognizing a contradiction at the heart of capitalism, that Marxism has some natural, ontological commitment to duality or binaries in all areas of its analysis, or indeed, in the ways that these contradictions appear. The source of this conflation is understandable: both within and outside the Marxist tradition, the idea that class under capitalism is structured through an antagonism between the bourgeoisie and the proletariat seems to mark a natural affinity with the real contradictions of capitalism sketched above. When class structure is reduced to an opposition between the bourgeoisie and the proletariat, this can lead thinkers to assume that all other social positions are likewise structured according to binary characterizations. However, this easy linkage is possible only through conflating a series of terms that are at base, completely different kinds of formations and questions. Here, we need to make an important distinction, one that is often elided in contempo-

---

9 | Plumwood, *Feminism and the Mastery of Nature*, 42.
10 | Christina Crosby et al., "Queer Studies, Materialism, and Crisis," *GLQ: A Journal of Lesbian & Gay Studies* 18, no. 1 (2012): 144.

rary Marxism itself, and that produces a whole range of misapprehensions and confusions between Marxism and the non-Marxist left: the conflation between the polar character of the central contradictions of capitalism and the shape of particular social antagonisms.

Capitalism takes a variety of shapes and forms, responds to a variety of conditions, and encounters a wide variety of constraints and resistances; indeed, as we saw in Chapter Three, capitalism is a highly differentiated, global system. In marking out a series of real contradictions of capitalism, Marx never suggested that historical human beings negotiated these contradictions in the same ways; rather, politicians, bureaucrats, capitalists, diplomats, organizers, workers, and a whole host of real, historical individuals devised methods of arranging, managing, and responding to these contradictions. In this way, the existence of a contradiction at the heart of capitalist logic can never tell us in advance how capitalism, in any particular historical, national, political, or social moment, will be structured. It will not tell us in advance whether or not universal healthcare will be offered to members of the proletariat, it will not tell us at what rate corporations will be taxed if it all, it will not tell us if there are minimum wages or whether slavery will be legal, it will not tell us when and where the letter of laws against slavery will be enforced or de facto allowed to flourish. What historical materialist analysis allows us to do, however, is to understand the ways in which all of these contingent, historical negotiations are related to a logic of profit, accumulation, and dispossession; it provides a lens through which we can understand the ways in which all of the negotiations happen inside a system engineered for profit maximization rather than the fulfillment of human needs. It thus reveals how, within any conjunction of historical factors, certain outcomes are more likely than others, and how these deliberations will happen almost always in institutions and structures of power designed to propagate rather than disrupt systems of exploitation and oppression. Moreover, the circuits of resistance to capitalism are themselves part of the complex, historical, and differentiated process of negotiations. Just because a decision, a piece of legislation, or a workplace policy accelerates exploitation and oppression does not necessarily imply that those effected will organize against it. Even less can we know in advance whether resistance will be successful. An analysis of capitalism does not disclose in advance how structures of exploitation and oppression will play out in individual lives and the identities of those individuals. It is an error to conflate the polarities of fundamental capitalist contradictions with the shape of social antagonisms (which are figured in a variety of ways, including in and through race, gender, sexuality, etc.). Social antagonisms should always be figured as pluri-vocal, multiplicitous, and, what is more, unpredictable and contingent.

In all of these senses, Marxism thoroughly repudiates the Law of the Excluded Middle; in fact, we could say that Marxism—or at least a non-reductive Marxism—is a theory *of the Middle*. It assumes and works from the assumption that real contradictions appear in a variety of ways, and that any particular social, political, or economic formation is the result of negotiations between the contradictory poles of capitalism's logic. In this sense, not only does Marxism insist on the inclusion of the middle, it is fundamentally a theory about the plurality of the middle; we might even go so far as to suggest that Marxism is a philosophy of many included middles. In one sense, the 'middle' shows us the ways in which real contradictions pull us in multiple directions at once, making every place a space of compromise, erasure, fracture, or partiality. In another sense, the middle shows us the ways in which the binary options of contemporary capitalist society are themselves mutually implicated, two sides of the same coin. Dialectics holds that the two poles or 'sides' of the contradiction are actually *not* in opposition with one another, even if they are in tension. It foregrounds the ineluctable co-constitution of the poles, the way in which they are inescapably tied together, and this tenuous, dynamic link produces a plethora of outcomes, arrangements, and compromises.

In this sense, the polarity of capitalism's logic subtends the actual plurality of historical conditions under capitalism, rather than endorsing binary thinking. As a theory of the included middles, Marxist philosophy can provide an opening for thinking polarity and diversity at one and the same time, a path for negotiating the relationship between dualism and multiplicity. Even recognizing all of the real, important limitations of binary thinking and the Law of the Excluded Middle, we must also wrestle with the problem that anti-binary or anti-dualist assertions themselves are not wholly sufficient to transform the material and logical production of binaries on a structural level. Simply claiming my identity as a queer woman who is neither heterosexual nor homosexual—which I do, loudly and as often as possible!—does little to shift the terrain of heterosexism that often presents these identities as the only available options, even if, through my queer pride, I might sometimes open up the space for others to question their own assumptions of a binary understanding of sexuality. But the problem runs deeper than even this, as Holly Lewis explains:

Paradoxically, struggles against dichotomies present new dichotomies: binary versus multiple[...] Moreover, there are important political dichotomies that this language evades: there is racism and antiracism, there is the picket line and there is crossing it, there is the murder of queer/ trans people and there is the absence of those murders, there is welcoming immigrants who land on your shores and there is letting them drown. Of course, these antagonisms need to be understood dialectically – racism and antiracism aren't just abstract conceptual objects but relational processes in a material world. Strikebreakers can be brought into the fold, and strikers can betray solidarity. Moving from violence against queer people to the absence of violence is a process that involves transforming those who would harm queer and trans people into those who won't. However, this procedural complexity does not mean that the antagonisms aren't real.[11]

Lewis draws out a nexus of important questions around the structure of binaries and the strategies needed in order to overturn them. The first is the way in which anti-binary thinking produces its own binary conceptions (binary vs. multiple) in a way that often seems to betray its own fundamental insight. But moreover, the position of refusing to accede to a binary ever, for any reason, has often itself engendered its own form of quietism: in being unable to draw a stark boundary between what is right and wrong, acceptable or unacceptable, we have seen, especially in the academy, where rejecting binary logic is near-gospel (at least in the humanities), an actual uptick in right wing fascism, open white supremacy, and explicit transphobia on campuses. This isn't only a backlash effect, though there is certainly an element of it; the rise of the right on campus has been buoyed by liberal forms of anti-dualistic thinking that refuse to carve the realm of speech into acceptable and unacceptable categories. As Ciccariello-Maher portends,

By asymptotically approaching the inclusion of everyone, we run the risk of sliding into far more treacherous territory, moving from rupture, division, and opposition toward the aspirational recasting of a near-total unity. If anything, *this* is the most ideological gesture of all, one that seeks to reconcile rupture with its opposite, taking refuge in the comforting idea that we are all in this together rather than engaging in risky solidarity *against*.[12]

The lesson that Lewis and Ciccariello-Maher draw from this problem is, however, *not* the reductive recuperation of binaries; they do not argue that because anti-binary thinking leads itself to new binaries, that dualism is unproblematic. Rather, they argue that binary conceptualizations are real forces in the world, forces that cannot simply be wished away. In order to understand the limitations of these binaries, both Lewis and Ciccariello-Maher turn toward dialectics as a way forward.

Dialectics as a model of diagnosis can show us how, at one and the same time, binaries are reductive and harmful *and* can show that rather than simply reject them, we need to engage with them, because they continue to frame the structural conditions of the world. By embracing contradiction and the position of included middles, dialectics can provide a grounding for both taking binaries seriously as modes of exploitation and oppression, and for 'making room' for

---

11 | Lewis, *The Politics of Everybody*, 276.
12 | Ciccariello-Maher, *Decolonizing Dialectics*, 5.

the variety of human identity, responses, mobilizations, and resistances against a world that tells us that the middle is excluded in advance.

Synthesis, Sublation, and other Positivities

Rather than a theory of middles, dialectics is often characterized as the idea that oppositions or contradictions should be synthesized into a 'higher' unity. The skepticism of this position is entirely understandable, as it seems committed to the notion that the reconciled world would be one, not of difference, but of absolute sameness, that the path to overcoming the painful and oppressive conditions of contemporary life lay in divesting ourselves of differences for a total, unproblematic, utopian unity. The genesis of this understanding of dialectics can be traced to reductive readings of Hegel in which, so we are told, the thesis (or pole 1 of the binary) meets its antithesis (pole 2) and is then magically "sublated" into a synthesis (or unity) of the previous two positions.[13] The deterministic and progressive narrative of this process, completed over and over, also leads to its own problems, of which many thinkers are rightly skeptical.

However, there is a venerable and long-standing tradition of Marxist dialectics that specifically rejects the synthetic moment of dialectical analysis. As we saw in Chapter Three, Glen Coulthard has shown that while Marx at some point in his life and career endorsed a kind of progressivist, synthetic understanding of capital's contradictions, he specifically rejected this position by the end of his life. Unlike a 'positive dialectics' that works toward the sublation of differences into a unity, the Marxist tradition of 'negative dialectics' forecloses any possibility of such a resolution.[14] According to Adorno and Horkheimer, the desire for synthetic resolution of differences "ultimately into one" is characteristic of the Enlightenment tradition that Marxist dialectics intends to challenge and

---

13 | Whether or not this is an *adequate* reading of Hegel, I leave to the Hegelians to discuss.

14 | Theodor W. Adorno, *Negative Dialectics*, 2 edition (New York: Bloomsbury Academic, 1981).

unseat.[15] The "fetishization of the positive"[16] that so frequently characterizes Hegelian approaches to dialectics is, for these theorists, problematic both philosophically and politically, by valuing identity and sameness over and above the real differences between positions, things, and people in the world. Negative dialectics thus focuses on the "contradiction in things themselves" and within subjects themselves as a fundamental aspect of their constitution, without the desire to strip them of it.[17] In this sense to 'do' dialectics "means to break the compulsion"[18] to achieve unity between differences, and instead to read social formations, systems, and structures as fundamentally disharmonious and highly differentiated.[19] In understanding capitalism, then, "the essence of this model of an antagonistic society is that it is not a society *with* contradictions or *despite* its contradiction, but *by virtue of* its contradictions."[20] In this sense, "dialectics themselves are no eternal values,"[21] but are rather strategic modes of analyzing and foregrounding contradictions to better understand the fractures, divergences, and multiplicities as they are constituted in our world.

From these sections, it is clear that dialectics, at least in some versions of Marxism, are a far cry from the dualistic and synthetic versions present in many caricatures. Rather, multiple strands of Marxist dialectics mobilize contradictions as a strategy of reading and understanding the relationship between plurality and structure as they emerge in the contemporary world. But Marxism has not as often meditated on the difficulties of living immersed in contradiction, of the ways in which experience and identity are wrapped up in the tensions of this world. Intersectionality's great contribution, or one of

---

15 | Max Horkheimer and Theodor W. Adorno, *Dialectic of Enlightenment*, ed. Gunzelin Schmid Noerr, trans. Edmund Jephcott, 1 edition (Stanford, Calif: Stanford University Press, 2007), 4-5. Without delving too deeply into the complicated question of exactly to what extent Marx himself can be situated inside or outside the Enlightenment tradition, I broadly agree with Nancy Hartsock who locates Marx as ambiguously straddling both positions: "I see Marx as an anti-Enlightenment figure on balance, although it must be recognized that his relationship to the Enlightenment and the whole tradition of Western political through is that of both the inheriting son and the rebellious son." Hartsock, "Marxist Feminist Dialectics for the 21st Century," 403.
16 | Theodor W. Adorno, *Lectures on Negative Dialectics: Fragments of a Lecture Course 1965/1966*, 1 edition (Cambridge: Polity, 2008), 18.
17 | Ibid, 7.
18 | Adorno, *Negative Dialectics*, 157.
19 | 'Identity' and 'identitarian' here should not be read as relating to political, social, or group identities, but rather in the sense of unproblematic, complete unities of concepts, objects, or processes.
20 | Adorno, *Lectures on Negative Dialectics*, 8-9.
21 | Ibid, 10.

them, is in a deep commitment to living through contradiction, not as a death sentence, but as the fountain of creative possibility. It is this understanding of dialectics to which we now turn.

SECTION TWO: INTERSECTIONALITY AND DIALECTICS

While there have been recent calls from Marxist feminists to "dialecticize intersectionality,"[22] these calls have often taken place in the absence of any rigorous engagement with the status of dialectics within intersectionality's own tradition. Rather than simply apply a concept of dialectics from the Marxist tradition to intersectional concerns, imputing a kind of Marxist structure onto intersectionality, this section probes and explores the ways in which intersectionality has already developed an understanding of contradiction and dialectics as fundamental to its own understanding of difference. This is not to claim that the intersectional tradition's understanding of dialectics developed wholly autonomously from Marxism, as if there were no lines of inheritance, critique, or engagement; it is to say that the intersectional tradition develops unique and novel understandings of dialectics that significantly pushes the theory and practice of dialectics beyond many of the debates and conceptions of the Marxist tradition and deserves consideration in its own right. I stake out two levels of contribution of intersectional dialectics: the first concerns the *content* of dialectics, explaining, exploring and arguing for different kinds of contradictions that deserve attention in our understanding of capitalism, and the second concerns the *form* of dialectics, by which I mean the theoretical contributions to how we consider and think about what contradictions fundamentally mean and how they are structured.

A discussion of the history of intersectional concepts of dialectics can helpfully be grounded in the work of one of the figures discussed in Chapter Zero, Deborah King. While King's analysis falls short of a 'full blown' intersectional perspective, she does offer some helpful comments on dialectics that will be useful in understanding the dynamic changes that the concept underwent through intersectionality's development. King deploys the concept of dialectics in two ways, each of which continues to influence the contemporary intersectional tradition. In the first place, dialectics name, for King, the forms of a non-additive relation that hold between various axes of oppression and exploitation. Commenting on the multi-faceted and iconic question of Sojourner Truth's, King writes,

---

22 | Lena Gunnarsson, "Why We Keep Separating the 'Inseparable': Dialecticizing Intersectionality," *European Journal of Women's Studies* 24, no. 2 (2015): 114-27.

To reduce this complex of negotiations to an addition problem (racism + sexism = black women's experience) is to define the issues, and indeed black womanhood itself, within the structural terms developed by Europeans and especially white males to privilege their race and their sex unilaterally. Sojourner's declaration "ain't I a woman?' directly refutes this sort of conceptualization of womanhood as one dimensional rather than dialectical.[23]

For King, 'dialectical' denotes the character of relation between axes of identity categories. Indeed, it is the name for the non-additive, non-hierarchical, complex, interwoven understanding of relations that intersectionality argues obtains under the matrix of domination. Secondly, rather than allying dialectics with white masculinity, King explicitly understands dialectics—at least a true, relational, non-reductive kind of dialectics—to be precisely opposed to the kind of European heterosexist and white supremacist forms of thinking with which it is often conflated. This insight is helpful because it allows us to key into two important and foundational truths about dialectics that are necessary in order to rehabilitate it for the purposes of thinking race, gender, class, and sexuality as co-constituted under contemporary capitalism. King understands dialectics as a repudiation of hegemonic and Eurocentric thought. Radicalizing this insight, King's suggestions could constitute a potent intervention against capitalism, colonization, slavery, and other structures of domination. King also turns our attention to non-Eurocentric traditions of dialectical thinking, many of which developed autonomously from Marx or Marxism. Ciccariello-Maher in particular uplifts this tradition of dialectical thinking, which he explores in particular in the thought of Frederick Douglas and in the way that Cedric Robinson frames the legacy of African thought in the Black Radical Tradition.[24]

King also elaborates a second understanding of dialectics that continues to influence the intersectional tradition: dialectics as transformative activist practice. She characterizes the "dialectics" of liberation movements as needing to move beyond the "monism" of unicausal explanation or singular focus in discussing not only theories of identity, oppression, and exploitation, but also in understanding the history of social justice movements. On her account, it would be historically inaccurate to segment the movements for abolition and civil rights from those of women's suffrage or the feminist movement; she also argues that much of the Marxist and trade unionist movements were heavily intertwined with the anti-imperialist movement. Understanding movements as engaged in deeply-held creative tension with one another reframes activist

---

23 | King, "Multiple Jeopardy, Multiple Consciousness: The Context of a Black Feminist Ideology," 51.
24 | Ciccariello-Maher, *Decolonizing Dialectics*, 152–70; Robinson, *Black Marxism*.

histories away from commonly-held reductive schemas.[25] Movements connect with one another, forming alliances, coalitions, and critiques; activists change their focus of work; key figures, theories, and strategies may be shared among movements, but they also might not be, for a variety of reasons. Understanding the relationship between movements as 'dialectical,' King foreshadows what Angela Davis has recent called "movement intersectionality,"[26] the understanding that movements themselves are constituted through a complicated nexus of power, privilege, identity, and repression, both within and between movements. King thus recognized two central aspects of dialectical thinking continue to influence the intersectional tradition: dialectics as a helpful way to conceptualize relations within the matrix of domination *and* dialectics as a guiding principle for activism within movements for social justice.

Dialectics as Intersectional Relation

According to Vivian May, one of the hallmarks of "intersectional thought and practice" is its commitment to "contradictions as politically and epistemologically significant."[27] Though the political and the epistemological are deeply interrelated levels of analysis, it is helpful to show how the intersectional tradition has grappled with contradiction and dialectics in each of these registers.

From the epistemological side, the intersectional tradition focuses on the way that contradictions can helpfully illuminate the structures and systems that present irreconcilable demands, narratives, and choices for oppressed people. In this sense, the focus on contradiction forms the bedrock of a theory of knowledge that oppressed people already have, as well as constitutes a strategy of reading the impossible binds on their lives. Part of what intersectionality intended to do, according to Patricia Hill Collins, was to provide a theory that allowed Black women to "com[e] to terms with contradictions," especially those particular contradictions that frame black women's social position in the contemporary U.S.[28] Among the many contradictions that Collins traces is the contradiction between hypervisibility and invisibility that often constitutes black women's social position under the contemporary matrix of domination; she argues that while African American women continue to be "invisible as fully

---

25 | Examples of this are of the 'wave' metaphor for feminism or from narratives that assert that the queer movement grew out of the feminist movement which in turn grew out of the civil rights movement. Of course movements are connected to one another, but their lines of connection are more complicated than these narratives suggest.
26 | Davis and West, *Freedom Is a Constant Struggle*.
27 | Vivian May, *Pursuing Intersectionality, Unsettling Dominant Imaginaries* (New York: Routledge, 2015), 9.
28 | Collins, *Black Feminist Thought*, 99.

human," this invisibility is at least partially constituted through the ways in which "all U.S. black women [are] especially visible and open to the objectification."²⁹ Yet another contradiction Collins outlines emerges around the contradictory status of the family and motherhood under capitalism for black women, where at one and the same time motherhood can be experienced "as a truly burdensome condition that stifles their creativity, exploits their labor, and makes them partners in their own oppression" *and* can also be experienced "as providing a base for self-actualization, status in the Black community, and a catalyst for social activism."³⁰

What makes Collins' account dialectical here is that she explains the oppositional understanding of the status of black motherhood, not as mere individual variety—as would, for example, choice feminism—but as the outcome of political, economic, social, and psychological structures that produce both truths, oppositional as they may be, at one and the same time.³¹

Sharon Doetsch-Kidder explains how contradictions such as those explored above by Collins contribute to a distinctly intersectional epistemology that foregrounds contradiction as formative to individuals' understanding of their own position within societies based on domination. She writes:

> From the experience of fragmentation, one realizes the impossibility of knowing a unified self in a body mind that is inherently relational [...] From this loving form of consciousness, one can form meaningful alliances and act in social and political spheres to counter oppression and support the survival of marginalized people.³²

Unlike many (though not all) Marxist accounts of contradiction and dialectics, the intersectional tradition generates its epistemology from the real contradictions experienced by oppressed people, highlighting the ways in which experience is an epistemologically salient category that links structures to

---

29 | Ibid, 100.
30 | Ibid, 176.
31 | Much of the debate between black feminists and white Marxist feminists of the 1970s was centered on the latters' inability to understand the particular contradictions of the family as Collins explains them. In much of the Marxist feminist literature at this time, the family was figured *only* as a repressive, dominating, and exploitative formation, which was often enframed by the perspective and experiences of many white women who were often confronted with the position of housewifery. The failure to offer a truly dialectical analysis, and to understand the multiplicity of family and kinship forms, as well as relationships to these, illuminates a moment when Marxism, despite its commitment to dialectical analysis, has often fallen short of that goal.
32 | Sharon Doetsch-Kidder, *Social Change and Intersectional Activism: The Spirit of Social Movement* (New York: Palgrave Macmillan, 2012), 54.

identification and political activism. There is, thus, a kind of 'order of operations' difference between many Marxist and many intersectional accounts of contradiction; while many of the Marxist accounts explored above often begin from the structural contradictions of capitalism as a system and then proceed to explain lived contradictions on this basis, the intersectional tradition more often begins with the knowledge and experience of real contradictions as they are lived and then thematizes structural relations on this basis. Neither account is wholly individual or wholly structural; Marxism and intersectionality share the commitment that both levels of analysis and their interrelation are central to explanations of the operations of contradiction in contemporary life. Their procedural or methodological differences, however, are worth noting, because they bring different elements into the foreground.[33]

Intersectionality's embrace of the contradictory character of subject formation, all the way down to the level of experience, is a certain radicalization of the concept of dialectics, able to take the contradictions of the world and see how they are written on to the body, into our speech, into our desire. In this way, it is an account of the contradictions of the world in a deep and indeed material sense, perhaps even more so than that offered by some Marxists, who take contradiction to be generally an issue of social position abstractly, rather than of lived experience concretely.

Intersectionality also thematizes contradiction on a political and structural level. As Vivian May explains, "the value of intersectionality's capacity to attend to relational power and privilege, across and within intermingled systems" is its ability to embrace "both/and logics" as something more than "illogical contradictions."[34] Rather, intersectionality focuses specifically on those moments of really existing contradictions, in which, for example, one is both oppressed and oppressor at the same time, or perhaps more accurately, one is simultaneously given and denied advantages in the world as a product of the contradictory constitution of the structure of the world. Rejecting the search for a perfect or total synthesis of the myriad contradictions enframing social and political life, Uma Narayan suggests than any "dialectical synthesis" that subjects carry out, any moment of reconciliation, will always be a partial and imperfect one:

> The relation between the two contexts the individual inhabits may not be simple or straightforward. The individual subject is seldom in a position to carry out a perfect 'dia-

---

[33] | This methodological distinction has often led interpreters to wrongly assume that intersectionality can *only* generate insights about experience or identity in an individualized sense rather than generating theoretical and structural analysis. As is clear at this point in the book, this idea is simply false, as intersectionality has made numerous contributions to the understanding of structures and systems of power.

[34] | May, *Pursuing Intersectionality, Unsettling Dominant Imaginaries*, 217.

lectical synthesis' that preserves all the advantages of both contexts and transcends all their problems. There may be a number of different 'syntheses,' each of which avoids a different subset of the problems and preserves a different subset of the benefits.[35]

Individuals may be and often are both subjected to oppression and complicit with oppression at one and the same time. Combahee River Collective member Barbara Smith writes, "As women of color..[i]t's often hard for us to believe that we can be both oppressed and oppressive at the same time."[36] This is one of intersectionality's deepest contributions to understanding the structural operation of contradiction: living within a world structured by oppression means that each of us is made in and through those oppressive structures. While this principle of intersectionality is often thematized through the relationship between oppression and privilege—that is, that I may be oppressed through one aspect of my identity but privileged through another—Smith's insight runs even deeper. Fundamentally, what Smith thematizes is that I may be oppressed and complicit *in the same axis*; that is, while I may be oppressed as a woman, I might also have internalized the narratives, dictates, and structures of misogyny and may act in ways that reinforce rather than unseat the very structures that contribute to my own oppression. The very real contradictions that structure any form of oppression produce, continually, both resistance to and complicity with both oppression and exploitation at every turn.

Moreover, the intersectional perspective that oppressions are intermeshed with each other illuminates another central contradiction at the heart of contemporary social, political, and economic life: that oppressions are both constitutive of one another and they are different from one another. As Russell, explains, "Current scholarship seems to be caught in a bind between collapsing social categories together and separating them out as a list."[37] These two diametrically opposed tendencies offer one of the most helpful and illuminating contributions of intersectionality to the dialectical tradition. If race is always gendered, classed, and sexualized, then what is the utility in continuing to even have separate concepts for them? Doesn't the very act of using different terms

---

35 | Uma Narayan, "The Project of Feminist Epistemology: Perspectives from a Non-Western Feminist," in *Gender/Body/Knowledge: Feminist Reconstructions of Being and Knowing*, ed. Alison Jaggar and Susan R. Bordo (New Brunswick, NJ: Rutgers University Press, 1989), 267.
36 | Smith, *Home Girls: A Black Feminist Anthology*, xliii–xliv.
37 | Kathryn Russell, "Feminist Dialectics and Marxist Theory," *Radical Philosophy Review* 10, no. 1 (2007): 35. Russell does not seem to find this problem to be helpfully thematized by intersectionality; while I appreciate her formulation of this problem, she significantly misses the way in which intersectionality's own tradition has insightful and dialectical solutions to this quandary, turning instead to other traditions.

for these phenomena suggest that there is something different about them, that they can't all be collapsed into the same idea? The answer is yes, to both questions. One of the most important insights one can learn from the intersectional tradition is that while in common parlance, and indeed sometimes even in theoretical investigation, it may be expedient to use terms like race or gender, in reality, the deep fabric of each of these terms cannot be rendered without reference to a whole host of others: sexuality, ability, nationality, class, etc. Hence, one of the key contentions of the intersectional tradition is that when one says 'race', one is also referring to the complex relays and interactions of racist gendering, racist ableism, racist class structures, etc. As some have noted, the deep interpenetration of all systems of oppression is hardly captured by the use of any of these terms in isolation or by the use of all of these terms in conjunctive lists. While we must have a concept of race that is conditioned by the other axes of oppression, and hence is constituted by them, the continued use of the term race (and gender and sex and class etc.) is itself productive of the misapprehension that these terms are ultimately separate. A truly intersectional understanding of the structural relationship between axes of oppression must be sensitively attuned to the ways in which each term is both irreducibly different and wholly suffused with each of the others. This is one of the central contradictions highlighted by the intersectional approach, and one of its most dialectical insights.

Dialectics as Intersectional Activist Practice

It is from this multi-layered understanding of contradiction that the figure of dialectics appears within the intersectional tradition. As Audre Lorde writes, understanding the real and particular contradictions that individuals live, and hence that structure the world, means that approaches to difference must take on a radicalized and revolutionary form: "Difference must not merely be tolerated, but seen as a fund of necessary polarities between which our creativity can spark like a dialectic."[38] In Lorde's understanding, dialectics names a dynamic process in which difference opens up the space to see problems from new perspectives and to imagine alternative worlds that would not reproduce the systems of oppression and exploitation that currently structure it. Here difference, rather than shared position, is figured as an opening, a possibility, which gives it positive rather than negative content. Only through recognizing and revalorizing differences can a dialectical model ground the process of revolutionary social change. Dialectics thus marks a strategy of reading and a politics of intervening in the world that can push beyond the contemporary con-

---

38 | Audre Lorde, *Sister/Outsider: Essays and Speeches* (Freedom: Crossing Press, 1984), 111.

traditions that structure it and that presents difference as a barrier to rather than the condition of possibility of engaging in collective action.

In this context we can begin to understand Cherrie Moraga and Gloria Anzaldúa's proclamation that "contradictions" are "the root of our radicalism."[39] In the intersectional tradition, this "root" manifests itself in a variety of ways. In the first place, contradictions constitute powerful openings onto understanding the very structure of domination. In so doing, these contradictions can open up the space for the creative and dialectical process of radical action, now conceived as the kinds of deep transformational work, of ourselves and society, that would be required in order to overcome those structures of domination. In this sense, probing contradictions as we live and experience them, discloses both the deep and embedded roots of the problems we face and acts as a guide for what truly radical work would entail. Through Lorde, Moraga, and Anzaldúa, the intersectional tradition thus thematizes a profound understanding of the relationship between lived contradiction and collective action. It is in this sense that Patricia Hill Collins argues that we should conceive of the relationship between oppression and activism as a "dialectical" one.[40] The painful, fraught, and complicated experiences of oppression are bound together with the movements to intercede against it. But in this, the intersectional tradition generates a profound insight into the relationship between theory and activism: it is not only that theoretical work can and should inform movements, but also that academics and theoreticians should root their own understandings in the insights gained and learned in movements. This is not only to say that theory and practice are bound together (though this is also true), but also that movements themselves are profound wells of knowledge about the contradictions of contemporary life and of the strategies that can be usefully deployed against oppression and exploitation. It is in this sense that the two forms of contradiction the intersectional tradition focuses on—the epistemological and the political—are themselves dialectically related to one another in the works of these authors.

CONCLUSION: TOWARDS A DIALECTIC OF DIFFERENCE

In both Marxist and intersectional traditions, dialectics figures as a potent and powerful way to render the differences in identity and position that so powerfully undergird the formation of contemporary capitalism. At its base, dialectics provides the theoretical tools for refusing the impasse of contemporary cap-

---

39 | Cherrie Moraga and Gloria Anzaldúa, eds., *This Bridge Called My Back: Writings by Radical Women of Color* (New York: Kitchen Table Press, 1983), 5.
40 | Collins, *Black Feminist Thought*, 22.

italism that furnishes us with two irreconcilable propositions about the nature of difference. The first proposition, what we might call the liberal stance, insists that we are all essentially the same, our differences are illusory, the fount of false politics, the sower of division. The liberated world, for the liberal critic, is one in which our differences melt away to reveal the underlying fundament of humanity shining forth from each one of us. The second proposition, what we might call the neoliberal stance, insists that we are all in fact different, that these differences make us each individual, unique, singular. On this view difference is all we have, the only truth, the only possibility.

In true dialectical fashion, while each of these propositions individually is false, there is something true about their conjunction: through its regimes of oppression and exploitation, capitalism does at one and the same time engage in homogenization and differentiation as structural features of the process of accumulation. In this sense, unilateral valorizations of either difference or sameness are strategies complicit with the production, reproduction, and maintenance of capitalist norms. It is in this sense that both liberal erasures of difference and neoliberal appeals to reductive understandings of identity maintain rather than contest capitalism. Speaking of the latter position, Himani Bannerji cautions, "the notion of 'identity' also, similar to many other useful notions, can become an ideological tool—and perform the same function that ideology has to, namely make the connections invisible."[41] This invisibility of connections is what queer Marxist Daniel Bensaïd referred to as "a shifting shimmer of singularities," in contrast to the notion of absolute singularity, mobilizing against the structures of exploitation and oppression requires understanding the connections between identities and positions, the structures that simultaneously homogenize and differentiate us, bringing us simultaneously, sometimes painfully, closer together and farther apart at the same time. What is necessary now, Bensaïd, argues, is "a dialectic of difference, which is essential to establishing a relationship of forces in the battle against oppression."[42]

Both the Marxist and the intersectional traditions turn toward versions of what might called a dialectic of difference to articulate the structures of oppression and exploitation that structure the contemporary world. This dialectic, deeply rooted in the productive, creative possibilities opened by affirming both differences and relations, can only be helpfully grounded through integrating some of the insights of both the Marxist and the intersectional traditions. To concretize a notion of this dialectic of difference, I would like to turn to three

---

41 | Himani Bannerji, *Thinking Through: Essays on Feminism, Marxism, and Anti-Racism* (Canada: Women's Press, 1995), 38.

42 | Drucker's translation. Daniel Bensaïd, *Les Irréductibles: Théorèmes de La Résistance à l'air Du Temps* (Paris: Textuel, 2001), 42; Drucker, *Warped*, 17.

potential models, one from the Marxist tradition and two from the intersectional tradition that each gesture toward what this might look like.

One of these models comes from Patricia Hill Collins, who explains that oppression and exploitation are constituted together in what she calls "the matrix of domination." The image of a matrix is a powerful and expansive one. It renders simultaneously the relations and provisional unity of multiple points within a figure without erasing the particularities of the positions that constitute it. The matrix of domination thus signifies that "for any given sociohistorical context" that social locations are "structured via a system of interlocking race, class, and gender oppression[s]", each of which "needs the others in order to function." Thus each site inside a matrix is relational, constituted in and through the other points within it. Moreover, the matrix shows the ways in which the dialectic of difference plays out simultaneously on multiple levels: "the level of personal biography; the group or community level ... and the systemic level of social institutions. Black feminist thought emphasizes all three levels as sites of domination and as potential sites of resistance." The multi-faceted and mutli-layered matrix renders the dialectic of difference as simultaneously constituting the structures that wound and the possibilities of transformative action. It is also able to weave together the individual and the structural at one and the same time, insisting on both the necessity of "individual empowerment" and recognizing that "only collective action can effectively generate lasting social transformation of political and economic institutions."[43] The matrix as a metaphor shows simultaneously how an overall social, political, and economic structure of domination frames the differential possibilities of life with contemporary capitalism and highlights the specificities, positions, and individual experiences that are related to but never reductively determined by those structures. The matrix, as an image that holds fast both to individual points and to the structure that surrounds those points and, to some extent, makes those points legible and connected, thus figures the dialectic of difference in a powerful way.

From the Marxist tradition of negative dialectics comes another model, that of the constellation. Emerging out of Adorno, Benjamin, and other Frankfurt School theorists, a constellation is, in one sense, a unity, but only a provisional one; one that is wholly constituted through the relations between the stars within it. Likewise, in looking at a constellation, we can see something about the individual stars that we could not perceive by simply taking each one in complete isolation from one another. There is something both objective and interpretive about constellations as well: some stars are closer to each other, and this objective condition is the condition of the possibility of seeing any given constellation. But how one looks at the stars, what shapes emerge for the

---

43 | Collins, *Black Feminist Thought*, 221-38.

viewer, how far is 'too far' apart for stars to be part of the same constellation—these are all contingent on the frames that the viewer brings with them. It is in this sense that many Marxist theorists, like David Harvey, have illuminated that each pole of a given contradiction is not a static, uniform, or unchanging 'thing', but is the incarnation of processes: each pole of the contradiction does not "exist outside of or prior to the processes, flows, and relations that create, sustain, or undermine them."[44] The constellation thus might serve as another model of the dialectic of difference.

A third model of a dialectic of difference might be the prism, a figure that emerges in both the intersectional and the Marxist traditions as ways of marking the ways in which any concept, figure, or position, is a unique, multifaceted confluence of relations.[45] While both the matrix and the constellation foreground the ways in which individual points relate in order to constitute a whole, the prism brings into relief the multiplicity that inheres in any individual point. It provides a way of reading each individual, each social location, each structure of oppression or exploitation as itself a manifold, an internal heterogeneity that is constituted in and through other structures of power:

> Imagine a ray of light—which to the naked eye, appears to be only one color—refracted through a prism onto a white wall. To the eye, the result is not an infinite, disorganized scatter of individual colors. Rather, the refracted light displays an order, a structure of relationships among the different colors—a rainbow. Similarly, we propose to use the 'prism of difference' [...] to analyze a continuous spectrum of people, in order to show how gender is organized and experienced differently when refracted through the prism of sexual, racial/ethnic, social class, physical abilities, age, and national citizenship differences.[46]

The image of the prism thus brings the dialectic of difference into each and every site, highlighting the ways in which relations between individual points are related internally as well as externally, are constituted in and through each other.

---

44 | David Harvey, *Justice, Nature, and the Geography of Difference* (New York: Blackwell Publishing, 1996), 49.

45 | In addition to the passage quoted just below, we should remember that prisms are a particular important metaphor for Adorno's understanding of negative dialectics. See, for example: Theodor W. Adorno, *Prisms*, trans. Shierry Weber Nicholsen and Samuel Weber, Reprint edition (Cambridge, Mass.: The MIT Press, 1983).

46 | Maxine Baca Zinn, Pierrette Hondagneu-Sotelo, and Michael Messner, "Gender through the Prism of Difference," in *Race, Class, and Gender: An Anthology*, ed. Patricia Hill Collins and Maragret Anderson, 4th ed. (Belmont, CA: Wadsworth, 2001), 169.

In a non-reductive reading of capitalism, all of these models are present, overlapping on one another. Every particular socio-historical moment is defined by its particular matrix of domination. Matrices of domination differ from one another, across time or space, not only through the individual points in the matrix, but also through the particular contours of their arrangement, or the shape of their constellation. Each point within the matrix is itself a prism, which, when approached in the right light, has the capacity to unveil a whole series of relations.

Thus, a dialectical understanding of difference approaches the individual and the structural, the experiential and the theoretical as two poles of creative tension, irreducibly different, often counter-posed, but both distinctly necessary. As David McNally explains,

> Dialectics [...]grasp[s] human activity as the moment of *intersection* and interpenetration of subject and object. This is why world-changing and self-changing are moments of a single process. Revolutionary transformation of society simultaneously entails tremendous processes of individual and collective learning.[47]

The dialectic of difference is thus both an analysis and part of an organizing strategy, both descriptive and prescriptive. While this chapter has focused primarily on explaining a dialectical *understanding* of the world, the following chapter answers the questions: how do we organize from these contradictions? How do we put the dialectic of difference into transformative practice?

---

47 | David McNally, "Language, Praxis, and Dialectics: Reply to Collins," *Historical Materialism* 12, no. 2 (2004): 149-50. Emphasis mine.

Chapter Seven: Solidarity in the House of Difference

> "If you let them red-bait, they'll race-bait, and if you let them race-bait, they'll queen-bait."
> - 1930s slogan of the National Union of Marine Cooks and Stewards[1]

> "I have often wished I could spread the word that a movement committed to fighting sexual, racial, economic, and heterosexist oppression, not to mention one which opposed imperialism, anti-Semitism, the oppressions visited upon the physically disabled, the old and the young, at the same time that it challenges militarism and imminent nuclear destruction, is the very opposite of narrow."
> - Barbara Smith[2]

> "Until I am Free, You are Not Free Either."
> - Fannie Lou Hamer[3]

In August 2013, Mikki Kendall started the hashtag #SolidarityIsForWhite Women, forcing debates about the politics of visibility and social location into the mainstream. In the months that followed, Twitter devotees founded #BlackPowerIsForBlackMen and #NotYourAsianSidekick, initiating a series of responses to the persisting tendency of women of color to be erased by both

---

[1] | Cited in: Allan Bérubé, *My Desire for History: Essays in Gay Community and Labor History* (Chapel Hill: University of North Carolina Press, 2011), 310.
[2] | Smith, *Home Girls: A Black Feminist Anthology*, xxxi.
[3] | Fannie Lou Hamer, *To Tell It Like It Is: The Speeches of Fannie Lou Hamer*, ed. Maegan Parker Brooks and Davis W. Houck (Jackson, MS: University Press of Mississippi, 2010), 121-30.

mainstream feminist movements and people of color movements. In so doing, through Twitter, a broader popular discourse provoked a series of prescient and complicated questions that both theorists and activists are obliged to work through: how have previous attempts at solidarity failed so thoroughly as to provoke the notion that solidarity is a fundamentally racialized and gendered concept, perhaps stabilizing institutions of power rather than unsettling them? To this conversation, we should counter-pose similar viral hashtags: #IAmTrayvonMartin and #WeAreAllTrayvon. Initially the hashtags, used mostly by black people, demonstrated the ways in which being subjected to armed violence and terror is a constitutive feature of anti-black racism in the contemporary United States; many other young black men could just as easily have faced Trayvon's fate because his murder was motivated by racism, not by anything particular to him as a unique individual. In that sense, any young black man could face his own George Zimmerman, because the system produces and foments the conditions for vigilante violence against people of color. What started as a group of black Twitter users highlighting the structural forces of anti-black racism began to be taken as a call for *all people* to use it without interrogating the status of the 'I' or the 'We' in the original hashtags. White social media users saw the hashtag as an opportunity to express solidarity with anti-racist struggle. The backlash was predictable: the very real fact that those of us who are white simply *are not* Trayvon Martin—and hence are not subjected to the specific modes of violence, terror, and coercion that constitute anti-Black racism—was seen to be disavowed by the use of the hashtag. White people's use of the hashtag seemed to square rather well with liberal notions of what has been called "colorblind racism," in which anti-racism is figured as a refusal to foreground the very real differences of experience, position, and power across racial groups.[4] In this sense, the Twitterverse roundly condemned this pseudo-solidarity as cooption and disavowal largely consistent with rather than destructive of racism in the USA.

With these two #SolidarityFails in mind, this chapter aims to reconceputalize what solidarity might mean in the context of the discussions of previous chapters. If solidarity does not and cannot be grounded in the pathetic liberal pleas of our 'ultimate' sameness, how can we navigate political relationships of coalition, alliance, and allyship across the dialectic of difference? What does solidarity look like when it is refigured as an outgrowth of, rather than a challenge to, the very real differences of position and experience that capitalism

---

4 | Eduardo Bonilla-Silva, *Racism without Racists: Color-Blind Racism and the Persistence of Racial Inequality in America*, 3 edition (Lanham: Rowman & Littlefield Publishers, 2009); Leslie G. Carr, *"Color-Blind" Racism* (Thousand Oaks: SAGE Publications, Inc, 1997); Michelle Alexander, *The New Jim Crow: Mass Incarceration in the Age of Colorblindness* (New York: The New Press, 2012).

depends on? We do not have to say that 'we are all Trayvon Martin' to express that we are all subjected to and live through the systems that killed Trayvon, even if capitalism, colonization, racism, and heteropatriarchy affect us in radically different ways.

This chapter proceeds in three sections. In the first section, I argue that part of the traditional Marxist conception of solidarity has historically relied on a notion of commensurability, that is, that solidarity can be expressed as the recognition of the moments of unity, shared situation, or commonality as the basis for mobilizing the power of movements. The problem with this orientation, however, is that it forces us, both politically and analytically, to mobilize from the lowest common denominator of our situation, implicitly or explicitly conceiving of moments of non-unity, non-similarity, or unshared condition as secondary, subsequent, epiphenomenal, or at worst irrelevant to the project of uprooting capitalism. In this model, we see two possibilities operative: either that differences are ultimately commensurable or that they are eliminable. There are different problems with each approach, but neither of them can speak to the specificities of subject position or social location in their deep imbrication with capitalism. The second section argues that the issue of incommensurability was actually quite sensitively thought by Marx, if not by many subsequent Marxists. Mobilizing Dipesh Chakrabarty's reading of Marx, we can see how Marx himself located a significant part of the problem of capitalism as producing a logic of commensurability, which is, according to Marx, part of what an anti-capitalist project must refuse. Marx gives us some of the necessary tools for thinking about capitalism's production of commensurability, but he himself does not adequately conceive the true extent of the problem, specifically the ways in which it constitutes oppressive as well as exploitative relations. Rather, as we will have seen in the first section, differences within the constitution of oppression and exploitation are also made commensurable by a capitalist logic. Hence, much of the contemporary Marxist approach to solidarity replays rather than subverts capital's production of commensurability. Despite this, a Marxist anti-capitalism is necessary for understanding how differences are produced as commensurable in the first place and how capitalism is the grammar for the erasure of incommensurable logics of oppression. The third section turns to intersectionality to radicalize and deepen the understanding of incommensurability as a way of reformulating solidarity. Intersectionality's theorizing of oppressed identities as coalitions allows us to think about relations as ways that conserve incommensurability *and* can serve as the basis for solidarity. Rather than falling prey to the liberal or post-structuralist versions of incommensurability that deny the role of relation, intersectionality articulates a model in which differences are conserved as the condition of the possibility of relation. Hence, this chapter as a whole argues that by integrating the insights of the Marxist and intersectional traditions, we can reformulate the concept of solidarity under capitalism as grounded in the incommensurable differences of social location.

CAPITAL'S LOGICS OF INCOMMENSURABILITY

The problem of commensurability in the Marxist tradition has taken numerous forms. On the one hand, certain directions in both Marxist theory and activism point toward a logic of commensurability, that is, of recognizing certain shared conditions (of labor exploitation, for example) as the basis for organizing broad-based groups of people against structures of exploitation and oppression. This supposedly shared position has often been used as the basis for the articulation of broad-based, 'universal' demands like the elimination of child labor, the reduction of the working day, the rights to unionize and strike, demands for universal healthcare, and, ultimately, for the abolition of an economic system that accumulates wealth for the few through the immiseration of the many. On the other hand, certain currents within Marxist theory and activism point to the many ways in which capitalism produces and reproduces differences under capitalism, as a central and structural condition of its possibility. The recognition of these differences has often been used as the basis for 'particular' demands like reparations, wages for social reproduction, indigenous land rights, and many others.

These tendencies within Marxism have often come into deep conflict with one another, with proponents of the former position arguing that focus on particular demands undermines projects of solidarity by committing us to a form of irreconcilable relativism, and proponents of the latter arguing for the necessity of rectifying the specific harms that oppressed groups face under capitalism. Critiques of the relativist position are well-worn and need not be rehearsed here, except to note that while the problems with the relativist position are numerous, left forms of relativism do themselves respond to an incredibly pressing problem: the contestation of universal notions that hide rather than expose oppression and exploitation and that adhere to a politics of assimilation. One of the most pressing concerns for philosophies of liberation must be the development of framework that can steer a path between the Scylla of universalizing human experience and the Charybdis of what Steven Best has called "the dictatorship of the fragments."[5] Holly Lewis' attempt to do so is to introduce a distinction between a "universalism from above" and a "uni-

---

5 | Steven Best, "Jameson, Totality, and the Poststructuralist Critique," in *Postmodernism/Jameson/Critique*, ed. Douglas Kellner (Washington, DC: Maisonneuve Press, 1989), 361.

versalism of below."[6] The former, for Lewis, is the form of universalism that is problematic in all of the ways that feminist, queer, anti-racist and disabled theorists have contested for centuries; it operates by covering over the diversity of social location and human experience through the assumption of a universal Man and hence a universal Politics. As opposed to this framework, Lewis' "universalism of below" seeks to chart an alternative path, grounded in the commonality of being subjected to the brutal regime of accumulation and dispossession under capitalism. This universalism from below, she argues, is grounded in the notion of commensurability that must be present in order to forge a politics of solidarity and recognize common cause.[7] However while Lewis' attempt is helpful, ultimately, basing a politics of emancipation in commensurability is precisely the problem that many intersectional theorists have located in a variety of leftist movements and theories of emancipation. Because social locations are actually not commensurable, any universalism, even from below, will come at the expense of adequately conceiving the specificity of capital's particular formations.

Take, for example, the differential logics of racialization that are evident in the historical construction of blackness and of indigeneity, respectively. While many contemporary accounts of race err by considering one or the other of these positions to the be the *ur*-form of racial construction (and hence the model to which all other structures of race ultimately refer), much contemporary scholarship from ethinic studies, Asian and Pacific Islander studies, African and Black Diaspora studies, Indigenous studies, and Latinx studies, have shown that the actual logic of racial regimes is itself not nearly so consistent. Iyko Day helpfully distinguishes between two logics of racism under settler colonial capitalism, one based on the "logic of elimination" and one based in the "logic of exclusion."[8] In her account, the logic of exclusion refers to the way in which racial hierarchy is upheld specifically through the reproduction of race in order to continue to exclude racialized populations from certain forms of labor, as well as from central political institutions of citizenship, recognition, and social power. This form of racialization is specifically oriented toward increasing the racialized population as a permanent underclass of workers, contributing to the intergenerational continuity of precarity and vulnerability, both in terms of exposure to high rates of exploitation and in lack of access to social and political power. The logic of exclusion is the organizing logic for those whose structural position under capitalism is primarily organized through racialized and gendered modes of subjection based in labor power; on her account, this logic is particularly applied to what she calls "alien labor", that is, in racialized

---

6 | Lewis, *The Politics of Everybody*, 11.
7 | Ibid.
8 | Day, *Alien Capital*, 25.

non-indigenous groups like black, Latinx, and Asian groups who are continually produced and reproduced as laborers in particularly precarious positions. In order for this logic to operate, the stability of capitalism's regime of accumulation requires the continual reproduction of the racialized group, especially, though not exclusively, in terms of the gendered and sexualized logics of generational replacement.

One concrete way to understand this requirement is in thinking about how the racial logic of blackness in the United States context. It is well known that, particularly in the United States, but also elsewhere, black racialization was governed by a 'one-drop rule', meaning, that from a legal classification perspective, anyone with any amount of black ancestry was considered black and hence subjected to all of the rules, regulations, dispossessions, and restrictions of all black people. In this sense, the logic of US anti-blackness was predicated on the idea that it is impossible to 'assimilate' out one's racial status as a black person. Historically, this in-assimilability was organized through the maternal inheritance of the status of slavery, and in the contemporary world continues through the way in which, colorism notwithstanding, mixed-race black people are consistently read 'as black'; Barack Obama for example, a person of mixed white and black heritage is considered the first black president, not just another white president or even, the first mixed-race president. This can only be understood inside a racial regime that continues the collective technology of race in ways that consider the 'heritability' of blackness and whiteness along completely counterposed logics, based in the continuation of a 'one-drop' logic.

By contrast, the logic of elimination manifests specifically in the case of indigenous racialization under settler colonial capitalism. The logic of elimination is organized specifically around the extermination of indigenous people, a multi-faceted program of violence in order to drive the dispossession of land which is necessary to the continuation of settler colonial capitalism in the form of ongoing primitive accumulation. Historically, this took the form of the intentional genocide of indigenous people through direct means: genocide disguised as war, the invention of biological weapons of annihilation, the systematic destruction of indigenous communities. Direct genocide is only one manifestation of the logic of elimination however; especially in the twentieth and twenty-first centuries, the logic of elimination takes the form of a technology of "biological absorption" that seeks to eliminate native people through intermarriage and cultural assimilation.[9] As Day reminds us, though these techniques are rather different, in the context of racialization genocide and assimilation they are "contradictory—but complementary—means" of attempting to eradicate the indigenous population.[10] In direct contrast to the one-drop rule

---

9 | Day, 25.
10 | Ibid.

developed in the case of blackness, a sophisticated system of blood quantum, traced through eugenic notions of parentage and inheritance, determined that a person was no longer indigenous if their 'blood quantum' reached below a certain threshold.[11] An entire system of forced assimilation, including rampant child abduction and relocation to white families, was part of a strategy that viewed race—for indigenous, but not black people—as something that could be "diluted" or "bred out."[12] In this case, the logic of capitalist accumulation primarily depends not on the reproduction of a racialized underclass of workers for the accumulation of surplus value, but rather on the white settlers' need to continue to dispossess indigenous people of their land.

---

11 | The first 'blood quantum' rule introduced in North America was passed by the Colony of Virginia in 1705. Under that piece of legislation, a person was deemed a racialized subject and excluded from citizenship if they were '1/2' or more indigenous (which generally meant if they had 1 indigenous parent or two indigenous grandparents). Between 1705 and 1933, various states, territories, and localities enacted a wide variety of racial classification laws, many of which relied on an idea of blood quantum, though in places that explicitly adhered to a binary racial classification (white or non-white), indigenous people were often subject to one-drop rules as well. The idea of a specific form of blood quantum that applied specifically to indigenous people, and not to any other racial or ethnic groups, was further entrenched by the U.S. Federal Government through both the Dawes Act of 1887 and the Indian Reorganization Act of 1934. Both pieces of legislation have been continually critiqued by indigenous activists and academics for entrenching the idea of blood quantum in order to determine indigenous membership, often in specific contradistinction to how indigenous tribes had themselves organized community membership before these dates. After 1934, many native tribes have been forced to adopt ideas of blood quantum into their own structures of tribal recognition, membership, and government. For more on this history, of the complicated legacy of blood quantum on multiple indigenous communities, see: Se-ah-dom Edmo, Jesse Young, and Alan Parker, *American Indian Identity: Citizenship, Membership and Blood* (Santa Barbara, California: Praeger, 2016); Katherine Ellinghaus, *Blood Will Tell: Native Americans and Assimilation Policy* (Lincoln: University of Nebraska Press, 2017); Norbert S. Hill and Kathleen Ratteree, *The Great Vanishing Act: Blood Quantum and the Future of Native Nations* (Colorado: Fulcrum Publishing, 2017); Kim Tallbear, *Native American DNA: Tribal Belonging and the False Promise of Genetic Science* (Minneapolis: University of Minnesota Press, 2013).
12 | Andrea Smith, "Heteropatriarchy and the Three Pillars of White Supremacy: Rethinking Women of Color Organizing," in *Color of Violence: The Incite! Anthology* (Cambridge: South End Press, 2006), 66-73; J. Kehaulani Kauanui, *Hawaiian Blood: Colonialism and the Politics of Sovereignty and Indigeneity* (Durham, NC: Duke University Press, 2008).

While Day locates these two logics of racialization, there seems also rather to be a third logic that, at least until the mid-twentieth century was operative, specifically in relationship to Latinx people. While many groups face targeted racialization, in at least some cases, settler colonial capitalism developed a strategy of denying the reality of racialization altogether. Until the landmark court case of *Hernandez v. Texas* (1954), for example, the State of Texas refused to recognize that Latinx people could possibly be subjected to racial violence, exclusion, or prejudice. According to the Treaty of Guadalupe Hidalgo, all Latinx people were considered by law to be "white," despite, of course, being subject to structural, constant, and ongoing evidence that they were not treated as white citizens.[13] Based in a historical narrative that citizens of Mexico and their descendants (and, by extension, citizens of all of Latin America and their descendants) were themselves the descendants of Spanish and Portuguese conquerors, courts repeatedly alleged that Latinx people were in fact, as Euro-descendent people, white, and hence could not be discriminated against on the basis of race.[14] While this was the position of institutional structures of law, this was clearly not born out in daily practice. Latinx people faced segregation, employment discrimination, jury exclusion, and immigration restrictions in ways that clearly testified to the fact that Latinx people certainly were not treated as white, often on the basis of simply having Spanish-sounding surnames and/or speaking Spanish as a first language.[15] In refusing to recognize the racialization of Latinx people, courts and laws prevented Latinx people from accessing the meager legal protections against racism. Denying Latinx people's status as racialized was used to justify and perpetuate their vulnerability and precarity. We might supplement Day's argument then, by highlighting that in addition to a logic of elimination and a logic of exclusion, race in the United States context also developed a *logic of inclusion*, one that specifically denies the racialized

---

13 | There are obvious limitations to relying on the law, legal institutions, or, as below, the Census, as the basis for discussions of race and racialization. My argument here is illustrative, showing that, even internal to very limited and circumscribed arena of the law, race is structured in a disunified and internally contradictory way.

14 | It seems not to have entered the realm of possibility for the United States courts that some Latinx people were indigenous, black, or of mixed race. Various legal systems in Latin America have erected numerous racial classification schemes that have varied throughout time and place in the hemisphere.

15 | These practices were further complicated by the fact that black Latinx people were assumed to be black and treated accordingly. There are, of course, also white Latinx people, and the argument posed here should not be read as denying that fact. Rather, it is to say that until the 1950s the morphological technologies of racial ascription and passing was often not available even to white or white-passing Latinx people on the basis of their surnames, national origin, immigration status, and native language.

status of certain groups in order to continue to produce and reproduce populations who are subjected to extreme vulnerability and precarity. This logic of inclusion might be seen in the contemporary landscape in the ways in which, at least according to the United States Census data, individuals of Middle Eastern descent are also classified as 'white', despite the continued logics of racialized violence directed at people of Middle Eastern descent, especially those who are black, Arab, and/or Muslim.[16]

That these three logics—elimination, exclusion, and inclusion—were instituted unevenly, inconsistently, and sometimes, in overlapping ways, is further testament to the internal tensions, contradictions, and differences in the relationship of racialization to the logic of capital.[17] It is clear that, as argued previously, capitalism requires both access to land and access to exploitable labor in order to function; this conversation clarifies the ways in which a historically-situated and empirically robust understanding of racialization must account for the simultaneity and incommensurability of these modes of producing white access to land and labor. The incommensurability of these logics has led to radically different legislation, experiences, social codes, administrative surveillance, and modes of dispossession for multiple racialized groups. Capitalism simultaneously relies on racialized exploitation *and* non-commensurable mechanisms of racialization.

These three logics of racialization were themselves deeply intertwined in techniques of gendering and sexualization. As Andrea Smith and others have

---

16 | These positions and identities should not be at all collapsed, as the Middle East is itself a vibrant, internally heterogeneous, and incredibly diverse area. But it is precisely this diversity that is occluded in the institutional designation of all people of Middle Eastern descent as white, despite the various ways in which multiple different Middle Eastern populations are and continue to be racialized. For an incredibly compelling historical account of the development of race and racism against Arab-Americans has developed, see Jamal's work in particular. For helpful accounts of the structure of Anti-Arab racism in the U.S., see Salaita and Bayoumi. Steven Salaita, *Anti-Arab Racism in the USA: Where It Comes From and What It Means for Politics Today* (London: Pluto Press, 2006); Moustafa Bayoumi, *How Does It Feel to Be a Problem?: Being Young and Arab in America* (New York: Penguin Books, 2009); Amaney Jamal, *Race and Arab Americans Before and After 9/11: From Invisible Citizens to Visible Subjects* (Syracuse, New York: Syracuse University Press, 2008).

17 | In speaking of these logics, I am, of course, speaking rather generally; this account should not be taken to constitute a reductive account of race, or to deny other arrangements of racial logics, complicated intersections, or the existence of racial formations that diverge from these general outlines; my account here is illustrative, not exhaustive, seeking only to show that racialization, when taken as a single, undifferentiated category, reveals multiple, incommensurable organizations and logics.

argued, the logic of elimination was deeply imbricated in sexual violence as a mode of terror that contributed to the dictates of biological absorption.[18] Many theorists of black feminism and black sexuality have shown how the logic of exclusion was possible only through the reproduction of widespread sexual violence.[19] While it might be tempting to think about sexual violence between these logics as similar, this tendency should be refused. Within a logic of elimination, sexual violence, especially inflicted by white men on women of color, might be organized so as to create the conditions in which children are born with increasingly less indigenous blood and hence fewer legal claims to the land. Within a logic of exclusion, sexual violence perpetuated by white men on women of color might be organized so as to continually reproduce a new generation of highly precarious, vulnerable, exploitable workers. Of course, sexual violence is always organized in a variety of ways, with multiple manifestations and organizations; tracing these logics should not be seen as (over)determinative. Rather, it highlights the necessity of developing a theory of capitalism that can be attentive to these divergent logics in their specificity.

The relationship between sexual violence and race cannot be exhaustively thematized, however, in discussions of white men raping women of color, though of course no account would be tenable without it. Sexual violence was also an aspect of the way in which conquering, settler men of the colonial state exercised power and violence over colonized men, especially those who were interpreted as deviating from a European understanding of masculinity. Moreover, the forced imposition of European norms of sex, gender, and sexuality onto communities of color constituted another aspect of this dense web.[20] Non-heteronormative and non-binary ideas of gender were also historically used in order to justify enslavement, dispossession, and appropriation, and were thus, in a variety of ways, completely interwoven in the narratives and ideas of race. These are not mere historical artifacts, but rather continue to enframe the contemporary matrix in which race, gender, and sexuality are interwoven categories.

---

18 | Smith, *Conquest: Sexual Violence and American Indian Genocide*.
19 | Davis, "Rape, Racism, and the Myth of the Black Rapist"; McGuire, *At the Dark End of the Street: Black Women, Rape, and Resistance—A New History of the Civil Rights Movement from Rosa Parks to the Rise of Black Power*; Roberts, *Killing the Black Body*.
20 | Paula Gunn Allen, *The Sacred Hoop: Recovering the Feminine in American Indian Traditions* (Open Road Media, 2015); Lugones, "Heterosexualism and the Colonial / Modern Gender System"; Oyeronke Oyewumi, *The Invention of Women: Making an African Sense of Western Gender Discourses*, 1 edition (Minneapolis: University of Minnesota Press, 1997).

Regimes of forced sterilization are also interwoven in this history.[21] Indigenous women, black women, and Latinx women have been and continue to be subjected to constant infringements on their own bodily autonomy through the performance of a variety of sterilization procedures that have taken place either against the patients' will, without their consent, or under conditions of extreme duress. While many accounts of forced sterilization wrongly consign this practice to the past, an investigative report in 2013 showed that these procedures were still being performed in California prisons, on people who did not consent to these procedures; nearly all of those subjected to them were women of color.[22] In 2017, Judge Sam Benningfield was actively offering reduced sentences to those convicted of a crime if they agreed to get vasectomies or birth control implants.[23] At first glance, the common practices of forced sterilization might seem at odds with the logic of exclusion, which relies on the reproduction of racialized groups. We can thus see a tension in the racialized logic of gender violence emerge through the counter-position of sexual assault and forced sterilization; one form increases the chances of biological reproduction and the other specifically aims to prohibit it. How can we read this duality within the regimes of racialized gender violence? This is just one example among thousands of the ways in which any potent or useful theory of oppression must account for the divergent logics that structure race, gender, class, sexuality, ability, and nationality in the contemporary world. What this discussion shows us is that not only are broad categories like "racialization" imbricated in dense, differential logics that cannot be reduced to one another, but so too are specific strategies of domination like sexual violence or forced sterilization. Any attempt to pin down any of these categories under one unified logic will miss the heterogeneity of its manifestations and will systematically erase the central contradictions between these logics as they play out in practice. They

---

21 | Karen Stote, *An Act of Genocide: Colonialism and the Sterilization of Aboriginal Women* (Halifax and Winnipeg: Fernwood Publishing, 2015); Sally J. Torpy, "Native American Women and Coerced Sterilization: On the Trail of Tears in the 1970s," *American Indian Culture and Research Journal* 24, no. 2 (2000): 1-22; Angela Davis, "Racism, Birth Control, and Reproductive Rights," in *Feminist Postcolonial Theory: A Reader* (New York: Routledge, 2003); Andrea Smith, "Beyond Pro-Choice Versus Pro-Life Women of Color and Reproductive Justice," *NWSA Journal* 17, no. 1 (Spring 2005): 119-40.
22 | Corey G. Johnson, "Female Inmates Sterilized in California Prisons without Approval," *The Center for Investigative Reporting*, July 7, 2013, http://cironline.org/reports/female-inmates-sterilized-california-prisons-without-approval-4917.
23 | Kalahan Rosenblatt, "Judge Offers Inmates Reduced Sentences in Exchange for Vasectomy," *NBC News*, July 21, 2017, https://www.nbcnews.com/news/us-news/judge-offers-inmates-reduced-sentences-exchange-vasectomy-n785256.

will thus be impoverished frameworks, ones that will, explicitly or implicitly, privilege certain groups' experiences and realities over others'.

What is sketched above is clearly indexed, empirically and historically, to the particular traditions of the United States. The historical operations of the interpenetration of gender, race, and sexuality under capitalism were not constant in all contexts, even if there may be linkages between the U.S. and other formations, especially vis-à-vis the US's particular neocolonial and neoimperial position in contemporary global geopolitics. This analysis is specifically generated in the context of what Iyko Day calls "the settler colonial mode of production" under capitalism. Different histories and techniques of this operation were evident in the mode of production under capitalism within the colonial and European non-settler metropoles. Moreover, both of these modes differ significantly from the ways in which oppression was organized, in what Patrick Wolfe has called "franchise colonies:" non-settler formations of imperial and colonial capitalism in which large-scale settler projects were never themselves developed.[24] As Sanyal argues, these two structures also differ from the development of "post-colonial capitalism."[25] These different modes of capitalist production, development, and reproduction not only give rise to various logics of gender, race, and sexuality, but also to the very structure and constitution of capital itself. Just as the forms of oppression under the settler colonial mode of capitalist production operate in incommensurable ways, so too are the various modes of capitalist production, each of which interact with vectors of oppression in unique ways.[26]

Obviously, a full account of historical specificities cannot be answered generally or theoretically; an analysis of specific cases and arrangements will always have to be contextualized, revised, and expanded in light of the particular instance under consideration. Theory cannot answer every question, and even less can it answer them in advance. Theories do however need to be responsive to, and generated out of, the actual arrangement of diversity and contradiction in the construction of oppression and exploitation, if they are to be useful and illuminating. As Lise Vogel reminds us, "Only in the analysis of an actual situation will abstraction spring to life, for it is history that puts flesh on the bare bones of theory."[27] As we can see from just the few issues traced

---

24 | Patrick Wolfe, "Settler Colonialism and the Elimination of the Native," *Journal of Genocide Research* 8, no. 4 (December 2006): 387–409.

25 | Kalyan Sanyal, *Rethinking Capitalist Development: Primitive Accumulation, Governmentality, and Post-Colonial Capitalism* (London and New Delhi: Routledge, 2013).

26 | An exhaustive explanation of each of these modes of production, their differences, and the multiple organizations of oppression under each is certainly outside the scope of this project, though a worthy and necessary endeavor on its own.

27 | Vogel, *Marxism and the Oppression of Women*, 9.

above, the interrelationships between gender, race, and sexuality manifest themselves rather differently and incommensurably, not only between groups, but also within groups, not only between societies, but also within them. Crucially, what this shows this that any analysis of race, gender, and sexuality cannot reduce these oppressions to single logic or to a single set of relations to capitalism. We thus need a theory that can, at minimum, respond to these differences *in their incommensurability*, rather than, as is far too often the case, taking one arrangement of forces as the model for all others.

CAPITAL'S PRODUCTION OF COMMENSURABILITY

Dipesh Chakrabarty offers an understanding of Marx's conception of capitalism that embraces rather than rejects this commensurability.[28] Chakrabarty shows that the most common responses to incommensurability—either assuming "an absence of relationship between dominant and dominating forms" or of producing "equivalents that successfully mediate between differences"—is a choice that, internal to the Marxist tradition, can be refused.[29] Specifically, Chakrabarty argues that revisiting the distinction between concrete and abstract labor reveals a method of relating to difference beyond commensurability.

Abstraction forms a central concern in Marx's own writing. Though this problem emerges at multiple points in his work, there are three central concerns with abstraction that are relevant here: the character of the commodity, the character of labor, and the conditions of labor. Abstraction emerges in Marx's discussion of the commodity in the following way: in order for goods to be exchanged, there must be something in those goods that is somehow seen to be equivalent or equal. Marx stages this problem through a reading of Aristotle, but we could just as easily turn to the common dictum that one 'cannot compare apples to oranges.' In common parlance, this signifies that comparisons cannot be made between unlike objects, but in our actual daily lives, the fruit picker may well exchange the apples she picks for a wage in

---

28 | His concern might initially seem to be significantly be located outside of the debate between Marxism and intersectionality, as he is concerned with the relationship between Marxism and subaltern studies. I do not in any way seek to collapse the different trajectories, texts, questions, or histories of Subaltern Studies and intersectionality, though there are certainly places in which these traditions themselves have overlapped and influenced each other. Rather, I seek to mobilize Chakrabarty's understanding of how Marxism can think the problem of difference in order to think about how we might use this version of Marxism to relate to intersectionality.
29 | Chakrabarty, *Provincializing Europe*, 17.

order to buy oranges. There is something true, Marx would tell us, in the idea that one 'cannot compare apples to oranges' in the sense that there are a whole series of differences, not only in the apples and oranges themselves, but also in the process necessary to grow, nurture, harvest, and eat them. And yet, despite the absolutely different, sensuously particular character of both the commodities themselves and the labor undertaken to produce them, capitalism is committed to the idea that they *can* be, indeed that they *must* be exchangeable. This is possible only, Marx tells us, through the process of abstraction, in peeling away the situated, concrete, sensuous, and specific character of labor in order to reveal something that is similar: the fact that labor, or the expenditure of human energy, went in to both the apple and the orange. This is, for Marx, what makes exchanging them possible.

This labor is what Marx referred to as 'abstract labor' and it is one of the most consistently misinterpreted concepts in Marx's work, both in relation to its meaning and in regard to its significance. Rather than positing abstract labor as the answer, Chakrabarty explains that abstract labor is rather a grounding and defining problem for Marx:

> The question for Marx was: if human beings are individually different from one another in their capacities to labor, how does capital produce out of this field of difference an abstract, homogeneous measure of labor that makes the generalized production of commodities possible?[30]

Rather than accepting abstract labor as the *goal* of anti-capitalism, Chakrabarty explains that for Marx, the concept of abstract labor is actually a form of "critique."[31] Marx uses abstract labor in order to show how capitalism is committed to the production of sameness, similarity, and equivalence, that is, to the sublation, eradication, or erasure of difference, and it is this tendency that Marx identifies as one of the central *problems* of capitalism. Life, labor, personhood, subjectivity, desire—all of these are ineliminably particular for Marx, and this particularity is not an obstacle to be overcome. Rather, the project of abolishing capitalism is undertaken in order to rescue particularity from the constant homogenization to which it is subject. In Chakrabarty's words, "Life, in Marx's analysis of capital, is... a 'standing fight' against the process of abstraction."[32]

As many queer, feminist, and anti-racist Marxists have shown, there is also a process of differentiation endemic to capitalism. Capitalism is historically and logically dependent on a whole series of differentiations: not only bourgeoisie and proletariat, but the historical construction of race, and multiple new

---

30 | Chakrabarty, 91.
31 | Chakrabarty, 58.
32 | Chakrabarty, 61.

configurations of gender, sexuality, nationality, and ability. But of course, *pace* the intersectional critique of the supposed internal stability of these categories, capitalism produces these differences as group-based uniformity, not as expressions of individual particularity. By this, I mean that while capitalism, for example, relies on a highly differentiated regime of racial divisions, it does so, at least partially, by homogenizing those who are subjected to racializing narratives, by reducing people to their racial identification. Part of the repressive function of various differentiations then, is the ways in which members of oppressed groups are subjected to homogenization. While capitalism certainly contributes to the production of difference, it recognizes only an anemic form of difference, which systematically militates against the recognition of any real, creative particularities between individuals. In order to function, capitalism must both produce and reproduce differences (in the character of the labor performed, the commodities produced, *and* in the subject-positions who perform it) *and* it must continually produce sameness. To be more precise, capitalism thus relies on intergroup differentiation and intragroup homogenization at one and the same time. An intersectional reading of capitalism must take this problem as one of capital's central contradictions.

This contradiction between capitalism's production of difference and similarity plays out in particularly poignant ways in contemporary critiques of neoliberal diversity management. Neoliberal capitalism has attempted to domesticate the radical critical potential of the academic and activist emphasis on difference by turning toward multicultural diversity management.[33] In this contemporary formation, seeking to stabilize the diametrically opposed demands of re/producing sameness and difference, neoliberal diversity programs have sought to conserve the reproduction of the same (dispossession, structural violence, marginalization, capital accumulation) through highlighting its commitment to difference. In this sense, the capital accumulation predicated on sameness is conserved, even intensified by the commodification of difference. We can thus see how the difference between neoliberal diversity capitalism and other formations of capitalism choose different strategies in order to manage the same contradictory tendency in capitalism: to produce sameness and difference at one and the same time.

It is true that, in the same breath that Marx critiques capitalism's structural reliance on abstraction, much of his philosophical method utilizes abstraction as a mode of analysis and diagnosis, and it is arguably this dual status of

---

33 | Sara Ahmed, *On Being Included: Racism and Diversity in Institutional Life* (Durham: Duke University Press, 2012); Roderick Ferguson, *The Reorder of Things: The University and Its Pedagogies of Minority Difference* (Minneapolis: University of Minnesota Press, 2012); Jodi Melamed, "The Spirit of Neoliberalism: From Racial Liberalism to Neoliberal Multiculturalism," *Social Text* 24, no. 4 (2006): 1-24.

abstraction in his work that has led to much of the confusion about his position. Since capitalism is always caught in the double-bind of difference and commensurability, the philosophical and theoretical practice of abstraction for Marx is not fundamentally about abstracting *from* differences in order to produce commensurability, but rather *using* abstraction in order to illustrate how capitalism relies on the production of commensurability from difference.

As Marx explains in *The German Ideology*, capitalism in part functions by obscuring the ways in which even the most concrete and specific circumstances are related to an internal logic of capitalist development. When I purchase a mug for my coffee, for example, that mug only comes to me through a whole series of operations: the labor of producing it, the creation of the ceramic it is made from, the laws that regulate the import of goods (the bottom of this particular mug reads 'Made in China'), the historical relations that produced the circumstance of US-China trade relations, etc. In looking at the mug, this object of "the simplest sensuous certainty,"[34] I do not immediately see the ways in which whole social and economic systems contributed it its production or indeed, I do not even see the ways in which my own work and labor furnished the income I used in order to purchase it. In this sense, any particular object is the product of "social development, industry, and commercial intercourse" in ways that are not immediately apparent in the particularity of the mug itself.[35] In order to *really see* this mug—or any other object—in this dense network of relations, in all of the historical determinations that made my encounter with it possible, I must, in some sense abstract from it, see the broad relations that make it possible and that constitute its real meaning, to situate myself and it and our encounter. In this sense, abstraction can be used in order to better understand the concrete, to reveal it as a particular thing that emerges in the conjunction of a whole host of social, political, and economic processes.

It is for this reason that Marx argues in the *Grundrisse* that, while it is necessary to militate against the structures of that treat us as abstract and commensurable, there can be a certain use of abstraction against itself. If we begin and remain only in the realm of the concrete, he tells us, it will be impossible to discern the connections, relations, structures and histories that tie individual moments of the concrete together. It is this "concentration of many determinations"[36] that must be explained by an anti-capitalist analysis, but in order to do so, one must, provisionally and performatively, mobilize theory *in order to better explain the connections in and among the various actually existing phenomena.*

---

34 | Karl Marx and Friedrich Engels, *The German Ideology* (New York: International Publishers, 1967), 62.

35 | Ibid.

36 | Karl Marx, *Grundrisse: Foundations of the Critique of Political Economy*, trans. Martin Nicolaus, Reprint edition (London; New York: Penguin Classics, 1993), 101.

Marx does not, as modern economists might, take a variety of configurations, use them as data points, and then generate a theory. In this operation, the production of the theory seems to be the goal of such an activity. Rather, for Marx, the goal of analysis, critique, and theory, is understanding the connections and relations among different things actually existing in the world. The goal is not to dissolve the differences of specific cases into an overarching or totalizing theory, quite the opposite; the goal for Marx is to use relatively abstract concepts in order to better explain the "rich totality of many determinations and relations" that make up the world.[37] The test of the theory and its goal is in preserving, explaining, and understanding, the many determinations and relations.

As Teresa Ebert explains this moment in Marx, "the process of knowing the concrete is... an analysis or unpacking of the layered components, moving to ever more simple, that is, ever more fundamental concepts [...] Only now are we able to conceptualize the concrete—not as a simple sensible object—but as the complex 'concentration of many determinations.'"[38] In other words, as Himani Bannerji articulates, the concrete is, for Marx, both a "'point of departure' (as the social) and 'a point of arrival' (as theory)."[39] This is what Richard A. Lee Jr. continually emphasizes in his reading of Marx's philosophical method,[40] in which one must use abstraction in order to "rise to the level of the concrete."[41] Abstraction is here specifically about a process of being able to thematize, explain, understand, illustrate the role of structures, institutions, and histories in each and every individual case, rather than a subsumption of the individual case into the universal or the structural. Because of the deep, material interconnections of the world, *every* specific case can tell us something important about the constitution of the world; this is what the metaphor of the prism developed in the previous chapter sought to illuminate. Because each person, each position, each case emerges inside the intersectional matrix of capitalism, when seen through the right lens, it sheds light on the system as a whole. Each star in the constellation is its own privileged site in understanding the world because it is through the actual diversity of particulars that the whole range of possible structural conjunctions becomes possible. The goal, in rising to the level of the concrete, is being able to understand the specific and the particular,

---

37 | Ibid, 100.
38 | Teresa L. Ebert, "The Spectral Concrete: Bodies, Sex Work, and (Some Notes on) Citizenship," in *Maxism, Queer Theory, Gender*, ed. Mas'ud Zavarzadeh, Teresa L. Ebert, and Donald Morton (Syracuse, New York: The Red Factory, 2001), 283.
39 | Bannerji, "Building from Marx: Reflections on Class and Race," 150.
40 | Richard A. Lee, *The Thought of Matter: Materialism, Conceptuality, and the Transcendence of Immanence* (New York: Rowman & Littlefield, 2015).
41 | Marx, *Grundrisse*, 100.

and thus also to begin to build a world in which the particular is recognized as the source of value.

Since the goal is rising to the level of the concrete, anti-capitalist resistance must be specifically about protecting the incommensurable *as incommensurable*, about refusing the way in which non-exchangeable, non-equivalent human beings are constantly treated as exchangeable and commensurable (or, alternatively, about refusing the way in which human beings are treated as *different* in order to make them more easily exchangeable and in order to deny their vitality, subjectivity, and agency). Chakrabarty critiques the way in which some Marxists' approach to thinking about difference misses this point completely in Marx, trying to produce a "universal equivalent" that could mediate between these differences. Though Chakrabarty does not thematize it in this way, in some contemporary versions of Marxist politics, solidarity is often thought of as this universal equivalent, the concept that can produce, whether performatively or in reality, that kernel of sameness that can form the basis of broad mobilizations. While the concern here is the right one—how do we build mass movements capable of challenging power—ultimately solidarity conceived in this way falls radically short of sensitively addressing difference or oppression under capitalism, as it is redeploying capitalism's insistence on commensurability (and hence, missing one of Marx's central insights).

Chakrabarty offers translation as an alternative framing to the universal equivalent. Under this model, one could think about using the concept of solidarity in order to *translate* rather that *equate* various positions under global capitalism. Just as when one produces linguistic translation, the sentiment in the original language and in the translated version are never *exactly* the same, one can approach questions of incommensurable positions under capitalism in the same way: translation would turn solidarity into a common language through which to express the differences in our position. In this sense, the reason that solidarity would be necessary is precisely *because* there is a gap or a breach between our situations. Solidarity specifically in this case signifies that though our situations are not the same, I can make sense of your position because I can empathize with it, because I can extend myself and my situation beyond the grammar of my own particularity. Solidarity as translation thus thematizes a way "writ[ing] and think[ing] in terms of this breach"[42] or gap between us.

While Chakrabarty's diagnosis of the problem of commensurability under capitalism and his reading of Marx's utility in thinking this problem are incredibly rich, the model of translation is an insufficient corrective. While it has the benefit of fidelity to the incommensurable, ultimately, it leaves unthematized the question of *what makes translation possible across incommensurability*, and it is unclear to me how this possibility could be grounded in anything

---

42 | Chakrabarty, 96.

other than some form of similitude, even if a performative and provisional one. Though Chakrabarty has incredibly helpful resources for explaining the limitations thinking about commensurability under capitalism, translation seems to re-entrench the idea that capitalism simply produces differences that must be bridged, thematized, and made translatable. This is where intersectionality has an incredibly sensitive and thoughtful response. One of the most crucial insights from intersectionality is precisely that solidarity does not have to be based in commensurability. Indeed, some of the most careful and sensitive analyses that come out of the intersectional tradition chart a path for thinking about solidarity as the affirmation of non-commensurability through, to borrow a term from Éduard Glissant, a politics and a poetics of relation.[43] The non-commensurability of the experiences and structures of racialization does not have to be erased in order to give an account of their structural, logical, and historical *relation*. Rather than positing incommensurable differences as the starting place for analysis, intersectionality rather approaches this problem in the way most consonant with Marx's analysis, that is, in rising to the level of the concrete.

INTERSECTIONAL COALITIONS AND REFUSING COMMENSURABILITY

In many ways, the problem of commensurability is at the heart of intersectional critique. Crenshaw's concept of intersectionality, as elaborated in the now-famous 1989 article, took as its point of departure the landmark 1976 case *DeGraffenreid v. General Motors*. The auto-giant had never hired a black woman before the passage of the 1964 Civil Rights Act (CRA); in the economic downturn of the early 1970s, all of the black women employed at the corporation lost their jobs, ostensibly, management claimed, because they had the least seniority. Five of the fired black women filed suit, arguing that the claim to seniority in this case merely allowed the conditions of the pre-CRA era to continue unabated and that, therefore, their right to equal protection had been violated. Because not all women had been fired (there were still white women employed) nor had all black people been fired (some black men were still employed), the plaintiffs alleged that they had been discriminated against specifically *as black women*, on the basis of a distinct combination of racism and sexism. The court rejected this basis, saying instead that the aggrieved could file suit alleging that they had been discriminated against *either* as women *or* as black people, but not both. In explaining this decision, the court explained

---

43 | Édouard Glissant, *Poetics of Relation*, trans. Betsy Wing (Ann Arbor: University of Michigan Press, 1997).

that it could not condone creating "a new classification of 'black women' who would have greater standing than, for example a black male. The prospect of the creation of new classes of protected minorities, governed only by the mathematical principles of permutation and combination, clearly raises the prospect of opening the hackneyed Pandora's box."[44] The Court's reason for denying labor protections to black women, thus, was predicated on the specter of a 'Pandora's box' of recognizing the specific ways in which black women are marginalized, oppressed, and exploited under contemporary capitalism and the ways in which the histories of racist and sexist policy continue to frame their lives after the passage of liberal anti-discrimination policy. Crenshaw's intervention was to highlight the way in which the contemporary liberal legal framework operates, in this case, in and through the assumption and insistence that black women's position is essentially *commensurable* with black men and/or white women. Crenshaw's version of intersectionality was thus developed specifically in order to diagnose a problem in the way that various subject positions, from a liberal civil rights framework, is situated inside a false commensurability that the intersectional approach highlights, critiques, and seeks to transform.

Despite Marxists' longstanding critiques of liberal approaches to legal anti-discrimination statutes and their clear and demonstrable interests in the workplace as an anchor of both exploitation and oppression under capitalism, the ironic tendency in Marxist receptions of intersectionality has been to replay the anxiety about this 'Pandora's box' in nearly the same terms as the Court. The deep irony of this position cannot be overstated. Marxist critiques of intersectionality have frequently worried that intersectionality, in foregrounding the particular situations of women of color, detracts from the ultimate recognition of capitalism as a system that weaves together the oppression and exploitation of women of color, men of color, queer people, working class white people, and the '99%' more generally. In its broadest terms, the worry stems from an analysis that undue meditation on differences within the working class will obscure the ties that bind the working class together in a struggle against capitalist accumulation, exploitation, and dispossession, weakening the bonds of solidarity and the momentum of movement work. This conception is rather foreign—at least in some places—to Marx's own approach to diagnosing capitalism. There are, however, deeper problems with this approach than mere textual infidelity.

In the first place, the Pandora's box approach suggests that not all subject-positions are 'equally different.' Rather, it suggests that the situation or demands of women of color are somehow *uniquely* particular, in ways that those of white male factory workers are not. The truth of the matter is, however, that all of these situations *are particular*, are enframed by the positionality, the unique

---

44 | Crenshaw, "Demarginalizing the Intersection of Race and Sex: A Black Feminist Critique of Antidiscrimination Doctrine, Feminist Theory, and Antiracist Politics," 143.

histories of each of these positions. In this sense, the Pandora's box approach reproduces, implicitly and insidiously, the perspective that there is something uniquely universalizable about straight, white, male, factory workers, which is, just simply, undigested racism and heterosexism.

But moreover, the Pandora's box approach becomes particularly problematic in trying then to erect a concept of solidarity. The notion of solidarity operative here is profoundly unilateral: it seems to require, as political principle, that women of color *ignore* grounding elements of their lives and their structural relationship to capital as a gift of solidarity to the white, male, waged factory workers who are never asked to reciprocate. While solidarity *does* require showing up, throwing down, and taking risks on issues that *do not immediately appear* to affect us negatively in *individual* and *personal* ways—white people must show up for indigenous rights, men will have to militate against systematic sexism, Latinx people must oppose Islamophobia, cis people must oppose transphobia, etc.—solidarity can never be based on the expectation that it flows unidirectionally.

Ultimately, the theoretical and political principle underlying the Pandora's box narrative on the left restricts both theory and praxis to a politics of the lowest common denominator. It is worth asking whether this politics of the lowest common denominator, which only requires political action in the much-circumscribed arena of that which the working class (supposedly) *shares*, is even solidarity at all. But lastly, the Pandora's box theory does not actually take seriously the grounding principle of intersectionality or even much of the insight of the queer, feminist, anti-colonial, and anti-racist Marxisms explored in Chapter Three; the idea that oppressions are mutually constructed and that the differential positions within each axis are reciprocally conditioned. In contradistinction to the Pandora's Box narrative, Crenshaw and the entire intersectional tradition have developed an incredibly sensitive heuristic for addressing the problem of commensurability, one that can be thematized through a variety of axioms about intersectional organizing. I explain each of these principles in turn.

1. Identities are already coalitions.

Rather than taking social locations as already-constituted unities, it is helpful to approach the question of identity through the understanding of coalitions. Intersectionality pioneered thinking of identity categories *themselves* as coalitions, in ways that can helpfully inform discussions of solidarity and coalitional thinking. Crenshaw herself specifically conceived of identities this way, arguing that intersectionality "provides a basis for reconceptualizing race as a coalition between men and women of color....[and a] coalition of straight and gay people of color."⁴⁵ As Grace Kyungwong Hong explains, the intersectional tradition "envisions 'African American' not as essential and unchanging, but as always already a coalition of different, sometimes competing formations, it implies the possibility of alliances among a variety of racial, gendered, sexualized, and national differences."⁴⁶ Carastathis offers that rather than "a narrow identitarianism," the intersectional critique "reveals identities to be coalitions: internally heterogeneous, complex unities constituted by their internal differences and dissonances and by internal as well as external relations of power."⁴⁷ Thinking about identities as coalitions helpfully resists the politics of commensurability because it refuses a unified understanding of how identity categories are constituted. It is not only across groups, but within groups as well, that difference emerges as a central and important consideration. Thinking about identities this way is precisely the response to dialectical diagnosis Marx generates: that difference and sameness are produced constantly and in relationship to one another. Thinking about identities as coalitions allows us to see these differences as central to, rather than distractions from, sensitive analyses of the role that identity plays in the structure of the contemporary world. In this way, thinking about identities as coalitions opens the space for refusing the ways in which capitalism homogenizes intragroup relations.

2. Identity itself is a contested and contradictory category.

Identities, though they are often the result of systems of domination and oppression, cannot be simply reduced to those systems. We need to recognize the multiple, contradictory ways in which identity is understood, mobilized, chosen, defended, or disavowed in order to really understanding the complex ways in which identities shape our lives. As queer Marxist Peter Drucker contends,

> Identities need to be analysed concretely case by case, particularly distinguishing imposed identities from freely chosen ones, fixed identities from fluid ones, monolithic identities from crosscutting ones. Identities' potential as sources of strength and sites of resistance needs to be acknowledged. The possibility needs to be held open of deploying identities in ways that do not petrify them, but rather seize upon whatever in them is most dynamic and open ended. And non-class identities cannot

---

45 | Crenshaw, "Mapping the Margins: Intersectionality, Identity Politics, and Violence Against Women of Color," 1299.
46 | Hong, *The Ruptures of American Capital: Women of Color Feminism and the Immigrant Culture of Labor*, xxvii–xxviii.
47 | Anna Carastathis, *Intersectionality: Origins, Contestations, Horizons* (Lincoln: University of Nebraska Press, 2016), 7.

be fully grasped if seen only as divisions sown by the ruling class in the interests of perpetuating its rule.[48]

In order to ground an emancipatory and liberatory politics that can mobilize against the simultaneous homogenization and differentiation central to capitalism, identity cannot be reduced to a mere instrument of oppression; indeed, some of the most successful social movements have been grounded in the valorization of oppressed and exploited subject positions. Too often this valorization is reduced, in Marxist circles, to constituting a dangerous redeployment of capitalism's own logic, as if recognizing and finding power in group identities somehow plays into and reinforces this logic. What is interesting in these accounts is that class is never figured this way; on the contrary, most Marxist organizing strategies *depend on* working class people recognizing their status as exploited workers and mobilizing from this basis. If we read capitalism in the non-reductive way I argue we ought to, then we must recognize that mobilization from other identity positions can be the source of strength, power, resilience, and community that are necessary to contest capitalism's repressive use of these differences.

Building the capacity for vibrant coalitional politics may, in some circumstances, require not only multi-group alliances, but also spaces to explore intragroup differences. As Alison Bailey writes, "episodic segregation ... provides us with a conceptual vocabulary to start the difficult conversations required for successful coalition building."[49] If our understanding of coalitional politics includes the recognition of incommensurable differences, it may be necessary for healthy, vibrant coalitions for its members to engage in probing, explaining, exploring, naming, and vocalizing those differences; without this piece, solidarity may falter into its 'lowest common denominator' formations. Episodic segregation may, in some instances, provide the platform to articulate the differential demands that will be necessary for uprooting the deeply entrenched systems of differentiation groups are subjected to; it may also be necessary in order to articulate a vision of what emancipation would look like, what a true valorization of identity might feel like, and what paths to emancipation will be most consonant with those visions. Identity thus must be approached in solidarity organizing as deep wells of possibility at the same time that they may also be tied up with experiences of oppression, pain, exploitation, and frustration.

---

48 | Drucker, *Warped*, 28.
49 | Bailey, "On Intersectionality, Empathy, and Feminist Solidarity: A Reply to Naomi Zack," 25–26.

3. Solidarity requires unity, not uniformity.

Audre Lorde names the location of a coalition "the house of difference." In response to the attempts of organizing only on the basis of shared position, Lorde explains that because each of us is an incommensurable, irreducibly singular individual, located at the cross section a variety of systems and positions, the only possibility for effective organizing is beginning from the assumption of incommensurability:

> Being women together was not enough. We were different. Being gay-girls together was not enough. We were different. Being Black together was not enough. We were different. Being Black women together was not enough. We were different. Being Black dykes together was not enough, we were different[...] It was a while before we came to realize that our place was in the very house of difference rather than the security of any one particular difference.[50]

The concept of the house of difference is particularly illustrative and important for reformulating the concept of solidarity from a coalitional perspective. The house is itself a structure, one imbued with notions of intimacy, but also, for many of us, with violence. The home is a deeply ambivalent notion and deeply contradictory structure, just as identity is ambivalent, contradictory, simultaneously empowering and painful. White people and indigenous people, intersex people and ciswomen, queer men and transwomen, all of us are connected because, whatever the content of our particular identities, the concepts, structures, histories, and violences that have produced these positions are themselves connected. We do not have to invent relationships between people in various social locations; the matrix of domination has already produced us as interrelated. My position as a queer, working class, white, Jewish ciswoman is already connected to and contingent upon others' locations because, whatever our relative positions of power within these determinations, the structures of white supremacy, Christian hegemony, capitalism, heterosexism, and patriarchy effect all of us *albeit in distinctly and incommensurably different ways*. I do not need to find or manufacture common ground with people of other genders; we have all been subjected to the violent vicissitudes of oppositional sexism.[51] The common structure already exists, even if my own experience of racist heteropatriarchal sexism will position me to understand certain facets of the structure with more ease than others. To put this another way, we do not have to bridge our differences; we already live together in the house of difference.

---

50 | Lorde, *Zami*, 226.
51 | For a particularly moving account of how men are affected by patriarchy, as just one example of this kind of analysis see: hooks, *The Will to Change*.

We need to understand how systems, structures, institutions, and histories have constructed these differences in order to mobilize against the violence, inequality, exploitation, and oppression we experience on the basis of those differences.

It is on this basis that the intersectional tradition significantly contributes to the concept of solidarity. As Ange-Marie Hancock notes, this version of solidarity understands coalitional demands to be predicated on an understanding that uprooting systems of oppression and exploitation relies on "group unity without group uniformity."[52] Understanding the distinction between group unity and group uniformity thus discloses a variety of novel strategic coalitional possibilities; once we dispense with the idea that solidarity is based in shared position, we can, according to Angela Davis begin to form the "unpredictable or unlikely coalitions grounded in political projects" that will be necessary in order to uproot the deeply entrenched systems of domination that structure our world.[53] Working on shared political projects across and between groups allows us to stake out a terrain of struggle in which solidarity is figured as the recognition in a political project of dismantling systemic exploitation and oppression, without assuming that each participant holds a shared position in relation to systems of power. Coalitions provide a potent political formation in which "solidarity, not sameness, is essential."[54]

4. Coalitional Solidarity Necessitates Praxis.

Chela Sandoval suggests that there is something particularly strategic and effective about the dislocation of a single center for anti-capitalist struggle: when no oppression "is privileged over any other" this means that "each site is as potentially effective in opposition as any other"; pluralizing the potential sites for anti-capitalist mobilization and leverage is "particularly effective under late capitalist and post-modern cultural conditions in the United States."[55] This mode of understanding the oppression and exploitation is what Sandoval calls "differential consciousness", which she identifies as coming out of the "U.S. Third World Feminist" tradition from the 1970s on, a tradition that she argues centers both a militant Marxist anti-capitalism *and* centers women of color in

---

52 | Hancock, "W.E.B. Du Bois: Intellectual Forefather of Intersectionality?," 80.

53 | Angela Davis, "Reflections on Race, Gender, and Class in the U.S.A," in *The Politics of Culture in the Shadow of Capital*, ed. Lisa Lowe and David Lloyd (Durham, NC: Duke University Press, 1997), 322.

54 | Vivian May, *Pursuing Intersectionality, Unsettling Dominant Imaginaries* (New York: Routledge, 2015), 50.

55 | Chela Sandoval, "U.S. Third World Feminism: The Theory and Method of Oppositional Consciousness Int He Post-Modern World," *Genders*, no. 10 (1991): 12.

the integrated critiques of imperialism, sexism, and racism.⁵⁶ Audre Lorde reveals another valence to this strategic benefit, which on her analysis is located in the ability of activists to bring their whole selves to organizing when projects are no longer based in lowest common denominator politics:

> As a Black lesbian feminist, I find I am constantly encouraged to pluck out some one aspect of myself and present this as the meaningful whole, eclipsing or denying the other arts of self. But this is a destructive and fragmenting way to live. My fullest concentration of energy is available to me only when I integrate all the parts of who I am, openly [...] Only then can I bring myself and my energies as a whole to the service of those struggles which I embrace as part of my living.⁵⁷

Coalitions must thus be rethought, not as the natural coalescence of groups who have a natural affinity, but rather as an important, strategic investment of time, energy, resources, learning, and reflection. Elizabeth Cole argues that we should think about "shared interests instead of shared identity."⁵⁸ Chandra Mohanty underscores this point, explaining that solidarity does not need to imply sameness: "the practice of solidarity foregrounds the communities of people who have chosen to work and fight together... [and] is always an achievement, the result of active struggle."⁵⁹ Audre Lorde writes, "I do not have to be you to recognize that our wars are the same. What we must do is commit ourselves to some future that can include each other and to work toward that future with particular strengths of our individual identities."⁶⁰

Grounding anti-capitalist activism in coalitions thus opens up the space to explore the possibilities of social transformation in broader ways than traditional class politics or in lowest common denominator mobilizations. Approaching this work from the perspective that multiple groups have strengths that can be leveraged and understandings that might speak to different constituencies expands the terrain of what is possible. When we embrace a political perspective that allows us to enter into organizing spaces in all of our particularities, without forcing ourselves to be reduced to that which is shared with others, we unleash the creativity that comes from being our whole selves, as complex, contradictory, or broken as those selves might be. With this creativity comes not only novel approaches, deeper diagnoses, and the experiences of multiple histories of struggle, it potentially lays the foundation for building new com-

---

56 | Ibid.
57 | Lorde, *Sister/Outsider: Essays and Speeches*, 120-21.
58 | Cole, "Coalitions as a Model for Intersectionality: From Practice to Theory," 447.
59 | Mohanty, *Feminism without Borders: Decolonizing Theory, Practicing Solidarity*, 78.
60 | Lorde, *Sister/Outsider: Essays and Speeches*, 142.

munities, ones in which difference is taken as a source of strength rather than as barriers to collective action. As Himani Bannerji remarks, "Communities of resistance, therefore, are or need to be much more than imagined."[61] Coalitional politics can begin to stretch our political imaginations in such a way that these communities of resistance can become the foundations for bringing into being the worlds we truly need.

CONCLUSION: TOWARDS A SOLIDARITY OF RELATION

In light of this discussion, solidarity must be something more than locating a lowest common denominator. If solidarity cannot be grounded in that which we share, or in that which constitutes some ground of our similarity, how are we to reconceputalize solidarity? In a 1971 speech, Fannie Lou Hamer said, "You know I work for the liberation of all people because when I liberate myself, I'm liberating other people... [The white woman's] freedom is shackled in chains to mine."[62] Hamer insists that groups cannot be liberated piecemeal, one by one. As she continues in the speech, "none of us is free until we all are." This insistence discloses possibility and necessity of a non-reductive solidarity.

Cherrie Moraga explained, speaking of her position as a woman of color, "As Third World Women we clearly have a different relationship to racism than white women, but all of us are born into an environment where racism exists."[63] There is, thus, by virtue of inhabiting a world shaped by oppression and exploitation, a certain inevitability that all people will be shaped by it, whatever the form of that shaping. We are bound together, "shackled" as Hamer says, to people with different experiences because we are made by these conditions. And while the conditions of our shaping, our access to institutions of power, our individual trials and tribulations, our particular social locations may all be different, we cannot escape the fundamental fact that all of these are constituted relationally.

This is as true for white people as for people of color, for straight as for queer people, for disabled as for able folks, for people of various genders and agender people. Not being subjected to oppression does not mean that one has not been molded by oppression, by the various institutions, narratives, possibilities, choices, etc. that are opened and closed by oppression and exploitation. When Fannie Lou Hamer proclaims that her freedom is shackled to the freedom of

---

61 | Bannerji, *Thinking Through: Essays on Feminism, Marxism, and Anti-Racism*, 29.
62 | Gerda Lerner, *Black Women in White America: A Documentary History* (New York: Vintage, 1973), 609–11.
63 | Moraga and Anzaldúa, *This Bridge Called My Back: Writings by Radical Women of Color*, 62.

white women, it is because white women too have been molded by racism; our entire subject position has been framed by it. Just because we are not oppressed by white supremacy does not mean we have not been made by it. What is often called 'privilege' is in reality this molding, a conditioning that shapes certain groups to be comfortable with exploitation and oppression, to be unable to see it, to be unable to see how it has been present at every step, in every moment of our lives as well. If we believe that a truly emancipated humanity would recoil in horror at oppression and exploitation, then we must believe that there is some aspect of humanity that has been eroded through inhabiting positions of privilege. The shackle that binds multiple, irreducibly different experiences together is this.

Sara Ahmed speaks about this helpfully in regards to the racialized sexual politics of compulsory heterosexuality. In a world of structural homophobia and heterosexism, heterosexuality can be helpfully conceived as a "repetitive strain injury."[64] Compulsory heterosexuality, oppositional sexism, and binary conceptions of gender, sex, and sexuality, do not leave straight, cismen unscathed, as if the only ways their bodies and desires interacted with the system of power was of unabated and uninterrupted praise or confirmation. Just as Simone de Beauvoir once proclaimed, "One is not born, but rather becomes, a woman,"[65] we might say that 'one is not born, but rather becomes a white, straight, cisgender man'—and, as bell hooks, R.W. Connell, and other theorists have shown, the process of 'making' straight cisgender men is rife with its own form of violences, compulsions, and prohibitions that often sever cismen from any expression of their positions and identities from anything other than masculinity's most toxic manifestations.[66]

Let's be very clear though: there are both different *forms* of violence that are endured by those inhabiting positions of privilege and *radically different consequences for having survived them*. Thus, it is not accurate to say that compulsory heterosexuality harms the straight in the same way as the queer, that patriarchy harms cismen in the same ways as women, trans, and nonbinary people, or that white supremacy harms whites in the same ways as people of color. As Patricia Hill Collins explains, "while group experiences are interdependent, they are not equivalent."[67] There are multiple organizations of harm. It is altogether a

---

64 | Sara Ahmed, *Queer Phenomenology: Orientations, Objects, Others* (Durham: Duke University Press, 2006), 57, 91.

65 | Simone de Beauvoir, *The Second Sex*, ed. Constance Borde and Sheila Malovany-Chevallier (New York: Alfred A. Knopf, 2009).

66 | hooks, *The Will to Change*; R.W. Connell, *Masculinities* (Cambridge: Polity Press, 1995).

67 | Patricia Hill Collins, *Black Feminist Thought: Knowledge, Consciousness, and the Politics of Empowerment*, 1 edition (New York: Routledge, 2008), 247.

different process and position to undergo the processes of compulsory heterosexuality and to find oneself rewarded rather than to find oneself marginalized, oppressed, silenced, disowned, beaten, policed, and exploited. The difference cannot be overemphasized.

However, we also cannot afford to ignore the connection between them, the way in which the structures of power have written themselves onto us, our identities, our desires, ourselves. Toxic masculinity is so named because it is toxic not only to those who are not men, but precisely also *for* men; white supremacy is damaging not only to people of color but to white people's own understanding of themselves and their communities. Recognizing the way in which people inhabiting privileged social positions—straight, white, male, cis, able-bodied, neurotypical, citizen, etc.—have also been constituted through their interaction with oppressive systems is necessary if our politics and our philosophy is to aspire to more than mere inclusion in the system. If we are to have a politics that goes beyond wanting everyone to be treated 'as white' 'as the capitalist' as 'straight men', then we have to recognize and wrestle with the fundamental violences that constitute even privileged positions. As Lugones reminds us,

Our possibilities lie in communality rather than subordination; they do not lie in parity with our superiors in the hierarchy that constitutes coloniality. That construction of the human is vitiated through and though by its intimate relation with violence.[68]

If we are committed to revolutionary change, then one has to admit that those who have the most power in society are also deeply damaged by the system that gives them this power. Both privilege and oppression, both power and exploitation, sever the connections and communities we need in order to ground true projects of liberation. Capitalism thus links us together, in a tie that binds us, often painfully, in relation to one another. This moment of relation is the true ground of solidarity. Solidarity does not require the erasing our differences, or the rooting of our political projects in the moments that our interests are aligned. Solidarity is thus the name for affirming the differences that exploitation and oppression produce within and between us; it is also the name for recognizing that every time I fight against anyone's oppression or exploitation, I fight against my own, I fight against everyone's.

The politics of the lowest common denominator will not get us very far. If we work to unseat only the ways oppression and exploitation affect all of 'us', we will leave intact so much of what must be overcome. As David Roediger explains, much of the contemporary left operates on the assumption that "universal projects"—like the elimination of capitalist markets, the institution of universal healthcare, the elimination of student debt, etc.—and "race-specific

---

68 | María Lugones, "Toward a Decolonial Feminism," *Hypatia* 25, no. 4 (2010): 752.

demands"—like reparations, affirmative action, racial self-determination, the return of indigenous land—are somehow incompatible.[69] This choice is false, and like many choices offered to us under capitalism, it must be refused. We cannot afford to choose whose needs are met, whose liberation is central, whose struggles we uplift. We must rather mobilize the dialectical insight that community specific demands *are already* working toward the liberation of all, and that supposedly 'universal' projects always already impact communities in different ways.

Solidarity is about mobilizing the transformational power of differential communities; it is about speaking and working from the position of our connections; it is about refusing the politics of commensurability that capitalism engenders; it is about noticing in ourselves the places in which our positions and experiences are partial and particular; it is about finding strength in difference and possibility in community. It is about recognizing that groups know more about their own positions and thus have valuable, unique perspectives to offer and specific needs that must be met in any project of liberation worth the name.

As Assata Shakur wrote from a prison cell in 1973:

> It is our duty to fight for our freedom. It is our duty to win.
> We must love each other and support each other
> WE HAVE NOTHING TO LOSE BUT OUR CHAINS![70]

If we think about them in the way that Fannie Lou Hamer suggests, a vibrant, creative solidarity is our *only* chance of losing these chains. Solidarity is the way we fight; it is the prefiguration of our freedom; it is the name of activist duty. It is the only mechanism through which we can love and support each other in deep, honest, and transformative ways. It is the only way that undermining the systems of exploitation and oppression will not lead to new sets of chains, for ourselves or for others. It is only through a relational solidarity that we will truly bring to bear a new world from the ashes of the old, to build the only world worth fighting for.

---

69 | Roediger, *Class, Race, and Marxism*, 15.
70 | Assata Shakur, "To My People," July 4, 1973, http://www.assatashakur.org/mypeople.htm.

Bibliography

Adorno, Theodor W. *Lectures on Negative Dialectics: Fragments of a Lecture Course 1965/1966*. 1 edition. Cambridge: Polity, 2008.
———. *Negative Dialectics*. 2 edition. New York: Bloomsbury Academic, 1981.
———. *Prisms*. Translated by Shierry Weber Nicholsen and Samuel Weber. Reprint edition. Cambridge, Mass.: The MIT Press, 1983.
Aguilar, Delia. "Tracing the Roots of Intersectionality." *Monthly Review Zine*, April 12, 2012.
Ahmed, Sara. *On Being Included: Racism and Diversity in Institutional Life*. Durham: Duke University Press, 2012.
———. *Queer Phenomenology: Orientations, Objects, Others*. Durham: Duke University Press, 2006.
Alcoff, Linda Martín. "An Epistemology for the Next Revolution." *Transmodernity* 1, no. 2 (2011): 67–78.
———. "Epistemologies of Ignorance: Three Types." In *Race and Epistemologies of Ignorace*, edited by Shannon Sullivan and Nancy Tuana, 39–58. Albany: State University of New York Press, 2007.
Alexander, Michelle. *The New Jim Crow: Mass Incarceration in the Age of Colorblindness*. New York: The New Press, 2012.
Alexander-Floyd, Nikol. "Disappearing Acts: Reclaiming Intersectionality in the Social Sciences in a Post-Black Feminist Era." *Feminist Formations* 24, no. 1 (2012): 1–25.
Ali, Kamran Asdar. *Communism in Pakistan: Politics and Class Activism 1947-1972*. I.B. Tauris, 2015.
Allen, Paula Gunn. *The Sacred Hoop: Recovering the Feminine in American Indian Traditions*. Open Road Media, 2015.
Allen, Theodore W. *The Invention of the White Race, Volume 1: Racial Oppression and Social Control*. Second Edition edition. London ; New York: Verso, 2012.
———. *The Invention of the White Race, Volume 2: The Origin of Racial Oppression in Anglo-America*. Second Edition edition. London ; New York: Verso, 2012.

Anderson, Kevin B. "Karl Marx and Intersectionality." *Logos: A Journal of Modern Culture and Society* 15, no. 2–3. Accessed January 10, 2017. http://logosjournal.com/2015/anderson-marx/.

———. *Marx at the Margins: On Nationalism, Ethnicity, and Non-Western Societies*. Chicago: University Of Chicago Press, 2010.

Anievas, Alexander, and Kerem Nisancioglu. *How the West Came to Rule: The Geopolitical Origins of Capitalism*. London: Pluto Press, 2015.

Anzaldúa, Gloria. *Borderlands/ La Frontera*. San Francisco: Aunt Lute Books, 1987.

Aricó, José. *Marx and Latin America*. Chicago: Haymarket Books, 2014.

Aristotle. *Metaphysics*. Bloomington: Indiana University Press, 1966.

Arruzza, Cinzia. *Dangerous Liaisons: The Marriages and Divorces of Marxism and Feminism*. Pontypool, Wales; London: Merlin Press, 2013.

———. "Remarks on Gender." *Viewpoint Magazine*, September 2, 2014.

Baca Zinn, Maxine, Pierrette Hondagneu-Sotelo, and Michael Messner. "Gender through the Prism of Difference." In *Race, Class, and Gender: An Anthology*, edited by Patricia Hill Collins and Maragret Anderson, 4th ed. Belmont, CA: Wadsworth, 2001.

Bagchi, Amiya Kumar, and Amita Chatterjee. *Marxism: With and Beyond Marx*. Delhi: Routledge India, 2014.

Bailey, Alison. "On Intersectionality, Empathy, and Feminist Solidarity: A Reply to Naomi Zack." *Journal of Peace and Justice Studies* 18, no. 2 (2009): 14–37.

Banks, Katherine Bell, and Robert C. Hayden. *W.E.B. Du Bois, Family, and Friendship: Another Side of the Man, Letters, and Memories*. Littleton, MA: Tapestry Press, 2004.

Bannerji, Himani. "Building from Marx: Reflections on Class and Race." *Social Justice* 32, no. 4 (2005): 144–60.

———. *Thinking Through: Essays on Feminism, Marxism, and Anti-Racism*. Canada: Women's Press, 1995.

Barlow, Tania. *New Asian Marxisms*. Durham: Duke University Press, 2002.

Batrlovich, Crystal, and Neil Lazarus, eds. *Marxism, Modernity and Postcolonial Studies*. Cambridge, UK ; New York: Cambridge University Press, 2002.

Bayoumi, Moustafa. *How Does It Feel to Be a Problem?: Being Young and Arab in America*. New York: Penguin Books, 2009.

Beal, Frances. "Double Jeopardy: To Be Black and Female." In *Black Woman's Manifesto*, 19–34. New York: Third World Woman's Alliance, 1970.

———. "Double Jeopardy: To Be Black and Female (1970)." *Meridians: Feminism, Race, Transnationalism* 8, no. 2 (2008): 166–76.

Beauvoir, Simone de. *The Second Sex*. Edited by Constance Borde and Sheila Malovany-Chevallier. New York: Alfred A. Knopf, 2009.

Belkhir, Jean Ait, and Berenice McNair Barnett. "Race, Gender, and Class Intersectionality." *Race, Gender and Class* 8, no. 3 (2001): 157–74.

Benería, Lourdes. "Reproduction, Production, and the Sexual Division of Labour." *Cambridge Journal of Economics*, no. 3 (1979): 203–25.
Benn Michaels, Walter. *The Trouble with Diversity: How We Learned to Love Identity and Ignore Inequality*. New York: Holt, 2006.
Bensaïd, Daniel. *Les Irréductibles: Théorèmes de La Résistance à l'air Du Temps*. Paris: Textuel, 2001.
Bérubé, Allan. *My Desire for History: Essays in Gay Community and Labor History*. Chapel Hill: University of North Carolina Press, 2011.
Best, Steven. "Jameson, Totality, and the Poststructuralist Critique." In *Postmodernism/Jameson/Critique*, edited by Douglas Kellner. Washington, DC: Maisonneuve Press, 1989.
Betancourt, Michael. "Immaterial Value and Scarcity in Digital Capitalism." *CTheory*, 2010. http://www.ctheory.net/articles.aspx?id=652.
Bezanson, Kate, and Meg Luxton. *Social Reproduction: Feminist Political Economy Challenges Neoliberalism*. Montreal and Kingston: McGill-Queen's University Press, 2006.
Bhattacharya, Tithi, ed. *Social Reproduction Theory: Remapping Class, Recentering Oppression*. London: Pluto Press, 2017.
Bilge, Sirma. "Whitening Intersectionality: Evanescence of Race in Intersectionality Scholarship." In *Racism and Sociology: Racism Analysis Yearbook 5-2014*, edited by Wulf D. Hund and Alana Lentin, 175–205. Berlin: Lit Verlag/Routledge, 2014.
Bonilla-Silva, Eduardo. *Racism without Racists: Color-Blind Racism and the Persistence of Racial Inequality in America*. 3 edition. Lanham: Rowman & Littlefield Publishers, 2009.
Bosteels, Bruno. *Marx and Freud in Latin America: Politics, Psychoanalysis and Religion in Times of Terror*. London ; New York: Verso, 2012.
Boyce Davies, Carole. *Left of Karl Marx: The Political Life of Black Communist Claudia Jones*. Durham: Duke University Press, 2008.
Brenner, Johanna. *Women and the Politics of Class*. New York: Monthly Review Press, 2000.
Brodkin, Karen. *How Jews Became White Folks and What That Says about Race in America*. New Brunswick, N.J: Rutgers University Press, 1998.
Brown, Heather. *Marx on Gender and the Family: A Critical Study*. Chicago: Haymarket Books, 2013.
Brown, Rita Mae. "The Last Straw." In *Class and Feminism*. Diana Press, 1974.
Butler, Judith. *Frames of War: When Is Life Grievable?* London: Verso, 2016.
———. *The Psychic Life of Power: Theories in Subjection*. Stanford University Press, 1997.
Cabral, Amilcar. *Resistance and Decolonization*. Translated by Dan Wood. London: Rowman & Littlefield, 2016.

Carastathis, Anna. *Intersectionality: Origins, Contestations, Horizons*. Lincoln: University of Nebraska Press, 2016.
Carby, Hazel. *Race Men*. Cambridge: Harvard University Press, 1998.
———. *Reconstructing Womanhood: The Emergence of the Afro-American Woman Novelist*. New York: Oxford University Press, 1987.
Carr, Leslie G. *"Color-Blind" Racism*. Thousand Oaks: SAGE Publications, Inc, 1997.
Cesaire, Aime. *Discourse on Colonialism*. New York: Monthly Review Press, 1973.
Chakrabarty, Bidyut. *Left Radicalism in India*. London: Routledge, 2014.
Chakrabarty, Dipesh. *Provincializing Europe: Postcolonial Thought and Historical Difference*. New edition with a New preface by the author edition. Princeton, N.J.: Princeton University Press, 2007.
Chakravarti, Sudeep. *Red Sun: Travels in Naxalite Country*. London and New Delhi: Penguin Books, 2008.
Chibber, Vivek. *Postcolonial Theory and the Specter of Capital*. 1 edition. London: Verso, 2013.
Cho, Sumi K. "Post-Intersectionality: The Curious Reception of Intersectionality in Legal Scholarship." *Du Bois Review* 10, no. 2 (2013): 385–404.
Cho, Sumi K., Kimberlé Crenshaw, and Leslie McCall. "Toward a Field of Intersectionality Studies: Theory, Applications, and Praxis." *Signs: Journal of Women in Culture & Society* 38, no. 4 (2013): 785–803.
Ciccariello-Maher, George. *Decolonizing Dialectics*. Durham and London: Duke University Press, 2017.
Cole, Elizabeth. "Coalitions as a Model for Intersectionality: From Practice to Theory." *Sex Roles* 59, no. 5–6 (2008): 443–53.
Collins, Patricia Hill. *Black Feminist Thought: Knowledge, Consciousness, and the Politics of Empowerment*. 1 edition. New York: Routledge, 2008.
———. "Comment on Hekman's 'Truth and Method: Feminist Standpoint Theory Revisted': Where's the Power?" *Signs* 22, no. 2 (1997): 375–81.
———. "Du Bois's Contested Legacy." *Ethnic and Racial Studies* 39, no. 8 (2016): 1398–1406.
———. *Fighting Words: Black Women and the Search for Justice*. Minneapolis: University of Minnesota Press, 1998.
———. "Gender, Black Feminism, and Political Economy." *The Annals of the American Academy of Political and Social Science* 586 (2000): 41–53.
———. "Intersectionality's Definitional Dilemmas." *Annual Review of Sociology*, no. 41 (2015): 1–20.
———. "On West and Fenstermaker's 'Doing Difference.'" In *Women, Men, and Gender: Ongoing Debates*, edited by Mary Roth Walsh, 73–75. New Haven: Yale University Press, 1997.

Collins, Patricia Hill, and Sirma Bilge. *Intersectionality*. 1 edition. Cambridge, UK ; Malden, MA: Polity, 2016.

Combahee River Collective. "A Black Feminist Statement." In *Capitalist Patriarchy and the Case for Socialist Feminism*, edited by Zillah Eisenstein, 362–72. New York and London: Monthly Review Press, 1979.

Conaghan, Joanne. "Intersectionality and the Feminist Project in Law." In *Intersectionality and Beyond: Law, Power, and the Politics of Location*, edited by Emily Grabham, Davina Cooper, Jane Krishnadas, and Didi Herman. Abingdon, UK: Routledge Cavendish, 2009.

Connell, R.W. *Masculinities*. Cambridge: Polity Press, 1995.

Coogan-Gehr, Kelly. "The Politics of Race in US Feminist Scholarship: An Archaeology." *Signs: Journal of Women in Culture & Society* 37, no. 1 (2011): 83–107.

Coulthard, Glen Sean. *Red Skin White Masks: Rejecting the Colonial Politics of Recognition*. Minneapolis: University of Minnesota Press, 2014.

Crawford, William H., and Carl G. Rosberg. *African Socialism*. Palo Alto, California: Stanford University Press, 1964.

Crenshaw, Kimberlé. "Demarginalizing the Intersection of Race and Sex: A Black Feminist Critique of Antidiscrimination Doctrine, Feminist Theory, and Antiracist Politics." *University of Chicago Legal Forum*, no. 140 (1989): 139–67.

———. "Mapping the Margins: Intersectionality, Identity Politics, and Violence Against Women of Color." *Stanford Law Review* 43, no. 6 (1991): 1241–99.

———. "Postscript." In *Framing Intersectionality: Debates on a Multi-Faceted Concept in Gender Studies*, edited by Helma Lutz, Maria Theresa Herrera Vivar, and Linda Supik, 221–34. Farnham, UK: Ashgate, 2011.

———. "Twenty Years of Critical Race Theory: Looking Back to Move Forward." *Connecticut Law Review* 43, no. 5 (2011): 1253–1352.

Crosby, Christina, Lisa Duggan, Roderick Ferguson, Kevin Floyd, Miranda Joseph, Heather Love, Robert McRuer, et al. "Queer Studies, Materialism, and Crisis." *GLQ: A Journal of Lesbian & Gay Studies* 18, no. 1 (2012): 127–47.

Dalla Costa, Giovanna Franca. *The Work of Love: Unpaid Housework, Poverty & Sexual Violence at the Dawn of the 21st Century*. Edited by Mariarosa Dalla Costa. Translated by Enda Brophy. Autonomedia, 2008.

Dalla Costa, Mariarosa. *Women, Development, and Labor of Reproduction: Struggles and Movements*. Edited by Giovanna F. Dalla Costa. Trenton, NJ: Africa World Press, 1999.

Dalla Costa, Mariarosa, and Selma James. *The Power of Women and the Subversion of the Community, 3rd Edition*. 3rd edition. Bristol: Falling Wall Press, 1975.

Davis, Angela. *Are Prisons Obsolete?* New York: Seven Stories Press, 2003.

———. "Racism, Birth Control, and Reproductive Rights." In *Feminist Postcolonial Theory: A Reader*. New York: Routledge, 2003.

———. "Reflections on Race, Gender, and Class in the U.S.A." In *The Politics of Culture in the Shadow of Capital*, edited by Lisa Lowe and David Lloyd, 303–23. Durham, NC: Duke University Press, 1997.

———. *Blues Legacies and Black Feminism: Gertrude "Ma" Rainey, Bessie Smith, and Billie Holiday*. 1st Vintage Books Ed edition. New York: Vintage, 1999.

———. "Rape, Racism, and the Myth of the Black Rapist." In *Women, Race, & Class*, 1st Vintage Books edition. New York: Vintage, 1983.

———. "Reflections on the Black Women's Role in the Community of Slaves." *Black Scholar* 12, no. 6 (1971): 2–15.

———. "The Approaching Obsolescence of Housework: A Working Class Perspective." In *The Angela Y Davis Reader*, 193–209. Oxford: Blackwell Publishing, 1998.

———. *Women, Race, & Class*. 1st Vintage Books edition. New York: Vintage, 1983.

Davis, Angela Y., and Robin D. G. Kelley. *The Meaning of Freedom: And Other Difficult Dialogues*. San Francisco, Calif.: City Lights Publishers, 2012.

Davis, Angela Y., and Elizabeth Martínez. "Coalition Building Among People of Color." *Inscriptions* 7 (1994). https://culturalstudies.ucsc.edu/inscriptions/volume-7/angela-y-davis-elizabeth-martinez/.

Davis, Angela Y., and Cornel West. *Freedom Is a Constant Struggle: Ferguson, Palestine, and the Foundations of a Movement*. Edited by Frank Barat. Chicago: Haymarket Books, 2016.

Davis, Kathy. "Intersectionality as Buzzword." *Feminist Theory* 9, no. 1 (2008): 67–85.

Dawson, Michael C. *Blacks In and Out of the Left*. Cambridge, Mass.: Harvard University Press, 2013.

Day, Iyko. *Alien Capital: Asian Racialization and the Logic of Settler Colonial Capitalism*. Durham: Duke University Press Books, 2016.

Degras, Jane, ed. *The Communist International Documents 1919-1943*. Vol. 2. 3 vols. London: Routledge, 2013.

Dill, Bonnie Thornton. "Race, Class, and Gender: Prospects for an All-Inclusive Sisterhood." *Feminist Studies* 9, no. 1 (1983): 130–50.

Dill, Professor Bonnie Thornton, and Professor Ruth Enid Zambrana, eds. *Emerging Intersections: Race, Class, and Gender in Theory, Policy, and Practice*. New Brunswick, N.J: Rutgers University Press, 2009.

Doetsch-Kidder, Sharon. *Social Change and Intersectional Activism: The Spirit of Social Movement*. New York: Palgrave Macmillan, 2012.

Draper, Hal, and Anne G. Lipow. "Marxist Women versus Bourgeois Feminism." *Socialist Register*, 1976, 179–226.

Drucker, Peter. *Warped: Gay Normality and Queer Anti-Capitalism*. Historical Materialism, 2015.
Du Bois, W.E.B. *Black Reconstruction in America, 1860-1880*. New York: Free Press, 1992.
———. *Darkwater: Voiced from Behind the Veil*. New York: Prometheus Books, 2003.
———. *The Autobiography of W.E.B. Du Bois: A Sololoquy on Viewing My Life from the Last Decade of Its First Century*. New York: International Publishers, 1968.
Dussel, Enrique. *The Invention of the Americas: Eclipse of "the Other" and the Myth of Modernity*. Translated by Michael D. Barber. New York: Continuum Publishing Company, 1995.
Ebert, Teresa L. "The Spectral Concrete: Bodies, Sex Work, and (Some Notes on) Citizenship." In *Maxism, Queer Theory, Gender*, edited by Mas'ud Zavarzadeh, Teresa L. Ebert, and Donald Morton, 275–305. Syracuse, New York: The Red Factory, 2001.
Edara, Dileep. *Biography of a Blunder: Base and Superstructure in Marx and Later*. Cambridge: Cambridge Scholars Publishing, 2016.
Edmo, Se-ah-dom, Jesse Young, and Alan Parker. *American Indian Identity: Citizenship, Membership and Blood*. Santa Barbara, California: Praeger, 2016.
Ellinghaus, Katherine. *Blood Will Tell: Native Americans and Assimilation Policy*. Lincoln: University of Nebraska Press, 2017.
Erevelles, Nirmala, and Andrea Minear. "Unspeakable Offenses: Untangling Race and Disability in Discourses of Intersectionality." *Journal of Literary & Cultural Disability Studies* 4, no. 2 (2010): 127–45.
Farris, Sara. *In the Name of Women's Rights: The Rise of Femonationalism*. Durham: Duke University Press, 2017.
Federici, Silvia. *Caliban and the Witch: Women, the Body and Primitive Accumulation*. 1st edition. New York; London: Autonomedia, 2004.
———. *Revolution at Point Zero: Housework, Reproduction, and Feminist Struggle*. 1 edition. Oakland, CA : Brooklyn, NY : London: PM Press, 2012.
Ferguson, Roderick. *The Reorder of Things: The University and Its Pedagogies of Minority Difference*. Minneapolis: University of Minnesota Press, 2012.
Ferguson, Sue. "Intersectionality and Social-Reproduction Feminisms: Toward an Integrative Ontology." *Historical Materialism* 24, no. 2 (2016): 38–60.
Firestone, Shulamith. *The Dialectic of Sex: The Case for Feminist Revolution*. New York: Farrar, Straus and Giroux, 2003.
Floyd, Kevin. *The Reification of Desire: Toward a Queer Marxism*. Minneapolis: Univ Of Minnesota Press, 2009.
Foucault, Michel. *Discipline & Punish: The Birth of the Prison*. Translated by Alan Sheridan. 2nd edition. New York: Vintage Books, 1995.

———. *The Birth of Biopolitics: Lectures at the Collège de France, 1978-1979.* Reprint edition. Basingstoke England; New York: Picador, 2010.

———. *The History of Sexuality, Vol. 1: An Introduction.* Translated by Robert Hurley. Reissue edition. Vintage, 1990.

García, Alma, ed. *Chicana Feminist Thought: The Basic Historical Writings.* New York: Routledge, 1997.

Gedalof, Irene. "Sameness and Difference in Government Equality Talk." *Ethnic and Racial Studies* 36, no. 1 (2013): 117–35.

Geerts, Evelien, and Iris van der Tuin. "From Intersectionality to Interference: Feminist Onto-Epistemological Reflections on the Politics of Representation." *Women's Studies International Forum* 41, no. 3 (2013): 171–78.

Gibson-Graham, J.K. *The End Of Capitalism (As We Knew It): A Feminist Critique of Political Economy.* 1st University of Minnesota Press Ed., 2006 edition. Minneapolis: Univ Of Minnesota Press, 2006.

Gimenez, Martha. "Marxism and Class, Gender and Race: Rethinking the Trilogy." *Race, Gender and Class* 8, no. 2 (2001): 22–33.

Gines, Kathryn T. "Race Women, Race Men, and Early Expressions of Proto-Intersectionality." In *Why Race and Gender Still Matter: An Intersectional Approach*, edited by Namita Goswami, Maeve O'Donovan, and Lisa Yount, 13–26. London: Pickering & Chatto, 2014.

Glenn, Evelyn Nakano "From Servitude to Service Work: Historical Continuities in the Racial Division of Paid Reproductive Work." *Signs: Journal of Women in Culture & Society* 18, no. 1 (1992): 1–43.

Glissant, Edouard. *Poetics of Relation.* Translated by Betsy Wing. Ann Arbor: University of Michigan Press, 1997.

Golash-Boza, Tanya. "The Parallels between Mass Incarceration and Mass Deportation: An Intersectional Analysis of State Repression." *Journal of World-Systems Research* 22, no. 2 (2016): 484–509.

Gómez-Barris, Macarena. *The Extractive Zone: Social Ecologies and Decolonial Perspectives.* Durham and London: Duke University Press, 2017.

Gonzáles, Marcial. "Postmodernism, Historical Materialism, and Chicana/o Cultural Studies." *Science and Society* 68, no. 2 (2004): 161–86.

Gotanda, Neil. "A Critique of 'Our Constitution Is Color-Blind.'" *Stanford Law Review* 44, no. 1 (1991): 1–68.

Grech, Shaun. "Disability and the Majority World: A Neocolonial Approach." In *Disability and Social Theory: New Developments and Directions*, edited by Dan Goodley, Bill Hughes, and Lennard Davis, 52–69. New York: Palgrave, 2012.

Griffin, Farah Jasmine. "Black Feminists and Du Bois: Respectability, Protection, and Beyond." *Annnals of the American Academy of Political Science*, no. 568 (2000): 28–40.

Grosfoguel, Ramón, Laura Oso, and Anastasia Christou. "'Racism', Intersectionality and Migration Studies: Framing Some Theoretical Reflections." *Identities* 22, no. 6 (2015): 635–52.

Grzanka, Patrick R. *Intersectionality: A Foundations and Frontiers Reader.* 1 edition. Boulder, CO: Westview Press, 2014.

Guidroz, Kathleen, and Michele Tracy Berger, eds. "A Conversation with Founding Scholars of Intersectionality: Kimberlé Crenshaw, Nira Yuval-Davis, and Michelle Fine." In *The Intersectional Approach: Transforming the Academy through Race, Class, and Gender*, 61–78. Chapel Hill: University of North Carolina Press, 2009.

Gunnarsson, Lena. "A Defense of the Category 'Women.'" *Feminist Theory* 12, no. 1 (2011): 23–37.

———. "Why We Keep Separating the 'Inseparable': Dialecticizing Intersectionality." *European Journal of Women's Studies* 24, no. 2 (2015): 114–27.

Habib, Irfan. "Capitalism in History." *Social Scientist* 23, no. 7/9 (1995): 15–31.

Hall, Kim F. *Things of Darkness: Economies of Race and Gender in Early Modern England.* 1 edition. Ithaca: Cornell University Press, 1995.

Hamer, Fannie Lou. *To Tell It Like It Is: The Speeches of Fannie Lou Hamer.* Edited by Maegan Parker Brooks and Davis W. Houck. Jackson, MS: University Press of Mississippi, 2010.

Hancock, Ange-Marie. *Intersectionality: An Intellectual History.* 1 edition. New York, NY: Oxford University Press, 2016.

———. "W.E.B. Du Bois: Intellectual Forefather of Intersectionality?" *Souls* 7, no. 3–4 (2005): 74–84.

———. "When Multiplication Doesn't Equal Quick Addition: Examining Intersectionality as a Research Paradigm." *Perspectives on Politics* 5, no. 1 (2007): 63–79.

Haraway, Donna. "Situated Knowledges: The Science Question in Feminism and the Privilege of Partial Perspective." *Feminist Studies*, no. 14 (1988): 575–99.

Harding, Sandra. *Whose Science? Whose Knowledge? Thinking from Women's Lives.* Ithaca: Cornell University Press, 1991.

Hardt, Michael, and Antonio Negri. *Multitude: War and Democracy in the Age of Empire.* Reprint edition. New York: Penguin Books, 2005.

Hartman, Heidi. "The Unhappy Marriage of Marxism and Feminism." In *Women and Revolution*, edited by Lydia Sargent. Boston: South End Press, 1981.

Hartsock, Nancy. "Marxist Feminist Dialectics for the 21st Century." *Science and Society* 62, no. 3 (1998): 400–413.

———. "The Feminist Standpoint: Developing the Ground for a Specifically Feminist Historical Materialism." In *Discovering Reality: Feminist Perspectives on Epistemology, Metaphysics, Methodology, and the Philosophy of Science*, edited by Sandra Harding and Merrill Hintikka, 283–310. Dordrecht, Netherlands: D. Reidel, 1983.

Harvey, David. *Justice, Nature, and the Geography of Difference.* New York: Blackwell Publishing, 1996.

———. "Response to Alex Dubilet." *Syndicate*, April 1, 2015. https://syndicate.network/symposia/theology/seventeen-contradictions-and-the-end-of-capitalism/.

———. *Seventeen Contradictions at the End of Capitalism.* Oxford and New York: Oxford University Press, 2015.

Hemmings, Clare. *Why Stories Matter: The Political Grammar of Feminist Theory.* Durham, NC: Duke University Press, 2011.

Hennessy, Rosemary. *Profit and Pleasure: Sexual Identities in Late Capitalism.* New York: Routledge, 2000.

Henry, Paget. "Caribbean Marxism Adter the Neoliberal and Linguistic Turn." In *New Caribbean Thought: A Reader.* Kingston: University of the West Indies Press, 2001.

Hill, Norbert S., and Kathleen Ratteree. *The Great Vanishing Act: Blood Quantum and the Future of Native Nations.* Colorado: Fulcrum Publishing, 2017.

Holcomb, Gary. "A New Spelling of Her Name: Audre Lorde's Queer Black Marxism." Washington, DC, 2014.

———. *Claude McKay, Code Name Sasha: Queer Black Marxism and the Harlem Renaissance.* Gainsville, FL: University Press of Florida, 2009.

Holstrom, Nancy. "Introduction." In *The Socialist Feminism Project: A Contemporary Reader in Theory and Politics*, edited by Nancy Holstrom. New York: Monthly Review Press, 2003.

Hong, Grace Kyungwon. *The Ruptures of American Capital: Women of Color Feminism and the Immigrant Culture of Labor.* Minneapolis: University of Minnesota Press, 2006.

hooks, bell. *Ain't I a Woman: Black Women and Feminism.* Boston, Mass.: South End Press, 1999.

———. Challenging Capitalism & Patriarchy: An Interview By Third World Viewpoint. Accessed August 1, 2017. http://soaw.org/component/content/article/110-gender-sexuality/910?format=pdf.

———. *Feminist Theory: From Margin to Center.* Routledge, 2014.

———. Media Education Foundation Interview, 1997. http://www.mediaed.org/transcripts/Bell-Hooks-Transcript.pdf.

———. *The Will to Change: Men, Masculinity, and Love.* New York: Atria Books, 2004.

Horkheimer, Max, and Theodor W. Adorno. *Dialectic of Enlightenment.* Edited by Gunzelin Schmid Noerr. Translated by Edmund Jephcott. 1 edition. Stanford, Calif: Stanford University Press, 2007.

Ignatiev, Noel. *How the Irish Became White.* New York: Routledge, 2008.

Jamal, Amaney. *Race and Arab Americans Before and After 9/11: From Invisible Citizens to Visible Subjects.* Syracuse, New York: Syracuse University Press, 2008.

James, C. L. R. *The Black Jacobins: Toussaint L'Ouverture and the San Domingo Revolution.* 2 edition. New York: Vintage, 1989.

James, Joy. *Seeking the Beloved Community: A Feminist Race Reader.* SUNY Press, 2013.

Jameson, Fredric. *Valences of the Dialectic.* London: Verso, 2009.

Johnson, Corey G. "Female Inmates Sterilized in California Prisons without Approval." *The Center for Investigative Reporting,* July 7, 2013. http://cironline.org/reports/female-inmates-sterilized-california-prisons-without-approval-4917.

Jones, Claudia. "An End to the Neglect of the Problems of the Negro Woman! (1949)." In *Words of Fire: An Anthology of African-American Feminist Thought,* edited by Beverly Guy-Sheftall, 107–23. New York: The New Press, 1995.

Jordan-Zachary, Julia S. "Am I a Black Woman or a Woman Who Is Black? A Few Thoughts on the Meaning of Intersectionality." *Politics & Gender* 3, no. 2 (2007): 254–63.

Kauanui, J. Kehaulani. *Hawaiian Blood: Colonialism and the Politics of Sovereignty and Indigeneity.* Durham, NC: Duke University Press, 2008.

Kelley, Robin D. G. *Hammer and Hoe: Alabama Communists During the Great Depression.* Chapel Hill: University of North Carolina Press, 1990.

———. *Race Rebels: Culture, Politics, and the Black Working Class.* New York: Free Press, 1994.

King, Deborah K. "Multiple Jeopardy, Multiple Consciousness: The Context of a Black Feminist Ideology." *Signs* 14, no. 1 (1988): 42–72.

Knapp, Gundrun-Axeli. "Race, Class, Gender: Reclaiming Baggage in Fast Travelling Theories." *European Journal of Women's Studies* 12, no. 3 (2005): 249–85.

Lee, Richard A. *The Thought of Matter: Materialism, Conceptuality, and the Transcendence of Immanence.* New York: Rowman & Littlefield, 2015.

Lenin, V.I. "Imperialism and the Split in Socialism." *Marxists Internet Archive,* October 1916. https://www.marxists.org/archive/lenin/works/1916/oct/x01.htm.

Lerner, Gerda. *Black Women in White America: A Documentary History.* New York: Vintage, 1973.

Lewis, Holly. *The Politics of Everybody: Feminism, Queer Theory and Marxism at the Intersection.* Zed Books, 2016.

Lindsay, Beverly. "Minority Women in America: Black American, Native America, Chicana, and Asian American Women." In *The Study of Woman: Enlarging Perspectives of Social Reality,* edited by Eloise C. Snyder, 318–63. New York: Harper and Row, 1979.

Lipsitz, George. *The Possessive Investment in Whiteness*. Philadelphia: Temple University Press, 1998.
Liss, Sheldon B. *Marxist Thought in Latin America*. Berkeley and Los Angeles: University of California Press, 1984.
Liu, Petrus. *Queer Marxism in Two Chinas*. Durham ; London: Duke University Press Books, 2015.
Lorde, Audre. "Age, Race, Class, and Sex: Women Redefining Difference." In *Sister/Outsider*. Berkeley: Crossing, n.d.
———. *Sister/Outsider: Essays and Speeches*. Freedom: Crossing Press, 1984.
———. *Zami: A New Spelling of My Name - A Biomythography*. First edition. Berkeley, Calif.: The Crossing Press, 1982.
Losurdo, Domenico. *Liberalism: A Counter-History*. Translated by Gregory Elliott. London ; New York: Verso, 2014.
Lowe, Lisa. *Immigrant Acts: On Asian American Cultural Politics*. Durham, NC: Duke University Press, 1996.
———. *The Intimacies of Four Continents*. Chapel Hill: Duke University Press, 2015.
Lowy, Michael. *Ecosocialism: A Radical Alternative to Capitalist Catastrophe*. Chicago: Haymarket Books, 2015.
Lugones, María. "Heterosexualism and the Colonial / Modern Gender System." *Hypatia* 22, no. 1 (2007): 186–209.
———. "Hispaneando y Lesbiando: On Sarah Hoagland's 'Lesbian Ethics.'" *Hypatia* 5, no. 3 (1990): 138–46.
———. *Pilgrimages = Peregrinajes: Theorizing Coalition against Multiple Oppressions*. Lanham, Md.: Rowman & Littlefield, 2003.
———. "Toward a Decolonial Feminism." *Hypatia* 25, no. 4 (2010): 742–59.
Lukács, Georg. *History and Class Consciousness: Studies in Marxist Dialectics*. Translated by Rodney Livingstone. Cambridge: The MIT Press, 1972.
Lutz, Helma, Maria Theresa Herrera Vivar, and Linda Supik. *Framing Intersectionality*. Farnham, UK: Ashgate, 2011.
Luxemburg, Rosa. *The Accumulation of Capital*. 2 edition. London ; New York: Routledge, 2003.
Ly, Abdoulaye. *Les Masses Africaines et l'actuelle Condition Humaine*. Éditions Présence Africaine, 1956.
Lykke, Nina. *Feminist Studies: A Guide to Intersectional Theory, Methodology, and Writing*. New York: Routledge, 2010.
———. "Intersectional Analysis: Black Box or Useful Critical Feminist Thinking Technology?" In *Framing Intersectionality: Debates on A Multi-Faceted Concept in Gender Studies*, edited by Helma Lutz, Maria Theresa Herrera Vivar, and Linda Supik, 207–21. Farnham, UK: Ashgate, 2011.
Magdoff, Fred, and John Bellamy Foster. *What Every Environmentalist Needs to Know about Capitalism*. Monthly Review Press, 2011.

Maingot, Anthony P. *Race, Ideology, and the Decline of Caribbean Marxism*. University Press of Florida, 2015.
Malm, Andreas. *Fossil Capital: The Rise of Steam Power and the Roots of Global Warming*. London: Verso, 2016.
Mann, Susan Archer. *Doing Feminist Theory: From Modernity to Postmodernity*. 1 edition. Oxford ; New York, NY: Oxford University Press, 2012.
———. "Third Wave Feminism's Unhappy Marriage of Poststructuralism and Intersectionality Theory." *Journal of Feminist Scholarship*, no. 4 (2013): 54–73.
Marable, Manning. "Reconstructing the Radical Du Bois." *Souls* 7, no. 3–4 (2005): 1–25.
Marable, Manning, and Leith Mullings. *How Capitalism Underdeveloped Black America: Problems in Race, Political Economy, and Society*. Haymarket Books, 2015.
Marini, Ruy Mauro. *Dialéctica de Dependencia*. Mexico: Ediciones Era, 1973.
Martínez, Elizabeth. "Beyond Black/White: The Racisms of Our Time." *Social Justice*, no. 20 (1993): 22–34.
———. "What Is White Supremacy?" *Catalyzing Liberation Toolkit: Anti-Racist Organizing to Build the 99% Movement*, n.d., 16–21.
Marx, Karl. *Capital: Volume 1: A Critique of Political Economy*. Translated by Ben Fowkes. Reprint edition. London ; New York, N.Y: Penguin Classics, 1992.
———. *Capital, Volume III*. Harmondsworth, England: Penguin Books, 1981.
———. *Contribution to the Critique of Political Economy*. Translated by N.I. Stone. Chicago: Charles H. Kerr & Company, 1904.
———. *Grundrisse: Foundations of the Critique of Political Economy*. Translated by Martin Nicolaus. Reprint edition. London; New York: Penguin Classics, 1993.
———. *The Eighteenth Brumaire of Louis Bonaparte*. 6th ed. Moscow: Progress Publishers, 1972.
———. *The Poverty of Philosophy: A Reply to M. Proudhon's Philosophy of Poverty*. New York, n.d.
Marx, Karl, and Friedrich Engels. *The German Ideology*. New York: International Publishers, 1967.
Marx, Karl, Friedrich Engels, and V.I. Lenin. *On Historical Materialism: A Collection*. Moscow: Progress Publishers, 1972.
May, Vivian. *Pursuing Intersectionality, Unsettling Dominant Imaginaries*. New York: Routledge, 2015.
———. "'Speaking into the Void?: Intersectionality Critiques and Epistemic Backlash." *Hypatia* 28, no. 1 (2014): 94–112.
Mayer, Adam. *Naija Marxisms: Revolutionary Thought in Nigeria*. London: Pluto Press, 2016.

Mbembe, Achille. "Necropolitics." Translated by Libby Meintjes. *Public Culture* 15, no. 1 (n.d.): 11–40.

McCall, Leslie. "The Complexity of Intersectionality." *Signs: Journal of Women in Culture & Society* 30, no. 3 (2005): 1771–1800.

Mcclintock, Anne. *Imperial Leather: Race, Gender, and Sexuality in the Colonial Contest*. 1st edition. New York: Routledge, 1995.

McDuffie, Erik S. "'No Small Amount of Change Could Do': Esther Cooper Jackson and the Making of a Black Feminist Left." In *Want to Start a Revolution? Radical Women in the Black Freedom Struggle*, edited by Dayo Gore, Jeanne Theoharis, and Komozi Woodard, 25–46. New York: New York University Press, 2009.

———. *Sojourning for Freedom: Black Women, American Communism, and the Making of Black Left Feminism*. Durham: Duke University Press, 2011.

McGuire, Danielle L. *At the Dark End of the Street: Black Women, Rape, and Resistance—A New History of the Civil Rights Movement from Rosa Parks to the Rise of Black Power*. Reprint. New York: Vintage Books, 2011.

McIntosh, Peggy. "White Privilege: Unpacking the Invisible Knapsack." *Independent School* 49, no. 2 (Winter 1990): 31–37.

McKay, Nellie Y. "The Souls of Black Women Folk in the Writings of W.E.B. Du Bois." In *Reading Black Reading Feminist: A Critical Anthology*, edited by Henry Louis Gates Jr., 227–43. New York: Meridian Books, 1990.

McNally, David. "Language, Praxis, and Dialectics: Reply to Collins." *Historical Materialism* 12, no. 2 (2004): 149–67.

———. *Political Economy and the Rise of Capitalism*. Berkeley and Los Angeles: University of California Press, 1988.

McNally, David, and Sue Ferguson. Social Reproduction Beyond Intersectionality: An Interview. Viewpoint Magazine, October 31, 2015. https://www.viewpointmag.com/2015/10/31/social-reproduction-beyond-intersectionality-an-interview-with-sue-ferguson-and-david-mcnally/.

McWhorter, Ladelle. *Racism and Sexual Oppression in Anglo-America: A Genealogy*. Bloomington: Indiana University Press, 2009.

Melamed, Jodi. "The Spirit of Neoliberalism: From Racial Liberalism to Neoliberal Multiculturalism." *Social Text* 24, no. 4 (2006): 1–24.

Mies, Maria. *Patriarchy and Accumulation On A World Scale: Women in the International Division of Labour*. 2nd edition. London; Atlantic Highlands, N.J., USA; Atlantic Highlands, N.J.: Zed Books, 1999.

Mills, Charles W. "White Ignorance." In *Race and Epistemologies of Ignorace*, edited by Shannon Sullivan and Nancy Tuana, 39–58. Albany: State University of New York Press, 2007.

Ming Francis, Megan. "Ida B. Wells and the Economics of Racial Violence." *Items: Insights from the Social Sciences*, January 24, 2017. http://items.ssrc.org/ida-b-wells-and-the-economics-of-racial-violence/.

Mintz, Sidney W. *Sweetness and Power: The Place of Sugar in Modern History.* Reprint edition. New York: Penguin Books, 1986.

Mitchell, Eve. "I Am a Women and a Human: A Marxist Feminist Critique of Intersectionality Theory." *Libcom.Com*, 2014. https://libcom.org/library/i-am-woman-human-marxist-feminist-critique-intersectionality-theory-eve-mitchell.

Mohanty, Chandra Talpade. *Feminism without Borders: Decolonizing Theory, Practicing Solidarity.* Durham: Duke University Press, 2003.

Molyneux, John. "Marxism and the Environmental Crisis." *Climate & Capitalism*, November 25, 2011. http://climateandcapitalism.com/2011/11/25/marxism-and-the-environmental-crisis/.

Moore, Jason W. *Capitalism in the Web of Life: Ecology and the Accumulation of Capital.* London: Verso, 2015.

Moraga, Cherrie, and Gloria Anzaldúa, eds. *This Bridge Called My Back: Writings by Radical Women of Color.* New York: Kitchen Table Press, 1983.

Morgan, Edmund. *American Slavery, American Freedom.* Reissue edition. New York: W. W. Norton & Company, 2003.

Morton, Peggy. "A Woman's Work Is Never Done, or: The Production, Maintenance and Reproduction of Labor Power." In *From Feminism to Liberation*, edited by Edith Altbach, 211–27. Cambridge: Schenkman Books, 1971.

Munroe, Trevor. *Jamaican Politics: A Marxist Perspective in Transition.* Kingston: Heinemann and Boulder, 1990.

Naison, Mark. *Communists in Harlem During the Great Depression.* New York: Grove Press, 1983.

Narayan, Uma. "The Project of Feminist Epistemology: Perspectives from a Non-Western Feminist." In *Gender/Body/Knowledge: Feminist Reconstructions of Being and Knowing*, edited by Alison Jaggar and Susan R. Bordo, 256–72. New Brunswick, NJ: Rutgers University Press, 1989.

Nash, Jennifer. "Home Truths on Intersectionality." *Yale Journal of Law and Feminism* 23, no. 2 (2011): 445–70.

Nava, Yolanda. "Myths, the Media, Minority Groups, and Women's Liberation: An Overview." presented at the Santa Monica College Women's Week, California, March 21, 1973.

Nieto Gómez, Anna. "La Feminista." *Encuentro Femenil* 1, no. 2 (1974): 34–47.

———. "Sexism in the Movimiento." *La Gente de Aztlán* 6, no. 4 (1976).

Ocen, Priscilla A. "Unshackling Intersectionality." *Du Bois Review* 10, no. 2 (2013): 471–83.

Ofari, Earl. *The Myth of Black Capitalism.* New York: Monthly Review Press, 1970.

Onesto, Li. *Dispatches from the People's War in Nepal.* London: Pluto Press, 2005.

Oyewumi, Oyeronke. *The Invention of Women: Making an African Sense of Western Gender Discourses.* 1 edition. Minneapolis: University of Minnesota Press, 1997.

Painter, Nell Irvin. *The History of White People.* New York: W. W. Norton & Company, 2010.

Parks, V., and D. Warren. "Contesting the Racial Division of Labor from Below: Representation and Union Organizing among African American and Immigrant Workers." *Du Bois Review* 9, no. 2 (2012): 395–417.

Patterson, Orlando. *Slavery and Social Death: A Comparative Study.* 1st edition. Cambridge, Mass.: Harvard University Press, 1982.

Plumwood, Val. *Feminism and the Mastery of Nature.* London and New York: Routledge, 1993.

Puar. *Terrorist Assemblages: Homonationalism in Queer Times.* Durham: Duke University Press Books, 2007.

Puar, Jasbir. "I Would Rather Be a Cyborg than a Goddess: Becoming-Intersectional in Assemblage Theory." *Philosophia* 2, no. 1 (2012): 49–66.

Quijano, Anibal. "Colonialidad de Poder y Clasificacion Social." *Journal of World-Systems Research* 1, no. 2 (Summer/Fall 2000): 342–86.

———. "Coloniality and Modernity/ Rationality." *Cultural Studies* 21, no. 2/3 (2007): 168–78.

———. "Coloniality of Power, Eurocentrism, and Latin America." Translated by Michael Ennis. *Nepantla: Views from South* 1, no. 3 (2000): 533–80.

Rancière, Jacques. *Proletarian Nights: The Workers' Dream in Nineteenth-Century France.* Second Edition edition. London ; New York: Verso, 2012.

Rancière, Jacques. *The Politics of Aesthetics.* Translated by Gabriel Rockhill. London; New York: Bloomsbury Academic, 2006.

Roberts, Dorothy. *Killing the Black Body: Race, Reproduction, and the Meaning of Liberty.* New York: Vintage, 1998.

Robinson, Cedric J. *Black Marxism: The Making of the Black Radical Tradition.* 2nd ed. Chapel Hill: University of North Carolina Press, 2000.

———. *Black Movements in America.* New York: Routledge, 1997.

Rodney, Walter. *How Europe Underdeveloped Africa.* Washington, D.C.: Howard University Press, 1982.

———. "Marxism and African Liberation." In *Yes to Marxism.* Georgetown, Guyana: People's Progressive Party, 1975.

Roediger, David R. *Class, Race, and Marxism.* London: Verso, 2017.

Roediger, David R., and Elizabeth D. Esch. *The Production of Difference: Race and the Management of Labor in U.S. History.* Oxford University Press, 2012.

Romero, Mary. "The Inclusion of Citizenship Status in Intersectionality: What Immigration Raids Tell Us about Mixed-Status Families, the State, and Assimilation." *International Journal of Sociology of the Family* 34, no. 2 (2008): 131–52.

Rosenblatt, Kalahan. "Judge Offers Inmates Reduced Sentences in Exchange for Vasectomy." *NBC News*, July 21, 2017. https://www.nbcnews.com/news/us-news/judge-offers-inmates-reduced-sentences-exchange-vasectomy-n785256.

Roth, Benita. *Separate Roads to Feminism: Black, Chicana, and White Feminist Movements in America's Second Wave*. Cambridge, UK ; New York: Cambridge University Press, 2003.

Russell, Kathryn. "Feminist Dialectics and Marxist Theory." *Radical Philosophy Review* 10, no. 1 (2007): 33–54.

Salaita, Steven. *Anti-Arab Racism in the USA: Where It Comes From and What It Means for Politics Today*. London: Pluto Press, 2006.

Sandoval, Chela. *Methodology of the Oppressed*. Minneapolis: University of Minnesota Press, 2000.

———. "U.S. Third World Feminism: The Theory and Method of Oppositional Consciousness in the Post-Modern World." *Genders*, no. 10 (1991): 1–24.

Sankara, Thomas. *Thomas Sankara Speaks*. Pathfinder Press, 2007.

Sanyal, Kalyan. *Rethinking Capitalist Development: Primitive Accumulation, Governmentality, and Post-Colonial Capitalism*. London and New Delhi: Routledge, 2013.

Severs, Eline, Karen Celis, and Silvia Erzeel. "Power, Privilege, and Disadvantage: Intersectionality Theory and Political Representation." *Politics* 36, no. 4 (2016): 346–54.

Shakur, Assata. "To My People," July 4, 1973. http://www.assatashakur.org/mypeople.htm.

Shifferd, K.D. "Karl Marx and the Environment." *Journal of Environmental Education* 3, no. 4 (1972): 39–42.

Singh, Jakeet. "Religious Agency and the Limits of Intersectionality." *Hypatia* 30, no. 4 (2015): 657–74.

Smith, Andrea. "Beyond Pro-Choice Versus Pro-Life Women of Color and Reproductive Justice." *NWSA Journal* 17, no. 1 (Spring 2005): 119–40.

———. *Conquest: Sexual Violence and American Indian Genocide*. Chapel Hill: Duke University Press, 2015.

———. "Heteropatriarchy and the Three Pillars of White Supremacy: Rethinking Women of Color Organizing." In *Color of Violence: The Incite! Anthology*, 66–73. Cambridge: South End Press, 2006.

Smith, Barbara, ed. *Home Girls: A Black Feminist Anthology*. New York: Kitchen Table Press, 1983.

———. "Introduction to Home Girls: A Black Feminist Anthology." In *Identity Politics in the Women's Movement*, edited by Barbara Ryan, 146–62. New York & London: New York University Press, 2001.

Smith, Barbara, and Beverly Smith. "Across the Kitchen Table: A Sister-to-Sister Dialogue." In *This Bridge Called My Back: Writings by Radical Women of*

Color, edited by Cherrie Moraga and Gloria Anzaldúa, 2nd ed., 113–27. New York: Kitchen Table Press, 1983.

Smith, Dorothy E. "Women's Perspective as a Radical Critique of Sociology." *Sociological Inquiry*, no. 44 (1974): 7–13.

Smith, Sharon. "A Marxist Case for Intersectionality." *Socialist Worker*, August 1, 2017. https://socialistworker.org/2017/08/01/a-marxist-case-for-intersectionality.

———. "Black Feminism and Intersectionality." *International Socialist Review*, no. 91 (Winter -2014 2013). http://isreview.org/issue/91/black-feminism-and-intersectionality.

Smith, Valerie. "Black Feminist Theory and the Representation of the 'Other.'" In *The Woman That I Am: The Literature and Culture of Contemporary Women of Color*, edited by D. Soyini Madison, 671–87. New York: St. Martin's, 1994.

Snorton, C Riley. *Black on Both Sides: A Racial History of Trans Identity*. Minneapolis: University of Minnesota Press, 2017.

Soloman, Mark. *The Cry Was Unity: Communists and African Americans 1917-1936*. Jackson: University of Mississippi Press, 1998.

Somerville, Siobhan B. *Queering the Color Line: Race and the Invention of Homosexuality in American Culture*. Chapel Hill: Duke University Press, 2000.

Spade, Dean. *Normal Life: Administrative Violence, Critical Trans Politics, and the Limits of Law*. Chapel Hill: Duke University Press, 2015.

Stewart, Maria, and Marilyn Richardson. *Maria W. Stewart, America's First Black Woman Political Writer*. Bloomington: Indiana University Press, 1987.

Stote, Karen. *An Act of Genocide: Colonialism and the Sterilization of Aboriginal Women*. Halifax and Winnipeg: Fernwood Publishing, 2015.

Tallbear, Kim. *Native American DNA: Tribal Belonging and the False Promise of Genetic Science*. Minneapolis: University of Minnesota Press, 2013.

Thompson Patterson, Louise. "Toward a Brighter Dawn (1936)." *Viewpoint Magazine*, October 31, 2015. https://www.viewpointmag.com/2015/10/31/toward-a-brighter-dawn-1936/.

Tomlinson, Barbara. "Colonizing Intersectionality: Replicating Racial Hierarchy in Feminist Academic Arguments." *Social Identities* 19, no. 2 (2013): 254–72.

Torpy, Sally J. "Native American Women and Coerced Sterilization: On the Trail of Tears in the 1970s." *American Indian Culture and Research Journal* 24, no. 2 (2000): 1–22.

Tronti, Mario. *Arbeiter Und Kapital*. Frankfurt: Verlag Neue Kritik, 1962.

Truth, Sojourner. *Sojourner Truth: Ain't I a Woman?* Edited by Patricia C. McKissack. Southfield, Mich.: Scholastic Paperbacks, 1994.

Vogel, Lise. *Marxism and the Oppression of Women: Toward a Unitary Theory*. Edited by Susan Ferguson and David McNally. Reprint edition. Historical Materialism, 2014.

Wadsworth, Nancy. "Fractured Believers: Race and Religion as Intersectional Aspects of United States Political Development." In *Race and U.S. Political Development*, edited by Joseph Lowndes, Julie Novkov, and Dorian Warren, 312–36. New York: Routledge, 2008.

Walby, Sylvia. *Gender Segregation at Work*. Open University Press, 1988.

Washington, Mary Helen. "Alice Childress, Lorraine Hansberry, and Claudia Jones: Black Women Write the Popular Front." In *Left of the Color Line: Race, Radicalism, and the Twentieth-Century Literature of the United States*, edited by Bill V. Mullen and James Smethurst, 183–204. Chapel Hill: University of North Carolina Press, 2003.

Waters, Kristin B. "Some Core Themes of Nineteenth Century Black Feminism." In *Black Women's Intellectual Traditions: Speaking Their Minds*, edited by Kristin B. Waters and Carol B. Conway, 365–92. Lebanon, NH: University Press of New England, 2007.

Weeks, Kathi. *The Problem with Work: Feminism, Marxism, Antiwork Politics, and Postwork Imaginaries*. Durham: Duke University Press Books, 2011.

Weinbaum, Alys Eve. "Gendering the General Strike: W.E.B. Du Bois's Black Reconstruction and Black Feminism's 'Propaganda of History.'" *South Atlantic Quarterly* 112, no. 3 (2013): 437–63.

Wells-Barnett, Ida B. *On Lynching: Southern Horrors and Other Writings*. Edited by Jacqueline Jones Royster. Boston, MA: Bedford/ St. Martin's, 1997.

Williams, Eric. *Capitalism and Slavery*. 1 edition. Chapel Hill: The University of North Carolina Press, 1994.

Winston, James. "Being Red and Black in Jim Crow America: Notes on the Ideology and Travails of Afro-America's Socialist Pioneers." *Souls* 1, no. 4 (1999): 45–63.

Wolfe, Patrick. "Settler Colonialism and the Elimination of the Native." *Journal of Genocide Research* 8, no. 4 (December 2006): 387–409.

Wood, Ellen Meiksins. "Capitalism and Human Emancipation." *New Left Review*, no. 167 (February 1988).

———. "The Uses and Abuses of Civil Society." In *The Retreat of the Intellectuals: Socialist Register 1990*, edited by Ralph Miliband and Leo Panitch. London: Merlin Press, 1990.

Wright, Erik Olin. *Class Counts*. London: Verso, 1997.

———. *Interogating Inequality*. London: Verso, 1994.

Young, Iris Marion. *Justice and the Politics of Difference*. Princeton, N.J: Princeton University Press, 1990.